D1539459

iF communication design award
yearbook 2009

Herausgeber, Editor. iF International Forum Design GmbH, Messegelände, Hannover, Germany; Sandstr. 33, München, Germany Phone: + 49.511.8932402, Fax: + 49.511.8932401, www.ifdesign.de, info@ifdesign.de iF Geschäftsführung, Managing Director. Ralph Wiegmann iF communication design award. Anja-Martina Kirschning, Carmen Wille, iF communication design award yearbook. Korinna Gramsch iF Team. Anne-Kathrin Aumann, Dirk Bartelsmeier, Gabriele Bertemann, Sabine Böhmer, Rylana Büter, Louisa Erbguth, Sandra Fischer, Heike Meier, Petra Nordmeier, Anna Reissert, Andrea Schewior, Birgit Schultz, Rainer Schwarz, Annegret Wulf-Pippig, Frank Zierenberg, iF Branch Office Taiwan. Sean C.K. Lee, Joan Wu, Tobie Lee, 3F., Bldg. G, 3–1 Park Street, Nangang Taipei 115, Taiwan iF Representative Office Korea. Sowon Koo, Design House Inc., Taekwang Building, 162-1 Jangchung-Dong 2-GA, Jung-Gu, Seoul 100-855, Korea iF Press Office. Claudia Neumann Communication GmbH, Claudia Neumann, Silke Becker, Sandy Pfeßdorf, Eigelstein 103–113, 50668 Köln, Germany, Phone: +49.221.9139490, Fax: +49.221.91394919, iF@neumann-luz.de

Projektmanagement Birkhäuser, Project management. Elena Dinter Produktion Birkhäuser, Production. Amelie Solbrig Gestaltung aktuelle Ausgabe, Design current Edition. Muriel Comby, Basel Satz und Lithografie, Typesetting and Lithograph. Jung Crossmedia Publishing GmbH, Lahnau Druck, Print. Kösel, Altusried-Krugzell Fotografie Jury, Jury Photography. Dirk Meußling, Isernhagen, KB Textredaktion, Copy Editing. Kristina Irmler, Großburgwedel; Dr. Tuuli Tietze, Winsen Übersetzung, Translation. Lennon.de Language Services, Münster Corporate Design iF communication design award. helke brandt communication, Hannover

© 2009 iF International Forum Design GmbH
Verlag, Publisher. Birkhäuser Verlag AG
Basel · Boston · Berlin
P.O. Box 133, 4010 Basel, Switzerland
Member of Springer Science+Business Media
www.birkhauser.ch
Printed in Germany
ISBN: 978-3-0346-0058-3

Bibliographic information published by the Deutsche Nationalbibliothek. The Deutsche Nationalbibliothek lists this publication in the Deutsche Nationalbibliografie; detailed bibliographic data are available on the Internet at http://dnb.d-nb.de
This work is subject to copyright. All rights are reserved, whether the whole or part of the material is concerned, specifically the rights of translation, reprinting, re-use of illustrations, recitation, broadcasting, reproduction on microfilms or in other ways, and storage in data bases. For any kind of use, permission of the copyright owner must be obtained.

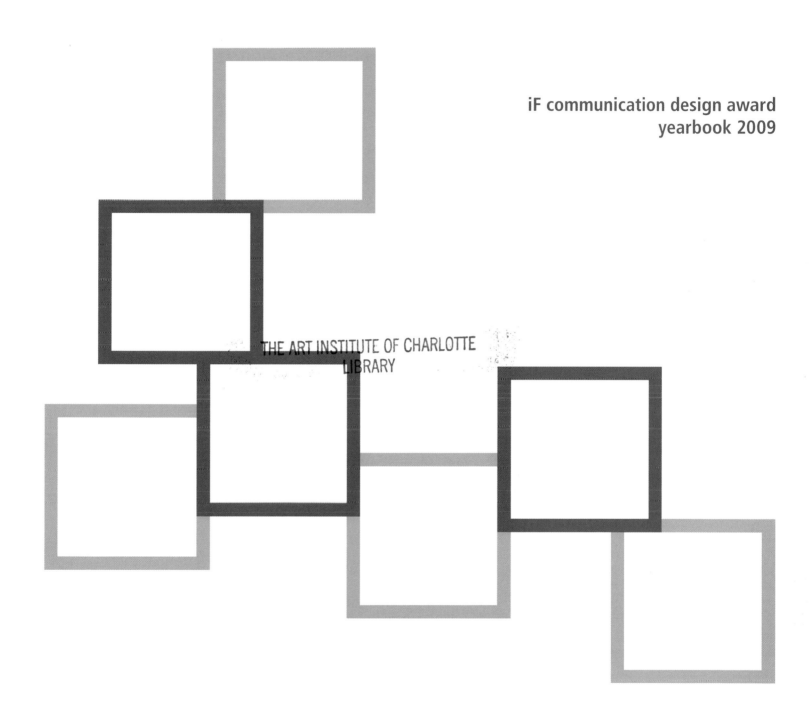

iF communication design award
yearbook 2009

THE ART INSTITUTE OF CHARLOTTE
LIBRARY

Birkhäuser
Basel · Boston · Berlin

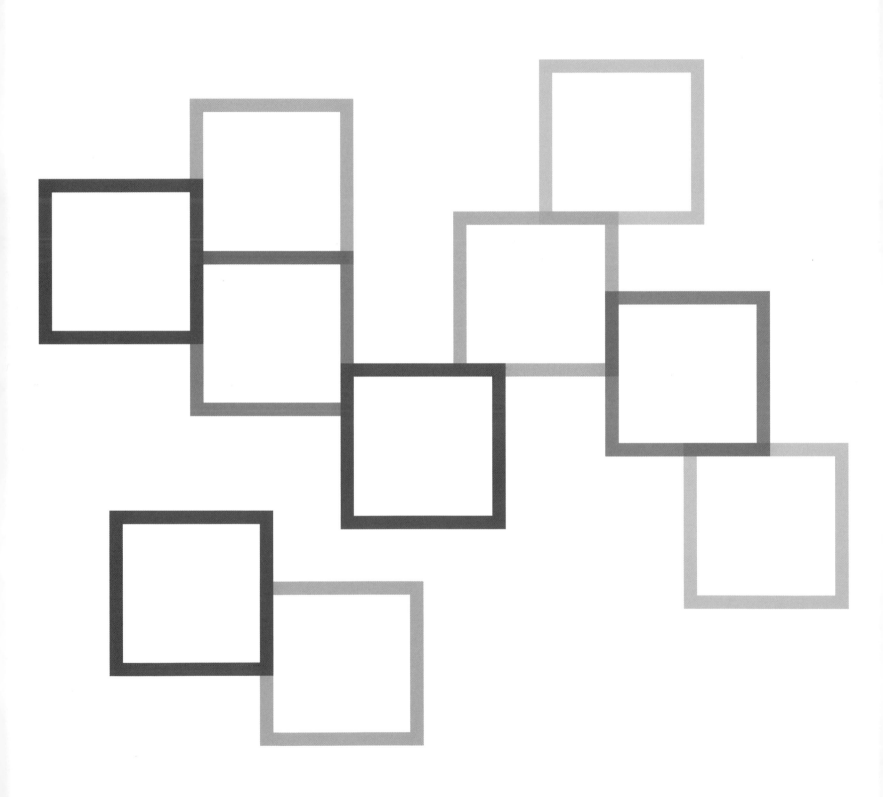

Von Evolution und Revolution

Ralph Wiegmann

Sicher nicht unversehens ähneln sich die Begriffe „Evolution" und „Revolution" bis auf einen einzigen Buchstaben: „R" wie radikaler Wandel ergänzt die Evolution, könnte man fast vermuten.

Dabei haben beide Wörter, fernab ihres eigentlichen Kontextes, längst in die Welt der Kampagnen, Produktbeschreibungen und viralen Marketingaktivitäten Eingang gefunden. Nichts überzeugt Konsumenten mehr, als der Umsturz der Dinge, so die Theorie – und seien es mittels digitaler Bearbeitung auferstandene Revolutionäre, die in einem aktuellen TV-Spot sinnierend mit einem neuen Automobil in Verbindung gebracht werden sollen.

Doch welche Taktik, angewendet auf den technologischen Fortschritt, auf die Erhaltung und Pflege des Lebensraums, auf die ökonomischen Grundpfeiler, auf soziologische wie kulturelle Bezie-

hungen ist die richtige? Die langsame, von Generation zu Generation weitergegebene Veränderung – oder eher die plötzliche, auch gewaltsame Umwandlung der Verhältnisse?

Mit der Parallelität der Entwicklungen, mit der Intensität der Ereignisse, die wir in der globalen Weltengemeinschaft zu erfassen in der Lage sind, haben wir neue Aufgaben zugewiesen bekommen. Wir können nicht mehr länger Augen und Ohren verschließen und in einem vermeintlich geschützten Raum agieren. Die Menge der Informationen und, dies ist zunehmend wichtiger, die Qualifizierung der Daten und Meldungen, erfordert Zeit und Quellen, denen wir vertrauen, die wir als glaubwürdig einstufen. So gehen Innovation und Selektion Hand in Hand und bedingen einander, entwickeln sich vom Spaßmedium, das über Glamour und Banalitäten berichtet, zu einem ernstzunehmenden, weiteren Tool, um das aktuelle Zeitgeschehen abzubilden: In die politischen Unruhen, die die Wahlen im Iran nach sich gezogen haben, wurden sowohl die Staatengemeinschaft als auch die jenseits aller Grenzen agierende Internetgemeinde einbezogen. Twitter ist, nicht erst seit den Anschlägen in Bombay, ein Medium, auf das Journalisten angewiesen sind, um die Öffentlichkeit in Kenntnis zu setzen. Auch die Lage im Iran macht aus der neuesten medialen Errungenschaft nicht nur eine Technologie, die es zu entdecken und weiterzuentwickeln gilt. Vielmehr beweist der Mut, sich in einem öffentlichen Raum zu äußern, und der „Erfolg", den die unzähligen, weltweiten Follower der dokumentierenden Demonstranten belegen, wie wenig bisher unter solchen Bedingungen möglicherweise „nach außen" dringen konnte.

Dass falsche Fährten einerseits von Irrläufern der Gegenseite gelegt werden, zum Teil auch von Verfolgten gelegt werden müssen, um die eigene Identität zu verschleiern, erschwert sicherlich die Wahrnehmung politischer und brisanter Wahrheiten auf den ersten Blick. Auf den zweiten Blick lassen sich jedoch intelligente Schwärme ausmachen, die selbst in der ausufernden Welt des Internets Korrekturen und Einschätzungen erkennen lassen – wenn man so will, eine Art gruppendynamische Qualitätskontrolle. Twitter ist, wie andere Web-Medien oder ein einfaches Brotmesser, das seinen Zweck erfüllt, Brot zu schneiden, oder eine gefährliche Waffe darstellt, ein Ding mit zwei Gesichtern. Man kann es als bedrohliche Revolution betrachten, dass nunmehr Nachrichten jedweder Relevanz als kommunikative Gruppenbildung direkt auch in Handlungen, im Netz oder außerhalb, umgesetzt werden, oder als Evolution, die längst überfällig ihre bisherigen Erfahrungen in ein neues Medium eingespeist hat.

Diese Beispiele belegen sowohl die Chancen als auch die Brisanz interaktiver Medien – aber auch die dafür notwendigen, vernetzten Denkstrukturen, die sich User und Gestalter dieser Dienste täglich aneignen müssen. So stellte das Institut zur Zukunft der Arbeit (IZA) im Juni dieses Jahres als Ergebnis einer Studie vor, dass sich mithilfe des Internetsuchdienstes Google die Entwicklung der Arbeitslosigkeit prognostizieren lässt. Bestimmte Suchbegriffe, die von Google-Nutzern eingegeben wurden, wie beispielsweise „Arbeitsamt" oder „Jobbörse", wurden in ihrer Häufigkeit analysiert und mit den statistischen Daten verglichen. Der Zusammenhang, den das IZA hergestellt hat, soll bald in verlässliche Vorhersagen münden. Hier zeigt sich, dass sowohl Ergebnis als auch die Frage selbst als Treffer zu generieren sind – und wiederum eine Überfülle an Datenmaterial produzieren. Die Schnelligkeit und Vernetzung, die Synchronität aller sich ereignenden Dinge erfordert freie Kapazitäten in unseren Köpfen – zum Denken, Nachdenken, Überdenken, und vor allem zum Sortieren und Qualifizieren. Wir sind von der crossmedialen Welt, in der die Wege noch hin- und wieder herführen, zu einer „infinitemedialen" Welt gelangt, in der

sich die Dinge zwar kreuzen können, nicht jedoch zwingend müssen, sondern unendlich parallel nebeneinander laufen und sich dennoch bedingen – und das womöglich noch in Lichtgeschwindigkeit.

Die Einschätzung der Jury im diesjährigen iF communication design award wurde erneut intensiv, genau, und immer in Vernetzung, nämlich in steter Diskussion, getroffen. Dass manches Mal nicht von der Revolution des Designs, sondern von der Evolution bestimmter Teilaspekte gesprochen wurde, kann alle Preisträger, insbesondere die der 30 iF gold awards, mit Stolz erfüllen. Denn am Ende braucht es viele kleine Dinge, um das Große zu bewirken – und das ist im iF communication design award 2009 eindrucksvoll gelungen.

Allen Preisträgern gilt unser Glückwunsch und den Juroren unser herzlichster Dank!

Ralph Wiegmann
iF Geschäftsführer

Of Evolution and Revolution

Surely it is no coincidence that the terms "evolution" and "revolution" are identical but for a single letter: "R" as in radical change supplements evolution, or so one could surmise.

At the same time both of these words, far removed from their original context, have long since entered the world of campaigns, product descriptions and viral marketing activities. Nothing is more convincing to consumers than upheaval, or so the theory goes – even to the point where revolutionaries, resurrected by means of digital editing, are found musing in a current TV spot connecting them to a new car.

But which tactic, applied to technological progress, to maintaining and caring for our living space, to the economical cornerstones, to sociological and cultural relationships is the right one? Slow change passed on from generation to generation – or rather the sudden change of circumstances, even through the use of force?

With the parallelism of developments, with the intensity of events we are able to grasp in the global community, we have been assigned new responsibilities. No longer are we able to cover our eyes and ears, operating in a supposedly protected space. The amount of information and – this is becoming increasingly important – the qualification of data and reports requires time as well as sources that we trust and consider credible. And so innovation and selection go hand in hand, one being conditional on the other, developing from an entertainment medium reporting on glamour and banalities into a serious new tool to depict the events of the day: Both the community of states and the internet community, which operates beyond all borders, have been drawn into the political unrest following the elections in Iran. Twitter is a medium journalists depend on in order to inform the general public – and not just since the attacks in Bombay. The situation in Iran also turned the latest media accomplishments into more than just a technology to discover and develop further. Rather, the courage to express oneself in a public arena and the "success" confirmed by countless worldwide followers of the protestors documenting their efforts prove just how little may have filtered through to the "outside" under such conditions in the past.

The fact that false trails are, on the one hand, laid by the opposing side and, on the other hand, sometimes also have to be laid by those being persecuted in order to conceal their own identity certainly does impede the perception of explosive political truths at first glance. But upon closer inspection, intelligent clusters can be identified who, even in the rampant world of the internet, make corrections and offer evaluations – a sort of group dynamics quality control, one might say. Like other web media or like a simple bread knife that serves its purpose of slicing bread or represents a dangerous weapon, Twitter has two different faces. The fact that messages of any relevance, through communicative group formation, are now also directly implemented as actions on the internet or outside of it may be viewed as a threatening revolution or as evolution that is long overdue and has fed its past experiences into a new medium.

These examples prove both the opportunities and the explosive nature of interactive media – but also the required networked thought structures which the users and designers of these services have to acquire from day to day. In June of this year the "Institut zur Zukunft der Arbeit" (IZA) (Institute on the Future of Employment) presented the results of a study indicating that unemployment trends can be forecast by using the Google internet search engine. The frequency of certain search terms entered by Google users, such as "employment office" or "job exchange", was analyzed and compared to statistical data. The relationship established by the IZA should result in reliable forecasts in the near future. This shows that both the results as well as the query itself can be generated as hits – and in turn produce an overabundance of data. The speed and networking, the synchronicity of all events taking place requires free capacity in our minds – to think, consider, reconsider and above all to sort and qualify. We have come from the cross-media world, where paths still led there and back, to an "infinite media" world where things may cross paths but not necessarily have to, instead running parallel to infinity and yet causing each other – and that, possibly, at the speed of light.

The decision of the jury in this year's iF communication design award was once again reached after intensive, precise, and always networked – that is, constant – discussion. All of the laureates, especially the recipients of the 30 iF gold awards, can be proud of the fact that it was frequently not the revolution of the design but the evolution of specific aspects that was debated. Because in the

end, many small things are required to achieve great things – and the iF communication design award 2009 achieved this in an impressive manner.

Congratulations to all of the laureates and our sincere thanks to the jurors!

Ralph Wiegmann
iF Managing Director

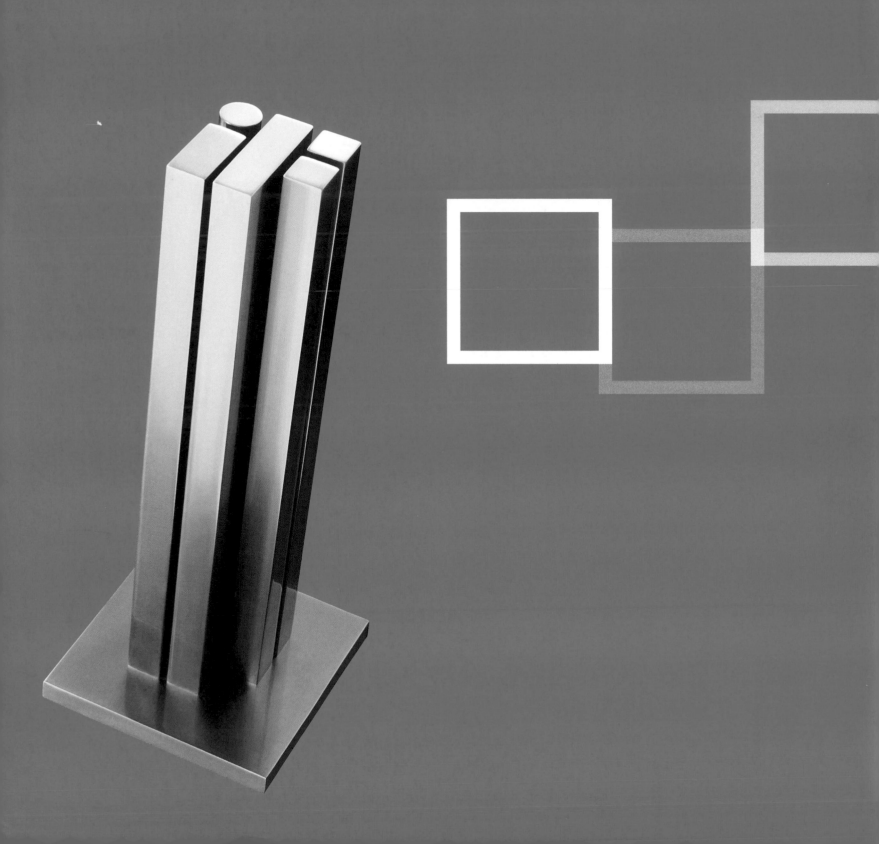

iF gold selection
2009

Eine Auszeichnung in einem der iF Wettbewerbe ist seit mehr als fünfzig Jahren ein Gütesiegel für herausragendes Design. Wer im iF product design award, im iF communication design award, im iF material award oder im iF packaging award von der jeweils fachkundigen, internationalen Jury das begehrte iF Label erhält, gehört zu den Besten seiner Branche. Zudem gibt es in jedem iF Wettbewerb die Chance, eine ganz besondere Trophäe nach Hause zu tragen: einen der iF gold awards. Diese eigens von Herbert H. Schultes entworfene iF Skulptur ist der Preis für die Besten des Wettbewerbs – und wer ihn erhält, hat mit einem ganz besonderen Produkt, einer Materialinnovation, einer Kommunikationsleistung oder einem Packaging die Jury überzeugt und sich so an die Spitze der Ausgezeichneten gesetzt. Alle Gewinner der iF gold awards bilden die iF gold selection des Jahres, die noch einmal in besonderer Form in der iF online exhibition dargestellt und auch als repräsentative Ausstellung zu sehen sein wird.

For over 50 years winning an iF award has served a symbol of outstanding design achievement. Anyone who manages to convince our international jury of experts to issue an iF product design award, an iF communication design award, an iF material award or an iF packaging award belongs to the crème de la crème in their sector. And every iF competition also offers its contestants a chance to win a special trophy as well: the iF gold award. These iF statuettes are a special creation of Herbert H. Schultes, and are considered to be for the best. Winning one of them means the recipient was particularly successful in convincing the jury of the exquisiteness of his or her product, material innovation, communication or packaging project, and therefore deserving of a special status among the other winners. All winners of an iF gold award automatically become members of the distinguished group known as the iF goldselection for the year, which is specially featured in the iF online exhibition and forms the basis of a high-class exhibition as well.

3M Svenska AB   adidas International Marketing BV   Adiri, Inc.   Air Berlin PLC & Co. Luftverkehrs KG
ALL STAR D.A.CH. GmbH   Amnesty International   Aperto AG   Apple, Inc.   Arco Meubelfabriek b.v.
argonauten G2 GmbH – a member of Grey | G2 Group   ART + COM   Art Directors Club für Deutschland
Atelier Oï   Baltensweiler AG
Bassier, Bergmann & Kindler Digital Sales and Brand Specialists Ludwigsburg GmbH   Bauerfeind AG
Baumann, Beck, Bergmann, Nowitzki   BEGA   BEGA · Produktgestaltung   BMW Group
Bolwin Wulf Architekten Partnerschaft   BSN medical GmbH   Canon Inc.   Catalyst Design Group
chilli mind GmbH   CITROËN Deutschland AG   Claudia Kempf Fotografie   color inc.
Crown Equipment Corp.   Crown Gabelstapler GmbH & Co. KG Industrial Design   D. Swarovski & Co
DAIKO ELECTRIC Co., Ltd.   DAIKO ELECTRIC Co., Ltd. PLCT   Daimler AG Business Unit Mercedes-Benz Vans
Daimler Financial Services AG / Intercom GmbH   Das Ding   DECATHLON   Demirden Design   DESSO
Deutsche Telekom AG   Dividium Capital Ltd.   Doro   Dr. Ing. h. c. F. Porsche AG   Elastique. We design.
Ergonomidesign   Euro RSCG Düsseldorf   Eye-Biz Pte Ltd.   fiftyfifty – Das Obdachlosenmagazin
Formation Design Group   formidable design   Fricke inszeniert. Dreidimensionale Kommunikation GmbH
fries & zumbühl   FSB Franz Schneider Brakel GmbH + Co KG   Graphische Betriebe Eberl GmbH
Haushoch   Hesse Design GmbH   Hilti Corporation   Hochschulinitiative Neue Bundesländer
Huawei Technologies Co. Ltd.   ilio   iriver Ltd.
Jonathan Herrle   Josef Niedermeier   Knog Pty Ltd.   Kolle Rebbe / KOREFE
Kunst am Bau und Leitsystem Ingeborg Kumpfmüller Mag. Art.   Kunsthochschule Weißensee
Kverneland Group   Laerdal Medical AS   LG Electronics, Inc. Corporate Design Center   Lothar Böhm GmbH
Lumini   Lyra Bleistiftfabrik GmbH   Martin et Karczinski GmbH   Marxen Wein GmbH & Co. KG
Miele & Cie. KG   MOOBEL GMBH   Mutabor Design GmbH   New Cat Orange Gestaltung und Kommunikation
Nils Frederking   Nippon Connection e. V.   Notions Publishing
ORNAMIN Kunststoffwerke W. Zschetzsche GmbH & Co. KG   Otto Bock HealthCare GmbH
Otto Bock Healthcare Products GmbH   Overath GmbH   Pacific Cycles, Inc.   Panasonic Corporation
Panasonic Corporation Design Company   Paperlux GmbH   Philips Design   Philips Healthcare Cardiac Care
POC Sweden AB   Powerflasher GmbH   PULS Design und Konstruktion   Ralf Kittmann
Rokitta, Produkt & Markenästhetik   Roset Möbel GmbH   Röthlisberger Schreinerei AG
Royal Philips Electronics   Ryohin Keikaku Co., Ltd.   Sal. Oppenheim jr. & Cie.   Samsung Electronics
SANYO Electric Co., Ltd.   SANYO Electric Co., Ltd. Advanced Design Center   Scholz & Friends Identify
SENZ Umbrellas BV   SilVER SEIKO   Simon & Goetz Design GmbH & Co. KG   Sirona Dental Systems GmbH
SNA Europe   Sonos   Sony Corporation   Sparkasse Berchtesgadener Land   Stefan Diez Industrial Design
Strichpunkt GmbH   Symo NV   Syzygy AG   the garage winery e.k.   The Art Box Collection   Thonet GmbH
TULP Products GmbH   Tobias Berneth, Shane Schneck   T-Systems Enterprise Services GmbH
Urband Asia Pacific   VanBerlo strategy+design   Veech Media Architecture (VMA)   Volkswagen AG
Whipsaw, Inc.   wirDesign communications AG   wirDesign / Fricke inszeniert.   Y Studios LLC
zweimaleins werbeagentur GmbH

Kathryn Best ist Beraterin, Autorin sowie Dozentin in den Bereichen Design, Management und Markenentwicklung. Ihre Aufgabe ist es, Marken in dreidimensionale Konzepte zu übersetzen und diese bis zur Realisierung zu betreuen. Bisher hat sie an der Bartlett School of Architecture, dem Royal College of Art in London und der Parsons School of Design in New York unterrichtet sowie ein Buch über Design Management veröffentlicht. Momentan doziert sie am University College for Creative Arts im Bereich Design Management.

Kathryn Best works as consultant, author and teacher in the fields of design, management and branding. Her role involves translating brands into three-dimensional environments and ensuring that design concepts were carried through to completion. She has lectured at the Bartlett School of Architecture, the Royal College of Art in London and the Parsons School of Design in New York and published a book on Design Management. Recently she is a Course Leader in Design Management at the University College for the Creative Arts.

Boris Lakowski (*1977) absolvierte ein Studium der Medienwirtschaft. Nach 3-jähriger Tätigkeit als Account Manager, Unitleiter und Geschäftsführer bei der Internet-Agentur Scholz & Volkmer in Wiesbaden gründete er zusammen mit Björn Sternsdorf die Strategieberatung für digitale Markenführung Sternsdorf Lakowski & Partner. Seit über vier Jahren unterrichtet er an den Hochschulen Wiesbaden und Düsseldorf in den Bereichen Informations- und Kommunikationstechnologie, Neue Technologien und Marketing-Kommunikation.

Boris Lakowski (*1977) graduated from Media-Management and afterwards worked for the Internet-Agency Scholz & Volkmer. Together with Björn Sternsdorf he founded the strategy consulting for digital brand management Sternsdorf Lakowski & Partner. Besides this Boris Lakowski is teaching information and communication technology, new technologies and marketing-communication at the universities of Wiesbaden and Duesseldorf for over four years now.

Gregg Heard machte 1988 seinen Bachelor-Abschluss in Graphic Design an der Kent State University. Heute arbeitet er als Senior Creative Director für Royal Philips in Amsterdam. Bevor er zu Philips kam, war er für Nesnadny & Schwartz in Cleveland, Mark Anderson Design in Palo Alto, Think New Ideas in Los Angeles, Clement Mok Designs, Studio Archetype in San Francisco sowie Sapient in Atlanta und London tätig. Während seiner 20-jährigen Berufserfahrung sind seine Designlösungen von zahlreichen Designpublikationen und -institutionen gewürdigt worden.

Gregg Heard graduated from Kent State University in 1988 with a BFA in Graphic Design. Today he works as a Senior Creative Director for Royal Philips in Amsterdam. Before coming to Philips Heard worked at Nesnadny & Schwartz in Cleveland, Mark Anderson Design in Palo Alto, Think New Ideas in Los Angeles, Clement Mok Designs and Studio Archetype in San Francisco and Sapient in their Atlanta and London offices. During his 20 years of work experience his design-solutions have been recognized by numerous design publications and institutions.

Kathryn Best

Boris Lakowski

Gregg Heard

Thomas Hirt

Markus Lüdemann

Prinz M. Pinakatt

Thomas Hirt studierte von 1993 bis 1997 Produktgestaltung an der HTW Dresden sowie berufsbegleitend im Jahr 2001 Strategisches Management, Marketingplanung und Organisation/Führung an der Fernuniversität Hagen. Ab 1998 arbeitete er als Projektleiter und schließlich als Gesamtleiter der Digitalen Kommunikation bei der ERCO Leuchten GmbH. Seit 2002 unterrichtet er an der FH Düsseldorf sowie an chinesischen Universitäten und hält regelmäßig Vorträge bei Institutionen wie dem Management Circle, dem Design Center Stuttgart und vielen mehr.

Thomas Hirt studied Product Design at the Dresden University of Applied Sciences and extra-occupational in 2001 strategic management, marketing planning, organisation/leadership at the distance university Hagen. Since 1998 he has worked for ERCO GmbH as project manager and finally as manager of digital communication. Since 2002 he teaches at the FH Düsseldorf as well as at Chinese universities and gives lectures at institutions such as the Management Circle, the Design Center Stuttgart and many more.

Markus Lüdemann (*1976) studierte von 1997 bis 2001 Design an der Fachhochschule für Design & Medien in Hannover. Nach Beendigung seines Studiums arbeitete er als User Interface Designer bei Sony International und SonyEricsson in München und anschließend als User Experience Manager bei Vodafone Global in Düsseldorf und Tokyo. Seit 2006 ist er als Head of User Experience bei LG Electronics Mobile in Düsseldorf tätig und leitet dort das User Interface Team.

Markus Lüdemann (*1976) graduated from the FH for Design & Media Hanover in Design. Past to his studies he worked for Sony International and SonyEricsson as User Interface Designer in Munich and afterwards at Vodafone Global in Duesseldorf and Tokyo as User Experience Manager. Since 2006 he is the Head of User Experience at LG Electronics Mobile in Duesseldorf, where he leads the User Interface team.

Prinz M. Pinakatt arbeitet seit 2007 für die Coca-Cola Company. Vorher war er als Interactive Marketing Manager in Deutschland tätig, wo er Mobilfunk- und Onlinekonzepte entwarf. Er arbeitete als Brand Manager für Marken wie Coca-Cola light und Fanta. Bei der Coca-Cola Company kümmert er sich um paneuropäische sowie globale digitale Initiativen. Er konzentriert sich dabei auf innovative digitale Markenerlebnisse und entwickelte für Deutschland den bekannten Launch www.cokefridge.de sowie www.cokezone.co.uk für Großbritannien.

Prinz M. Pinakatt works for the Coca-Cola Company since 2007. Prior to this he was Senior Interactive Marketing Manager in Germany delivering several mobile and online programs. He worked as Brand Manager for brands like Coca-Cola light and Fanta. His role within the Coca-Cola Company began in a European function dedicated to pan-european and global digital initiatives. He focuses on innovative digital brand experiences and developed the famous launch of www.cokefridge.de in Germany as well as www.cokezone.co.uk for Great Britain.

Anne Kurth (*1972) absolvierte ihr Designstudium an der International School of Design in Köln als Diplom-Designerin. Von 1996 bis 1998 arbeitete sie freiberuflich für Werbeagenturen und Designbüros wie kdh+p sowie Zintzmeyer & Lux. Seit 1998 ist sie Inhaberin und Geschäftsführerin der formfindung GmbH & Co. KG in Köln und war darüber hinaus von 2001 bis 2004 Vorstandsvorsitzende des Vereins KISD Club (ehemals Verein der Freunde und Förderer des Fachbereich Design e.V.).

Anne Kurth (*1972) graduated from the International School of Design Cologne with a Diploma in Design. From 1996 to 1998 she worked as an independant Designer for agencies like kdh+p and Zintzmeyer & Lux. Since 1998 Anne Kurth is he owner and manager of the formfindung GmbH & Co. KG in Cologne. Furthermore she held the office of the chairwoman of the KISD Club e.V. from 2001 to 2004.

Carsten Gluth studierte Betriebswirtschaftslehre. Nach unterschiedlichen Stationen bei Werbeagenturen in Düsseldorf und Hamburg gründete er 1997 die Kommunikationsagentur C3 CARPE CONNECT COMMUNICATIONS. C3 entwickelt Live-Marketing Konzepte für internationale Unternehmen und setzt diese weltweit um. Als aktives Mitglied in Kommunikationsverbänden und Fachgremien hat er sich zur Aufgabe gemacht, die Bedeutung des Live-Marketing im interdisziplinären Kontext zu stärken. Ein besonderes Augenmerk legt Gluth auf die Nachwuchsförderung in der Kommunikationsbranche.

Carsten Gluth studied economics. He worked for different advertising agencies in Düsseldorf and Hamburg. In 1997 he established the communication agency C3 CARPE CONNECT COMMUNICATIONS with offices in Hamburg and Hanover. C3 designs live-marketing concepts for clients all over the world. He takes an active part in organizations for communication and professional panels to boost the interest of live-marketing in a interdisciplinary context. He makes it his business to promote young people in the communication sector.

Alessandro Balossini Volpe studierte Rechtswissenschaften in seiner Heimatstadt Mailand und absolvierte anschließend seinen Master im Bereich Marketing. Seine berufliche Laufbahn wurde nach Beendigung seines Studiums vor allem von internationalen Unternehmen geprägt, die mit weltweit bekannten Marken wie Mattel, Sergio Tacchini, Fila, Salvatore Ferragamo, Upim und Artemide operieren. Als selbstständiger Berater legt Alessandro Balossini Volpe seinen beruflichen Fokus auf die Vermarktung von Premium-Marken im Bereich Mode, Luxus und Design.

Alessandro Balossini Volpe studied law in his home town Milan and afterwards took an MBA in Marketing. His professional career was developed through several multi-national companies, operating through internationally leading brands, like Mattel, Sergio Tacchini, Fila, Salvatore Ferragamo, Upim and Artemide. As an independant consultant Alessandro Balossini Volpe's professional focus lies on the management of premium brands in fashion, luxury and design industries.

Anne Kurth

Carsten Gluth

Alessandro Balossini Volpe

Andreas Rotzler

Dr. Andreas Siefke

Markus Rachals

Markus Rachals war von 1996 bis 1999 als Group-Brandmanager bei Viag Interkom/O2 Germany tätig. Von 2000 bis 2003 arbeitete er als Geschäftsstellenleiter der Sportsponsoring Agentur Zimmermann in München. Mit seiner langjährigen Erfahrung begann er 2004 seine Tätigkeit bei der adidas AG, wo er 2006 die Position des Head of Brand Marketing im Bereich Area Central übernahm.
Markus Rachals worked at Viag Interkom / O2 Germany as Group-Brandmanager from 1996 to 1999. From 2000 until 2003 he was the branch manager of the sport-sponsoring agency Zimmermann in Munich. In 2004 he started his career at the adidas AG, where he became Head of Brand Marketing in the field of Area Central.

Andreas Rotzler schloss sein Design-Studium an der Grafikfachklasse Basel mit Auszeichnung ab. Nach einigen Jahren als freier Künstler und Designer arbeitete er von 1992 bis 1994 als freier Illustrator, unter anderem für Leib+Gut in Bern, Rucker Huggins in Kalifornien und für Designalltag in Zürich. Seit 1996 ist Andreas Rotzler bei Interbrand Zintzmeyer & Lux tätig, heute ist er dort Chief Creative Director. Zu seinen wichtigsten Kunden zählen u.a. die Deutsche Telekom, Schindler, MINI, BMW, DOW XLA, Lucern Festival, graubünden, Jura, Roche.
Andreas Rotzler graduated from his design studies in Basel with distinction. After a few years as an independent artist and designer he specialized as an illustrator and worked for various companies and agencies such as Leib+Gut in Bern, Rucker Huggins in California and Designalltag in Zurich. Since 1997 he joined Interbrand Zintzmeyer & Lux and was appointed Chief Creative Director in 2007. His most important clients are Deutsche Telekom, Schindler, MINI, graubünden, BMW, DOW XLA, Lucerne Festival, Franke, Jura, Roche, to name just a few.

Dr. Andreas Siefke (*1967) beendete 1993 sein Studium der Betriebswirtschaftslehre mit Prädikatsexamen – 1997 erlangte er die wirtschaftswissenschaftliche Doktorwürde. Nach seiner wissenschaftlichen Mitarbeit von 1993 bis 1998 am Institut für Marketing der Universität Münster übernahm er 1998 die Geschäftsführung der Forschungsstelle Bahnmarketing in der Wissenschaftlichen Gesellschaft für Marketing und Unternehmensführung e.V. in Münster. Seit 2000 ist er beim HOFFMANN UND CAMPE VERLAG GmbH in Hamburg tätig, dort hat er seit 2004 die Geschäftsführung inne.
Dr. Andreas Siefke (*1967) graduated with distinction in business economics in 1993 – in 1997 he obtained the degree of doctor in this field. After his scientific collaboration at the Muenster University's Institute for Marketing he became manager for the Research Center in Bahnmarketing of the Academic Society for Marketing and Business Leadership, in Muenster. Since 2000 he works at HOFFMANN AND CAMPE Corporate Publishing in Hamburg, where he holds the position of the manager since 2004.

Jennifer Tsai

Arne Schultchen

Jennifer Tsai ist seit 1987 Geschäftsführerin sowie Kreativdirektorin bei Proad Identity in Taiwan. Ihr berufliches Schaffen hat sie der Verbindung östlicher mit westlichen Kulturen verschrieben – in ihren Entwürfen kombiniert sie östliche Elemente mit westlichen Designs. Darüber hinaus setzt sie sich für die Verbindung internationaler Bündnisse und Assoziationen ein, wie u. a. der Global Design Source, der Pan European Design Association. Jennifer Tsai wurde als herausragende Frau Chinas geehrt und gewann für ihr Markendesign zahlreiche Preise.

Jennifer Tsai is managing and creative director of Proad Identity since 1987. In order to the fusion of eastern and western culture, she devoted herself to present eastern elements in western design and to work on linking the international alliance and association, such as Global Design Source, Pan European Brand Design Association and many more. She has been honoured as "China Outstanding Woman" and won numerous prizes in branding design.

Arne Schultchen (*1965) studierte Design an der Hochschule für bildende Künste Hamburg. 1994 gründete er gemeinsam mit seinem Partner André Feldmann die feldmann+schultchen design studios GmbH. Gemeinsam mit seinem Team erarbeitete Schultchen von Beginn an Design-Lösungen für verschiedenste Bereiche, von Architektur über Marke und Produkt bis hin zu Verpackung. Zahlreiche internationale Preise und Patente im Design-Bereich zeichnen die feldmann+schultchen design studios heute aus.

Arne Schultchen (*1965) obtained a degree in design at the University of Fine Arts of Hamburg. In 1994 he founded the feldmann+schultchen design studios GmbH together with his partner André Feldmann. From that moment Schultchen and his team created design solutions for several fields of design, from architecture and product to branding or packaging. Today the feldmann+schultchen design studios can be characterized by numerous prizes and patents within the field of design.

Hubert Grothaus studierte Kommunikationsdesign in München. 1988 gründete er die Design Company Agentur GmbH, eine Agentur für Markenführung und Markenentwicklung. Als Creative Director arbeitet er heute mit 35 Architekten, Innenarchitekten und Designern für Kunden, wie Audi, Sony Ericsson, Salewa, APC und Fischer. Hubert Grothaus gewann Design-Preise für diverse Messe- und Shopprojekte, wie den iF exhibition design award in Gold und Silber, den contractworld.award und den ddc award.

Hubert Grothaus studied communication design in Munich. In 1988 he founded the Design Company Agentur GmbH, an agency for brand management and brand development. Today he works as Creative Director in a team with 35 interior designers, architects and designers for clients such as Audi, Sony Ericsson, Salewa, APC and Fischer. Hubert Grothaus won numerous design prizes for his exhibition and shop projects, like the iF exhibition design award in gold and silver, the contractworld.award as well as the ddc award.

Jou Min Lin studierte Architektur und Urban Design an der Tam Kang University in Taiwan sowie an der Columbia University in New York. 1995 gründete er J.M.Lin Architect, P.C in New York. Zwei Jahre später kam J.M.Lin Architect/The Observer Design Group in Taipei hinzu. Jou Min Lin ist der führende Architekt beider Büros, die für nachhaltige Werte in Architektur und Design stehen. Sein Team setzt sich aus Spezialisten in den Bereichen Architektur, Innenarchitektur, Landschaftsarchitektur, Grafikdesign sowie Kommunikationsdesign zusammen.

Jou Min Lin studied architecture and urban design at Tam Kang University Taiwan and at Columbia University New York. In 1995 he founded J.M.Lin Architect, P.C. in New York. Two years later J.M.Lin Architect/The Observer Design Group was founded in Taipei. Jou Min Lin is the principle architect for both offices, which strive for lasting value in architecture and design. His team works in the fields of architecture, interior design, landscape design, graphic design, communication design and research-based design.

Hans-Henrik Sørensen schloss sein Studium in den Bereichen Marketing und Wirtschaftswissenschaften ab. Seine berufliche Laufbahn begann er als Web-Designer, seitdem arbeitet er sowohl in der kreativen als auch der kommerziellen Entwicklung von Design. Heute ist Sørensen Director of Interactive Design bei der Design-Beratung Designit AS. Sein Fokus liegt auf der Konzept- und Geschäftsentwicklung im multidisziplinären Umfeld bei Designit, indem er sowohl hocheffiziente als auch kreative Lösungen für internationale Kunden entwickelt.

Hans-Henrik Sørensen graduated in marketing and economics. He began his career as a web designer and since then has been managing both the creative and the commercial side of design development. Today Sørensen is Director of Interactive Design at the design consultancy Designit AS. His focus lies on concept and business development in a multi-disciplinary environment at Designit, delivering high-impact and creative solutions for international clients.

Jou Min Lin

Hubert Grothaus

Hans-Henrik Sørensen

Thomas Hirt

Gregg Heard

Markus Rachals

Arne Schultchen

Carsten Gluth

Jennifer Tsai

Hans-Henrik Sørensen

Alessandro Balossini Volpe

Markus Lüdemann

Prinz M. Pinakatt

Andreas Rotzler

Hubert Grothaus

Dr. Andreas Siefke

Boris Lakowski

Kathryn Best

J.M. Lin

Anne Kurth

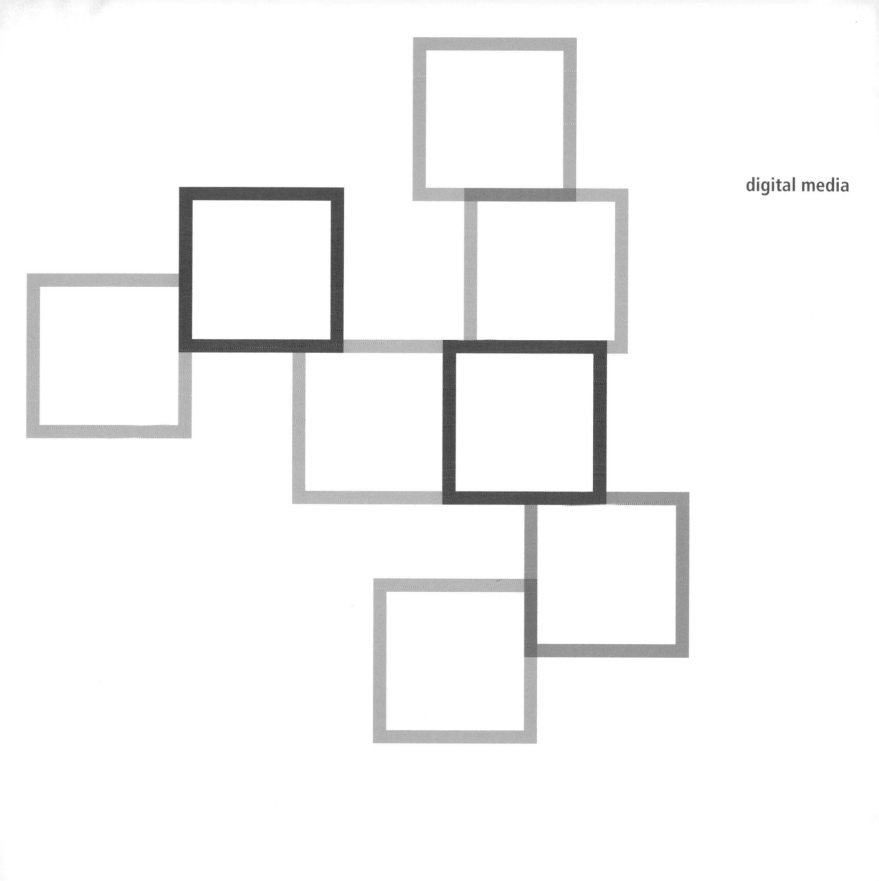

digital media

„Kommunikationsdesigner als ‚Designdenker'"

Die Integration von Marke, Technik, Inhalt, Medien und Erzählkunst ist einer der schönsten Aspekte des Kommunikationsdesigns digitaler Medien als Plattform für die Verbreitung von Botschaften sowie für das Knüpfen gezielter Kontakte zu Individuen und einem in Einzelpersonen aufgeteilten Publikum – die Kultur der Partizipation wird mehr und mehr vom Internet bestimmt. Heutzutage finden Kommunikationsdesigner im Bereich der kreativen Dienstleistung immer mehr Geschäftsfelder vor: als „Vermittler" von Konversationen und Ideen ebenso wie als „Designdenker" mit tangentialen, Problem lösenden Ansätzen zur Bewältigung der in Beruf, Gesellschaft und Umwelt gestellten Aufgaben.

In diesem Jahr gab es in der Kategorie digitale Medien insgesamt 79 Beiträge, aufgeteilt in die Unterkategorien Animation, Atmosphäre, Benutzeroberfläche, Bildschirmdesign, Struktur, Viralität, digitale Werbung und Humor. In lebhaften, zuweilen intensiven Diskussionen beurteilte die Jury für digitale Medien jeden Beitrag nach den folgenden Kriterien: Zielgruppenansprache und Inhalte, Usability, „Look and Feel", Einzigartigkeit.

Einsender der Beiträge waren zahlreiche Organisationen auf der ganzen Welt – von Designabteilungen großer Firmen über Designberater und Agenturen für digitale Medien bis hin zu unabhängigen kreativen Unternehmen. Die Beiträge – Online-Umgebungen, Bannerwerbung, webbasierte, virale Marketingkampagnen, E-Commerce-Produkte, Service-Kataloge, Werbepräsentationen und -filme für Unternehmen, Online-Magazine und animierte Fernsehtrailer – zeugen in all ihrer Vielfalt von originellen Methoden, wie man sein Publikum durch die animierte, interaktive Kraft digitaler Medien fesseln kann. Der quer durch alle Beiträge feststellende Reichtum an Designsprache, Format und Inhalten war äußerst bemerkenswert. Diese Art von werthaltiger Kreativität garantiert dem Kommunikationsdesign einen gesicherten Platz in der Geschäftswelt. Dieses mächtige Instrument nimmt erheblichen Einfluss darauf, wie das Publikum eine Marke, eine Botschaft, eine Erfahrung oder eine Aussage aufnimmt und ob diese Aussage letztlich ernst genommen oder zurückgewiesen wird.

"Communication designers as 'design thinkers'"

The integration of brand, technology, content, media and storytelling is one of the most satisfying aspects of digital media communication design, as a platform for conveying a message and, in our increasingly web-enabled participative culture, building customised relationships with individuals and audiences, one person at a time. Today, there are evidently an increasing number of opportunities for communication designers to engage with and in business, creatively offering their services as 'facilitators' of conversations and ideas, and as 'design thinkers', taking a tangential, problem-solving approach to the challenges faced by business, society and the environment.

This year saw a total of 79 entries in the digital media category, a wide range of work entered across the sub-categories of animation, atmosphere, interface, screendesign, structure, virality, digital advertising and humor. Through lively discussion and at times intense debate, the digital media jury considered how each entry addressed the following criteria: Targeting and content, usability, look and feel, uniqueness.

The entries originated from a wide range of organisations across the world – from in-house design teams of major corporations, to design consultancies and digital media agencies, through to independent creative enterprises. The diversity of applications – from on-line environments, banner ads, web-based viral marketing campaigns, e-commerce product and service catalogs, company promotional presentations and films, online magazines and animated television trailers – each demonstrated a wide range of inventive approaches in how to engage audiences, compellingly, through the animated and interactive power of digital media. The richness of design language, format and content displayed across the range of entries was really quite remarkable. It is this kind of value-adding creativity that guarantees communication design a firm place in business. It is an enormously powerful means of influencing how a brand, a message, an experience or a story is received by an audience, and whether that story is ultimately accepted, or rejected.

Kathryn Best

Digitale Kommunikation ist unabdingbarer Bestandteil eines jeden Kommunikationsmixes

Die diesjährigen Bewerbungen um einen iF communication design award kamen zahlreich und gleichermaßen aus der B2C als auch dem B2B Bereich. Dies stellte auf der einen Seite eine Herausforderung für die Juroren dar, schließlich ist es nicht leicht faire Kriterien für die Ansprache beider Kundengruppen zu definieren, andererseits belegt dies auch, dass digitale Kommunikation ein unabdingbarer Bestandteil eines jeden Kommunikationsmixes geworden ist – sei es für ein alkoholisches Getränk oder für den Anbieter von Scharnieren

Grundsätzlich ist festzustellen, dass eine gewisse Standardisierung im Bereich Userführung und Usability erreicht wurde. Dies ist absolut im Sinne des Users, da er sich mehr auf die Inhalte einer Site konzentrieren kann, als auf das Abrufen dieser konzentrieren muss. Darüber hinaus ist die Einbindung von multimedialem Content ein immer häufiger genutztes Mittel zur Steigerung der „Stickiness" einer Site oder einer Applikation geworden. Dies geht einher mit einer stärkeren Vernetzung verschiedener Medien und Kanäle, was die Komplexität für den User teilweise vergrößert, aber, wenn es gut gemacht ist, zu einer wesentlich intensiveren Interaktion mit der Marke und/oder dem Produkt führt.

Ein Kritikpunkt, den es anzumerken gibt, ist, dass es leider kein Feuerwerk an Kreativität und Innovationen gab. Dies mag an der vorher genannten Nivellierung oder den dieser Tage üblichen, gekürzten Budgets liegen.

Abschließend ist zu sagen, dass es den Juroren in den zwei Tagen sehr viel Spaß gemacht hat die Arbeiten anschauen, zu „erfahren" und zu bewerten, und dass die speziell mit dem iF gold award prämierten Arbeiten absolut überzeugt haben.

Digital communication is an essential component of any communication mix

This year's numerous submissions for the iF communication design award came from both the B2C and the B2B segments. On the one hand, this represented a challenge for the jurors since it is not easy to define fair criteria to address these two customer groups. On the other hand, it also confirms that digital communication has become an essential component of the communication mix – for everything from alcoholic beverages to a supplier of hinges.

In general, a certain level of standardization has been achieved in terms of user guidance and usability. This definitely benefits the user, since he or she can focus more on the content of a site rather than concentrating on how to access it. Furthermore, the integration of multimedia content is increasingly being used as a means to increase the "stickiness" of a site or application. This goes hand in hand with the ongoing convergence of various media and channels, which sometimes increases the level of complexity for users but, when it is done well, leads to much more intensive interaction with the brand and/or the product.

One notable point of criticism is that there are, unfortunately, no fireworks of creativity and innovation. This may be due to the leveling trend identified above or the reduced budgets common these days.

In conclusion, it can be said that the jurors very much enjoyed examining, "experiencing" and evaluating the entries over the course of two days and that the submissions honored with the iF gold award in particular were absolutely convincing.

Prinz M. Pinakatt

Project
Mercedes-Benz Narnia
Microsite

Design
Syzygy AG
Dirk Ollmann, Daniel Richau,
Alexander Meinhardt,
Wolfgang Schröder,
Christina Metzler, Thorsten Binder
Bad Homburg, Germany

Client
Daimler AG
Business Unit Mercedes-Benz Vans
Stuttgart-Untertürkheim, Germany

Wenn Mercedes-Benz und Disney gemeinsame Sache machen, dann ist die Welt nicht genug. Deshalb hat Syzygy zur Kooperation von Viano und „Die Chroniken von Narnia" eine Parallelwelt entstehen lassen – eine Web Wide World für Viano und Narnia, die das Beste aus beiden Welten zusammenbringt, es medienadäquat inszeniert und dabei nicht nur Kinder, sondern auch Eltern anspricht. Die Microsite ist eine runde Sache geworden – dank des Zusammenspiels von innovativer Technik und Kreation. Auf dem 3-D-Globus können Viano-Reisende in sechs spannenden Szenarien fantastische Abenteuer erleben – powered by Flash, 3-D, Motion Design, After Effects und Photoshop.

The world is not enough when Mercedes-Benz and Disney cooperate. Therefore Syzygy created a new and better world as an online communication platform for the Mercedes Viano and Disney's "The Chronicles of Narnia". On this 3D globe the user experiences fantastic adventures while travelling with the Viano. After a lesson in archery the user meets his new travelling companion in the deeps of the forest: the Viano. He can also dub someone to knighthood, challenge the Narnians to an ear waving contest or take a glimpse into the future. Whatever he does, he is always in the best place for heroes – a world where adventures lure behind every corner.

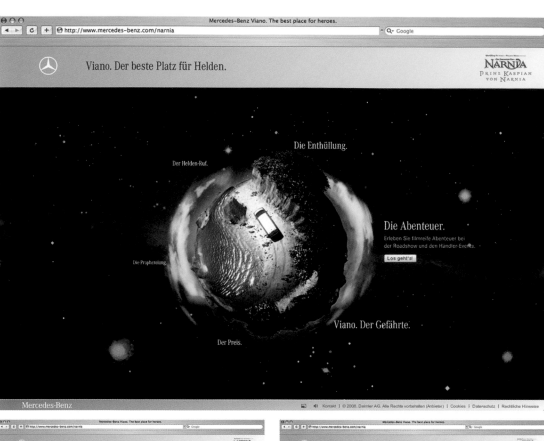

Project
Converse.de Relaunch
Website

Design
Powerflasher GmbH
Constanze Leinweber, André Britz,
Malte Beyer, Nico Zimmermann,
Timo Langpeter, Sven Sonntag,
Mattes Groeger, Stephan Partzsch,
Jens Halm, Carlo Blatz
Aachen, Germany

Client
ALL STAR D.A.CH. GmbH
Neuss, Germany

ALL STAR D.A.CH. beauftragte Powerflasher mit dem Design, der Konzeption und der Umsetzung der Webseite www.converse.de für den deutschsprachigen Markt. Die neue Seite wurde unter strenger Berücksichtigung des Converse-typischen „Look" und „Style" entwickelt. Im Zentrum stehen der „Spirit" der Marke und das Logo – der Stern. Alle Produkte, wie Schuhe, Bekleidung und Accessoires, werden in einem sternförmigen Showroom – realisiert in Flash – präsentiert. Ein menschlicher Avatar – gefilmt und digital nachbearbeitet – betreut die User. Die intuitive Bedienung sowie die Einbindung von Kampagnen, News und der Geschichte von Converse machen den Besuch zum Erlebnis.

ALL STAR D.A.CH. entrusted Powerflasher with the design, conception and realization of www.converse.de. The new website for the German-speaking market was designed in due consideration of the brand's unique style and feel. It's all about the typical logo and the casual spirit. All products like shoes, apparel and accessories are presented in a star shaped showroom, completely based on Flash. A realistic avatar – filmed and digitally altered afterwards – assists users in finding a specific product. Consistent usability, special campaigns, news and valuable insight in Converse's history make sure the visit will be an extraordinary experience.

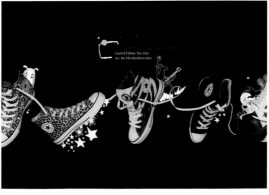

Project
Volkswagen2028.com
Webspecial

Design
argonauten G2 GmbH
– a member of Grey l G2 Group
Jan Pautsch, Matthias Trick,
Larissa Honsek, Tobias Richter,
Jens Wettlaufer, Roland Schweighöfer
Berlin, Germany

Client
Volkswagen AG
Wolfsburg, Germany

Wie wird die automobile Welt des Jahres 2028 aussehen? Die Website www.volkswagen2028.com wagt einen Ausblick in die Zukunft und gibt mögliche Antworten auf diese komplexe Frage. Hier vermittelt Volkswagen den Kunden seine Vision für das Jahr 2028 – einfach, unterhaltsam, auf Augenhöhe. Zuerst führt ein interaktiver Film den User in die Informationsebenen. Dabei bietet der „Digital Butler" dem Nutzer nach Belieben immer wieder Interaktionsmöglichkeiten. Experteninterviews, Animationen zu Technologien, Zukunftsautos in 3D und vertiefende Texte erörtern anschaulich und für jedermann verständlich die Frage: „Wie werden wir in Zukunft Auto fahren?"

What will the world of driving feel like in 20 years? This complex question requires very human answers – both from VW and from the Flash website we designed to deliver them. So the site brings the present and the future together, using text, animation and a short film to show how VW engineers, designers and researchers are developing breakthrough answers to the question: "How will we drive?" It's an elegant combination of lean-forward and lean-back scenarios, accompanied by a "digital butler", and built to be human rather than sci-fi – to provoke, not just inform; to feel sticky, not slick.

 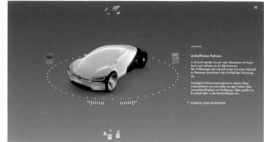

Project
F1-Noise Race
Online Game

Design
zweimaleins werbeagentur GmbH
Jochen Martens (Art Direction)
Christoph Hänold (Art Direction/
Design)
Christoph Kluge (Grafik)
Berlin, Germany

Client
T-Systems Enterprise Services GmbH
Frankfurt a. M., Germany

Die Kommunikation des ICT-Portfolios von T-Systems richtet sich meist an ein Fachpublikum. Im Umfeld der Formel 1 sollte aber ein breiteres Publikum emotional erreicht und eine überzeugende Brücke zu den Kernkompetenzen des Unternehmens geschaffen werden. Im Sinne dieser Anforderung haben wir im Rahmen der Komplett-Umsetzung der F1-Online-Präsentation das „F1-Noise Race" entwickelt. Das Online-Multiplayer-Game wird per Telefon gesteuert und zeigt, welchen wesentlichen Beitrag die ICT im Hintergrund des Renngeschehens leistet. Aus dem kommunikativen Gedanken „IT + TK + Lautstärke = Geschwindigkeit" entstand das Motto: „Je lauter, desto schneller."

The ICT portfolio from T-Systems communicates mainly to a specialist audience.
In connection with Formula 1 it is intended to reach a broader-based audience on an emotional level and to build a convincing bridge to the company's areas of core competence. To meet this requirement we have developed the "F1-Noise Race" as part of the overall F1 online presentation. The online player game is controlled by phone and demonstrates what an essential contribution ICT makes in the background to the race. The communicative idea of "IT + TC + Volume = Speed" gave rise to the motto: "The louder, the faster."

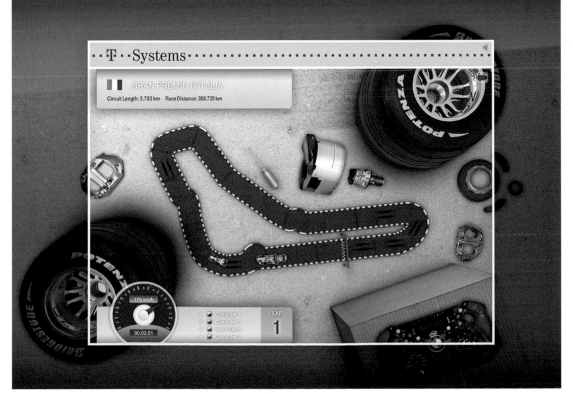

Project
Studieren in Fernost
Studiensuchmaschine
Study search engine

Design
Aperto AG
Moritz Otto
Berlin, Germany

Client
Hochschulinitiative Neue Bundesländer
Berlin, Germany

Herkömmliche Studientests und Hochschulsuchen sind langweilig: Suchmasken oder lange Tests mit Textfragen. Die Hochschulstudiensuchmaschine der Kampagne „Studieren in Fernost" ist anders: Sie ist laut, schrill, spannend und verrückt. Zugeschnitten auf die Zielgruppe der 16- bis 20-Jährigen unterstützt die unter www.studieren-in-fernost.de und auf schülerVZ erreichbare Applikation Studieninteressierte bei der Auseinandersetzung mit dem Thema Studieren in Ostdeutschland. Die Maschine schafft Aufmerksamkeit durch Irritation und Unterhaltung. Das komplexe Interaktions-Design ist schrill, laut und modern, aber trotzdem einheitlich und authentisch.

Conventional study tests or college searches are boring: search forms or long tests with text questions. The college study search engine for the "Studying in the Far East" campaign is different: it is loud, flashy, exciting and crazy. Aimed at the target group of 16 to 20-year-olds, the application available at www.studieren-in-fernost.de and on schülerVZ helps interested students with the topic of studying in Eastern Germany. The search engine attracts attention by means of irritation and entertainment. The complex interaction design is flash, loud and modern but nevertheless uniform and authentic.

Project
Porsche: Sturm und Drang.
Die neuen Cayman Modelle.
Webspecial

Design
Bassier, Bergmann & Kindler
Digital Sales and Brand Specialists
Ludwigsburg GmbH
Martin Spies, Mario Stockhausen (Art
Direction)
Andreas Herde (Concept)
Dennis Borgemehn (Project Manage-
ment)
Michael Weh, Pacal Knoske (Flash)
Ludwigsburg, Germany

Client
Dr. Ing. h. c. F. Porsche AG
Ludwigsburg, Germany

Das Webspecial präsentiert die neuen Cayman Modelle als moderne Technologieträger in nächtlicher,
städtischer Umgebung. Musik spielt eine tragende
Rolle. Über sowohl visuell als auch musikalisch unterschiedlich inszenierte Routen taucht der Nutzer
in die „stylish-urbane" Welt der Cayman Modelle
ein. So ermöglicht das Webspecial die Identifikation
verschiedenster Nutzertypen. Die Message lautet:
„Der Cayman passt zu Dir." Eine Besonderheit des
Webspecials ist das Modul „Ihr Cayman Mix" – eine
Möglichkeit, seinen persönlichen, individuellen „Cay-
man-Clip" zusammenzustellen. Das Ergebnis kann
auf Handy/iPhone (und Desktop) heruntergeladen
werden.

This webspecial presents the new Cayman models
as modern prototypes in an urban, night-time setting. The music plays a supporting role here. Through
visually as well as musically different staged routes,
the user is immersed in the stylish, urban world of
the different Caymans. In this way, the webspecial
enables the identification of a wide variety of user
types and conveys the message: "The Cayman suits
you." A special feature of the webspecial is "Your
Cayman Mix". The module offers the option of "mix-
ing" your personal, individual "Cayman Clip". The
result can be downloaded to a mobile phone/iPhone
(and desktop).

Project
fiftyfifty – Das Obdachlosenmagazin
„Transparent Man"
Digitale Medien
Digital media

Design
Euro RSCG Düsseldorf
Felix Glauner, Torsten Pollmann,
Florian Meimberg, Jean-Pierre Gregor,
Till Köster
Düsseldorf, Germany

Client
fiftyfifty – Das Obdachlosenmagazin
Düsseldorf, Germany

Die Aufgabe:
Sensibilisieren und zum Kauf des Obdachlosenmaga-
zins „fiftyfifty" animieren.
Die Lösung:
Obdachlose fühlen sich, als würde man durch sie hin-
durch sehen. Das demonstrieren wir mit einer spektakulären Aktion zur Weihnachtszeit.
Die Umsetzung:
Eine Kamera nimmt die Szenerie hinter dem Obdach-
losen auf. Ein Beamer projiziert das Bild auf ihn. Live!
So erhalten die Fußgänger den Eindruck, der Obdachlose sei unsichtbar. Seine Botschaft: „Ignorier' mich
nicht!"
Das Resultat:
Umfangreiche regionale und überregionale Bericht-
erstattung und eine ausverkaufte Ausgabe der „fiftyfifty".

The brief:
Sensitize the public and incite them to buy the home-
less magazine "fiftyfifty".
The solution:
Homeless people often feel like pedestrians look right
through them. We visualize just that with an amazing
promotion during the Christmas season.
The execution:
A camera captures the scenery behind a homeless
man. A video projector projects the picture onto him.
Live! Pedestrians get the impression that the home-
less is invisible. His message: "Don't ignore me!"
The result:
Extensive regional and nationwide TV and press coverage and a sold-out issue of the homeless magazine
"fiftyfifty".

Project
BMW 7 Series Configurator
Website

Design
Interone Worldwide GmbH
Patrick Fonger, Jochen Röhling,
Svenja Wiegemann, John DuBois,
Serdar Sahin, Robert Schulke,
Hannes Stockner, Sven Busse,
Chris Amon, Sebastian Vogt
Hamburg, Germany

Client
BMW AG
München, Germany

Für den neuen „BMW 7er" sollte ein Konfigurator entstehen, der sich perfekt in Kampagne und Web-special einfügt – und der dem Flaggschiff von BMW in jedem Detail gerecht wird. Der „BMW 7 Series Configurator" erlaubt dem User, sein persönliches Fahrzeug bis ins Detail zusammenzustellen, verzichtet dabei jedoch auf umfangreiche Menüs und komplexe Navigation. Erleben und Erkunden stehen im Vordergrund, wenn der User seine Wunsch-Ausstattungen direkt am gezeigten Fahrzeug auswählt. Großformatige Bilder und 360-Grad-Darstellungen liefern bestechende Eindrücke und erlauben eine intuitive Fahrzeug-Konfiguration.

For the new "BMW 7 Series Sedan", a configurator was to be created that would fit perfectly into the campaign and online multimedia highlight – as well as meet in every detail the standards set by the flagship model from BMW. The "BMW 7 Series Configurator" allows users to create their own personal vehicle down to the finest detail, yet at the same time, it does away with extensive menus and complex navigation. The focus is placed on experiencing and exploring when users select the equipment they desire directly on the vehicle. Large-format images and 360-degree views deliver captivating impressions and allow for an intuitive vehicle configuration.

49

Project
Daniel Libeskind
Website

Design
Elastique. We design.
Betty Schimmelpfennig,
Andreas Schimmelpfennig,
Karz von Bonin, Wolfgang Schmitz,
Peter Pannes, Thomas Ganter
Köln, Germany

Client
proportion GmbH
Berlin, Germany

Die limitierten „Signature Series of Private Homes"
sind luxuriöse Villen, die die besondere Handschrift
des Star-Architekten Daniel Libeskind tragen. Um
diese persönliche Note im Internet zu transportieren, führt Daniel Libeskind als Gastgeber durch die
gesamte Website. So erfahren Betrachter alles über
das Projekt aus erster Hand: von der Idee bis hin zu
Details über das Haus. Inspiriert von Papiermodel-
len, mit denen der Architekt bevorzugt arbeitet, greift
die visuelle Gestaltung der Website den Entwurfs-
prozess in abstrakter Form auf: Papierähnliche Flächen formen sich immer wieder zu Objekten, die an
die Form des Hauses erinnern.

The limited "Signature Series of Private Homes"
stands for luxurious villas, bearing the hallmarks
of their creator: star architect Daniel Libeskind. In
order to transfer this personal connection to the
corresponding internet presence, Libeskind himself
is guiding users through the website. By means of
several interviews he gives a firsthand impression
of underlying ideas and interesting details regarding the project. The visual language of the website
is inspired by hundreds of paper models the famous
architect uses during the design process: paper-like
white shapes, animated and forming diverse sculp-
tures, always reminding of the villa.

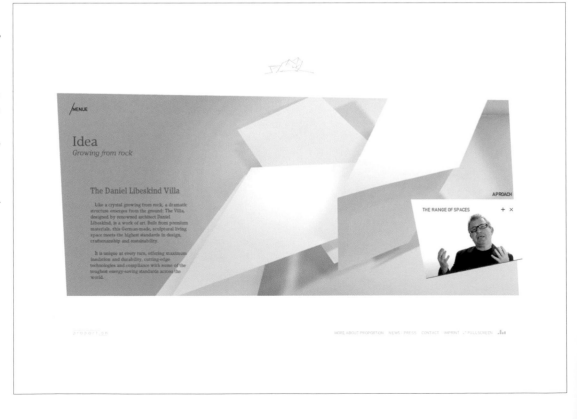

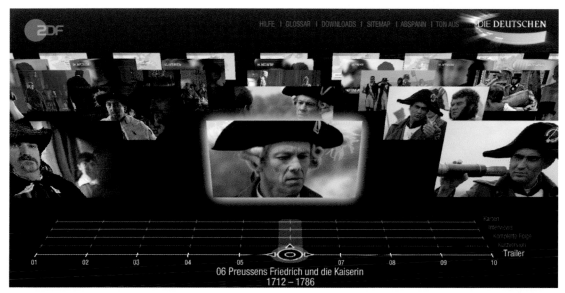

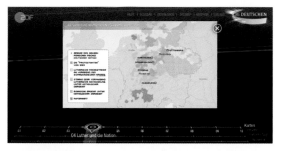

Project
DIE DEUTSCHEN
Microsite

Design
form one – visuelle kommunikation
Niels Bünemann (Creative Direction &
Concept)
Michael Rieble (Concept)
Hamburg, Germany

Client
ZDF – Zweites Deutsches Fernsehen
Mainz, Germany

Die 10-teilige ZDF-Dokumentarreihe DIE DEUTSCHEN lässt 1.000 Jahre deutscher Geschichte lebendig werden. Sie wird durch eine umfassende, interaktive Flash-Applikation erlebbar gemacht, die es dem Nutzer erlaubt, eine Zeitreise durch die wechselvolle deutsche Geschichte zu unternehmen. Alle Folgen sind als Kurztrailer, Kurzversionen und Komplettfolgen abrufbar. Außerdem stehen historische Karten und Experteninterviews bereit. Dies alles kann der Nutzer mithilfe eines „Zeitschiebers" direkt „erfahren", indem er zu den Folgen, Interviews und Karten navigiert, die als Bildsymbole dreidimensional und chronologisch auf einem Gitter aufgereiht sind.

The 10 episodes of the ZDF documentary THE GERMANS revive 1,000 years of German history. An accompanying extensive and interactive Flash application makes it possible to travel through the changeful history of the Germans. All episodes are available as different short trailers and can also be viewed in full length. In addition historic maps and interviews with experts stand by. All these components can be experienced by the user by using the so-called "time slider" to navigate through the episodes, interviews and maps, which are arranged chronological and in 3D on a baseline grid.

Project
E.ON – focussing on your needs.
Vertriebstool
Sales tool

Design
avcommunication GmbH
Nikola Wischnewsky (Gesamtleitung)
Sonja Westfeld (Projektleitung
Design)
Martin Fuchs (Design/Programmie-
rung)
Ludwigsburg/München, Germany

Client
E.ON Energie AG
München, Germany
E.ON Energy Sales GmbH
München, Germany
E.ON Ruhrgas AG
Essen, Germany
E.ON Vertrieb Deutschland GmbH
München, Germany

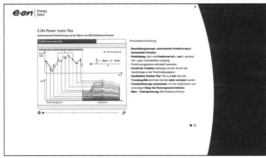

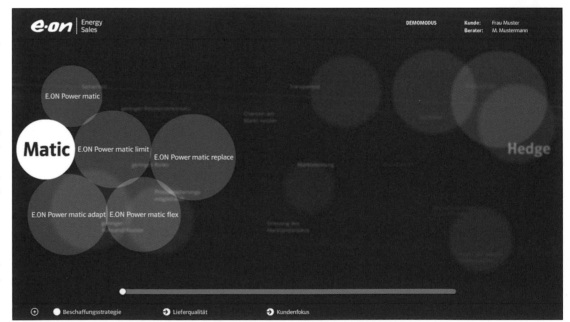

Mit dem multimedialen Tool „E.ON – focussing on your needs." nimmt E.ON die für seine Kunden passenden Produkte und Dienstleistungen in den Fokus und stellt seine weltweite Kompetenz in Erzeugung, Beschaffung, Handel und Transport heraus. Bereits mit der Eingabe einer individuellen Kundennummer konzentriert sich das Tool auf den Kunden mit all seinen Bedürfnissen und Fragen, für die E.ON maßgeschneiderte Lösungen auf Augenhöhe mit dem Kunden entwickelt. Begriffe der Kundenanforderungen und der Produkte werden in einer lockeren Anordnung im Zusammenhang dargestellt. Die klare Struktur lässt die Kundenbedürfnisse in den Vordergrund treten.

With the multimedia tool „E.ON – focussing on your needs." E.ON is concentrating on the adequate products and services and is also accentuating the worldwide competence in creation, acquisition, trade and transport. Starting with the entry of a customer ID the tool is focussing on the client with all his needs and questions and for which E.ON is developing tailored solutions on eye-level with the client. Terms of customer demand and of the products are put in context by a loose visual arrangement. The client's needs become important through the clear structure of the design.

Project
RWE E-Mobility
Microsite

Design
GETIT GmbH
Susanna Beckmann (AD)
Sandra Jacob (Junior AD)
Matthias Bätz (AD Flash)
Klaus Koch (3D)
Dirk Ostkamp (Compositing)
Teigelkämper (Imagefilm)
Dortmund, Germany

Client
RWE AG
Essen, Germany

RWE plante ein Online-Portal zum Thema E-Mobility. Das Design unterstützt das Thema und vermittelt es auf emotionale und intellektuelle Art. Animierte Grafiken, Flash-Specials und Filme erklären die technischen Funktionen. Die Bildwolke ermutigt den User, eigene Ideen zum Thema zu entwickeln und zu posten.
Beide Seiten sind unterschiedlich gestaltet, um den verschiedenen Anforderungen der Zielgruppen und Inhalte gerecht zu werden. „B2C" zeigt eine Nachtoptik als Kontrast zu den „Lightstrokes", die Energieströme darstellen. „B2B" hat einen klaren Fokus auf Informationen.
GETIT ist verantwortlich für Konzept, Design, Flash-Specials, 3-D-Umsetzung sowie die Bildwolke.

RWE wanted to create an online portal about electric mobility. The design supports the subject and realizes it in an emotional and intellectual way. Animated graphics, Flash specials and films explain the technical context. The picture cloud encourages the user to develop and post his own idea of the subject.
The two sites are designed differently to point out the different demands of the target groups and contents of each site. "B2C" has a night optic as contrast to the light strokes representing the electricity. "B2B" is clearly focusing on the information.
GETIT is responsible for concept, design, Flash-specials including 3D and the picture cloud.

Project
Miles & More
Website Relaunch

Design
Ray Sono AG
Ilona Kühn, Marc Althoff,
Jens-Volker Schmidtke (Konzept)
Andrea Sondermeier (Creative
Direction)
Chris Hansert (Art Direction)
Ilona Kühn (Projektleitung)
München, Germany

Client
Deutsche Lufthansa AG,
Miles & More
Frankfurt a. M., Germany

Ein hohes Maß an Emotionalität ist das Ergebnis der Konzeption und Gestaltung des Relaunches. Die neue Struktur orientiert sich stark an den Bedürfnissen der Teilnehmer: Meilen sammeln/einlösen, Programminfos, Kundenbereich. Meilen-Angebote können über eine komfortable Funktion gefiltert werden. Es wurde großen Wert auf die persönliche Ansprache der verschiedenen Zielgruppen gelegt. Absolute Neuheit ist hierbei die virtuelle „Lounge", deren Besonderheit in ihrer kompletten Personalisierung besteht. Sie bietet eine Vielzahl an individualisierten Angeboten und Informationen. Als zentrales Navigationselement dient die stilisierte Teilnehmerkarte.

The result of the concept and design of the relaunch is a high degree of emotionality. The new structure is more in line with members' needs: collect/cash in miles, program information, customers area. There is a comfortable function to filter bonus offers. Great importance is attached to the individual approach to different target groups. The real novelty is the virtual "lounge" which is absolutely unique in its complete personalization. It provides a variety of individualized offers and information. The central navigation element is a stylized membership card that is colored according to the customer's status and contains account details.

Project
Networksim
Interaktive Installation
Interactive installation

Design
WHITEvoid interactive art & design
Christopher Bauder (Creative Director)
Joreg Diessl, Sebastian Gregor (Software Development)
Robert Henke (Audio Engine / Sound Design)
Berlin, Germany
Dan Pearlman Markenarchitektur
Marcus Fischer
Berlin, Germany

Client
Deutsche Lufthansa AG
Köln, Germany

Im Tower der Lufthansa Markenakademie in Frankfurt-Seeheim erfahren Besucher die lokalen und globalen Zusammenhänge des internationalen Luftverkehrs. Eine 14 m breite 180-Grad-Projektion lässt den Besucher in eine frei navigierbare 3-D-Datenvisualisierung der täglichen 16.000 Flüge von Lufthansa und Star Alliance in Echtzeit eintauchen. Das intuitive Navigationsinterface – mit sechs Freiheitsgraden sowie unabhängig zu- und abschaltbaren Zeit- und Inhaltsfiltern – ermöglicht innerhalb weniger „Flugsekunden" einen Wechsel zwischen dem Makroblick auf lokale und nationale Zusammenhänge und der Gesamtansicht der weltweiten Flugverbindungen.

In the flight control tower of the Lufthansa Brand Academy in Frankfurt-Seeheim visitors learn about the local and global connections of international air traffic. A 14 meter wide 180 degrees projection lets the visitors dive into the fully navigable, realtime 3D visualization of 16,000 daily Lufthansa and Star Alliance flights. The intuitive navigation interface provides six degrees of freedom. Additional time and content filters can be activated with extra buttons and sliders. In just a few seconds of flight the user can move from a macro view of a local hub to a global overview of the worldwide air traffic routes.

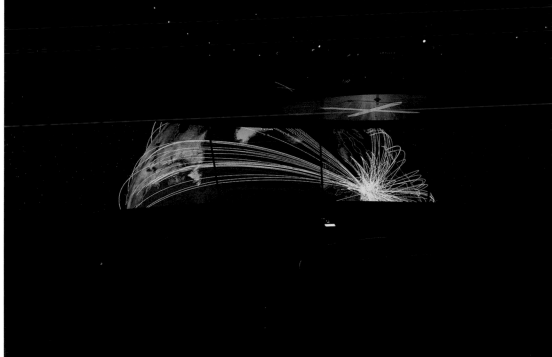

Project
Philips Consumer Website

Design
Philips Design
Philips Design Team
Eindhoven, Netherlands

Client
Royal Philips Electronics
Eindhoven, Netherlands

2008 gestaltete Philips Design die Philips-Kunden-Website völlig neu und entwickelte eine überaus benutzerfreundliche Lösung, die den Käufern beratend zur Seite steht. Die Website lässt sich sehr einfach bedienen. Über eine Auswahlfunktion können die Nutzer konkrete Kriterien eingeben, auf deren Grundlage ihnen dann das am besten geeignete Produkt empfohlen wird. Alle Erzeugnisse werden in einer Galerie dargestellt. Kunden können sich dann jedes Produkt im Detail ansehen. Die Website wurde so gestaltet, dass sie weltweit gleichermaßen genutzt werden kann. Seit Einführung stieg die Anzahl der Besucher um 36% auf jährlich etwa 90 Millionen an.

In 2008 Philips Design redesigned the Philips consumer website, creating a totally consumer-friendly solution which answers the shopper's needs at every step. The website allows easy navigation through the shopping process. An "elimination tool" allows specifying criteria so that you find the ideal product. A gallery is available for all products throughout the website and allows the visitor to explore each product in great depth. The site is engineered to provide a seamless experience globally. Since the redesign the number of website visitors went up to 90 million a year – an increase of 36%.

Project
uniquedigital
DARWIN Produktfilm
DARWIN trailer

Design
Syzygy Deutschland GmbH
Dominik Lammer (Creative Director)
Bad Homburg, Germany
A.R.T. Studios
Soundstudio
Matthias Heisig, Gordon Piedesack
Frankfurt a. M., Germany
ACHT FRANKFURT GmbH & Co. KG
digital solutions
ACHT FRANKFURT visual catering
Frankfurt a. M., Germany

Client
uniquedigital GmbH
Hamburg, Germany

DARWIN ist eine Media-Management-Suite zur Planung, Auswertung und Optimierung von Online-Kampagnen. Im September 2008 wurde sie erstmalig auf der OMD präsentiert. Der Trailer lief als Eyecatcher am Messestand. Er bringt technische Features auf den Punkt und gibt dem abstrakten Produkt „Media-Management" ein unverwechselbares Gesicht. Emotionales Storytelling statt technischer Vorteilskommunikation: So werden selbst ausgesprochene Fachthemen für Laien verständlich. Vor allem aber haken sie sich im Gedächtnis fest. Das Resultat: Ein starkes Instrument zur Markenbildung und Positionierung der Suite in einem hart umkämpften Wettbewerbsumfeld.

DARWIN is a media management suite for planning, evaluating and optimizing online campaigns. It was presented for the first time in September 2008 at the OMD. The trailer ran as an eye-catcher at the trade show booth, bringing together technical features and giving the abstract product "media management" an unmistakable face. Emotional storytelling instead of listing technological advantages: this makes difficult technical topics comprehensible to the average layperson. What's more, such stories are hard to forget. The result: A strong tool for branding and positioning the suite in a highly competitive field.

Project
3sat nano
Vorspann für TV
TV trailer

Design
ACHT FRANKFURT GmbH & Co. KG
visual catering
Christiane Jähnel (Creative Director)
Timo Wolf (Producer)
Mark Gläser (Regie/Realbild)
Diane Preyer (3D Artist)
Piet Hohl (3D Artist)
Frankfurt a. M., Germany

Client
3sat
Mainz, Germany

Vorspann zur täglich (montags bis freitags) auf 3sat ausgestrahlten, 30-minütigen Sendung nano: Die Sendung soll den Zuschauern durch unterhaltsame, spannende und informative Wissenschaftsfilme Einblicke in die Welt aus Technik, Forschung, Natur- und Geisteswissenschaften sowie in die Welt von morgen vermitteln. Die Idee des Vorspanns ist es, einen schnellen Eindruck über die Themenbereiche von nano zu geben. Dabei gehen die Bilder ineinander über (One Shots) und „fliegen" von einer Themenwelt in die nächste – vom Weltall bis zur Zelle.

Trailer for the daily (Monday to Friday) on 3sat broadcasted program nano: the program gives the viewer an insight into the world of technology, research, natural science and human discipline through exciting, entertaining and informative films. The idea of the trailer is to give a quick impression about the subject areas of nano. The images blend into each other (one shots) and "fly" from one theme into the next theme – from outer space through to the cell.

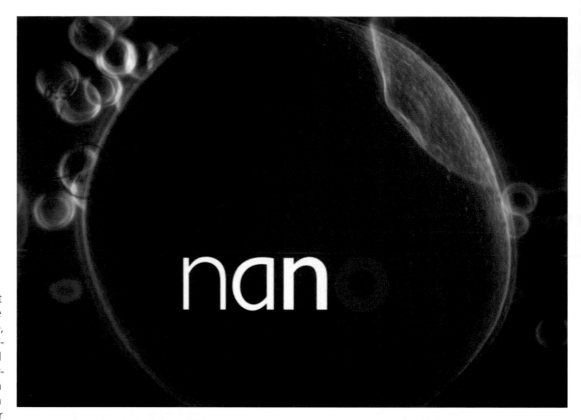

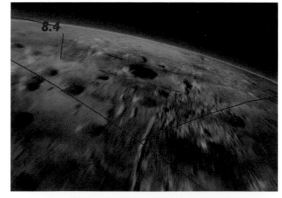

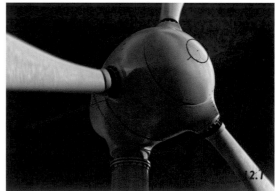

Project
IG-Transformer
Industriegetriebe von SEW
Industrial gear units from SEW

Design
madness GmbH
Axel Berne, Günter Zimmermann, Peter Ederer,
Richard Ballinger, Thorsten Kuttig, Silvio Schwarz
Sonja Schlichter
Göppingen, Germany

Client
SEW-EURODRIVE GmbH & Co. KG
Bruchsal, Germany

Zur Positionierung der neuen Industriegetriebe konzipierte „madness" einen eigenständigen Film mit
dem Projektnamen „Transformer". Der Film begeistert durch seine unglaubliche Geschwindigkeit und
Ausdruckskraft. In der Art der bekannten Spielzeug-
figuren „Transformers" verwandeln sich kubische
Elemente in Maschinen und Anlagen, in denen die
Industriegetriebe zum Einsatz kommen, wie zum
Beispiel riesige Kräne oder Bulldozer. In einer intensiven Postproduktion erhielten die Filme eine visuelle Brillanz. Der Film von SEW-EURODRIVE markiert
damit einen neuen Qualitätsstandard bei dieser Art
von „B2B"-Kommunikation.

For the positioning of the new industrial gear units
"madness" conceived a self-contained movie with the
project title "Transformer". The movie inspires with
its incredible velocity and impressiveness. Like the
well known toy figures "Transformers" cubistic elements transmute into machines and constructions in
which the industrial gear units are applied e. g. huge
tower cranes or bulldozers. In a very intensive post-
production the movies obtained a visual brilliance.
The movie from SEW-EURODRIVE brands a new quality standard in this field of "B2B" communication.

Project
Barrieren
Film

Design
Kolle Rebbe
Ulrich Zünkeler (Creative Direction)
Stefan Wübbe (Creative Direction)
Jörg Dittman (Art Direction)
Florian Ludwig (Text)
Hamburg, Germany

Client
Inlingua Sprachschule GmbH
Hamburg, Germany

Wer als Unternehmer einen Markt im Ausland er-
obern will, sieht sich oft mit einem erheblichen Hin-
dernis konfrontiert: der Sprache. Auf diesen Punkt
spielen Inlingua Language Schools mit einem Ani-
mationsfilm an, in dem englische Begriffe aus der
Geschäfts- und Finanzwelt zu militärischen Verteidi-
gungsanlagen mutieren.

When an entrepreneur wants to conquer a foreign
market, he or she is often presented with a consid-
erable obstacle: the language. Inlingua language
schools hint at this with an animation film in which
English business and financial terms mutate to mili-
tary defensive fortifications.

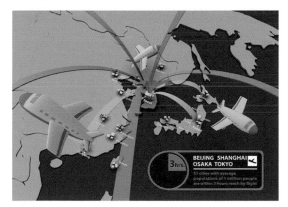

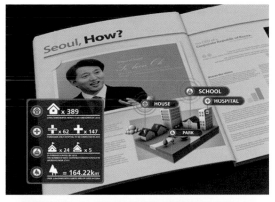

Project
SEOUL IFC
Overseas Publicity Film

Design
Fleishman-Hillard and domo
Communication Consulting Consortium
Andrew Lee, Eunice Lee, Sylvia Shin, Jack Kang
(Planning & Storyline)
Seoul, South Korea
PENTABREED
Kim Kyung-sik
Seoul, South Korea

Client
Seoul Metropolitan Government
Seoul, South Korea

Der Film soll Investoren davon überzeugen, dass Seoul aufgrund seiner wirtschaftlichen, kulturellen und geographischen Vorzüge als Finanzzentrum Ostasiens prädestiniert ist. Von herkömmlichen Werbefilmen unterscheidet er sich durch eine Kombination aus Animation und „Motion Graphics", wodurch die Erzählweise fesselnder wird. Tonfall und Stil des hochklassigen Films sind über die gesamte Länge einheitlich. Die Schlüsselszenen, durch lebhafte Farben und grafische Symbole hervorgehoben, fallen sofort ins Auge.

The movie is made appealing for investors as speaking of why Seoul should be the financial hub in East Asia in terms of economy, culture and geographical advantage. It shows differentiated style from other ordinary promotional movie by using a mix of animation and motion graphic techniques which helps story-telling more interesting. Entire tone and manner of the movie maintains same consistency and high quality atmosphere. Every key point of story is highlighted by using vivid colors and graphic icons for capturing attentions of customers.

Project
Lufthansa TravelWorld beta
Launch einer neuen Microsite
Microsite launch

Design
Ray Sono AG
Stefan Spiegel, Mick Schneider, Michael Konitzer
(Konzept)
Paul Schlichter (Design)
Benjamin Gutschik (Technik)
Stefan Spiegel (Projektleitung)
München, Germany

Client
Deutsche Lufthansa AG
Frankfurt a. M., Germany

Reise-Inspiration und praktische Empfehlungen auf hohem Niveau: Auf der TravelWorld beta stellt die Lufthansa beliebte Reiseziele aus spannenden Blickwinkeln vor. Inspirierende Full-frame-Videos und Slideshows zeigen das Reiseziel bildschirmfüllend in vielen Facetten und versetzen den Besucher in seine Wunsch-Destination. Eigens recherchierte Reiseberichte mit Empfehlungen zu Sehenswürdigkeiten, Shopping und Veranstaltungen ergänzen die virtuelle Entdeckungsreise. Zu vielen Themen bieten Web-Links zusätzliche Informationen. Die TravelWorld startet mit Barcelona, Hongkong und München als erste Destinationen.

Travel inspiration and practical tips on a high level: on TravelWorld beta Lufthansa presents popular destinations from interesting angles. Inspiring full-frame videos and slide shows bring many facets of a destination to the screen and take visitors to their dream destination. Carefully researched travel reports with tips for sightseeing, shopping and events complete the discovery tour. Web links with additional information are available for many topics. TravelWorld is starting out with Barcelona, Hong Kong and Munich as the first destinations.

Project
AIR-CRUISE CUBE
Projektionsraum
Movie zone

Design
Samsung C & T
Seungmin Kim
Seoul, South Korea
Seymourpowell Ltd.
Nick Talbot
London, United Kingdom

Client
Samsung C & T
Seoul, South Korea

Der AIR-CRUISE CUBE ist ein kubischer Schattenbild-Raum, in dem man den im Himmel schwebenden AIR-CRUISE sehen kann – einen innovativen Wohnungsentwurf für die Zukunft. Das Bild wird dreidimensional auf drei 6 m hohe Wände und ein Zwischengeschoss projiziert. Zwei begehbare Ebenen umgeben den Raum.
Im Erdgeschoss löst der riesige Umfang des Bildes beim Betrachter das Gefühl aus, an Board des AIR-CRUISE zu gehen. Im Obergeschoss fuhlt er sich, als ob er durch den Himmel reise. Die Animation und die Schattenbilder von Menschen an den Wänden kreieren eine neue Interaktions-Struktur zwischen Medien und Mensch.
Mit diesem visionären Projekt möchten wir Menschen Träume schenken.

The AIR-CRUISE CUBE is a theater cube exhibiting the AIR-CRUISE – the concept design for the innovative future residence cruising in the air. It projects in a three-dimensional way to three 6 m tall walls and the floor plane, taking two floors to surround the theater.
Viewers will be assimilated into the huge scale images on the first floor and feel as if they are boarding the AIR-CRUISE. On the second floor they will feel as if they are cruising in the sky. This animation and shadows of people reflected on the walls create new textures through the interaction between media and people.
This is a vision project of our company to give people dreams.

Project
ZDF Terra X
Vorspann für TV
TV trailer

Design
ACHT FRANKFURT GmbH & Co. KG
digital solutions
Frank Schneider / filmstyler pictures (Regie)
Timo Fritsche (Schnitt)
Heiko Leitsch (Compositing)
Michael Koch (3D)
Olli Schumacher (Colorgrading)
Frankfurt a. M., Germany

Client
filmstyler pictures GmbH
Frankfurt a. M., Germany

„Terra X" ist eine Serie des Zweiten Deutschen Fernsehens (ZDF) im Dokumentarfilm-Format. Die Themen sind hauptsächlich Fragestellungen aus historischen, zeitgenössischen und naturwissenschaftlichen Bereichen der Geschichte und Archäologie. Die gesamte Erd- und Menschheitsgeschichte zieht „gefühlt" am Betrachter vorbei. Dabei bleibt die vermeintliche Kamera immer in der gleichen Position und zeigt am Ende einen Ausblick in die Zukunft.
In ständiger gemeinsamer Absprache zwischen dem Filmproduzenten filmstyler pictures und ACHT FRANKFURT entstand aus real gedrehten Bildern mit Hilfe von 3-D-Animation und Compositing die „Terra X"-Welt.

"Terra X" is a serial in a documentary film format of the German TV station ZDF. The topics are mainly from the ancient, contemporaneous and scientific field of history and archaeology. In the trailer the viewer sees and "feels" passing by the entire history of earth and mankind. The pretended camera angle stays always in the same position and in the end it offers a sight into the future.
In close cooperation with our client, the film production company filmstyler pictures, we generated the "Terra X" world in the postproduction, by using the shot footage and creating an entire world in the compositing and 3D animation.

Project
adidas women's training
Website

Design
Neue Digitale / Razorfish GmbH
Elke Klinkhammer (Creative Direction)
André Bourguignon (Art Direction)
Sebastian Hilbert (Screendesign)
Andreas Diwisch, Heiko Schweickhardt (User Interface Development)
Frankfurt a. M., Germany

Client
adidas International Marketing BV
Amsterdam ZO, Netherlands

Die richtige Trainingsbekleidung für individuelle Bedürfnisse: Der Claim „Me, Myself." ist online durch große Close-up-Szenen umgesetzt, die Frauen bei und nach dem Sport zeigen. Mit dem „Mix & Match"-Tool kann sich die Nutzerin Kleidungsstücke anzeigen lassen, neu kombinieren und in dreifacher Bildschirmgröße betrachten, um auch die Stofflichkeit und Materialien sehen zu können. Das Webspecial erfüllt mit einer Mischung aus emotionaler und erlebnisreicher Sport- und Produktpräsentation die Bedürfnisse der weiblichen Nutzer. Sie erforschen auf kreative, emotionale und natürliche Weise die Produkte, interagieren damit und kombinieren sie frei.

Appropriate training gear for women's individual efforts to look good: online, the claim "Me, Myself." is translated into large emotional close-up scenes, which show women during their workout and afterwards. With the "Mix & Match" tool, users can view items, combine them in new ways and zoom in on products at three times the size – for a close-up look at the materials and their textures. With the combination of an emotional and exciting sports and product presentation the microsite meets the needs of female users. They experience the products in a creative, emotional and natural manner and may interact with the items.

digital media atmosphere

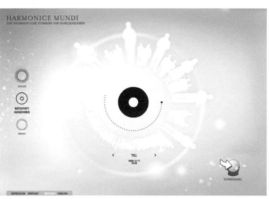

Project
S&V Harmonice Mundi
Xmas-Special 2008

Design
Scholz & Volkmer GmbH
Nicoletta Gerlach (Creative Direction)
Jens Fischer (Sound Design)
Susanne Wilhelm, Melanie Lenz, Michael Geissler
(Screendesign)
Peter Reichard (Technical Direction)
Marc Storch, Raphael Wichmann (Programming)
Jin Jeon, Tim Sobczak, Annette Jans (Text)
Peter Reichard, Nicoletta Gerlach (Konzept)
Sabine Schmidt (Project Management)
Mohshiour Hossain, Till Nowak (Video)
Wiesbaden, Germany

Client
Scholz & Volkmer GmbH
Wiesbaden, Germany

Das Xmas-Special „Harmonice Mundi" (lat. „Welt-harmonik") ist ein Soundtool, das den User dazu ein-lädt, weihnachtliche Klangbotschaften in einer virtu-ellen Schneekugel zu versenden. In Anlehnung an eine nostalgische Spieluhr sucht sich der User seine Spielfiguren zusammen. Jede Figur erzeugt einen eigenen Sound – kombiniert der User sie, entsteht Mu-sik. Die Spielfiguren bestehen – in bewährter Xmas-Special-Tradition – aus den S&V-Mitarbeitern, die gefilmt und mit individuellen Klangmotiven versehen wurden. Um den Gruß zu personalisieren, kann der User zur Musik eine Audiobotschaft aufnehmen und seine Komposition per E-Card an Freunde und Familie senden.

The 2008 Xmas special invites users to send Christ-mas sound messages in a virtual snowball. Similar to an old-fashioned music box, the user can select different figures. Each figure has its own individual sound motive and the user can combine the figures as desired to configure an individual Christmas sound. The figures represent the S&V employees, true to our Christmas tradition. They were all individually filmed and each assigned an own sound for the special. The user can personalize the Christmas greeting by re-cording an audio message and then send his own composition per e-card to friends and family.

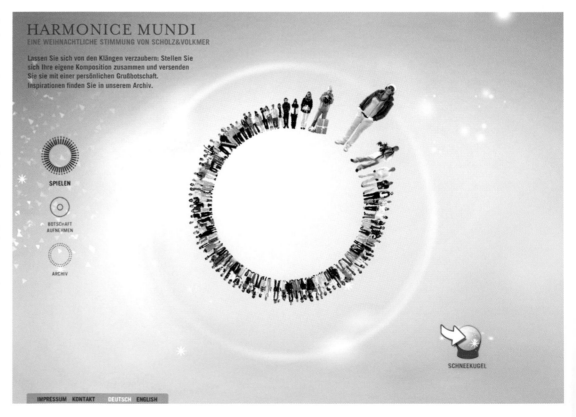

Project
Dell Design Studio
Interaktive Webseite
Interactive website

Design
Experience Design Group
Dell Inc.
Dell.com and Experience Design Center
Round Rock, TX, United States of America

Client
Dell Inc.
Round Rock, TX, United States of America

Als etablierter Hersteller personalisierter Produkte bietet Dell seinen Kunden die Möglichkeit, die Außenseite ihres „Studio Laptops" individuell zu gestalten. Auf Dells Design-Studio-Webseite findet man eine Auswahl von über 100 einzigartigen künstlerischen Designs. Die Gallerie ist wie ein Kunstatelier gestaltet. Besucher können sich mit Hilfe von Filtern problemlos in drei Kategorien bewegen oder das gesamte Angebot durchblättern. Wenn der Kunde eine Auswahl getroffen hat, kann er das Design auf seinem Laptop betrachten, näher heran zoomen, die Biografie des Künstlers einsehen oder einen Freund über Social Networking daran teilhaben lassen.

Continuing its history of personalization, Dell offers customers a unique way to make the exterior of their laptop PCs more personal. Through the interactive Dell Design Studio Website, customers can choose from over 100 unique artistic designs for their Studio laptop lid. The gallery is stylized like a downtown art studio. Visitors can easily browse by filtering through three categories or scroll through all of the offerings. Once customers choose, they can see the design on the laptop, zoom in closer, view the artist's bio or share with a friend through social networking sites.

Project
KMS TEAM Corporate Design
Film

Design
KMS TEAM GmbH
Knut Maierhofer (Creative Director)
Jörg Richter, Christian Schmid (Motion Designer)
Cecil V. Rustemeyer
(Technical Manager Motion Design)
Nadine Vicentini (Account Director)
Christian Ring (Sound Design)
München, Germany

Client
KMS TEAM GmbH
München, Germany

Der Film zeigt die Konzeption eines ganzheitlichen Erscheinungsbildes, das seine Kraft in unterschiedlichen Medien entfaltet. Ein schwarzer Balken, das zentrale Gestaltungselement von KMS TEAM, führt den Betrachter in einer facettenreichen Reise durch die KMS-TEAM-Welt. Der Balken verkörpert die „Leitidee" und nimmt verschiedene Formen und Funktionen an. Von der ersten Inspiration über unterschiedliche Anwendungen wird der Ideen-Balken zum Navigator in der digitalen Welt. Das visuelle Element ist die kraftvolle Konstante des Auftritts und präsentiert überraschende Anwendungsmöglichkeiten, die den Betrachter immer stärker in ihren Bann ziehen.

The video shows the conceptual design of an integrated image which unfolds its power in various media. A black bar, the central design element of KMS TEAM, leads the viewer on a multifaceted journey through the KMS TEAM world. The bar embodies the "guiding philosophy" and assumes various forms and functions. From the initial inspiration to various applications, the idea bar acts as a navigator through the digital world. This visual element represents the powerful constant of the design and presents surprising application options that increasingly cast a spell on the user.

Project
Mediatektur
Mediale Fassade
Media facade

Design
ART+COM
Prof. Joachim Sauter, Dennis Paul,
Susanne Traeger, Jens-Ove Panknin,
Christine Paech, Gerd Grüneis,
Tobias Gremmler, David Siegel,
Valentin Schunack, Gert Monath
Berlin, Germany
ATELIER BRÜCKNER
Prof. Uwe R. Brückner, Eberhard Schlag,
Michel Casertano, Dominik Hegemann
Stuttgart, Germany

Client
BMW Group
München, Germany

Aufgabe in einem Museum der Mobilität war es, mit gestalterischen Mitteln eine Atmosphäre der Dynamik zu vermitteln. Die „Mediatektur", eine Symbiose aus Medien und Architektur, erweitert den Raum visuell und versetzt die ausgestellten Fahrzeugexponate in Bewegung: zum einen durch ihre Relativbewegung zur Fassade, zum anderen durch die über die Oberflächen gleitenden Lichtreflexionen. Im reaktiven Modus reagiert die bespielte Fassade auf die Präsenz der Besucher, die so in das Geschehen im Museum einbezogen werden.

The approach was to create a dynamic environment for a museum of mobility. The "Mediatektur", a symbiosis of media and architecture, on one hand enlarges the space by extending it virtually through three-dimensional moving images. It also sets the exhibited "parked" cars into motion relative to the animated walls. In the switched reactive mode, the pattern of illumination changes according to the mere presence of visitors and thus actively involves them in the scenario.

Project
Concept FASCINATION
Animation / Revealfilm

Design
Elastique. We design.
Andreas Schimmelpfennig, Thomas von den Driesch,
Stefan Ditner, Hans Schultheiß, Marius Ruhland,
Waldek Szymkowiak, Christoph Wolf, Christian Basler
Köln, Germany
Deine Freunde
Postproduction
Swen Linde, Volker Heisterberg, Alexander Knörk,
Peter Pannes, Robert Leger, Alexander Hupperich,
Agniezka Kruczek, André Paulsen
Köln, Germany

Client
Oliver Schrott Kommunikation GmbH
Köln, Germany

Mit dem von der Presse als aufregende Design-Revolution gefeierten Showcar „Concept FASCIN-ATION" beginnt bei Mercedes-Benz eine neue De-sign-Ära. Zur Premiere des neuartigen Coupé-Kombi auf dem Pariser Autosalon entstand ein Animations-film, der so ungewöhnlich und spannend ist wie das Auto selbst. Mit einer Fahrt durch eine abstrakte grafische Welt setzt das formschöne Shooting-Brake die gesamte Umgebung in Bewegung, verändert die Farbwelten und präsentiert die innovative Design-Sprache von Mercedes-Benz aus atemberaubenden Blickwinkeln.

The film presents the start of a new Mercedes-Benz design era with the show car "Concept FASCIN-ATION". Shown at The Paris Motor Show 2008 this animation is as uncommon and exciting as the car itself. Driving through an abstract graphical world the car sets the whole environment in motion, changes the lightning and opens up breathtaking perspec-tives on the new and innovative Mercedes-Benz de-sign language. Dancers accompany the extremely dy-namic drive and start what is being continued right after the film on stage during the live show in Paris.

Project
Audi tv
Web TV Portal

Design
Neue Digitale/Razorfish GmbH
Daniel Klipfel (Information Architect)
Ulf Germann (Screendesigner)
Norbert Protzek (Senior Account Manager)
Berlin, Germany
TV NEXT Solutions GmbH
Nicolas Westermann (Product Manager)
Rico Slaby (Lead Software Engineer)
Berlin, Germany
ZIGGY mediahouse GmbH
Siegfried F. Nümann (Executive Producer)
Alexandra Wonko (Creative Director)
Carsten Funke, Wolfgang Jaschensky, Thomas Ruge,
Alexander Gerlts (Editors)
München, Germany

Client
AUDI AG
Ingolstadt, Germany

„Audi tv" setzt in Design, Technik und Nutzeran-sprache Maßstäbe im Automobilbereich: Durch den Relaunch erhält das Web-TV-Portal ein neues, inno-vatives Interface mit neuen Funktionen. Es geht auf die Wünsche des Nutzers ein, ist intuitiv bedienbar und begeistert durch emotionales Design sowie technische Highlights. Beiträge rund um Fahrzeuge, Events und Making-of werden in den unterschied-lichen Kanälen („On Air", „Behind the Scenes", „On the Road", „Sports Center", „Life and Style") the-matisch aufbereitet. Dabei ist das Interface auf die wesentlichen Funktionen reduziert, jederzeit stehen die „Audi tv"-Beiträge im Mittelpunkt.

"Audi tv" has set the bar in the automobile branch for design, technology and user approach: the web TV portal received a fresh, innovative interface with new functions with the relaunch. It speaks to the needs of the user, is intuitive and wows users with an emotional design and technical highlights. A multitude of content about the cars, events and mak-ing of videos are presented by topic ("On Air", "Be-hind the Scenes", "On the Road", "Sports Center", "Life and Style"). This allows the interface to be re-duced to its main features and keeps "Audi tv" con-tent in focus.

digital media interface

Project
SWR Gebührenchecker
Website

Design
feedback media design
Isabel Pettinato, Markus Müller, Jeanette Neumann,
Stefanie Kittel, Ralf Greiner
Hans Weidhofer
Stuttgart, Germany

Client
Südwestrundfunk
Abteilung Rundfunkgebühren
Stuttgart, Germany

Der Gebührenchecker richtet sich an junge Ziel-gruppen und soll Basisinformationen zum Thema Rundfunkgebühren vermitteln. Die Herausforderung bestand darin, das Thema zielgruppengerecht zu „verpacken" und einen spielerischen Umgang da-mit zu finden. Wir haben bewusst auf eine klare Menüführung verzichtet und das Wohnzimmer als Spielraum eingesetzt. Der Gebührenrechner lässt sich durch Klicken ein- und ausfahren. Über die Auswahl im Gebührenrechner kann sich der Nutzer anzeigen lassen, wie hoch die individuelle monatliche Rund-funkgebühr – unter Berücksichtigung der jeweiligen technischen Ausstattung – ausfällt.

Aimed at young target groups, the fee checker is in-tended to communicate basic information on TV and radio license fees. The challenge was to "package" the topic in a manner suited to the target group and to approach it playfully. We made a conscious deci-sion to avoid clear menu navigation and use the living room as a play space. The fee calculator is activated and deactivated by clicking. By making selections in the fee calculator, the user is able to determine the monthly cost of TV and radio license fees under con-sideration of the respective equipment.

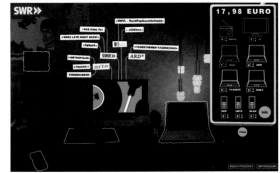

Project
Website www.bahn.de
Redesign, Konzept, Layout

Design
namics (deutschland) GmbH
Jan Hochbruck, Cornelia Franke,
Sandra Assfalg, Claus Medvesek
Frankfurt a. M., Germany

Client
namics (deutschland) GmbH
Frankfurt a. M., Germany

Das Vertriebsportal der Deutschen Bahn – www. bahn.de – ist eines der wichtigsten Portale für Bahn- und Reiseangebote. Um dem Kunden mehr Komfort zu bieten und die Prozesse schneller und angenehmer zu gestalten, wurde namics mit einem umfassenden (konzeptionellen und gestalterischen) Redesign beauftragt. Das neu gestaltete Portal wurde am 10. Dezember 2008 freigeschaltet. Die Konzentration auf den Nutzer stand bei jedem Entwicklungsschritt und jeder Gestaltungsphase im Mittelpunkt. Aus der Icon-Sprache der Bahn und der Innengestaltung des ICEs wurde eine typische Ästhetik abgeleitet, die dem Nutzer bei allen Innovationen und Neuerungen eine gewohnte Markenwelt präsentiert.

www.bahn.de – the commerce portal of Deutsche Bahn – is one of the chief distribution channels for all railroad products and travel offers. To create a platform that offers more comfort to the user and renders the processes on the website easier to use, namics was assigned with the task of a complete relaunch, which went online on December 10th, 2008. User-centered design and development was the key to every step taken. A very special look and feel was derived from the existing icon language and the ICE-train's interior design, which makes users feel at home with the brand in an all-new layout full of new functionalities and innovations.

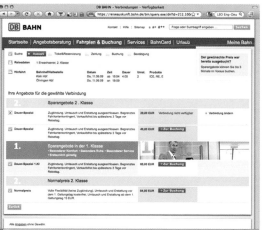

digital media interface

Project
Online Portfolio
3-D Online Portfolio System

Design
WHITEvoid interactive art & design
Christopher Bauder, Andre Stubbe, Markus Lerner
Berlin, Germany

Client
WHITEvoid interactive art & design
Berlin, Germany

Intuitiv visuell navigierbar und leicht verständlich – das sind die Maximen der Gestaltung der Portfolio-Website für das Design-Studio WHITEvoid. Der Präsentation der Leistungen und Projekte dient ein dreidimensional navigierbares Flash-Interface, das die zugrunde liegende Baumdiagramm-Struktur als gestalterisches Element nutzt. Menü und Inhalt bilden eine Einheit: Der Nutzer kann von jedem Punkt der Menüverzweigung aus übersichtlich zu jedem anderen Unterpunkt navigieren. Alle Elemente der Applikation wie Text, Bild und Video wurden bei der Gestaltung gleich gewichtet.

Intuitive visual navigability and easy understandability – these are the design maxims of WHITEvoid's portfolio website. The presentation of services and projects is based on a three-dimensional navigable Flash interface, which uses the underlying tree diagram structure as a design element. Menu and content form a whole: from any point in the clear menu structure users can easily navigate to any other point. All elements of the application such as texts, images and videos have been given equal weight in the design.

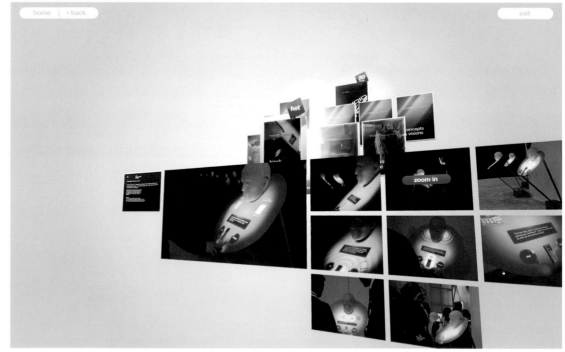

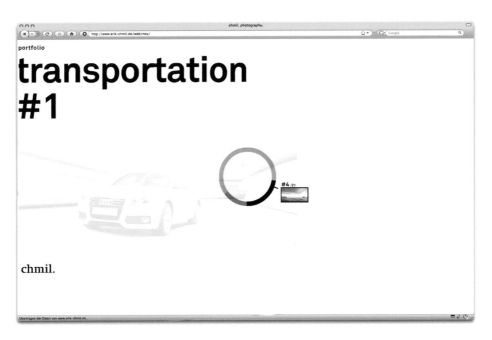

Project
Website des Fotografen E. Chmil
Corporate Website

Design
häfelinger + wagner design
Frank Wagner, Sascha Obermüller
München, Germany

Client
Chmil. Fotografie GbR
Köln, Germany

Im Mittelpunkt des Internetauftritts von Erik Chmil steht die Präsentation seiner Fotografien, auf die sich die gesamte Aufmerksamkeit des Betrachters konzentrieren soll. In dieser Absicht wurde auf die übliche Menüstruktur verzichtet. An ihre Stelle tritt auf der Homepage eine interaktive Ringnavigation, die über Vorschaubilder in die verschiedenen fotografischen Themenbereiche führt. Hier ist die Ringnavigation, als solche nicht sichtbar, hinter den großformatigen Motiven angelegt und tritt nur als dynamische Steueroption über den Mauscursor in Erscheinung. Optische Störer der fotografischen Arbeiten werden auf diese Weise vermieden.

In the center of Erik Chmil's website is the presentation of his photographs, which is designed to grab the visitor's full attention. With this in mind, a standard menu structure has not been used. In its place, the homepage features an interactive circle navigation, which uses thumbnails to take visitors to the different photographic subject areas. Here, the circle navigation as such is hidden behind the large-format motives and can only be accessed as a dynamic control option using the mouse cursor. Visual interference with the photographic work is thereby avoided.

Project
Multitouch-Screen
Interaktive Installation
Interactive installation

Design
Scholz & Volkmer GmbH
Philipp Bareiss (Senior Art Direction)
Konstantin von Rhein (Design)
Peter Reichard (Technical Direction)
Julian Koschwitz (Hardware/Programming)
Sebastian Müller, Henrike Goetsch (Filmschnitt)
Uwe Stellberger (Text)
Julian Koschwitz, Peter Reichard, Philipp Bareiss,
Thorsten Kraus (Konzept)
Christian Tamanini (Project Management)
Lichthorizonte GmbH (LCD-Displays)
Wiesbaden, Germany

Client
Caligari FilmBühne
Kulturamt Wiesbaden
Wiesbaden, Germany

Im Oktober 2008 veranstaltete die Caligari Film-Bühne in Wiesbaden das „Atlantis Natur- und Umweltfilmfestival". Eine begleitende Kampagne mit Fokus auf regionale Besucher sollte Aufmerksamkeit für das Festival erzeugen. Das Konzept: Der größte interaktive Multitouch-Screen Deutschlands bringt Passanten in Berührung mit der Natur. Ein normales Schaufenster wurde in einen Touchscreen verwandelt und lädt Passanten dazu ein, per Berührung mit dem Schaufenster zu interagieren und auf diese Weise in die Filme des Festivals einzutauchen. Durch die Multitouch-Funktion können mehrere Personen gleichzeitig die Anwendung bedienen.

The "Caligari FilmTheater" in Wiesbaden arranged the "Atlantis Nature and Environment Film Festival" in October 2008. An accompanying campaign should generate awareness and boost visitor numbers. The concept: the biggest interactive Multitouch-Screen in Germany brings pedestrians into contact with nature. A normal display window was transformed into a touch screen, inviting pedestrians to interact by touching the display window and thus immerse themselves in the festival's films. Due to the Multitouch function several people can use the application simultaneously.

Project
optovision Visioner
Brillenglassimulator
Lens simulator

Design
KAISER+MORE
Agentur für Kommunikation GmbH
Joe Kaiser, Thomas Poursanidis,
Friedemann Rink (Photography),
Anette Löwen (Set Styling)
Wiesbaden, Germany

Client
optovision Gesellschaft für
moderne Brillenglastechnik mbH
Langen, Germany

Wie sehe ich mit einem Premium-Gleitsichtglas? Wie wirken sich die Sehbereiche bei unterschiedlichen Gleitsichtgläsern aus? Welchen Seheffekt kann ich mit einer Veredlung erreichen?
Das Softwaretool „Visioner" visualisiert in hoher Darstellungsqualität die Wirkung von verschiedenen Brillenglasarten, Farben und Veredelungen in unterschiedlichen Sehsituationen. Der „Visioner" überzeugt durch eine hohe Qualität der Bildszenarien, eine authentische Darstellung der Sehwirkung sowie durch eine einfache, intuitive Handhabung und unterstützt den Augenoptiker bei Beratung und Verkauf hochwertiger Brillengläser.

How do I see through premium progressive lenses? What impact do the visual fields have when using different kinds of progressive lenses? Which optical effects can I achieve with a special coating?
The software tool "Visioner" visualizes in high quality the effects of different lenses, colorings and coatings for eyeglasses in diverse optical situations. The "Visioner" impresses with its high quality of the picture scenarios, the authentic representation of the optical effects, an easy and intuitive usability, and supports the optician during customer consultations for high quality glasses.

Project
GROHE Cube
3D Webspecial

Design
argonauten G2 GmbH
– a member of Grey | G2 Group
Markus Kleine-Vehn, Reinhard Dassel, Florian Mlodzik,
Christina Fiedler, Roland Schweighöfer
Berlin, Germany

Client
GROHE AG
Düsseldorf, Germany

Ein digitaler „Showroom" ist heute keine Besonderheit mehr. Für GROHE strebten wir deshalb nach einer
anderen innovativen Lösung und entwickelten den
dreidimensionalen GROHE Cube. Er lädt die Nutzer
der Website ein, GROHE's Wasserwelten spielerisch
in einer interaktiven, fotorealistischen 3D-Umgebung
zu erkunden. Außerdem ermöglicht der Cube dem
User individuell aus dem großen Angebot Produkte
auszusuchen, in virtuelle Badezimmer und Küchen ein-
zusetzen und die Gesamtwirkung verschiedener Stil-
richtungen und Raumgrößen zu testen. Der 3D-Cube
bietet Kontakt zu GROHE-Fachhändlern und vereint
Markenwerte, Produktinformationen und Design-In-
spirationen meisterlich.

These days pretty much every brand has a digital
showroom of some sort. For GROHE, we wanted
more. So instead of a sleek but flat studio, we built a
smart 3D Cube. The Cube invites visitors to explore
GROHE's worlds of water in dynamic, true-to-life, yet
playful fashion. It also allows them to select lifestyle-
appropriate fittings from GROHE's wide range of
products, and even to install and experience these fittings in virtual bathrooms and kitchens. Brand values,
product information and design inspiration in one,
the GROHE Cube completes the circle by connecting
shoppers to brick-and-mortar fittings outlets.

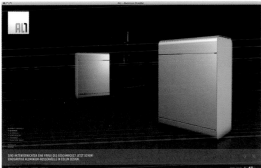

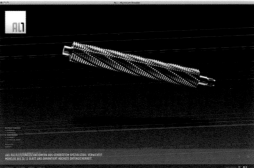

Project
Alushredder
Website

Design
Daniel Priester
Konzeption und Gestaltung
Balingen, Germany
Buero Simpatico
René Griesinger
Berlin, Germany

Client
IDEAL
Krug & Priester GmbH & Co. KG
Balingen, Germany

Der Aluminium-Shredder „AL1" ist ein Design-Objekt und Technologieträger aus dem Hause IDEAL, dem weltweit führenden Hersteller von professionellen Aktenvernichtern. Diese Microsite soll das Produkt präsentieren und spielerisch seine Wandlungsfähigkeit vermitteln. Die „Konzert-Funktion" macht die Hintergrundmusik „sichtbar" und soll als Plattform für wechselnde Künstler dienen.

The aluminum shredder "AL1" is both, design object and technology carrier. It is made by IDEAL, the worldwide leading manufacturer of professional document shredders. This microsite shall present the product and playfully translate its mutability. The "concert function" actually "visualizes" the background music and serves as platform for alternating artists.

Project
uniquedigital
Corporate Website

Design
Syzygy Deutschland GmbH
Dominik Lammer (Creative Director)
Bad Homburg, Germany

Client
uniquedigital GmbH
Hamburg, Germany

Die Website bringt Markenwerte und Persönlichkeit der Online-Marketing-Agentur auf den Punkt und ist ein zentraler Baustein der neuen Corporate Identity. Inhalte werden multimedial vermittelt, der Auftritt kommt mit wenigen Worten aus: Auf der „Home"-Seite präsentiert ein Power-Teaser aktuelle Projekte; die Geschäftsführer stellen sich in einem Fullscreen-Video persönlich vor; News werden in Form eines Blogs dargestellt; unter „Kontakt" findet der Nutzer die Standorte in London und Hamburg in interaktiven Satellitenbildern. Selbst ein komplexes Produkt wie die Media-Management-Suite DARWIN wird in einem Showreel abgebildet.

The website sums up the brand value and personality of the online marketing agency and is a key component of the new corporate identity. Multimedia presentations are used to communicate content and the website has little need for words: the homepage presents a power-teaser of current projects; management introduces itself personally in a full-screen video; news is presented in the form of a blog; under "Contact", the user finds the London and Hamburg locations in interactive satellite images. Even a complex product such as the DARWIN media management suite is illustrated in a showreel.

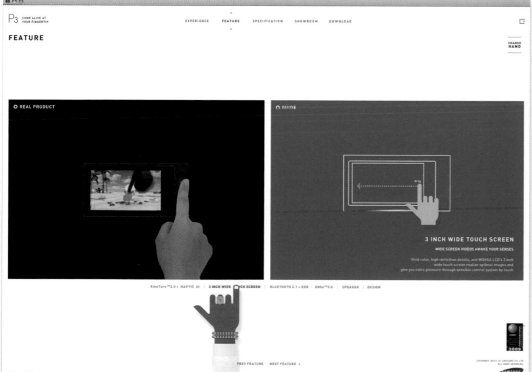

Project
Samsung mp3p P3
Promotion Site

Design
designfever
Seoul, South Korea

Client
Samsung Electronics Co., Ltd.
Suwon-City, South Korea

Auf dieser Website kann der Nutzer die haptischen Funktionen des „mp3p P3" persönlich entdecken. Dafür wurde eine Spaßkomponente eingebaut: Im Intro kann der Nutzer aus zwölf verschiedenen Händen „seine Hand" auswählen, um damit die Funktion des Geräts zu bedienen.

A site to personally experience the functions of haptic "mp3p P3". A fun component of the site is to select twelve hands from the intro and be able to use the widget function.

Project
www.reiz.net
Website

Design
Zum Kuckuck
Büro für digitale Medien
Daniel Rothaug, Werner Goldbach, Sebastian Lenz,
Alexander Dees, Vera Baierlein
Jan Winkler (Fotografie)
Würzburg, Germany

Client
REIZ Reutter und Gutbrod GbR
Wernau, Germany

REIZ fertigt seit 1996 hochwertige Brillen im einzigartig edlen Design am deutschen Produktionsstandort. Die Website greift die dreidimensionale Architektur der Brillen auf und verbindet klassisch-reduzierte Gestaltung mit visionärem Futurismus. Das klar strukturierte Menü sorgt für Übersicht. Im Hintergrund sorgen fortwährend ineinander übergehende Fotos für eine warme Retro-Atmosphäre. Dieser Überblendungseffekt wird in der Produktübersicht weitergeführt: Alle Modelle können bildschirmfüllend in allen verfügbaren Formen, Farben und Größen miteinander verglichen werden, so dass der Händler die Website auch als POS-Tool nutzen kann.

Since 1996, REIZ has been producing high-quality glasses with extraordinary classic design at the German production site. The homepage takes up the three-dimensional architecture of the glasses and combines classic reduced design with visionary futurism. The clearly structured menu ensures a comprehensive view. In the background constantly dissolving pictures create a warm retro atmosphere. This cross fade effect has also been applied in the product overview: all models can be viewed on full screen in all available shapes, colors and sizes and therefore easily compared so that the dealer can use this homepage as a POS tool as well.

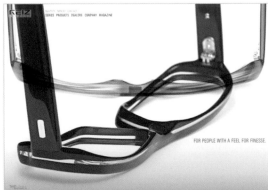

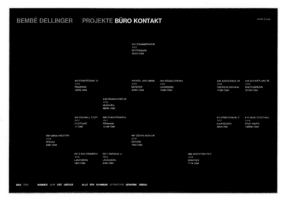

Project
bembe-dellinger.de
Website

Design
Zum Kuckuck
Büro für digitale Medien
Daniel Rothaug, Werner Goldbach,
Alexander Dees, Vera Baierlein
Würzburg, Germany

Client
bembé-dellinger architekten bda
Greifenberg, Germany

Im Stil eines fotografischen Kontaktabzugs liefert die digitale Werkschau einen Überblick über das vielfältige Schaffen des Architektur- und Stadtplanungsbüros bembé-dellinger. Mehr als 60 vergangene und aktuelle Projekte sind im Indexprint-Format archiviert und lassen sich nach diversen Kriterien sortieren und filtern. Der User hat die Wahl zwischen einem signifikanten Motiv oder der entsprechenden Kurzbeschreibung und gelangt so zu einer manuell bedienbaren Slideshow mit weiterem Bildmaterial. Die reduzierte Grundgestaltung und die ausdrucksstarke, plakative Typografie lehnen sich an die konstruktivistischen Entwürfe des Architektenteams an.

In the style of a contact print, the digital exhibition provides an overview of the varied creative works of the architecture and town planning office bembé-dellinger. More than 60 past and current projects have been archived in an index print format and can be sorted and filtered according to various criteria. The user can choose between a significant motive and the respective short description and subsequently gets to a manually operated slideshow that provides additional footage. The reduced basic design and the as much expressive as striking typography, follow the constructivist blueprints of the architect team.

Project
www.dessign.de
Website

Design
dessign. – Werbeagentur.
Ulrich Paulus, Christian Frick, Martin Dess,
Christina Sellner
Röckersbühl, Germany
Zum Kuckuck
Büro für digitale Medien
Daniel Rothaug, Christian Rudolph, Sebastian Lenz,
Steven Schmidt, Werner Goldbach, Alexander Dees
Würzburg, Germany

Client
dessign. – Werbeagentur.
Röckersbühl, Germany

Als „Die Jäger von Röckersbühl" geht die Werbe-agentur „dessign." auf Ideenjagd – und so zeigt die Website idyllische Landschaften und Jagdszenen mit subtilen Animationen und leisen Tiergeräuschen. Kunden als Jagdtrophäen, der steigende Leberkäs-Verbrauch des Teams und treffsichere Informations-Grafiken aus dem waidmännischen Erlebnishorizont – trotz Augenzwinkern kommen die Kernaussagen über Tätigkeitsfelder nicht zu kurz. Eine klare Typografie und ein übersichtlich gegliedertes Layout zeugen von strukturierter Arbeitsweise. Unterschwelliger Humor kombiniert mit seriösen Inhalten erzeugt den Eindruck einer Agentur mit hohem Kreativpotential.

As "The hunters of Röckersbühl" the ad agency "dessign." goes hunting for ideas – and so the website displays quaint landscape photos as well as hunting scenes with subtle animations and faint animal sounds. Customers as hunting trophies, rising "Leberkäs"-consumption and accurate information graphics from the huntsman-like horizon of experience – despite the humor, this site does not miss out on the core statements about the fields of activity. Clear typography and neatly articulated layout are proof of the structured working method. Humor and a serious content create the impression of an ad agency with high creative potential.

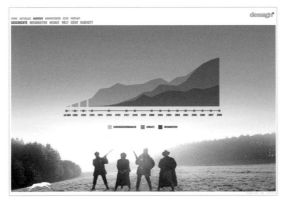

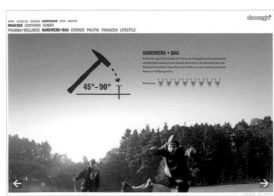

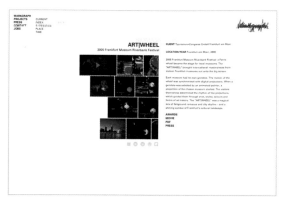

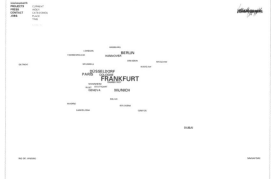

Project
www.markgraph.de
Website

Design
Atelier Markgraph
Stefan Weil, Kristin Trümper, Angela Kratz,
Sybille Schneider, Christina Loeffler-Kitzinger,
Christina Novak, Sebastian Pein
Frankfurt a. M., Germany
Zum Kuckuck
Büro für digitale Medien
Daniel Rothaug, Sebastian Lenz,
Werner Goldbach, Alexander Dees
Würzburg, Germany

Client
Atelier Markgraph
Frankfurt a. M., Germany

Die international renommierte Agentur „Atelier Markgraph" inszeniert Showrooms, Ausstellungen, Events und Messeauftritte. Das unverwechselbare Erscheinungsbild des Ateliers wird im digitalen Medium konsequent fortgeführt: Collagierte, typografische Navigationselemente gruppieren, überlagern, ergänzen sich immer wieder neu. Sie stehen in Opposition zu den kalligraphischen Signaturen der Projektmitarbeiter, die sich abhängig vom Inhalt immer neu zusammensetzen und die interdisziplinäre Arbeitsweise der Agentur symbolisieren. Das reduzierte Design der Seite lässt Raum für Beschreibungen der vielfältigen Projekte – nach Art, Ort und Zeit untergliedert.

The internationally renowned agency "Atelier Markgraph" produces showrooms, exhibitions, events and trade fair appearances. Its unique appearance continues consequently in the digital medium: typographic collaged navigation elements arrange, overlap and complement each other again and again and are in opposition to the calligraphic signatures of the team members, that – depending on the content shown – also repeatedly reconfigure. They symbolize the interdisciplinary working methods of the agency. The reduced design of the website leaves room for descriptions to be subdivided according to the kind, place and time of the diverse projects.

Project
adidas SLVR
Website

Design
Neue Digitale/Razorfish GmbH
Elke Klinkhammer (Creative Direction)
Jan Schlag (Art Direction)
Peyman Pakzad (User Interface Design)
Christoph Riebling (Interactive Sound Development)
Frankfurt a. M., Germany

Client
adidas International Marketing BV
Amsterdam ZO, Netherlands

adidas SLVR steht für Produkte in reduziertem Design aus zeitlosen, hochwertigen Materialien. In Anlehnung an die Kollektion besticht die Website durch minimalistisches Design, Schwarz-Weiß-Ästhetik und ein simples Navigationskonzept. Eine Besonderheit ist die „Jalousie-Navigation" als zentraler Part: Sie bietet einfachen und schnellen Zugang zu allen Produktabbildungen und zur Fashion-Fotografie. Durch eine extrem reduzierte Produktinszenierung gelingt es, die Attribute der Kollektion eins zu eins widerzuspiegeln. Denn der Fokus liegt auf einer Produktpräsentation, die mit der Ästhetik der Marke übereinstimmt.

adidas SLVR stands for reduced design and for timeless fabrics of high quality. According to the collection, the website is minimalistic and is set to impress with its black and white aesthetic and a simple navigational concept. A special feature is the "jalousie navigation": it provides easy and fast access to all product imagery and style beauty shots. Through an extremely reduced product presentation, the site is able to mirror the attributes of the collection exactly, so that the focus lies on a product presentation which corresponds to the aesthetic of the brand.

Project
NEOLOG Europe
Internetpräsenz
Corporate website

Design
Sagross Design
Arman Emami
Berlin, Germany

Client
Scopetime GmbH
Hamburg, Germany

Die Internetseite ist als Bestandteil des Corporate Designs an das Produkt und seine Zielgruppen angepasst. Ihre Gestaltung folgt der Zielsetzung, die Produkte in allen Facetten abzubilden – ohne dabei die Kunst der Reduzierung aus den Augen zu verlieren. Weitere Schwerpunkte neben der Profilbildung und dem Imageaufbau der Marke sind Übersichtlichkeit und Benutzerfreundlichkeit. Die gezielte Reduzierung und konsequente Einhaltung des Gestaltungsrasters soll zu einem harmonischen Gesamtbild führen. Die Ladezeiten sind durch rekursives Laden der Folgebilder im Hintergrund sehr kurz. Sämtliche Bilder sind bei einem In-house Fotoshooting entstanden.

As a component of the company's corporate design the internet presence is adapted to its product and target groups. The design pursues the objective of depicting all facets of the product without losing sight of the art of reduction. Additional focuses, alongside the development of the brand's profile and image, are clarity and usability. Deliberate reduction and consistent adherence to the design grid are to generate a harmonious overall image. Loading times are extremely brief, thanks to recursive loading of subsequent images in the background. All images were created during an in-house photo shoot.

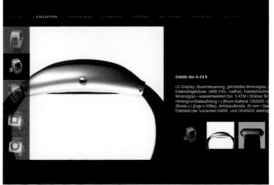

 digital media screendesign

Project
Andreas Mühe
Internetseite
Homepage

Design
Neue Gestaltung GmbH
Anna Bühler, Pit Stenkhoff
Berlin, Germany

Client
Andreas Mühe
Berlin, Germany

Der Fotograf Andreas Mühe arbeitet für die wichtigsten Magazine und Werbeagenturen. Er inszeniert seine Portraits und Gruppenbilder bis ins kleinste Detail. Sie sind nah und ehrlich.
Die Website versteht sich als Showcase, das sich durch ein einfaches Content-Management-System modifizieren lässt. Der Fotograf kann eigenständig Bilder hochladen, beschriften, durch „drag and drop" sortieren oder löschen. Die Auswahl und Zusammenstellung lässt sich auf diese Weise kurzfristig und ortsunabhängig gestalten.

Photographer Andreas Mühe works for the most prestigious magazines and advertising agencies. His elaborately staged portraits and group pictures are infused with closeness and honesty.
His website serves as a showcase, modified by means of an easy content management system which enables the photographer to upload, label, arrange by means of "drag and drop" and delete his own pictures. The website's selection and composition is thus altered at short notice and regardless of the photographer's location.

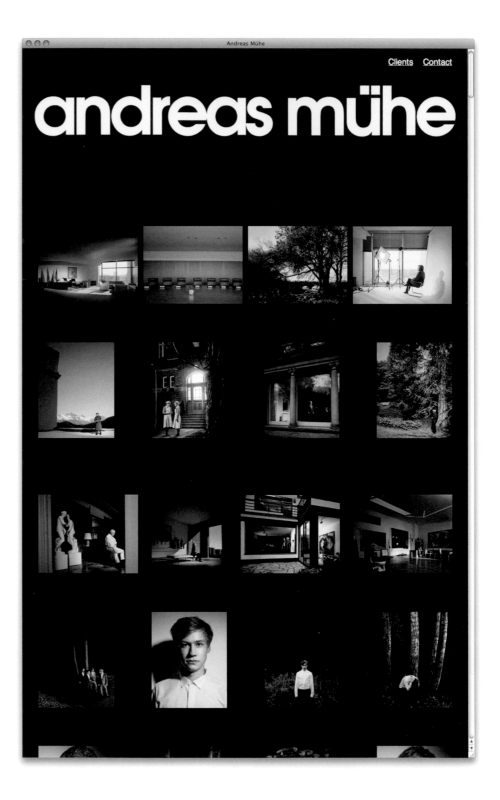

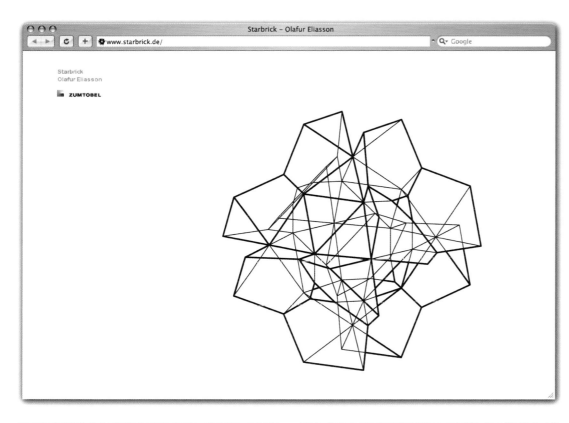

Project
Starbrick O. Eliasson
Internetseite
Homepage

Design
BOROS. INTERAKTIV GmbH
Ingo Maak, Christian Boros, Martina Schiffer,
Jochen Kronenberg, Alexander Schnitzler
Wuppertal, Germany

Client
Zumtobel Lighting Group
Dornbirn, Austria

Starbrick ist ein innovatives modulares Leuchtkörper-system, das von dem Künstler Olafur Eliasson ent-worfen wurde und von Zumtobel vermarktet wird. Eliasson beschreibt Starbrick als „ein Experiment aus Lichtmodulation und Raum". Einzelne Module lassen sich zu Gruppen beliebiger Größe zusammenfügen, die sich entlang verschiedener Vektoren im Raum weiterentwickeln können. Die Website stellt das Kon-zept in vier Sprachen vor. Die zurückhaltende Gestal-tung gibt Bildern und Texten den Raum zur Entfal-tung ihrer vollen Wirkung.

Starbrick is an innovative, modular luminary system which was designed by the artist Olafur Eliasson and marketed by Zumtobel. Eliasson describes Starbrick as "an experiment of light modulation and space". In-dividual modules may be connected to groups of any desired size which can also develop further alongside various vectors in the room. The homepage presents the concept in four languages. The modest design allows images and texts the room for development of their entire effect.

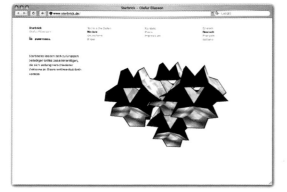
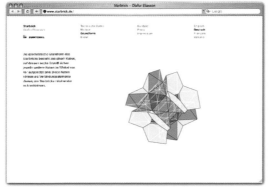

digital media screendesign

Project
VCH Group – Website
Corporate Website

Design
hauser lacour kommunikationsgestaltung GmbH
Laurent Lacour, Kai Bergmann, David Welbergen
Frankfurt a. M., Germany

Client
VCH Investment Group AG
Frankfurt a. M., Germany

Eine moderne, hochwertig elegante Gestaltung wird mit einer klaren, übersichtlichen Struktur verbunden. Durch die transparenten Flächen und den großzügigen Einsatz von Bildern – zusätzlich zu den Elementen Logo, Farbe und Schrift – werden die festgelegten Markenkernwerte – Transparenz und innovatives Unternehmertum – assoziativ vermittelt.

A modern, high-grade and elegant design will be combined with a clear, manageable structure. The transparent areas and generous use of images – in addition to the elements of logo, color and font – will communicate, by way of association, the fixed core brand values – namely transparency and innovative entrepreneurship.

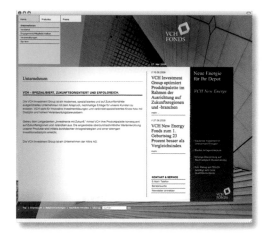
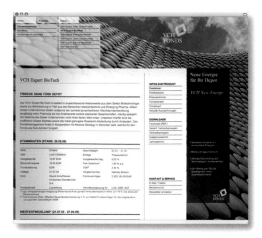
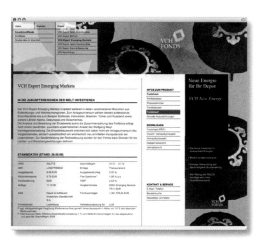
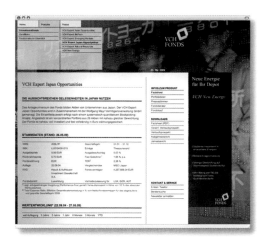
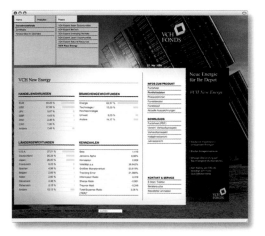
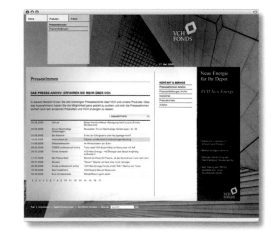

Project
FBG Online
Website

Design
Finest Branding Interactive
Marc Steinmetz (Creative Direction/Concept)
Tobias Ziegener (Art Direction/Flash)
Kanako Tada (Screens)
Nina Kaser (Screens)
Karlsruhe, Germany

Client
FINEST BRANDING GROUP
Karlsruhe, Germany

Die FBG – FINEST BRANDING GROUP – ist ein internationales Beratungs-, Marketing-, Kommunikations- und Design-Unternehmen, das führende B-to-C- und B-to-B-Marken betreut. Die Website der FINEST BRANDING GROUP wurde zum 1. April von Finest Branding Interactive konzipiert, gestaltet und programmiert. Die Website zeichnet sich durch einen hohen Anspruch an Anwendbarkeit, Screendesign und Interaktions- sowie Filtermöglichkeiten aus. Einige der zahlreichen Projekte der FBG werden detailliert in Case Studies vorgestellt und zum Teil mit eigens dafür produzierten Videosequenzen für den Betrachter erlebbar.

The FBG – FINEST BRANDING GROUP – is an international consulting, marketing, communication and design company, which assists leading B-to-C and B-to-B brands. The website of the FINEST BRANDING GROUP has been conceived, designed and programmed as of April 1st by Finest Branding Interactive. It features a high standard of usability, screen design and interaction as well as the possibility to filter the websites content easily. Some of the numerous projects of FBG are presented in detailed case studies. Partly, the user can experience them by watching especially produced video sequences.

Project
MTV Redesign 2008
Neues On-air-Design
New on air design

Design
MTV Networks Germany GmbH
Design Department
Etienne Heinrich, Robert Michael Brodmüller,
Justin Kruse, Nicole Schuster, Adrienne Matu,
Maren Knieling, Christina Chlapek
Berlin, Germany

Client
MTV Networks Germany GmbH
Berlin, Germany

01 TYPOGRAFIE:
FONT: Es galt, ein sich selbsterstellendes Design zu entwickeln.
SUBTITLE: Die Innovation: Untertitel passen sich generisch an den Sprachfluss des Originals an und unterstützen durch Farbcodes die Verständlichkeit.
02 BUG/BUGSYSTEM:
Das Ziel war es, das Markenlogo unterbewusst moderner wirken zu lassen und gleichzeitig die alte Ästhetik beizubehalten.
03 FARBEN:
MTV-Farbwelten erzeugen eine emotionale Verankerung in den Köpfen.
04 PROMOTIONENDINGS:
Der „Schlüsselloch-Effekt" bewirkt, dass die Aufnahme einer Textbotschaft durch die Verringerung von Störeindrücken erleichtert wird.
05 WERBETRENNER:
ALL EYES ON = Artist Touch.

01 TYPOGRAPHY:
FONT: We wanted to develop a self generating type design and make sure type information is comprehensible and independent of any background.
SUBTITLE: The innovation: subtitles are supporting the channel design and look.
02 BUG/BUGSYSTEM:
Our goal was to create a subliminally more fashionable MTV icon without destroying a 25 year old brand.
03 COLORS:
We wanted to generate an emotional anchoring in the viewers' minds by using a new "MTV color scheme".
04 PROMOTIONENDINGS:
We used research conclusions (eye tracking system) to reduce information communication gaps. The result: a "keyhole effect".
05 BRAKEBUMPER:
ALL EYES ON = Artist Touch.

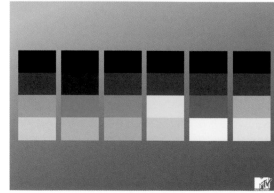

Project
Otto Schmid Metallbearbeitung:
www.otto-schmid-gmbh.de
Website

Design
Initial Kommunikationsdesign
Tanja Huber, Alex Müller,
Stephanie Niewienz, Tom Ziora (Fotografie)
Henk Blankenberg (Programmierung)
Alex Müller & Henk Blankenberg (Motion)
Ludwigsburg, Germany

Client
Otto Schmid Metallbearbeitung GmbH
Schwäbisch Gmünd, Germany

Otto Schmid Metallbearbeitung steht für Handwerks-
tradition und innovative Präzisionstechnologie. Diese
spannende Kombination wurde für die Website in
ein visuelles Gesamtkonzept aus Struktur, Farbigkeit
und Typografie übersetzt. Die filigran durchbrochene
Vordergrundebene „schwebt" über der plakativen
Hintergrundebene. Als Bindeglied fungiert die Typo-
Navigation, die bei Verwendung den Blick auf großformatige Fotos freigibt. Atmosphärische Bilder aus
der Produktionshalle wechseln sich mit ästhetischen
Nahaufnahmen ab. So werden interessante Einblicke
in die Arbeitswelt bei Otto Schmid möglich.

Otto Schmid Metallbearbeitung stands for traditional
craftsmanship and innovative precision technology.
For the purpose of the website, this exciting combination was translated into a visual master concept
through structure, colors and typography. The fili-
gree, open work foreground level "floats" over the
striking background level. Typo-navigation, which reveals a view of large-format photos upon activation,
acts as the link. Atmospheric images of the production facilities alternate with aesthetic close-ups. This
provides interesting insights into the working world
at Otto Schmid.

digital media screendesign

Project
PASTEL MUSIC
Website

Design
WEATHER DESIGN
Kim Sung-Lae (Art Direction)
Kim Hoo-Sung (Project Manager)
Kim Sung-Lae, Kang Do-Hoon, Kim Woo-Geun
(Design)
Kim Rack-Kyun (Programming)
Seoul, South Korea

Client
PASTEL MUSIC
Seoul, South Korea

www.pastelmusic.com ist eine offizielle Webseite der koreanischen unabhängigen Plattenfirma PAS-TEL MUSIC für alle Fans von warmer, erfrischender PASTEL MUSIC. Die Webseite besteht aus fünf Hauptelementen, die einen reichhaltigen musikalischen Genuss versprechen: Musik, Künstler, Konzerte, Kalender und Multimedia. Benutzer der Webseite können zwischen zahlreichen Optionen und Anwendungen wählen, sich Tracks von PASTEL MUSIC anhören und in ihre eigenen Blogs importieren. Wir hoffen, dass die Musik den Besuchern der Webseite ein freudiges, emotionales Erlebnis bereitet.

www.pastelmusic.com: this is an official website of PASTEL MUSIC which is a representative of Korean indie music record label. We try to make this website for those who love warm and refreshing PASTEL MUSIC. This is composed of five major contents: music, artists, gigs, schedule and multimedia. All of these contents will provide an opportunity of rich musical experience. It is equipped with varied devices to provide visitors with a variety of options for them to enjoy music. And visitors can easily listen to various tracks of PASTEL MUSIC album from the website and also share them with friends at their own blog. We hope visitors of the website enjoy the music and get emotional comfort from them.

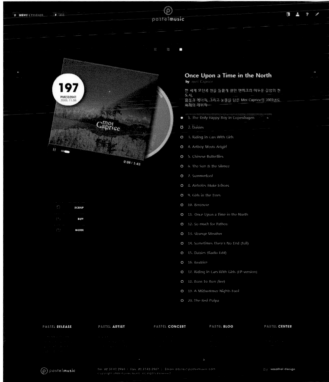

Project
Philips Online-Shop

Design
Philips Design
Philips Design Team
Eindhoven, Netherlands

Client
Royal Philips Electronics
Eindhoven, Netherlands

Der „Philips Online-Shop" ist unser Vorzeigege-schäft: Er enthält einen Katalog mit dem kompletten Produktangebot von „Consumer Lifestyle" und ver-schiedene nützliche Kauffunktionen, so dass er ein perfektes Einkaufserlebnis vermittelt. Die Website ist mit sehr wenigen Mausklicks zugänglich. Ihre Start-seite enthält ein robustes visuelles Navigationstool, mit dem die gesuchten Produkte schnell zu finden sind. Während eine Empfehlungsfunktion die Pro-duktauswahl entsprechend der konkreten Kunden-bedürfnisse erleichtert, hebt eine Vergleichsfunktion die Merkmale hervor, bei denen sich die ausgewähl-ten Erzeugnisse voneinander unterscheiden.

The "Philips Online-Shop" is a flagship experience: a complete consumer lifestyle product catalog with value added purchasing tools and a shopping experi-ence that answers the demanding needs of users. The site reduces click counts via a robust visual navigation tool on the homepage, which quickly navigates users to the product they are looking for. Product advisor tools select products based on user needs, while the compare tool can be used to highlight the features that are different across selected products. Since the first site launched, Net Promoter Scores are up across all countries, with one employee store registering a 30 point increase.

Project
gloss postproduction
Corporate Website

Design
SALON91 GmbH
Stefan Schröter (Design)
Christian Darsow (Flash)
Joscha Rüdel (Web Development)
Hamburg, Germany

Client
gloss postproduction GmbH
Hamburg, Germany

Mit Büros in Hamburg, Barcelona, Los Angeles, New York und Hong Kong ist gloss einer der gefragtesten Anbieter von Postproduktionen in Deutschland und weltweit. Kunden wie BMW, Procter & Gamble und die VOGUE, aber auch führende Werbeagenturen wie Jung von Matt, Goodby, Silverstein & Partners oder Crispin Porter & Bogusky setzen ihr Vertrauen in die Fertigkeiten von gloss. Für gloss entwarf Salon91 ein zeitgenössisches Screendesign in Hochglanz-Optik, das die atemberaubenden Arbeiten des Postproduktions-Hauses entsprechend in Szene setzt. Die bearbeiteten Fotografien bilden das Zentrum eines minimalistischen und zugleich sehr edel anmutenden Interfaces.

With offices in Hamburg, Barcelona, Los Angeles, New York and Hong Kong, gloss is one of the most sought-after post-production companies in Germany and around the world. Clients include BMW, Proctor & Gamble and the VOGUE, but also leading advertising agencies including Jung von Matt, Goodby, Silverstein & Partners and Crispin Porter + Bogusky, all of whom place their trust in gloss' skills. Salon91 produced a contemporary screen design in a highgloss look to showcase the post-production company's breathtaking work. Edited photographs form the heart of the interface for an impression that is both: minimalist and extremely elegant.

Project
i wie ida
Corporate Website

Design
//SEIBERT/MEDIA GmbH
Martin Riekert, Claudia Delang, Katja Wittrowski
(Konzeption und Design)
Torsten Groß (Realisation)
Marc Klaesius (Fotografie)
Mirko Schernickau (Videos)
Wiesbaden, Germany

Client
i wie ida GbR
Wiesbaden, Germany

Ausgangssituation: Das neu gegründete Modelabel „i wie ida" möchte sich im Internet präsentieren und dort Shirts verkaufen. Idee: Jedes Kind ist einzigartig und jedes Shirt von „i wie ida" ein Unikat. „Individualität" ist deshalb das zentrale Thema dieses Konzepts. Emotionale Hintergrundfotos und Imagefilme, bei denen Kinder ihr eigenes Shirt tragen, bringen dies auch im Design zum Ausdruck. Die Idee vom exklusiven und handbestickten Designer-Shirt wird für den Besucher erlebbar, der hier in eine für die „Baby-Branche" erfrischend ungewöhnliche Atmosphäre eintaucht.

Starting point: The newly founded fashion label "i wie ida" would like to be represented on the internet and sell its shirts online. Idea: Every child is one-of-a-kind and every shirt from "i wie ida" is unique. Therefore, "individuality" is the central theme of this concept. Background photos, loaded with emotion, and image films with children, wearing their own shirt, emphasize this theme – even within the design itself. The idea of exclusive, hand-stitched designer shirts may thus be experienced by the site visitors, who are immersed in a refreshingly unconventional atmosphere hitherto unknown by the "baby industry".

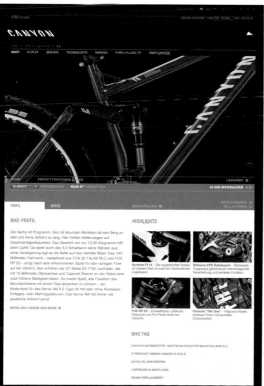

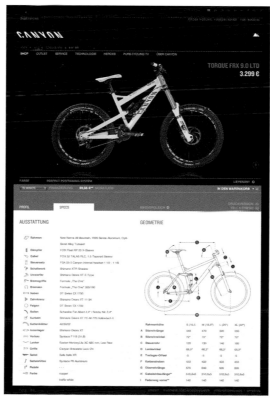

Project
Canyon Bicycles
Online-Shop

Design
wysiwyg* Software Design GmbH
Alex Koch, Maik Nischik, Bärbel Fritz,
Pattrick Kreutzer, Finn Jacobsen, Thomas Kaplanek,
Goetz Haselhoff, Andreas Stöber, Florian Breiter
Düsseldorf, Germany

Client
Canyon Bicycles GmbH
Koblenz, Germany

Für die ausschließlich im Direktvertrieb erhältliche Marke Canyon ist der Online-Shop die Vertriebsplattform Nummer 1 geworden. Es gilt, die anspruchsvolle Zielgruppe bei einem Höchstmaß an Übersichtlichkeit und Beratungskompetenz im Web mit allen wichtigen Informationen zu versorgen, ohne die Seite zu überfrachten. Die Produkte werden inszeniert und über einen Zoom unmittelbar erfahrbar. Alle möglichen Konfigurationen lassen sich darstellen. Der „Bike-Finder" vereinfacht die Modellwahl, das „Perfect Positioning System" liefert die richtige Größe und Sitzposition. Zudem wird die Marke über die „Heroes" und das „Pure Cycling TV" erlebbar.

For direct seller Canyon the online shop has become their major channel of distribution. Canyon seeks to supply fans and bicyclists online with all things for a bike, yet ensuring topmost clarity and advisory skills throughout the website. All products and their different setups are presented lavishly and feature a zoom-in on the respective product pages. Canyons "bike finder" allows easy selection of the desired model while the "Perfect Positioning System" provides correct size and seating configurations. Finally, "Pure Cycling TV" as well as Canyon "Heroes" adds to the overall brand experience.

digital media screendesign

Project
Wiedemann Werkstätten
Website

Design
KMS TEAM GmbH
Knut Maierhofer (Creative Director)
Markus Sauer (Art Director)
Stefanie Grüner (Account Director)
Andreas Paul, Oliver Rutzen (Programming)
München, Germany

Client
Wiedemann Werkstätten
Höchstädt, Germany

Präzision und Qualität prägen den gesamten Internetauftritt der „Wiedemann Werkstätten" – einer exklusiven Küchenmanufaktur, deren Maxime die Einzigartigkeit jeder ihrer Auftragsarbeiten ist. Die Besonderheit des Herstellers und der Auftraggeber wird durch eine neue Form der Inszenierung der planerischen und handwerklichen Kompetenzen der Wiedemann-Mitarbeiter zum Ausdruck gebracht. Die präzise Gestaltung und die klare Informationsvermittlung verbinden sich zu einer faszinierenden Markenwelt, in der exklusive Küchen Schritt für Schritt zum Leben erweckt werden. Durch Praxisbeispiele und viele persönliche Bilder wird das Unternehmen mit seinen Leistungen und Menschen erlebbar.

Precision and quality define the entire website of "Wiedemann Werkstätten" – an exclusive kitchen manufacturer whose motto is that each custom order is unique. The distinctiveness of the manufacturer and its customers is expressed through a new form of presentation for the planning expertise and craftsmanship of Wiedemann employees. The precise design and clear communication of information combine to form a fascinating brand philosophy which brings exclusive kitchens to life step by step. Through practical examples and many personal images, the company can be experienced with its performance and its people.

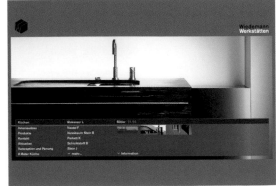

Project
KMS TEAM
Website

Design
KMS TEAM GmbH
Knut Maierhofer (Creative Director)
Bruno Marek (Design Director)
Stefanie Gruener (Account Director)
Till Bergs (Designer)
München, Germany

Client
KMS TEAM GmbH
München, Germany

Das gesamte KMS-TEAM-Erscheinungsbild wird durch eine klare Schwarz-Weiß-Gestaltung und eine dominante Balkensystematik geprägt. Auf der Website dient als Navigator durch die virtuelle Welt ein schwarzer Balken, der alle bildlichen und sprachlichen Inhalte gliedert und ordnet. Durch die reduzierte Gestaltung ist es möglich, die unterschiedlichen Markenwelten der Auftraggeber ohne ästhetische Einschränkungen darzustellen. Die Website lädt zur spielerischen Auseinandersetzung mit allen Inhalten ein. Dadurch dringt der Nutzer immer tiefer in die KMS-TEAM-Welt ein und entdeckt zahlreiche – auf den ersten Blick verborgene – Facetten und Funktionen.

The entire KMS TEAM image is defined by a clear black and white design and a dominant system of bars. A black bar serves as a navigator through the virtual world of the website, structuring and sequencing all images and text. Thanks to the reduced design, the different brands of the customers can be depicted without any aesthetic restrictions. The website invites playful interaction with all of its content. This allows the user to delve deeper and deeper into the world of KMS TEAM and discover numerous facets and functions that are concealed at first glance.

digital media screendesign

Project
Relaunch des internationalen Web-Auftritts der
MACKEVISION GmbH
Corporate Websites

Design
NOLTE & LAUTH GmbH
Kai Müller (Head of Business Unit Digital Experience)
Uta-Maria Jatzkowski (Design)
Stuttgart, Germany

Client
MACKEVISION GmbH
Stuttgart, Germany

Die Kernherausforderung war es, den hohen Quali-
tätsanspruch der MACKEVISION GmbH in Form von
hochwertigen Film- und 3-D-Produktionen bis zu
HD-Formaten auf das Medium Internet auszuweiten.
Wir realisierten einen internationalen Web-Auftritt
als Präsentationsmedium in der Kundenakquise, für
die Projektdokumentation und als Plattform für virale Kampagnen und Web-2.0-Aktivitäten. Die neue
Website ist zudem so aufgebaut, dass sie als porta-
bles Portfolio mit in Kundenpräsentationen genommen werden kann. Die Maxime „Passion & Technology" wird durch die weiße Welt und die schwarze
Welt mit ihren jeweiligen Eigenheiten transportiert.

The challenge was to expand the high quality standards such as the presentation of film and 3D productions to the point of HD formats of MACKEVISION
to the internet. We realized an international website
appearance as a presentation medium for customer
acquisitions, for project documentations and as a
platform for viral campaigns and web 2.0 activities.
To distribute their own performances we also integrated all computer generated images and visual results. The new website is based on a portable portfolio you can show in customer presentations. The
black and the white world transport MACKEVISION's
"Passion & Technology" philosophy to the web.

digital media screendesign

Project
Deutsche Reihenhaus AG
Website

Design
Die Firma GmbH
Wiesbaden, Germany

Client
DRH Deutsche Reihenhaus AG
Köln, Germany

Die Deutsche Reihenhaus AG ist als Partner bei der Stadtentwicklung auf hochwertige, schlüsselfertige Reihenhäuser spezialisiert. Das kommunikative Ziel der Internetpräsenz ist die Darstellung und Etablierung des Reihenhauses als attraktive und zukunftsfähige Lebensform im urbanen Raum. Weiterhin gilt es, die Bindung zu institutionellen Zielgruppen zu erhöhen und das Vertrauen in das Produkt Reihenhaus zu stärken. Durch reduzierte Form- und Farbgebung ist eine übersichtliche Präsentation der Haustypen gewährleistet. Die Präsenz ermöglicht einen einfachen Zugang zu aktuellen Bauprojekten des Unternehmens.

As an urban development partner, Deutsche Reihenhaus AG specializes in high-end turnkey row houses. The communication objective of the website is to present and establish the row house as an attractive and sustainable urban living choice. Additional goals include cementing relationships with institutional target groups and boosting confidence in the row house as a product. Reduced forms and coloring assure a concise presentation of row house styles. The website offers easy access to the company's current construction projects.

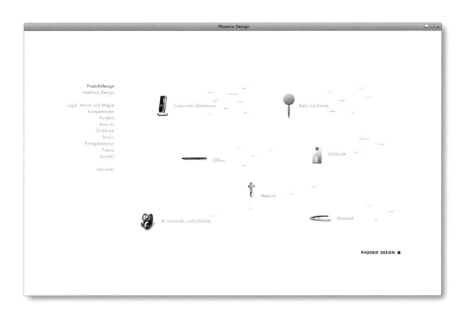

Project
Phoenix Design
Webdesign

Design
Phoenix Design GmbH & Co. KG
Team Phoenix Design
Stuttgart, Germany

Client
Phoenix Design GmbH & Co. KG
Stuttgart, Germany

Die Intention ist es, die unterschiedlichen Welten von Produkt- und Interface Design in einem schwebenden Kosmos aufzuzeigen. Das Corporate Design des Design-Studios ist geprägt von den Farben Rot, Lichtgrau und Weiß. Diese Farben spiegeln sich in Typografie und Bildkommunikation wider. Downloads sind nur im Pressebereich verfügbar. Die Firmenphilosophie „Logik, Moral und Magie" bildet neben Produkten und Interfaces einen wichtigen Schwerpunkt des Internetauftritts. Ebenso werden Einblicke in die Design-Prozesse sowie die Nachwuchsarbeit gegeben. Der Bereich „Aktuelles" zeigt nationale und internationale Aktivitäten, Awards und vieles mehr.

The intention is to present the different worlds of product and interface design in a floating cosmos. The design studio's corporate design is characterized by the colors red, light grey and white. These colors are reflected in the typography and in the way content is communicated. Downloads are only available in the press area. Besides products and interfaces, the company philosophy "Logic, Morality und Magic" is an important part of the website. Insights into design processes and the work with up-and-coming talents are also given. The area "Latest news" shows national and international activities, awards and much more.

Project
Iamsterdam.com
Website

Design
Fabrique Communications and Design
Sanne Wijbenga, Marlene Soulier, Wijbrand Stet,
Emko Bos, Filip van Harreveld
Delft, Netherlands

Client
Amsterdam Partners
Amsterdam, Netherlands

„I amsterdam" ist das Motto für Amsterdam. Es ist ein Citymarketing-Portal, das einen Überblick über all das verschafft, was Amsterdam zu bieten hat und was die Stadt so einzigartig macht. Die Website hält Informationen für Besucher („Visiting", „What's on"), Unternehmer („Business") und Einwohner von Amsterdam („Living") bereit. Das Angebot wendet sich an englischsprachige Besucher, jedoch sind die Informationen auch in deutscher, französischer und niederländischer Sprache verfügbar. Den Benutzern steht mit „my amsterdam" auch ein persönlicher Bereich zur Verfügung, in den Locations, Veranstaltungen und Artikel eingefügt werden können. Weitere interaktive Module werden in Kürze folgen.

"I amsterdam" is the motto for Amsterdam and the Amsterdam area. Fabrique developed one portal for all the different visitors to find their information. The website contains information for visitors ("Visiting", "What's on"), companies ("Business") and Amsterdam citizens ("Living"). The site is aimed at English speakers, but the information for visitors is also available in German, French and Dutch. Users are able to add locations, events and articles to "my amsterdam", which can be printed as a personal travel guide. Within several months more interactive modules will be added, such as responses to hotels and performances (user generated content).

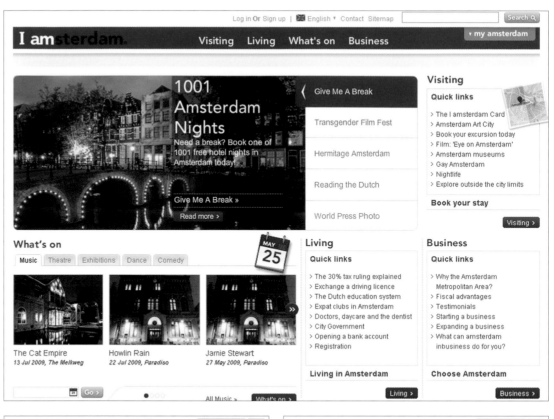

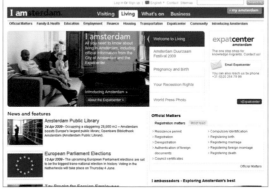

Project
DHL Logbook
Website

Design
Interone Worldwide GmbH
Martin Bauermeister, Martina Marzahn, Tim Liedtke,
Kevin Mitchell, Marcel Offermann, Christian Potthast,
Hans Schaale, Isabell Urban, Chris Wallon
Köln, Germany

Client
Deutsche Post World Net
Bonn, Germany

Logistik ist verstaubt und langweilig? Das Gegenteil beweist das „DHL Logbook": Das einzigartige, inter-aktive Logistik-Kompendium vermittelt durch seine intuitive Navigation und die multimediale Aufberei-tung komplexe Sachverhalte und exklusives Fachwis-sen auf einfache Art. Authentische Video-Porträts flankieren die Theorie mit fesselnden Lebensläufen junger DHL-Manager. So wird durch größtmögliches Nutzer-Erleben Logistik einfach erfahrbar und intui-tiv erlebbar – Logistik ist sexy.

Logistics is moldy and boring? The opposite proves the "DHL Logbook": the unique interactive logistics compendium offers a comprehensive logistics man-ual and exclusive know how in a very user friendly way. Authentic video portraits flank the theory with captivating vitas of young DHL-managers and create an atmosphere that makes users discover the logis-tics business in an intuitive, emotional and innovative way – logistics is sexy.

Project
BauNetz Relaunch
Website

Design
PROJEKTBUERO HENKEL.HIEDL
Robinson Meinecke (Designer)
Hubert Ilg (Art Director)
Andreas Henkel, Bärbl Hiedl (Creative Directors)
Berlin, Germany

Client
BauNetz Media GmbH
Berlin, Germany

Relaunch von BauNetz, dem heute führenden „B2B"-Medium für Architekten. Der Auftritt sollte optisch und funktional komplett überarbeitet werden: übersichtlich, mutig und jung – so der Wunsch des Kunden. Das Herzstück von BauNetz, die täglichen Branchenmeldungen „halb 4", wurden ins Zentrum des Auftrittes gerückt. Eine intuitiv bedienbare Navigation führt durch das Magazin und präsentiert täglich wechselnde Inhalte. Zum neuen Markenzeichen gehört der mit dem Magazintitel wechselnde Hintergrund.

Relaunch of BauNetz, today's leading "B2B" medium for architects. The optical and functional appearance should be reconditioned completely: clear, courageously and young – so the desire of the client. The heart from BauNetz, the branch's daily news "halb 4", was moved in the center. An intuitive operable navigation leads through the magazine and presents daily alternating contents. The background, changing with the magazine title, belongs to the new brand of BauNetz.

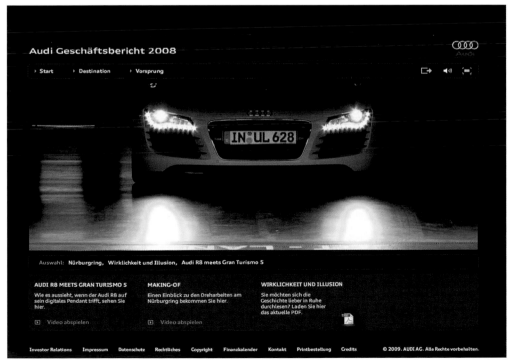

Project
AUDI Online-Geschäftsbericht 2008
Online annual report 2008

Design
BurdaYukom Publishing GmbH
Christian Ittner, Domenico Galizia
München, Germany

Client
AUDI AG
Ingolstadt, Germany

Mit der Online-Version des Geschäftsberichts 2008 verfolgt AUDI ein völlig neues Konzept der Visualisierung und Inszenierung von Inhalten. Die Microsite www.audi.de/gb2008 ist eine Kombination aus Mapping-Applikation und Videosite. Auf einem interaktiven Globus werden alle 23 Destinationen der Geschichten aus dem Geschäftsbericht abgebildet, zu denen Zusatzinfos abgerufen werden können. Für jeden Ort gibt es eine rasante Kamerafahrt aus dem Weltraum bis hinunter auf den Straßenzug. Hier kann der Nutzer die Geschichten als Audio, Video oder Slideshow erleben: das pure Kinoerlebnis im Cinemascope-Format.

With its online version of the 2008 annual report, AUDI pursues a completely new concept for visualization and orchestration of contents. The microsite www.audi.de/gb2008 is a combination of mapping applications and video site. On an interactive globe, all 23 locations of articles found in the annual report are displayed, for which additional information can be accessed. For each location, there is a high-speed camera tracking shot, starting in outer space and zooming down to the level of individual streets. Here the user can experience the article as audio, video or slideshow. It is pure cinematic experience in Cinemascope format.

digital media structure

Project
HyundaiCard
Website

Design
ACG Co., Ltd.
Astrum Creative Group
Seoul, South Korea

Client
HyundaiCard Co., Ltd.
Seoul, South Korea

Diese Neuerung führt eine innovative Website-Strukturierung ein. Kundenorientiert, einfach und praktikabel – mit der neu geordneten Website-Architektur mit optimierter Navigation lassen sich Schlüsselinhalte durch einfache Menüs und Datenintegration darstellen. Drei GNB-Sektionen bieten zielgruppengerechte Primärinformationen; dabei wurde die Auffassung von Bedienerfreundlichkeit reformiert, welche die meisten heimischen Websites und Finanzunternehmen vertreten. Ein Seitenbalken vereinfacht die Navigation in zweiter und dritter Ebene, wodurch sich verwandte Daten bequem anzeigen lassen.

This renewal begins an innovative structuring strategy. Based on "customers first", simplicity and practicality, site architecture reorganization aims for exposing key contents by simplifying menu and integrating information, realizing an optimized navigation process. The GNB was unified into three sections to offer primary information according to the purpose of target visitors. It changed the perception of convenience which most of domestic websites and financial companies have stuck to. To improve simply arranged second and third levels of navigation, side-bar section was introduced to optimize usability and efficiency by exposing related data effectively.

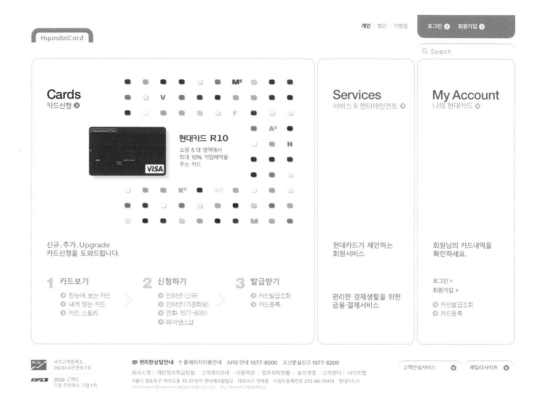

Project
Klangkiste
Website

Design
FEEDMEE DESIGN GmbH
Köln, Germany

Client
Westdeutscher Rundfunk
Köln, Germany

Musiker, Tontechniker und Orchesterwarte laden ihre jungen Zuhörer ein, hinter die Kulissen zu schauen und sich mit der Computermaus durch die Welt von Rundfunkorchester, Big Band, Sinfonieorchester und Rundfunkchor zu klicken. Die neue Kinderseite der WDR Klangkörper ist aus vielen Karten wie ein Quartett-Spiel aufgebaut. Wer einen der Musiker auf der Startseite mit einem Mausklick in Bewegung setzt, wird von ihm direkt in die Klangkiste geführt. Dort sind die Infokarten auf vier Laufbändern angeordnet. Mit einer Mausbewegung auf die einzelnen Karten können die Kinder Musik hören oder Filme anschauen.

Musicians, sound technicians and orchestra managers invite their young listeners to take a look behind the scenes and use their mouse to click through the world of the radio symphony orchestra, big band, symphony orchestra and radio choir. The new children's site from WDR-Klangkörper consists of multiple cards like a game of Happy Families. Making a musician on the homepage move with a click of the mouse takes you directly to the sound box. Here the information cards are arranged on four treadmills. By moving the mouse pointer over a card, children can listen to music or watch videos.

Project
Clipfish.de
TV trifft Web2.0
TV meets Web2.0

Design
Pixelpark Agentur Köln
Faden Baloglu, Iris Heidt, Lars Inselmann,
Rainer Lingmann, Stefan Schopp
Köln, Germany

Client
Clipfish GmbH & Co. KG
Köln, Germany

TV trifft Web2.0: Das Videoclip-Portal Clipfish.de bietet hochwertige Videoclips aus TV, Musik und Comedy sowie themenbezogene Talent-Aktionen in Kombination mit Community-Elementen. Nachwuchsfilmer werden in entsprechenden Channels präsentiert. Die User können interaktiv alle Clips „voten", kommentieren oder verschicken. Pixelpark hat mit dem Relaunch ein flexibles Rahmenwerk konzipiert, welches für variierende inhaltliche Schwerpunkte entsprechend angepasst werden kann. Für Clipfish war es wichtig, sich durch den Fokus auf professionelle Inhalte ihrer Partner RTL, Universal und Sony zu differenzieren.

TV meets Web2.0: the video clip portal Clipfish.de offers high-quality video clips from television, music and comedy sectors, as well as topical talent quest programs with community elements. Up-and-coming filmmakers are introduced on various channels. Users can comment and vote on all clips interactively, or forward them to other users. For its relaunch initiative, Pixelpark has developed a flexible framework which can be adapted to fit changing strategic objectives. It was essential to Clipfish that its profile was developed with a focus on the professional contents of its business partners RTL, Universal and Sony.

Project
MINI Cabrio Online Special
Website

Design
Interone Worldwide GmbH
Silke Gottschalck, Michael Ploj, Christoph Behm,
Patrick Decaix, Christoph Siebelt, Tina Leuthe,
Christian Amon, Björn Scholl, Hannes Stockner
Hamburg, Germany

Client
BMW AG
München, Germany

Das „MINI Cabrio" steht für radikale Offenheit und
maximalen Fahrspaß. Die Online-Branding-Kam-
pagne setzt diese Maxime kompromisslos um: mit
einer Website, die ihre Grenzen überschreitet – mit
interaktiven und authentischen Filmen in Full-Screen
und einer radikalen Visualität, die durch extreme
Weitwinkel-Optik den Fahrspaß im „MINI Cabrio" erlebbar macht.

The "MINI Cabrio" stands for radical openness and
maximum driving sensations. The online branding
campaign demonstrates this maxim in an uncompromising fashion: with a website that extends beyond its own limits – containing authentic, interactive
full-screen films and characterized by a radical visual-
ity whose wide-angled views provide a so-close-you-
can-touch-it experience of the thrills offered by the
"MINI Cabrio".

Project
Urlaubsverschmutzung
Umweltkennzeichnung
Environmental indicator

Design
Elephant Seven Hamburg GmbH
Kai Becker, Oliver Viets, Oliver Baus, Roman Pelz,
Nils Liedmann, Thorsten Becker
Hamburg, Germany

Client
Umweltbundesamt
Dessau-Roßlau, Germany

Das Banner macht auf ungesehene Weise klar, dass umweltschädigende Gefahren überall und vor allem zu jeder Zeit lauern. Besonders dort, wo man es am wenigsten erwartet. Als plakatives Beispiel wird der geschätzte schleichende Meeresöleintrag von 188.000 Tonnen pro Jahr (Quelle: GESAMP) thematisiert, an dem auch die Tourismusbranche einen erheblichen Anteil trägt. Auf diese Weise wird das Umweltschutzkennzeichen des „Blauen Engels" überraschend und aufmerksamkeitsstark in einem verbraucherrelevanten Kontext inszeniert. Das Banner sensibilisiert die Verbraucher für die Allgegenwärtigkeit von aktuellen Umweltgefahren und regt zum Hinterfragen an.

The banner illustrates, in an original and striking way, that environmental dangers are present everywhere, all the time – especially where you least expect them. It addresses one danger in particular: the amount of oil released into the ocean every year, which is estimated to be 188,000 tons (source: GESAMP), a significant amount of which is due to the tourism industry. The campaign presents the "Blue Angel" logo in a consumer-related context and in an unexpected, attention-grabbing way. The banner raises consumer awareness of the ever-present dangers to the environment and encourages consumers to question the status quo.

Project
Into the wild
Auto
Car

Design
Elephant Seven Hamburg GmbH
Kai Becker, Oliver Viets,
Mirko Gluschke, Stefan Roest
Hamburg, Germany

Client
Chrysler Deutschland GmbH
Berlin, Germany

„Raus aus dem Alltag. Rein ins Abenteuer." Wie einfach es ist, mit dem neuen „Jeep® Cherokee" das Zeitgeschehen hinter sich zu lassen, zeigt dieses Werbemittel auf überraschende Weise. Scrollt der Anwender die Nachrichtenseite nach rechts, springt der Cherokee aus dem Format und lässt den Alltag immer weiter hinter sich. In freier Wildbahn begibt er sich auf eine spannende Reise durch atemberaubende Landschaften und zeigt, dass er sich auf jedem Untergrund zu Hause fühlt. Ein Flashfilm ist auf eine maximale Breite von 2.880 Pixeln beschränkt, daher wurden hier drei Flashfilme zum größten Banner der Welt zusammengefügt.

"Leave your everyday life behind and embark on an adventure." This advertising medium demonstrates in an innovative way how easy it is to forget the daily grind with the new "Jeep® Cherokee". If the user scrolls to the right on the news page, the Cherokee jumps out of its position and drives on and on, leaving everyday life behind. It sets off on an exciting journey through wild and breathtaking landscapes, demonstrating that it's at home on any kind of terrain. Usually, a Flash animation is restricted to a maximum width of 2,880 pixels, but here three Flash animations have been woven together to create what is the world's biggest banner.

Project
Porsche: Die 4. Dimension. Der neue Panamera.
Webspecial

Design
Bassier, Bergmann & Kindler
Digital Sales and Brand Specialists
Ludwigsburg GmbH
Martin Spies (Art Direction)
Thorsten Weh (Concept)
Nils Hocke (Project Management)
Michael Weh (Flash)
Ludwigsburg, Germany

Client
Dr. Ing. h. c. F. Porsche AG
Ludwigsburg, Germany

Das Panamera Webspecial ist ein interaktives Online-Magazin, das aus zwei „Welten" besteht, die für den Nutzer über einen frei drehbaren, klappbaren Würfel zu betreten sind: Die weiße Welt repräsentiert Produkt und Marke, die schwarze Welt bietet Inspiration rund um den Panamera. Beide Welten laden den Nutzer ein, sich in den Dimensionen „Moment", „Ort" und „Zeit" zu informieren. Die „4. Dimension" – unterteilt in „Motivation", „Design", „Technologie" und „Sport" – dient als Filter für die Auswahl der verfügbaren Artikel, deren Anzahl bis zum Ende der Kampagne mehr als 100 umfassen wird.

The Panamera webspecial is an interactive online magazine, which is based on two "worlds": the white world represents product and brand, the black world provides inspiration around the Panamera. Both worlds invite the user into the dimensions "moment", "location" and "time". The user can access the webspecial via a freely turnable and tiltable cube. The "4th dimension" – which is separated into "challenge", "design", "technology", and "sportiness" – functions as a filter to select individual articles. More than 100 articles will be available until the end of the campaign in mid 2009.

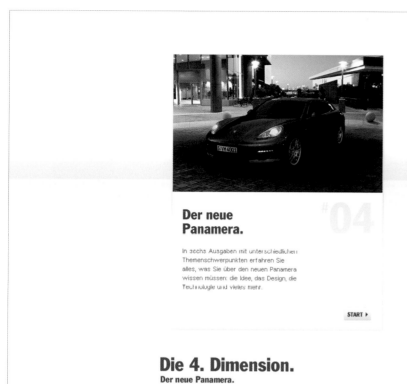

**Der neue
Panamera.**

In sechs Ausgaben mit unterschiedlichen
Themenschwerpunkten erfahren Sie
alles, was Sie über den neuen Panamera
wissen müssen: die Idee, das Design, die
Technologie und vieles mehr.

START ▶

Die 4. Dimension.
Der neue Panamera.

**Das Panamera
Magazin.**

START ▶

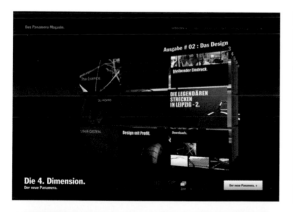

Project
Aus tiefstem Innern. Der neue 911 GT3.
Webspecial

Design
Bassier, Bergmann & Kindler
Digital Sales and Brand Specialists
Ludwigsburg GmbH
Martin Spieß, Mario Stockhausen (Art Direction)
Andreas Herde (Concept)
Michael Weh (Flash Development)
Ludwigsburg, Germany

Client
Dr. Ing. h. c. F. Porsche AG
Ludwigsburg, Germany

Das Webspecial „Aus tiefstem Inneren. Der neue 911 GT3." unterstützt die weltweite Vorstellung des neuen Porsche 911 GT3, der das „Racecar" unter den 911ern ist. Anhand von elf Fahrszenen werden Fahrspaß und Performance des neuen Fahrzeugs demonstriert und die wesentlichen Produkteigenschaften von Rennsportlegende Walter Röhrl persönlich erläutert. Der Nutzer nimmt die Ansicht eines Rennleiters auf einem Kommandostand ein. Seine Aufgabe ist es, den neuen Porsche 911 GT3 zusammen mit Walter Röhrl auf Herz und Nieren zu prüfen.

The webspecial "From the Inner Sanctum. The new 911 GT3." promotes the worldwide premiere of the new Porsche 911 GT3, the race car amongst the 911 cars. Eleven driving scenes are used to demonstrate the driving enjoyment and performance of the new car and the most significant product features are explained by racing legend Walter Röhrl. The user adopts the point-of-view of a race manager at the command post. His job, together with Walter Röhrl, is to examine the new Porsche 911 GT3 as thoroughly as possible.

Project
Samsung Refrigerator
Promotion-Film
Promotion movie

Design
designfever
Seoul, South Korea

Client
Samsung Electronics Co., Ltd.
Suwon-City, South Korea

Dieser Werbefilm beschreibt auf heitere Weise die Welt der Frische, die sich im Inneren des Samsung-Kühlschranks verbirgt – mit traumhaften 3-D-Animationen.

This is a promotional movie which describes delightfully a fresh world – hiding inside Samsung refrigerator – with dream-like images of 3D animation.

Project
wow! Manifesto
Website

Design
CHEIL Worldwide
Andrew Berglund (Creative Director)
Felix Genzmer, Yoon Jee Kang (Art Directors)
Seoul, South Korea
Sugarcube
Kiyoung Park (Executive Producer)
Sangil Moon (Designer)
Yoonhyeong Kim (Flash developer)
Seoul, South Korea

Client
Samsung Mobile
Seoul, South Korea

„Samsung Mobile wow!" ist die erste Samsung Web2.0-Kampagne. CHEIL Worldwide kreierte eine Video- und Fotoplattform in Kombination mit verschiedenen sozialen Netzwerken, die Nutzern die Möglichkeit bietet, Inhalte zu generieren und zu kommentieren. Dadurch, dass die Nutzer die Inhalte aktiv gestalten und darüber innerhalb der Community diskutieren können, haben wir einen Anreiz geschaffen, „Samsung Mobile wow!" regelmäßig zu besuchen – und gleichzeitig für Samsung eine Plattform bereitgestellt, die weitere Produkteinführungen in der Zukunft ermöglicht.

"Samsung Mobile wow!" is the first campaign ever for Samsung to create a truly web2.0 campaign integrating different social networks, discussion, video and photo platforms. By creating an emotional connection with the "wow! experience" in social networks, Samsung Mobile developed a community of existing and potential users of Samsung Mobile. By allowing users to actively interact in the community, it not only gives users a reason to come back but also creates a platform for Samsung Mobile to powerfully launch future products.

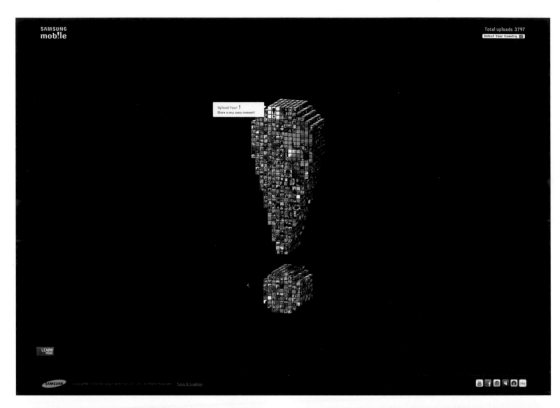

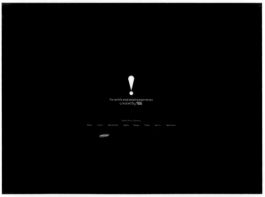

Project
Cialis „Happy Hours"
Medikament

Design
Elephant Seven Hamburg GmbH
Oliver Viets, Kai Becker, Oliver Baus,
Katharina Bender, Benjamin Bruno, Robin Wichmann
Hamburg, Germany

Client
Lilly Deutschland GmbH
Bad Homburg, Germany

Entwickelt wurde ein Bildschirmschoner für Fach-
ärzte, der das Nützliche mit dem Humorvollen verbindet. Denn was zunächst nach einer ungewöhnlichen
Uhr aussieht, entpuppt sich beim zweiten Hinsehen
als überraschende Inszenierung des Produktnutzens.
Durch die besondere Funktionsweise der Uhr wird
der Bildschirmschoner zum Blickfang: Statt der Zeiger
dreht sich das Ziffernblatt.

A screensaver for medical specialists was developed
that combines a useful tool with humor. What at first
looks like an unusual clock face turns out to be a
novel way of presenting the product benefit. Thanks
to the special way the clock works, the screensaver
becomes a real eye-catcher: instead of the hands
turning on the clock face, the clock face turns around
the hands.

Project
Hirn & Herz
Animation Hirn & Herz
Animation Brain & Heart

Design
Vogelsang Konzeptagentur GmbH & Co. KG
Miriam Damati, Christian Schaffrath, Dirk Schalis
blokstudio
Grevenbroich, Germany

Client
Vogelsang Konzeptagentur GmbH & Co. KG
Grevenbroich, Germany

„Mehr Nachdenken. Mehr Herzklopfen." Nur so kann gute Werbung entstehen, die nicht nur einfallsreich ist, sondern auch effektiv. Weil Hirn und Herz nun aber sehr unterschiedlich in ihrer Arbeitsweise sind, ist die Entwicklung einer richtig guten Kampagne manchmal sehr schwierig. Wir möchten mit diesen kurzen, aber sehr intimen Filmen Einblicke in die Welt der Kreativen geben und zeigen, warum gute Werbung manchmal etwas Zeit braucht.

"More thought. More heartbeat." This is our device for good and effective advertising. Because of the different function from brain and heart the process of a really good campaign is sometimes very difficult. These short videos give an impression of our daily business and how to create excellent advertising anyway.

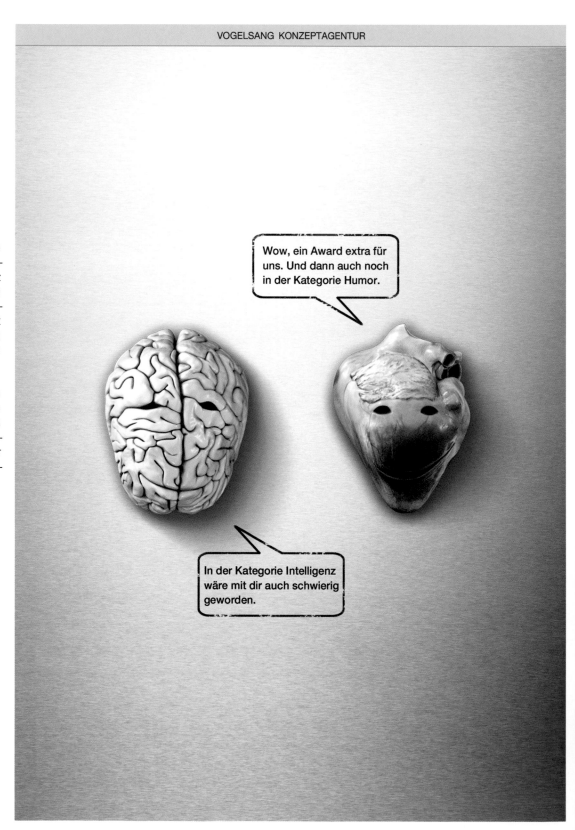

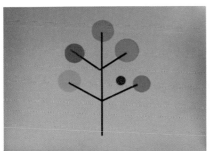

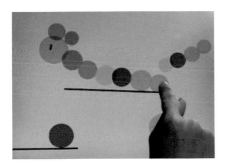
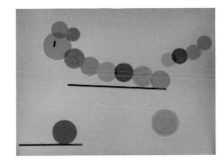

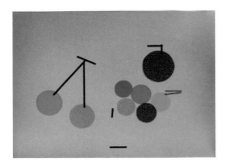
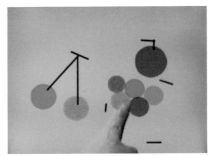

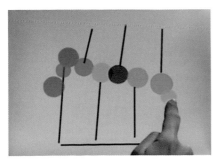
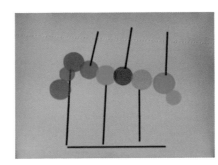

Project
SeeSaw
Pädagogisches Online-Spielzeug
Online educational toy

Design
Recruit Media Communications Co., Ltd.
Norikazu Yamashita
Osaka, Japan

Client
Recruit Media Communications Co., Ltd.
R&D Promotions Department
Tokyo, Japan

SeeSaw (zu deutsch: Wippe) ist ein pädagogisches Spielzeug, das eine neue Art der Kommunikation zwischen Kleinkindern mit unterschiedlichen Sprachen und Gepflogenheiten ermöglichen soll. Kinder aus aller Welt, die noch nicht gut sprechen oder gar mit einem Computer umgehen können, können gemeinsam auf einem Sensorbildschirm anregende Bilder gestalten, wie beim Bemalen einer Glasscheibe von beiden Seiten. Durch Berühren des Monitors entstehen bunte Bälle oder Linien. Dabei reagiert ein Kind auf das, was das andere Kind gemalt hat, und es entsteht eine intuitive Art der Rollenteilung. Die Kinder bauen ihre eigenen Bilder immer weiter aus und verleihen ihnen somit neue Bedeutungen und Formen.

SeeSaw is an educational toy aimed at fostering a new form of communication between toddlers with different languages and customs. SeeSaw invites toddlers from all over the world, who are not yet able to speak or operate a computer well, to use a touch panel and create stimulating visuals together. Touching the monitor creates colored balls or lines to appear on the screen much in the same way as if they were scribbling on opposite sides of sheet of glass. Responding to the shape drawn by one toddler creates an intuitive form of role-sharing. The toddlers continue to build on their own drawing giving it new meaning and form.

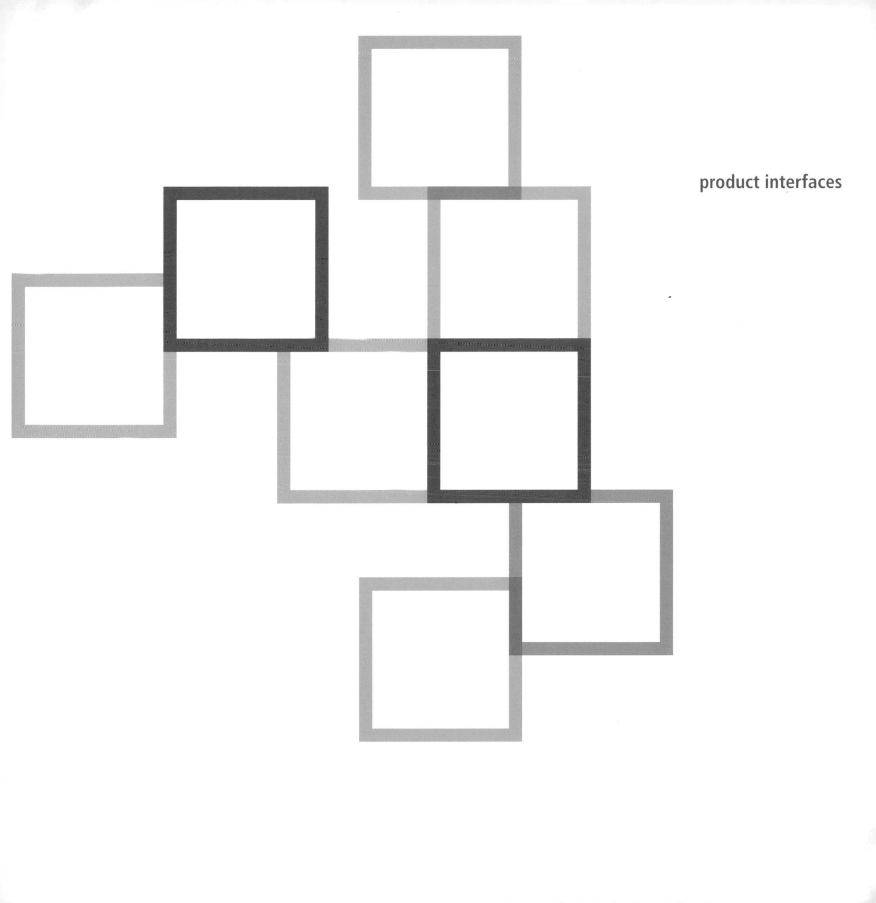

product interfaces

„product interface" als Erfolgsfaktor für Kundenbindung

"product interface" as a success factor for customer retention

„Product interfaces" ist keine neue Disziplin, doch scheint es ein Gebiet mit viel Wachstumspotenzial. Erst langsam erkennen Unternehmen die Bedeutung eines guten „product interface" und dessen Bedeutung als wichtigen Erfolgsfaktor für ihre Kundenbindung. Häufig wird das Interface eines Produktes lediglich als grafische Diziplin verstanden, doch bei einem gelungenen product interface geht es um mehr, nämlich um die Erfahrung der Oberfläche. Eine Vielzahl an Dimensionen, wie Grafik, Informationsarchitektur, (physische) Bedienelemente etc. sind miteinander zu kombinieren, um ein überzeugendes product interface zu erhalten – ein product interface, das besondere Kompetenzen schafft, die es ermöglichen, Kunden langfristig zu binden.

Auffällig ist, dass Kulturen sehr unterschiedlich mit dem Thema „product interface" umgehen. Eine perfekte Symbiose ergäbe sich aus einer Verbindung der technologischen Kompetenzen und Benutzbarkeit von Produkten asiatischer Firmen mit der guten Designqualität in der Markenführung deutscher Unternehmen. Nur sehr langsam gelingt es Herstellern, innovative Technologien mit einer konsequenten Markenführung zu verbinden.

Einige wenige Industrien, wie beispielsweise die Mobilfunk- und Kameraindustrie, sind besonders dynamisch und weisen eine gigantische Geschwindigkeit in der Weiterentwicklung ihrer product interfaces auf. Jedoch ist die Innovationsgeschwindigkeit im Bereich des product interface zur Zeit noch viel kleiner als in anderen Bereichen.

Es wäre zu wünschen, dass Unternehmen noch bewusster über ein gutes product interface nachdenken und dass insbesondere bedeutende Industrien, wie beispielsweise die Automobileindustrie, in Zukunft verstärkt eine Vorbildfunktion einnehmen und das Interface ihrer Produkte sowohl technologisch wie auch Marken relevant vorantreiben.

While "product interfaces" is not a new discipline, it appears to be a field with a lot of growth potential. Companies are gradually recognizing the importance of a good "product interface" and its significance as a key success factor for customer retention. While product interface design is frequently understood as a strictly graphical discipline, a successful product interface needs more; it requires experiencing the surface. Numerous dimensions such as graphics, information architecture, (physical) control elements etc. must be combined for a convincing product interface – a product interface that results in special qualities which promote long-term customer loyalty.

There are distinct cultural differences in the approach to the product interface. A combination of the technological sophistication and usability of products from Asian firms with the good design quality in brand management by German companies would result in a perfect symbiosis. Manufacturers are slow to succeed in combining innovative technologies with consistent brand management.

A few select sectors, such as the wireless communication and camera industries, are especially dynamic and exhibit incredible speed in the continuous development of their product interfaces. But the pace of innovation in the field of product interfaces is currently still much slower than in other areas.

It would be desirable for companies to put more conscious thought into a good product interface and for major industries in particular, such as the automobile industry, to increasingly take a leadership role and advance their product interfaces both in terms of technology and branding.

Thomas Hirt

Project
Digital IXUS 110 IS
Digitalkamera-Interface
Digital camera interface

Design
Canon Inc.
Ryu Wakui, Katsuhito Yoshio,
Akira Yoshino, Maiko Shibata,
Keita Takatani
Tokyo, Japan

Client
Canon Inc.
Tokyo, Japan

Das Digital IXUS „User-Interface" bietet Anfängern und Nutzern mit durchschnittlichen Kenntnissen Qualität und schnelle sichere Bedienung für leichtes Fotografieren. Wie die bisherigen Kamera-Rädchen rotiert das „User-Interface" glatt auf dem Schirm. Die schnelle Bedienung lässt keine Fotochance verpassen. Funktionshinweise, wo es wenig Blickbewegung gibt, ermöglichen eine glatte Führung. Dunkle Farben mit Kontrastorange heben Fotos hervor und sind auch für Personen mit Farbschwächen gut erkennbar. Feine Gradierungen und Animation erzeugen ein Gefühl von Qualität. Aus vielen Fotos können fix Favoriten gewählt und durch Schütteln der Kamera angesehen werden.

The Digital IXUS user interface comes with a sophisticated design and enables for fast and easy operations. A user interface that rotates smoothly on the screen was newly developed, allowing for swift operations and no missed shutter opportunities. Functional guidance is displayed in a strategic position on the screen, enabling for smooth operations. Orange is used against a dark background so that users can easily see and distinguish the items on the screens, which also appear sophisticated through subtle gradations and animations. During playback, users can select their favorites and view pictures easily, simply by shaking the camera.

Intuitive and enjoyable 3D CUBE UI

Direct access

Function   Information   Contacts   Contents

Quick transition

4-Way Homescreen

Project
ARENA GUI
Bedienungsbildschirm
Graphic user interface

Design
LG Electronics, Inc.
Corporate Design Center
Mee Yeon Choi, Kun Ho Lee,
Byung Nam Lee, Kang E. Lee,
Jin Whan Jung
Seoul, South Korea

Client
LG Electronics, Inc.
Corporate Design Center
Seoul, South Korea

Hier handelt es sich um einen Bedienungsbildschirm mit vier Flächen und mit kontextbezogenen Funktionen, Informationen, Personen und Inhalten. Der Bildschirm mit der bildlichen Benutzeroberfläche ermöglicht schnellen und direkten Zugriff und bietet dynamische Animationen für mehr Spaß bei der Bedienung. So können Lieblingsinhalte auf einfache Weise angepasst werden. Die Ergonomie setzt auf natürliche Fingerbewegungen und naturgetreue Aktionen beim Berühren des Displays.

This is a 4-way home screen with functions, information, persons and contents regarding the context. The screen with the visual user interface offers quick and direct access as well as dynamic motion which enhances the user's emotional satisfaction. Hence, users can easily customize their favorite contents. The ergonomics provide natural gesture and real touch feedback.

Natural gesture & Real feedback

Project
UNIT2S
User Interface

Design
iriver Ltd.
Yeong Kyu Yoo, Woo Sik Choi
Seoul, South Korea

Client
iriver Ltd.
Seoul, South Korea

Das iriver-UNIT2S ist ein Internet-Video-VoIP-Handy mit einer multimedialen Ausstattung. Das UNIT2S besteht aus einer Basisstation und einer Hörerein-heit. Das Display der Basisstation bietet den best-möglichen Blickwinkel für Video-Konferenzen und eine gute Orientierung bei Multimediainhalten. Die Hörereinheit passt nahtlos in die Basisstation, sodass beide Einheiten zusammen wie eine Einheit erschei-nen. Der Benutzer kann Notizen auf das Display schreiben, Bank-Transaktionen tätigen und über eine Internetverbindung Informationen aus Telefon- und Branchenbüchern abrufen. UNIT2S ist ein Endver-braucherprodukt, welches das Leben zu Hause berei-chern kann.

The iriver UNIT2S is an internet video VoIP phone plus a multimedia apparatus. The UNIT2S is com-posed of the base unit and the handset unit – the display on the base unit provides the best viewing angle for video conferencing and multimedia con-tents navigation, and the handset unit fits seamlessly into the base unit, making the two units appear as one. Also, the user can write down the memo on its display, make bank transactions; and, since it's an internet video phone, it can readily access the internet to fetch Yellow Pages and White Pages information. UNIT2S is a consumer product that can truly enrich life at home.

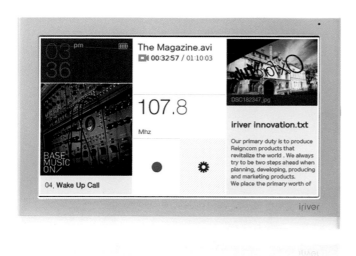

Project
P7-UI
User Interface

Design
iriver Ltd.
Yeong Kyu Yoo, Chang Hoon Lee
VINYL Inc.
Seoul, South Korea

Client
iriver Ltd.
Seoul, South Korea

Das UI-Design des Multimedia-Players P7 ist wie das Deckblatt eines Magazins aufgebaut. Es zeigt leicht überschaubar den gesamten Inhalt auf einer Seite. Durch die Anordnung der zuletzt gespielten Multimedia-Inhalte in dem Hauptmenü als animierte Miniaturbilder bekommen diese Miniaturbild-Symbole Platz im „User-Interface". Neben dem Einfallsreichtum des UI machen es auch der Berührungssensor und die große Anzeigefläche des P7 für den Anwender möglich, das zu tun, was immer er oder sie tun möchte, intuitiv und schnell, ohne den Menübaum durchsuchen zu müssen.

The UI design incorporated in iriver P7 mimics the cover of the magazine, which shows the inside contents all in one page with great accessibility. By placing the recently played multimedia contents on the main menu as animated thumbnails, these thumbnail icons become the part of the user interface. Beside its UI ingenuity, the touch sensor and the large display area of the P7 also make it possible for the user to get to whatever he or she wants, intuitively and quickly without navigating deep into the menu tree.

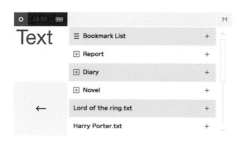

Project
YP-P3 Haptic UI
Interface zum Berühren und Fühlen
Touch and haptic interface

Design
Samsung Electronics
Jongsung Joo, Eunhye Lee, Joonho Won,
Byeongcheol Hwang, Joongsam Yun
Seoul, South Korea

Client
Samsung Electronics
Suwon-city, South Korea

Dieses Touch-UI auf DigiLog-Basis vermittelt ein analoges Gefühl. Haptisches Feedback (Vibrationen) erleichtert die Bedienung. Der Benutzer kann die Menüsymbole und Widgets auf dem Home-Screen anordnen und dabei aus drei verschiedenen Stilarten auswählen. UCIs (User Created Interfaces) tragen zur benutzerspezifischen Einstellung bei. Die Widgets und die verbesserte, stilvolle GUI (grafische Benutzeroberfläche) der Menüsymbole gewähren noch schnelleren Zugriff auf die Funktionen und sind ein echtes Erlebnis für die Sinne. Das „Quick-Tray" (Ablage für oft verwendete Funktionen) und der „Mini-Player" (Musik- und Radio-Player) können einfach und schnell bedient werden, so dass Multitasking zum Kinderspiel wird.

This is a DigiLog-based touch UI offering an analog feel. Clear one-hand operations are possible through haptic (vibration) feedback. The user can arrange menu icons and widgets together on the home screen, and store them in three different styles. User customization is maximized by UCIs (User Created Interfaces). The widgets and the newly-improved stylish GUI applied to the menu icons enhance accessibility to functions and sensual satisfaction. The "Quick Tray" ("tray" of frequently used functions) and the "Mini Player" (music/radio control player) can be called for easy and quick operations during multi-tasking.

Project
e-HOTEL Solution
Grafische Benutzerschnittstelle
Graphical user interface

Design
Samsung Electronics Co., Ltd.
Korea Headquarters
Juno Hwang, Sun Young Kim, Kyu Seok Kang
(Senior Designer),
Jung Bum Park (Designer)
Seoul, South Korea

Client
Samsung Electronics Co., Ltd.
Korea Headquarters
Seoul, South Korea

Die „Samsung e-HOTEL Solution" eröffnet den Gästen ein brandneues Hotelerlebnis. Die Gästezimmer sind mit einem Room-Pad mit 10-Zoll-Touch-Screen und intuitiver, dynamischer Benutzeroberfläche ausgestattet, während das Interface der Set-Top-Box mithilfe der Fernbedienung über den Fernsehbildschirm kontrolliert werden kann. Für einen nahtlosen Service verfügen beide Benutzeroberflächen über die gleiche Menüstruktur. Den Gästen bietet sich ein erfreuliches neues, digitales Hotelerlebnis mit hervorragender Grafik, dynamischer Bewegung und einem benutzerfreundlichen Menü. Das Manager-Interface besteht aus verschienen Modulen für unterschiedliche Management-Bedürfnisse. Durch die Verbindung zu anderen Managern wird ein ausgezeichneter Service für die Gäste ermöglicht.

"Samsung e-HOTEL Solution" provides all-new-hotel-experience to the guests. The Room Pad with 10 inch touch screen in guest rooms has instinctive and dynamic UI. Settop Box UI on TV screen can be controlled by using the remote controller. These two different UIs have the same menu structure for seamless services. For the guests, these UIs provide gentle and joyful new hotel digital experiences with gorgeous graphics, dynamic motions, and an easy-to-use menu. Manager UI consists of various modules for different needs of each manager. By connecting to each other, managers can provide excellent services for hotel guests.

Project
Presence Wheel Interface
Telefon-Interface
UI for office phones

Design
Samsung Electronics
Sihyoung Lee, Jung Go, Soyoung Shin,
WuJong Kwon, SangSung Woo
Seoul, South Korea

Client
Samsung Electronics
Suwon-city, South Korea

Das „Presence Wheel Interface" für Unified Communications ist ein intelligentes Interface in Form einer Drehscheibe, das es dem Benutzer ermöglicht, seinen Status einfach zu verändern und optimal zu kommunizieren. Drei Einstellungen stehen zur Verfügung. Das Display des Telefons passt sich der jeweiligen Einstellung an. Out-of-Office: Drehen Sie beim Verlassen des Büros das Rad nach links. Anrufe werden umgeleitet. Das Display zeigt einen Bildschirmschoner. Anwesend: Drehen Sie das Rad zurück in die Mitte, wenn Sie an Ihren Arbeitsplatz zurückkehren. Ihr Telefon ist jetzt online. Sie können verpasste Anrufe, Nachrichten und E-Mails abrufen. UC-Expert-Einstellung: Drehen Sie das Rad nach rechts, um das Telefon mit dem UC-Client Ihres Computers zu verbinden. Das Gerät kann nun für aktive Kommunikation verwendet werden.

"Presence Wheel Interface" of the unified communication is an intelligent wheel-based interface that allows the user to change status and communicate ideally. the user can chose out of three modes. The phone automatically changes the screen by selected mode. Out of Office – Turn the wheel to the left when you leave. Call is directed to your device. Screensaver will be displayed on the screen. In Office – Turn the wheel to the center when you come back. Mode turns into online. You can check missed calls, messages and e-mails. UC Expert Mode – Turn the wheel to the right to connect the PC's UC client function. Device can be used for active communication.

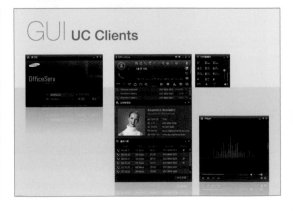

Project
CLW-Multitouch
Vernetztes Leben und Arbeiten CeBIT 2009
Connected life and work CeBIT 2009

Design
q-bus Mediatektur GmbH
Berlin, Germany

Client
Deutsche Telekom AG
Bonn, Germany

Moderne Kommunikationstechnologien vernetzen immer mehr Lebens- und Arbeitsbereiche – eine Entwicklung, maßgeblich vorangetrieben von der Deutschen Telekom. Der CLW-Multitouch stellt diese Aktivitäten heraus und führt sie in einem übergreifenden Präsentationskontext zusammen. Die Metapher: Schwarm – Fischschwärme bewegen sich selbstbestimmt durch einen virtuellen Teich, reagieren auf Interaktionen der Nutzer. „Tag-Ids" als „Futterstellen" generieren Navigationsmenüs für weiterführende Darstellungen.
Die Technologie: Multitouch – eine hochgradig intuitive Umgebung, „multiuserfähig", kombiniert mit atemberaubend lebensechter Darstellungsqualität.

Modern means of communication link ever more areas of our daily life and work – a development vigorously promoted by Deutsche Telekom. The CLW-Multitouch presentation illustrates these activities and merges them in a comprehensive presentational context. The metaphor: the swarm – fish self-determinedly swarm around in a virtual pond, responsive to user interactions. Tags acting as "feed" generate navigation menus that lead to further information. The technology: Multitouch – a highly intuitive presentational, multi-user environment, combined with breathtakingly authentic images.

Project
Tower HMI
Interface für Towerlotsen
Interface air traffic control

Design
Institut für Arbeitswissenschaft
TU Darmstadt
Thomas Hofmann, Christina König,
Dr.-Ing. Jörg Bergner, Hendrik Ebert
Darmstadt, Germany

Client
Deutsche Flugsicherung (DFS)
Langen, Germany

Diese neuartige digitale Benutzerschnittstelle unterstützt den Lotsen im Kontrollturm eines hoch belasteten Hub-Flughafens bei der sicheren und effizienten Kommunikation mit den Piloten der an- und abfliegenden Flugzeuge. Ermöglicht wird dies durch eine optimal angepasste Gestaltungslösung und die hoch integrierte Darstellung der Flugplan- und Planungsinformationen, die über mehrere Wahrnehmungskanäle bereitgestellt werden.
Als Hardware werden 21 „WACOM-Touchscreens mit Stifteingabe" verwendet.
Die vom BMWi geförderte gemeinsame Entwicklung von DFS und „delair ATS" soll an den Flughäfen Frankfurt, München und Berlin eingesetzt werden.

The unique digital human machine interface (HMI) supports the local-controller in the aerodrome tower of a busy hub airport in communicating safely and efficiently with the pilots of the arriving and departing aircrafts. This is achieved by a proper design according to the information needs and an innovative integration of the flight plan and sequencing information which is concisely presented on a 21 "WACOM pen controlled touch screen" in a multimodal way. This HMI, jointly developed by DFS and "delair ATS", was partly funded by the BMWi and will be introduced at the ATC towers in Frankfurt, Munich and Berlin.

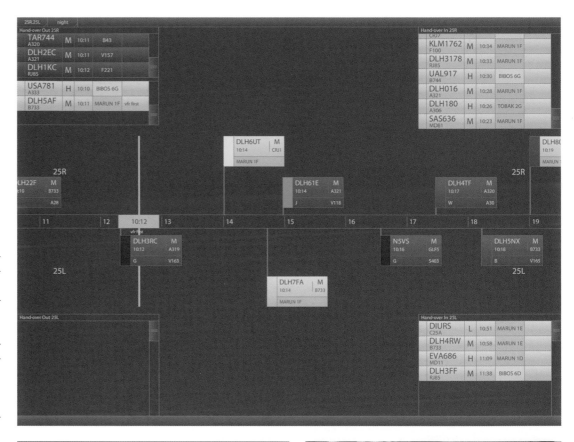

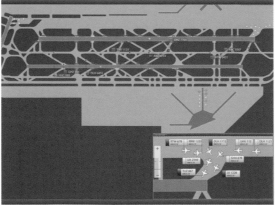

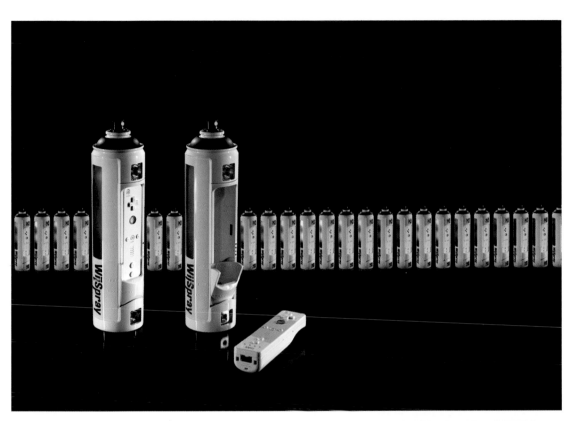

Project
Wii Spray
Digitales Graffiti
Digital graffiti

Design
Bauhaus Universität Weimar
Martin Lihs
Weimar, Germany

Client
Bauhaus Universität Weimar
Interface Design Group
Weimar, Germany

Wii Spray ist ein innovatives Interface mit räumlichem Interaktionskonzept für Spiele und kreative Anwendungen. Es basiert auf der „Nintendo Wii®" und ermöglicht es, digital Grafiken und Graffiti zu erstellen. Das Design entspricht in Form und Charakter einer, um elektronische Funktionen erweiterten, realen Sprühdose mit druckempfindlichem Sprühventil, interaktivem Farbdisplay sowie austauschbaren Sprühköpfen. Wii Spray wurde von Martin Lihs als Diplomarbeit unter der Leitung von Prof. Damm, Prof. Dr. Geelhaar und Jan Sieber am Lehrstuhl für Interface-Design der Bauhaus-Universität Weimar entwickelt und realisiert.

Wii Spray is a highly innovative interface for gaming and creative applications with new three-dimensional interaction concept. It's based on "Nintendo Wii®" and enables you to paint digital artworks and Graffiti. The experience design is based on the handling of real spray cans as used by graffiti artists. The controller provides a pressure sensitive valve, interactive color display and the option to interchange nozzles. Wii Spray was developed and realized by Martin Lihs in his Diploma Thesis under the guidance of Prof. Damm, Prof. Dr. Geelhaar and Jan Sieber, at the Interface Design Group, Bauhaus-University Weimar.

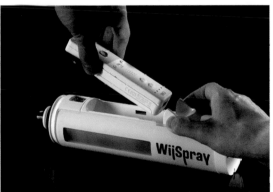

Project
smart Konfigurator
Farb-/Material Konfigurator
Color and trim configurator

Design
spek Design
Patrick Sauter, Eberhard Kappler,
Nadine Dopslaff, Alfe Toussaint, Caterina Idler,
Carola Unsöld, Devin Teachout
Stuttgart, Germany

Client
Daimler AG, smart
Stuttgart, Germany

Die Interface-Würfel tragen jeweils Muster der Lacke, Stoffe und Leder sowie Abbildungen der Felgenauswahl. Der Besucher wird eingeladen, mit den Würfeln seinen persönlichen smart am Bildschirm zu gestalten. Danach hat er die Gelegenheit, diesen smart als Postkarte für sich auszudrucken. Jede Karte ist vorgestanzt und kann in Sekundenschnelle in einen kleinen smart-Würfel verwandelt werden. Ein ausgeklügeltes „RFID-System" ermöglicht es, dass die Würfel als sympathisches Bedienungs-Interface die smart-Bildschirmdarstellung steuern. Diese kurzweilige und haptisch erlebbare Eingabemethode wirkt faszinierend und entspricht dem smart-Markenauftritt.

The interface cubes carry samples of color, textile and leather as well as images of the rim selection. Using these material cubes, visitors are invited to design their own smart car on the screen before printing out a postcard of this personal smart. Each precut card can be simply folded, turning it within seconds, into a miniature smart cube. "RFID technology" transforms the material cube into an inviting product interface, with which the car exterior and interior image on the screen can be "designed". This tactile and entertaining interface in shape of a simple cube suits the brand image and is enjoyable for the user.

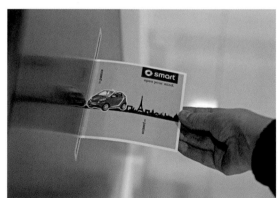

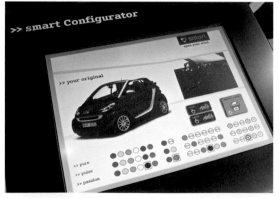

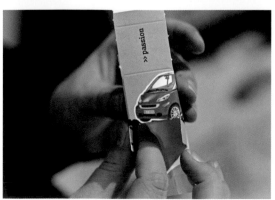

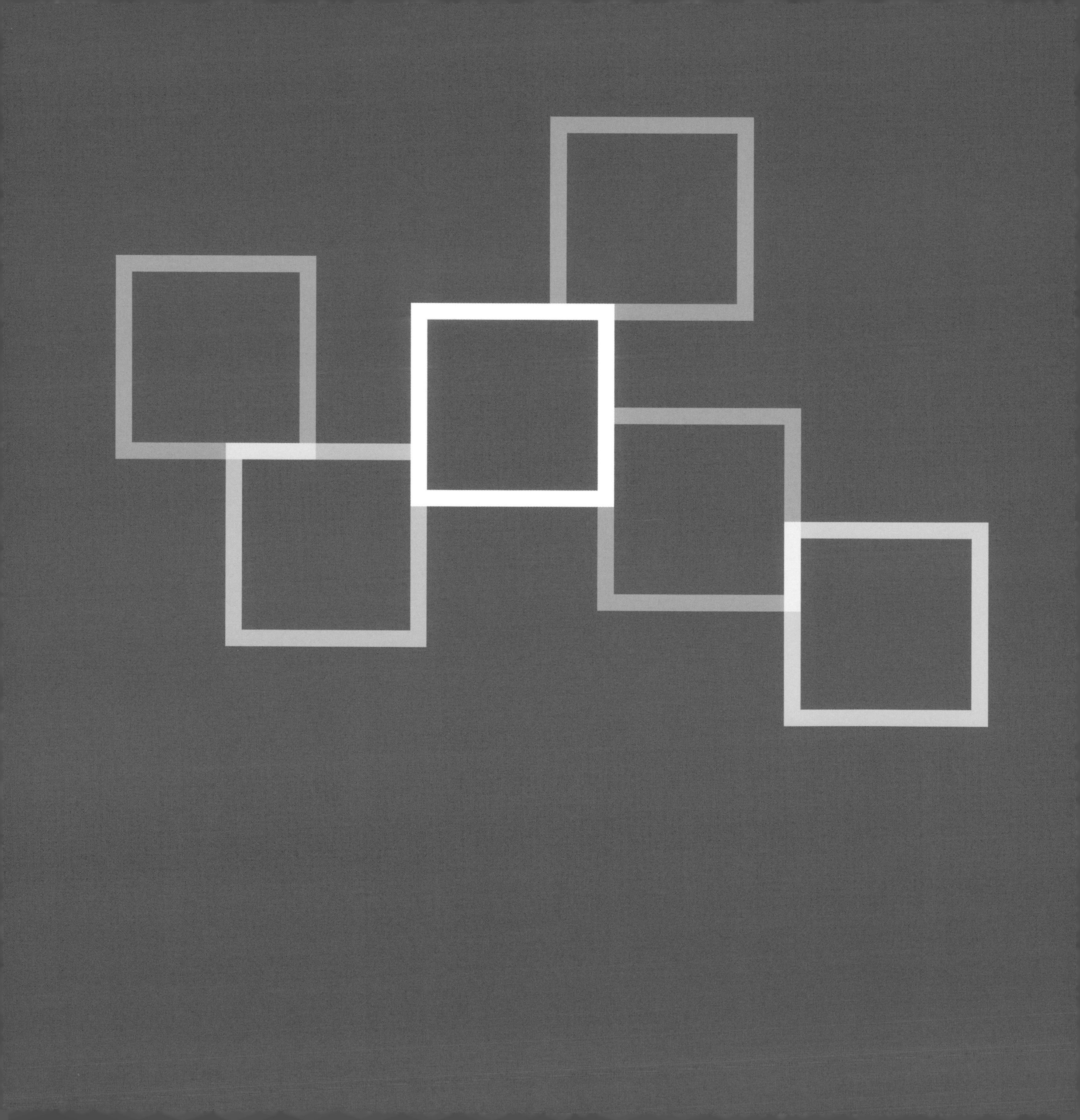

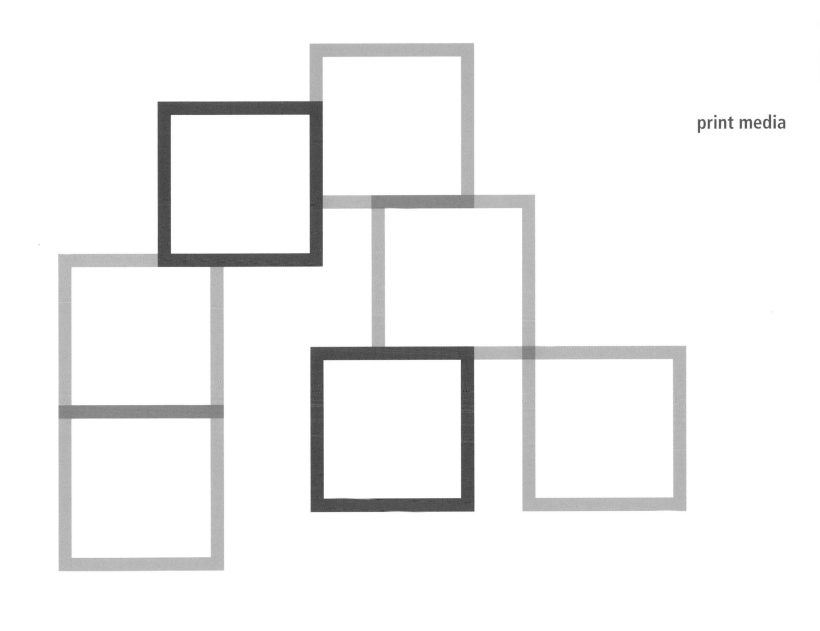

print media

Marken machen Geschichte. Geschichten machen Marken.

Brands tell a story. Stories make brands.

1987 hüpfte eine kleine Tischlampe einem Ball nach; beobachtet von der Mutterlampe staunte sie in die Kamera. Die Pixar Studios haben 1986 den ersten prämierten digitalen Film lanciert. 2009, 23 Jahre später, wurde das Filmfestival Cannes zum ersten Mal mit einem Digitalfilm eröffnet. Viele tolle Geschichten liegen zwischen diesen beiden Auftritten. Zwei Auftritte, die aus einem digitalen bewegten Bild eine Marke gemacht haben.

Marken machen Geschichte, wenn sie Geschichten erzählen. Heute hat jeder seine kleinen digitalen Unterhaltungsgeschichten bei sich. Und dennoch: Print lebt. Es gibt kaum eine Marke, die ihre Geschichten nicht auch im Printbereich erzählt.

Ist der fünfte Geschäftsbericht in hochstehendem, aber fast identischem Layout für fünf unterschiedliche Marken noch ein guter Geschäftsbericht? Soll sich eine Imagebroschüre an den Mafo-Resultaten zur Nutzerführung oder doch lieber an der spektakulären Inszenierung der Inhalte orientieren? Hintergrund hin oder her – was die internationale Jury begeisterte, waren große und kleine Geschichten. Souverän inszeniert und zelebriert.

Wenn Illustrationen, Name, Logo, Produkte, Sprache, Verpackung, Gebrauchsanweisung und Materialien die gleiche Geschichte nie gleich erzählen, dann berührt es. Dann bleibt es hängen. Dann ist es großartiges Print Design. Dann ist es Marke. Die Jury hat ausgezeichnet, wer nicht dogmatisch durchdekliniert, sondern erzählerisch souverän die wichtigen Inhalte auf den Punkt gebracht hat. Geschichten machen Marken. Marken machen Geschichte.

In 1987, a small table lamp hopped after a ball; watched by the mother lamp, it marveled at the camera. Pixar Studios launched the first award-winning digital film in 1986. In 2009, 23 years later, the Cannes Film Festival opened with a digital film for the first time. Many amazing stories were told in between those two performances. Two performances that turned a digital moving image into a brand.

Brands make history when they tell a story. Today, just about everyone carries their own little digital entertainment stories with them. Nevertheless: Print lives. There is scarcely any brand that does not tell its story in print media as well.

Is the fifth annual report of outstanding quality but with a nearly identical layout for five different brands still a good annual report? Should an image brochure be based on the market research results for user guidance, or rather on the spectacular presentation of the contents? Background notwithstanding – the international jury was inspired by stories great and small. Presented with confidence and celebrated.

When illustrations, the name and logo, products, language, packaging, instructions for use and materials tell the same story but never in the same way, that is what moves you. That makes an impression. That is brilliant print design. That is a brand.

The jury selected entries that confidently got to the point of important content rather than being dogmatically thorough. Stories make brands. Brands tell a story.

Andreas Rotzler

„krisis bedeutet auch ‚Wahl, Entscheidung'"

"Another meaning of krìsis is 'choice, decision'"

Krise. Eine der Bedeutungen des altgriechischen Wortes krìsis ist „Höhepunkt einer Krankheit." In der Tat – als im Mai 2009 die Jury-Sitzungen des iF-Preises Kommunikationsdesign stattfanden, befand sich die Weltwirtschaft mitten im Kampf gegen die härteste Rezession seit der großen Depression der Dreißiger. Da ist es kein Wunder, dass sich viele (wenn nicht die meisten) Beiträge in der Kategorie Printmedien vorsichtig, manchmal auch ängstlich oder gar konventionell präsentierten. Als Manager, Berater oder Marketing- und Kommunikationsprofis konnten sich die Juroren beim Bewerten von Katalogen, Anzeigen, Mail-Packs, Broschüren, Publikationen und all den anderen Wettbewerbsbeiträgen gut vorstellen, wie die Agenturen, deren Creative Directors und die Manager der Kunden bestrebt waren, konservativ zu bleiben und wenig oder gar nichts zu riskieren.

Eine weitere Bedeutung von krìsis ist „Wahl, Entscheidung." Trotz der harten Zeiten sah man einigen Beiträgen an, dass hier Agenturen und deren Kunden mutig genug waren, die Markenpositionierung in den Mittelpunkt zu rücken und mit ihren Kommunikationsinstrumenten offen zu unterstützen. In einer Welt niedrigen Konsumentenvertrauens, sinkender Absätze, unternehmerischer Rekordverluste und ungewisser Zukunftsaussichten haben nur Unternehmen mit klaren Strategien und starker Markenpositionierung eine Chance – vorausgesetzt, die Kommunikation mit Verbrauchern, Kunden, Geschäftspartnern, Anteilseignern und Interessenvertretern klappt. Doch wann „klappt" Kommunikation in diesen Krisenzeiten? Wir müssen wohl zurück zu den Wurzeln: Es geht um ungekünstelte Klarheit, Aufmerksamkeit für kleinste Details, Erforschung des Unerwarteten, Achtung der Markentradition. Und Entscheidungsfreude – mit all ihren Risiken und Chancen.

Crisis. One of the meanings of the ancient Greek word krìsis is "the peak of an illness". And in fact, when the jury sessions of the 2009 iF communication design award took place (May 2009), the global economy was struggling in the toughest recession after the Great Depression of the 30's. No wonder that many of the entries in the print media categories (if not the majority of them), were cautious if not sometimes shy or even conventional. The jurors, being managers, consultants or professionals in marketing and communication, while evaluating catalogues, advertisements, mail packs, brochures, publications and all the hundreds of entries competing for the award, could easily imagine the agencies, their creative directors and customers' managers, trying to be conservative and to take little or no risk.

Another meaning of krìsis is "choice, decision". Despite the harsh times, some entries were showing agencies and their customers bold enough to focus on the brand positioning and support it openly with their communication tools. In a world of low consumer confidence, declining sales, record company losses and uncertain future, only companies with clear strategies and strong brand positioning will have a chance, provided they are supported by good communication towards their consumers, customers, business partners, shareholders and stakeholders. But what is "good communication" going to be in this sharp crisis era? Probably we have to go back to the roots: crisp clarity, great care of details, research of the unexpected, consistency with the brand heritage. And taking the risk, and the chance, of making decisions.

Alessandro Balossini Volpe

Project
CITROËN „Abbiegelicht"
Anzeige
Advertisement

Design
Euro RSCG Düsseldorf
Felix Glauner, Martin Breuer,
Martin Venn, Ingmar Krannich,
Heiner Krauss
Düsseldorf, Germany

Client
CITROËN Deutschland AG
Köln, Germany

Kreative Zielsetzung:
Entwicklung einer Anzeige, die schnell und plakativ
das Abbiegelicht in vielen CITROËN-Modellen be-
wirbt.
Lösung:
Wir demonstrieren den Produktvorteil so, wie es kein
anderer tun kann – mit der Hilfe unseres Logos.

Brief:
Development of an ad, which dramatizes the cornering lights – a gadget of many CITROËN cars – in a
simple, fast and eye catching way.
Solution:
We demonstrate the benefit of the cornering lights
like nobody else can – via the CITROËN logo.

Abbiegelicht. Jetzt in vielen Citroën Modellen.

Project
ADC Creative Report
Buch
Book

Design
Hesse Design GmbH
Klaus Hesse (Art Director)
Sandra Stoffers (Designerin)
Uli Knörzer (Illustrator)
Düsseldorf, Germany

Client
Art Directors Club für Deutschland
(ADC)
Berlin, Germany

Der ADC veranstaltet nicht nur Deutschlands wichtigsten Kreativwettbewerb, sondern ist auch ein potenter Ausrichter von Seminaren für Profis, Junioren und Studierende. Zum ersten Mal gibt der Art Directors Club für Deutschland mit dem ADC Creative Report eine Art „Geschäftsbericht" heraus. Dieser Report zeigt nicht nur auf, was 2008 im Club passiert ist, sondern erinnert auch an große Vorbilder. Neuartig ist auch, dass alle Fotos durch Illustrationen ersetzt wurden.

Not enough the ADC hosts the most important creative competition, it also organizes professional workshops for creative pros, juniors and students. For the very first time the "Art Directors Club für Deutschland" publishes a kind of annual report, delivering insight into the club's work in 2008 and evoking great examples. Ground-breaking in the Creative Report is also that all photos are replaced by illustrations.

Project
Allblacks Rugby Box
Limitierte Editionsbox
Limited edition box

Design
Paperlux GmbH
F. Marco Kuehne (Creative Director)
Richard Lange (Art Director)
Hamburg, Germany
The Art Box Collection
Alex Sun
Berlin, Germany

Client
adidas International Marketing BV
Amsterdam, The Netherlands

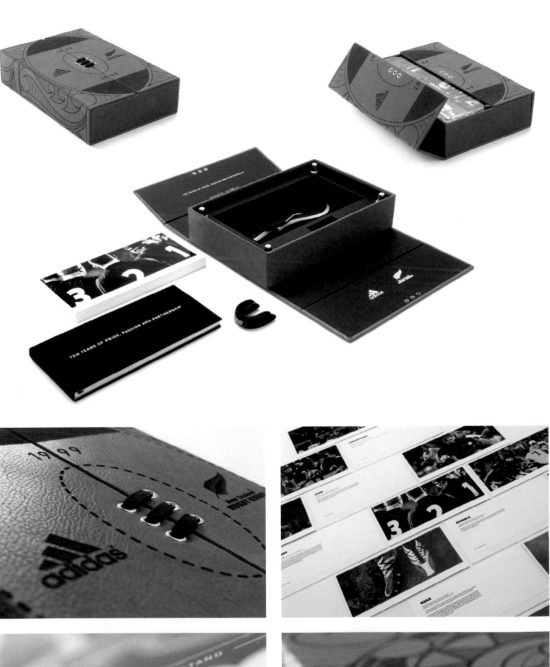

„Ten years of pride, passion and partnership."
Unsere Aufgabe bestand darin, eine kunstvolle Lösung für ein exklusives Geschenk für das obere Management zu entwickeln. Anlass war die zehnjährige Partnerschaft zwischen adidas und der New Zealand Rugby Union (NZRU)/All Blacks. Alle Details dieser in Leder gebundenen Box sind inspiriert durch wichtige Bestandteile eines Rugby Spieles und durch die zentralen Werte dieser Partnerschaft. Wir haben damit eine einzigartige, limitierte und personalisierte Publikation entwickelt, die den Empfänger überrascht und starke Emotionen hervorruft.

"Ten years of pride, passion and partnership."
The task was to develop a creative art inspired solution for an upper management present in dedication to the ten year partnership between adidas and the New Zealand Rugby Union (NZRU)/All Blacks. All elements and details of this leather-bound box are inspired by the relevant tools of a rugby game and the key values of this partnership. We created a unique, limited and personalized publication which is very surprising for the recipient and arouses a strong emotional experience.

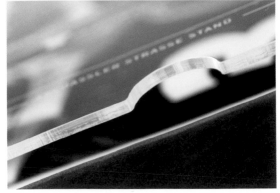

Project
ilio
Unternehmensidentität
Corporate identity

Design
Demirden Design
graphic design team
Sema Obuz (Creative Direction)
Esin Nalbantoglu, Banu Alpay,
Berk Okyay
Istanbul, Turkey

Client
ilio
Istanbul, Turkey

Das Wort „ilio" ist die altgriechische Bezeichnung für „Sonne" und steht für ein Geschirr- und Möbelunternehmen mit cleveren Ideen und Designs für eine kultivierte Lebensart. Die horizontal verwendeten Schriftzeichen sind eine stilisierte Darstellung der Sonne und ihrer Spiegelung im Wasser.
Wie die Produkte der ilio-Kollektion verfolgt auch das Logo einen spielerischen Ansatz, der die Dynamik und Energie des Design-Teams ebenso wie den Firmenslogan „The Story within" (auf deutsch etwa: „Die Geschichte dahinter") zum Ausdruck bringt. Das Corporate Design von ilio verkörpert die Marke auf zurückhaltende, doch elegante Weise.

The word "ilio", from the ancient Greek meaning of "sun" represents a tableware and furniture company committed to bright ideas and design for fine living. It is utilized horizontally, while its vertical format portrays a stylized representation of the sun and its reflection on water.
Just as with products within the ilio collection, the brand adopts a playful approach, symbolically reflecting the dynamism and energy within the design team while embodying the company slogan "the story within". ilio corporate materials reflect the brand in a modest yet elegant way.

Project
Nippon Connection 08
Katalog
Catalog

Design
Baumann, Beck, Bergmann, Nowitzki
Katja Baumann, Susanne Beck,
Kai Bergmann, Anne Nowitzki
Mainhausen, Germany

Client
Nippon Connection e. V.
Frankfurt a. M., Germany

Nippon Connection ist das größte japanische Filmfestival weltweit. Es findet jährlich im April auf dem
Frankfurter Universitätsgelände statt. Neben aktuellen japanischen Newcomer- und Underground-Pro-
duktionen, wird ein umfangreiches Kulturprogramm
angeboten. Nach zwei Jahren „zurückhaltenderer"
Kommunikation will Nippon Connection sich wieder
poppiger positionieren, ohne dabei den intellektuel-
len Anspruch zu vernachlässigen. Der Programmka-
talog ist hierbei das wichtigste Informationsmedium.
Neonfarbene Brücken materialisieren sich in unserer
(europäischen) Umgebung als Sinnbild für interkul-
turellen Austausch.

Nippon Connection is the largest film festival for
Japanese film worldwide. It takes place at the Frankfurt University every April. Beside the latest Japanese
newcomer and underground productions, there is a
large range of events. After two years of representing
itself in a rather contained fashion, Nippon Connection wanted to get a more striking communication
campaign but with a intellectual note. Pink bridges
materialise themselves in a (our) European scenery,
symbolising an inter-cultural exchange between Japan and us.

Project
Berlin 2008
Broschüre und Buch
Brochure and book

Design
New Cat Orange
Gestaltung und Kommunikation
HP Becker (CD)
Julia Maria Depis (Grafik)
Folker Wrage (Text)
Josef Hoelzl (Foto)
Wiesbaden, Germany

Client
Daimler Financial Services AG/
Intercom GmbH
Köln, Germany

West, Ost, Berlin, die Mauer. Es wäre zu einfach, sich auf die Inszenierung dieser Inhalte bei den Kommunikationsmitteln zu reduzieren. Das Thema „Tearing down the Walls" wurde vor allem mit dem Fokus „eigene Sichtweisen überdenken", also die Mauern in unseren Köpfen zu durchbrechen, inszeniert. Spielerisch kann man sich mit den Drucksachen auseinandersetzen, um immer wieder neue Facetten zu entdecken. Zudem haben alle Kommunikationsmittel einen relevanten Mehrwert. Es ist gelungen, die gewünschte Teilnehmerzahl zu generieren und auch die Bindung zum Veranstalter zu stärken. Mit großer Akzeptanz wurden die Kommunikationsmittel vor Ort genutzt.

East – West – Berlin – the Wall. It would be much too simple to limit the orchestration of the content to these few words. The subject "Tearing Down The Walls" was staged primarily with a clear focus on "rethinking your points of view", tearing down walls inside of our heads. All print material enabled the reader to interact with the subject, and to keep discovering new facets of it. Additionally, the communication elements all have been conceived to deliver a relevant added value. The communication program succeeded in generating the desired number of participants, and in strengthening relations with the host company.

Project
BERLIN HAUSHOCH
Magazin über Charlottenburg
Magazine about Charlottenburg

Design
Haushoch
Alexandra Bald, Ana Lessing,
Esra Rotthoff
Berlin, Germany

Client
Haushoch
Berlin, Germany

Berlin hat viele Gesichter. Die Vielseitigkeit zeigt sich nirgendwo deutlicher als in den 23 Stadtteilen. BERLIN HAUSHOCH fügt der Vielseitigkeit eine neue Facette hinzu. Das Magazin BERLIN HAUSHOCH porträtiert in jeder Ausgabe einen Berliner Stadtteil und schenkt ihm besondere Aufmerksamkeit. Nach Marzahn und dem Wedding steht in der dritten Ausgabe Charlottenburg im Mittelpunkt. Das Alltägliche und das Besondere des Stadtteils wird mit Fotografien, Illustrationen, Texten und einer dem Ort entsprechenden grafischen Sprache visualisiert. BERLIN HAUSHOCH zeigt Menschen, Wohn- und Lebensräume und schafft ein Bild von Berlin, das berührt.

Berlin has many faces. Nowhere does its diversity show more prominently than in its 23 different districts. BERLIN HAUSHOCH adds a fresh feature to the city's versatility. In each issue, the award-winning magazine BERLIN HAUSHOCH dives into the depths of one of these urban microcosms and reels in new prospects of a metropolis to be manifested within its pages. After Marzahn and Wedding, the 3rd issue portrays Charlottenburg. The everyday aspects as well as the particularity of this district are presented with photography, illustrations, texts, and a graphic language that is visually referential to its specific surroundings.

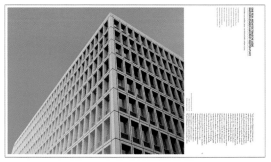

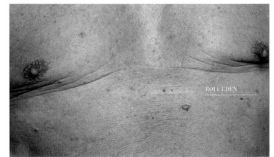

gold award: print media corporate communication

Project
„219 plus"
Kundenmagazin
Customer magazine

Design
Simon & Goetz Design GmbH & Co. KG
Dörte Fischer, Gerrit Hinkelbein,
Christina Schirm (Art Direction)
Frankfurt a. M., Germany

Client
Sal. Oppenheim jr. & Cie.
Köln, Germany

Ziel war es, ein hochwertiges, aufmerksamkeitsstarkes und unterhaltendes Magazin zu schaffen, welches dem anspruchsvollen Selbstverständnis des Hauses Sal. Oppenheim entspricht. Der Gestaltungsauftritt kommuniziert in unaufdringlicher Weise die bewusst gelebten Werte Tradition, Individualität, Exklusivität und Unabhängigkeit. Die Themenbereiche Ökonomie, Gesellschaft und Kultur repräsentieren die Haltung der Kölner Privatbankiers seit Gründung im Jahr 1789 – offen für neue Entwicklungen in Industrie und Wirtschaft, sensibel für gesellschaftspolitische Zusammenhänge, persönlich engagiert in vielen Bereichen der Kunst und Kultur.

The aim was to make a high-class, attention-grabbing magazine, which corresponds to the ambitious self-image of Sal. Oppenheim. The design should communicate the consciously lived values tradition, innovation, exclusiveness and independence in an unintrusive way. The topics economy, society and culture represent the attitudes of the private bank Sal. Oppenheim since the company's founding in 1789. They are open-minded for new industrial and economic developments, sensitive for sociopolitical issues and show personal commitment in many fields of art and culture.

Erkenntnis zwischen Buchdeckeln

VERLEGER SUCHEN DIE BALANCE VON
GELD UND GEIST.

--- Im Alter von sieben Jahren begann Benedikt Taschen, Comics zu sammeln. Er liebte die Duck-Familie, Donald und dessen drei Neffen Tick, Trick und Track. Vom frühen Enthusiasmus für die gezeichneten Bildergeschichten führte Taschens Weg zu einer Passion für Kunst und Fotografie in späteren Jahren. Heute besitzt der 47-jährige Kölner den größten Kunstverlag der Welt. Angetreten war er mit einer Vision: So erschwinglich, wie Comics für Kinder und Jugendliche waren, so erschwinglich wollte Taschen Kunstbände für Erwachsene machen.

Denn die waren bis dahin teuer, der Normalkäufer konnte sie sich nur selten leisten. Taschen wollte die elitäre Gattung allen Einkommensschichten verfügbar machen, den Markt gleichsam demokratisieren. Dazu brachte er zwischen 50 000 und 100 000 Exemplare heraus – statt, wie bis dahin üblich, nur wenige Tausend. Durch die hohen Auflagen konnte er die Bände zu günstigen Preisen auf den Markt bringen. Kunst, Fotografie, Comic, Mode und Design, Architektur, Film, Erotisches und Pornografisches, das alles produziert Taschen für die Massen.

DIE IDEE VOM GLOBALEN BUCH

Der Kölner Verleger wollte den Markt aber nicht nur demokratisieren – er wollte ihn auch internationalisieren. Sein Ziel war es, durch seine Bücher Menschen in den entlegensten Winkeln der Welt einen Zugang zu Kunst, Mode, Design oder Architektur zu verschaffen. Taschen ließ viele seiner Bücher in weit als 20 Sprachen übersetzen, baute ein globales Verkaufsnetzwerk auf. So kennt der niederländische Architekt Rem Koolhaas einmal verblüfft berichten, wie er eines seiner Bücher aus dem TASCHEN Verlag entdeckt hatte: in einer Flughafen-Buchhandlung in Lagos, Nigeria.

Neben dem Sendungsbewusstsein des Herausgebers merkt man Taschens Büchern auch einen Hang zum Auffälligen an – eine Vorliebe, die sich von seiner Persönlichkeit auf sein Programm übertragen hat: Der Verleger selbst trägt zum Beispiel Schuhe aus Froschleder und hält sich gerne in seinem Haus in Los Angeles auf, dem spektakulären, oktogonalen, raumschiffartigen Chemosphere-Haus des Architekten John Lautner, das auf einem einzigen Betonpfeiler direkt an einem Hang des San Fernando Valley ruht. Er produziert riesige, kostspielige Bände für Leute, die wie er dem Buch verfallen sind. Dabei setzt er nicht nur geografisch, sondern auch preislich und physisch neue Maßstäbe. Zum Beispiel mit seinem Schwergewicht „GOAT", einem rund 10.000 US-Dollar teuren und 30 Kilogramm schweren Bildband über den Boxer Muhammad Ali.

DIE GEISTIGE INNENAUSSTATTUNG DER REPUBLIK

Ein ganz anderer Gigant, „ein Verleger der Weltklasse", „der letzte Dinosaurier", wie es die Verlegerin Inge Feltrinelli formulierte, war Siegfried Unseld. Im Unterschied zu Taschen war sein Ziel, die geistige Atmosphäre der Bundesrepublik verlegerisch mitzuprägen. Und das ist ihm auf nie da gewesene Art gelungen: „Der Mann, der die Bundesrepublik war", so titelte die Hamburger Wochenzeitung „Die Zeit" über den Suhrkamp-Chef in einem Nachruf: Mit seinem Tod ist eine Geschichte der alten Bundesrepublik erst wirklich an ihr Ende gekommen. Er habe, so wurden viele Stimmen laut, das Land mehr geprägt als so mancher Kanzler.

Unseld verlegte die großen Dichter wie Paul Celan, Uwe Johnson, Hermann Hesse, Marcel Proust oder Max Frisch sowie Soziologen und Philosophen wie Jürgen Habermas, Theodor W. Adorno oder Peter Sloterdijk. Er wollte in seinem Verlag

Ob ausgeprägtes Sendungsbewusstsein, Liebe zum wissenschaftlichen Diskurs oder Mut zum Ungewöhnlichen – die Persönlichkeit des Verlegers bestimmt die Ausrichtung seines Hauses. Und beeinflusst damit in nicht wenigen Fällen die intellektuelle Atmosphäre ganzer Generationen.

INSPIRATION UND LEIDENSCHAFT TRIFFT KUNST UND GENIE

153

Project
Dividium Capital
Imagebroschüre
Image brochure

Design
Martin et Karczinski GmbH
Peter Martin, Marcus-Florian Kruse,
Constanze Kolbe, Rupert Stauder,
Tina Marusic, Karoline Grebe
München, Germany

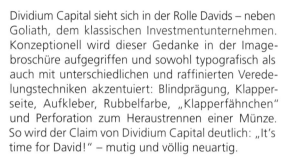

Client
Dividium Capital Ltd.
Frauenfeld, Switzerland

Dividium Capital sieht sich in der Rolle Davids – neben Goliath, dem klassischen Investmentunternehmen. Konzeptionell wird dieser Gedanke in der Imagebroschüre aufgegriffen und sowohl typografisch als auch mit unterschiedlichen und raffinierten Veredelungstechniken akzentuiert: Blindprägung, Klapperseite, Aufkleber, Rubbelfarbe, „Klapperfähnchen" und Perforation zum Heraustrennen einer Münze. So wird der Claim von Dividium Capital deutlich: „It's time for David!" – mutig und völlig neuartig.

Dividium Capital sees itself in the role of David against Goliath, who is the classic investment company. Conceptually this idea has been taken up in the image brochure typographically and is also accentuated by different and refined finishing techniques: blind embossing, flaps, stickers, scratch sections, "flap banners" and perforations to tear out a coin. In this way Dividium Capital has been successful in always staying one step ahead of the conventional investment company. The claim is clear: "It's time for David!"

Project
Air Berlin
Geschäftsbericht 2007
Annual report 2007

Design
Strichpunkt GmbH
Kirsten Dietz, Jochen Rädeker
(Creative Direction)
Kirsten Dietz (Art Direction)
Kirsten Dietz, Holger Jungkunz,
David Claassen (Designer)
Stuttgart, Germany
Graphische Betriebe Eberl GmbH
Ernst Gärtner (Druck)
Immenstadt im Allgäu, Germany
Claudia Kempf
Robert Brembeck, Oliver Jung,
Matthias Ziegler, Yvonne Seidel
(Fotografie)
Wuppertal, Germany

Client
Air Berlin PLC & Co.
Luftverkehrs KG
Berlin, Germany

Bei der weltweit am schnellsten wachsenden Flugge-
sellschaft stehen im aktuellen Geschäftsbericht neue
Destinationen auf der ganzen Welt im Mittelpunkt.
Die Banderole, der beigeheftete Aufkleberbogen zur
Bestückung des Reisekoffers auf dem Titel, ein Post-
kartenset und eine 24-seitige Imagestrecke zu den
neuen Destinationen visualisieren auf sympathische
Art „Air Berlin goes Global".

The world's fastest growing airline focuses on a number of new international destinations in its current
business report. Designed to look like a suitcase with
a baggage label on the cover, the first page consists
of a page of stickers, followed by 24 pages that create an image route to the new destinations and a set
of postcards in the cover – a friendly and appealing
visualisation of "Air Berlin goes Global".

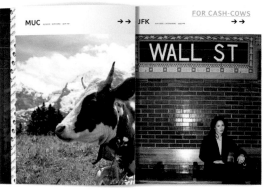

Project
Typotron-Heft 26,
Christian Fischbacher – der Stoff,
aus dem die Stoffe sind
Broschüre
Brochure

Design
TGG Hafen Senn Stieger
Visuelle Kommunikation
Dominik Hafen, Bernhard Senn,
Roland Stieger
St. Gallen, Switzerland

Client
Typotron AG
für die gedruckte Kommunikation
St. Gallen, Switzerland

Thema dieser Publikation ist die St. Galler Textilfirma Christian Fischbacher. Das weltweit tätige Unternehmen wird in Text und Bild durch ein Produktionsjahr begleitet. Die Publikation wurde als Schweizer Broschur ausgerüstet und kann kalenderartig geblättert werden. Die japanische Bindung mit einem Innendruck auf Dünndruckpapier erzeugt eine Haptik, welche an Stoffmuster erinnert. Der Umschlag ist in Anlehnung an einen Stoffmuster-Bügel gestaltet, wie er für Stoffkollektionen im Fachhandel verwendet wird. Daher kann das Büchlein auch aufgehängt werden.

The topic of this publication is the textile business of Christian Fischbacher from St. Gallen, Switzerland. The worldwide renowned enterprise was accompanied throughout one year's production cycle and the observations were documented in texts and photographs. The publication was manufactured as Swiss Brochure and the pages can be turned over in the same way as a calendar. The Japanese Binding with reverse print on folded super thin printing paper creates the feel and touch that reminds the reader of fabric samples. The cover is shaped like a fabric sample hanger, just as it is used for fabric collections in the fashion trade. That is why the brochure can be hang up.

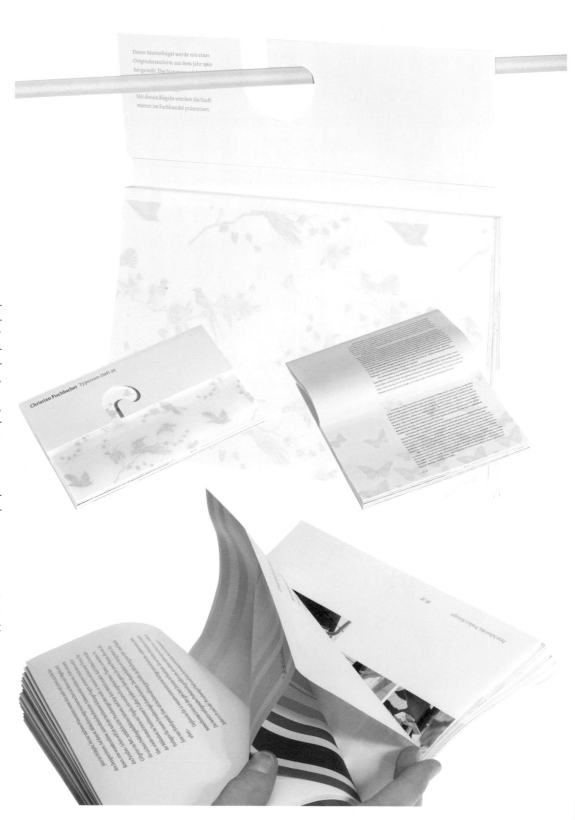

Project
Weltbewegend
Jahresbericht 2007
Annual report 2007

Design
RTS Rieger Team Werbeagentur GmbH
Michael Frank (Geschäftsführung)
Yvonne Wicht (Beratung/Projekt-
leitung)
Daniela Schäfer, Luisa Lueg
(Art Direction)
Marc Fielers, Stefan Linder (Text)
Düsseldorf, Germany

Client
FIEGE Stiftung & Co. KG
Greven, Germany

Die Aufgabe:
Entwicklung des Jahresberichts 2007 der FIEGE
Gruppe als hochwertiges Medium der Imagekommu-
nikation zur Information der Fachöffentlichkeit über
den Verlauf des Geschäftsjahres 2007 und Heraus-
stellung der internationalen Logistikkompetenz.
Die Idee:
Der Jahresbericht gibt „Weltbewegend" Einblick in
die Kontraktlogistik. Die drei heterogen gestalteten
Kapitel nehmen Leser mit auf die Reise von Tape-
tenrollen rund um den Globus, zeigen die weltweite
Aufstellung von FIEGE und die Aktivitäten in den Re-
ferenzbranchen.

The Challenge:
Development of the annual report 2007 of the FIEGE
Group as a high-quality image communication medium, which informs the specialist community about
the business year 2007 and the exhibition of international logistics competence.
The Idea:
The annual report provides a "moving the world"-
insight into contract logistics. The three heterogen-
eously-formed chapters invite the reader to accompany rolls of wallpaper on their journey around the
world, thereby demonstrating FIEGE's global set-up
and describing activities in the reference sectors.

Project
Energie Zukunft
Corporate Book

Design
BEHNKEN & PRINZ
Wolfgang Behnken, Constanze Lemke
Hamburg, Germany

Client
Viessmann Werke GmbH & Co. KG
Allendorf, Germany

Das Buch „Energie Zukunft. Effizienz und erneuerbare Energien im Wärmesektor" – Herausgeber ist der Journalist Jürgen Petermann, Auftraggeber das Unternehmen Viessmann – liefert Fakten und Einsichten zur Energiedebatte und zeigt Wege auf, wie sich brachliegende Effizienzreserven durch den Einsatz moderner Heiztechnik mobilisieren lassen. Das 246 Seiten starke Buch ist gegen eine Schutzgebühr von 22,50 Euro zu erwerben. Es wurde von Journalisten und Wissenschaftlern für eine breite Öffentlichkeit geschrieben und wartet mit einer Vielzahl moderner Infografiken auf. Neben der deutschen wird es 2009 auch noch eine englische Ausgabe geben.

The book "Energy Future. Efficiency and renewables in the heating sector" – publisher is the journalist Jürgen Petermann, Viessmann is the contracting company – provides facts and insights on the energy debate and shows ways of how to untapped reserves of efficiency through the use of modern heating technology can be mobilized. The book with its 246 pages is written by famous journalists and scientists for a wider public and presents a lot of modern graphics. The book is available on the homepage of the company Viessmann. An English edition will be released later in 2009.

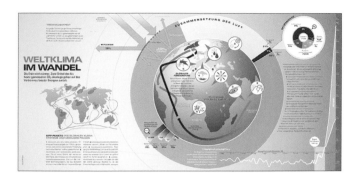

DIE HERAUS-FORDERUNGEN: KLIMASCHUTZ UND SICHERE ENERGIE

1

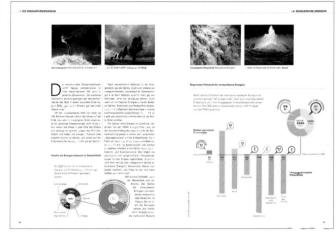

MUTTER ERDE IM FIEBER – DER KLIMA-WANDEL UND DIE FOLGEN

An die 800 Milliarden Tonnen CO_2 heben sich seit Beginn des Industriezeitalters in der Atmosphäre angesammelt. Die Symptome einer schleichenden Erderwärmung häufen sich. Gerät das Weltklima aus den Fugen? Was können wir tun, um den Temperaturanstieg zu bremsen und den drohenden Klimakollaps abzuwenden?

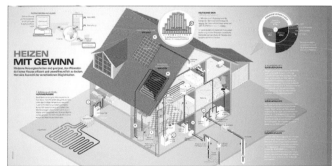

Project
Schwindende Ahnen
Mailing

Design
JUNO
Björn Lux, Frank Wache,
Wolfgang Greter, Nicole Klein
Hamburg, Germany

Client
Arctic Paper
Hamburg, Germany

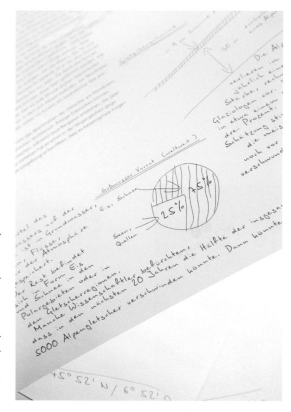

Im Auftrag von Arctic Paper, dem größten Hersteller von FSC-zertifiziertem Papier (FSC = Forrest Stewardship Council) in Europa, machen wir Werbung für Werber. Die Herausforderung: Begeisterung bei einer kritischen Klientel wecken. Und, die nachhaltigen Produkte des Papierherstellers preisen, ohne mahnenden Klima-Zeigefinger. Dazu benutzen wir Schwundbilder von Alpengletschern, die wir jeweils 1998 und 2007 innerhalb einer Langzeitdokumentation fotografiert haben. Zudem interviewen wir Glaziologen. Die Arbeit ist schön und schaurig zugleich. Als Booklet und XXL-Kunstdruck wird unsere Arbeit an 16.000 Adressen verteilt.

For Arctic Paper, Europe's biggest manufacturer of FSC-certified paper (FSC = Forrest Stewardship Council), we make advertising for advertisers. The challenge: To wow a critical and saturated clientele and, at the same time, to promote the sustainable products of arctic paper without a wagging finger. We use pictures of melting glaciers in the Alps, which we took in the years 1998 and 2007. Also we interview glaciologists. The work is beautiful and sad at the same time. As booklet and art print our work is distributed to 16,000 addresses.

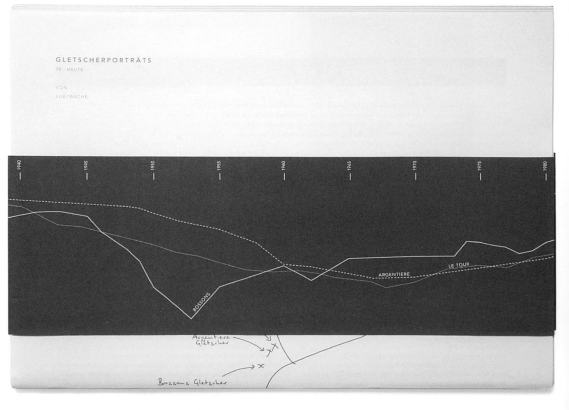

Project
The Sports Bible
Enzyklopädie
Encyclopedia

Design
MAGMA
Brand Design GmbH & Co. KG
Lars Harmsen, Boris Kahl,
Sabrina Behringer, Silke Hensel,
Patrick Hubbuch, Jill Wentz
Karlsruhe, Germany

Client
Sportswear International Magazine
Milan, Italy

MAGMA Brand Design gestaltete für Sportswear International The Sports Bible, eine detaillierte Enzyklopädie von sportlichen und von Sport inspirierten Styles. Das Werk enthält auf 400 Seiten nahezu 600 Begriffe aus der Sportmode. Durch den Einsatz einer speziellen Drucktechnik hat jede Ausgabe der Sports Bible eine andere Farbkombination auf dem Cover. Keine zwei Bücher sind gleich.

For Sportswear International MAGMA Brand Design designed The Sports Bible, an in-depth fashion-based encyclopedia of sport and sport-inspired style containing nearly 600 sports-fashion terms on 400 pages. By using a new and very special printing technique every copy of the Sports Bible presents a different color combination on the cover. No two books are the same.

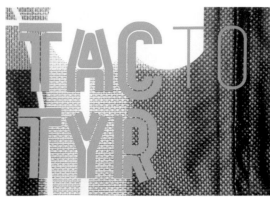

Project
Nicht neu.
Design classics Katalog
Design classics catalog

Design
Buttgereit und Heidenreich
Wolfram Heidenreich, Frank Gockel
Haltern am See, Germany

Client
mono – Seibel Designpartner
Mettmann, Germany

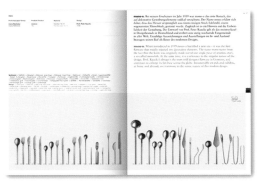

Der mono design classics Katalog „Nicht neu." schafft es, die teilweise schon seit 50 Jahren existierenden Produkte neu, interessant und begehrenswert in Szene zu setzen. Er spielt mit Charme, Wort- und Bildwitz mit dem Alter, der Zeitlosigkeit und Funktionalität der Designklassiker der mono-Tischkultur und macht deutlich: „Das Neue ist selten das Gute, weil das Gute nur kurze Zeit das Neue ist." (Arthur Schopenhauer)

The mono design classics catalog "Not new." presents products that are partly over 50 years old in a new, interesting and desirable way. Employing words and visuals full of charm and esprit, the catalog plays with the age, timelessness and functionality of the design classics by mono table culture. It gives clear expression to the adage: "The new is seldom the good, while the good does not long remain the new." (Arthur Schopenhauer)

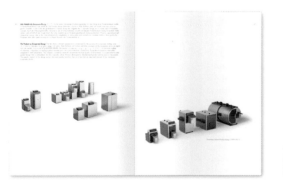

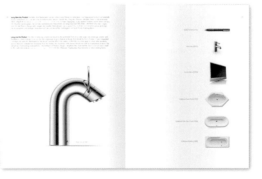

Project
Logik, Moral, Magie
Publikation/Imagebroschüre
Publication/image brochure

Design
Phoenix Design GmbH & Co. KG
Team Phoenix Design
Stuttgart, Germany
Tokyo, Japan

Client
Phoenix Design GmbH & Co. KG
Stuttgart, Germany

Publikation/Imagebroschüre über 21 Jahre Phoenix Design: Phoenix Design ist volljährig! Mit der Publikation Logik, Moral und Magie geben die Gründer und Inhaber Andreas Haug und Tom Schönherr von Phoenix Design in Stuttgart/Tokyo Einblicke in ihre Denk- und Arbeitsweisen. Auf mehr als 100 Seiten zeigen sie die Vielzahl an Faktoren, die in einem Gestaltungsprozess eine Rolle spielen, wie z.B. die Einbindung von Markenstrategien sowie die Verbindung von Produktdesign und Interface Design. Die Erfahrungen und der Erfolgsweg der letzten 21 Jahre werden in dieser Publikation sichtbar.

Publication/image brochure about 21 years Phoenix Design: Phoenix Design has come of age! In their publication "Logik, Moral, Magie" Andreas Haug and Tom Schönherr of Phoenix Design in Stuttgart/Tokyo give insights into their ways of thinking and working. On more than 100 pages they show the great number of factors which play a role in the design process, such as the integration of marketing strategies and linking product and interface design. Their experiences and their path to success over the last 21 years become visible in this publication.

print media image

Project
Weihnachtskarte 2008
Greeting card 2008

Design
Büro4
Gestaltung + Kommunikation
SF Gestaltung
Cordula Gieriet
Zürich, Switzerland

Client
Schweizer Fernsehen
Zürich, Switzerland

Die Weihnachtskarte des Schweizer Fernsehens ist zugleich eine geografische Landkarte der Schweiz im Maßstab 1 : 400.000. Funktion und Inhalt verbinden sich auf mehreren Ebenen: SF steht in engem Kontakt zur Schweiz, der Kultur und den Bürgern – direkt und vor Ort. Auf der Straßenkarte werden kommende Fernseh-Highlights geografisch positioniert. Auf Umschlag und Karten-Rückseite entwickelt sich aus der Topografie stimmungsvoll eine silberglänzende weihnachtliche Winterlandschaft.

The Swiss Television Christmas card is a combination of a greeting card and a roadmap of Switzerland with the scale: 1 : 400,000. Usability and content allow SF to communicate very close to the people of the country and their particular culture. On the road map several important upcoming television broadcasts are geographically marked. A topographical silver-shiny landscape is printed on the cover and on the back side that associates a specific feeling of Christmas time.

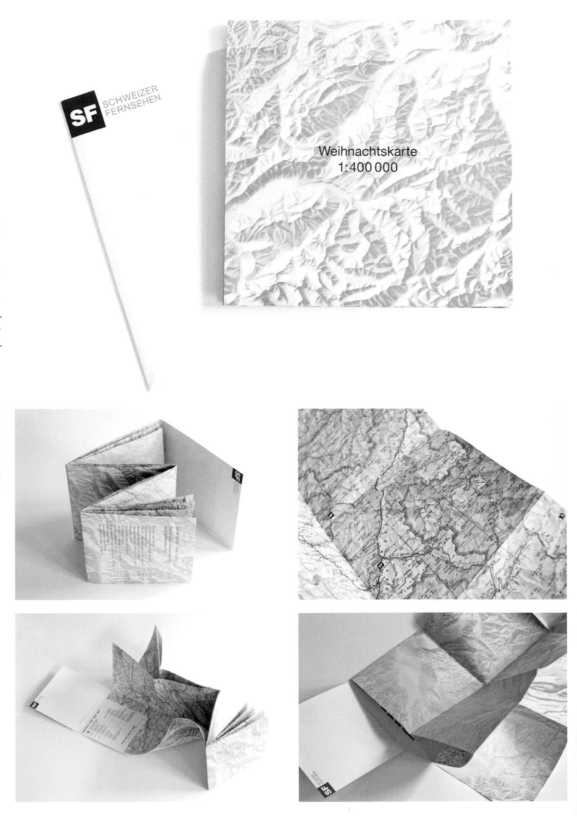

Project
Wannert Feuerschutz
Imagebroschüre
Imagebrochure

Design
Heine Warnecke Design GmbH
Cord Warnecke, Dirk Heine
Hannover, Germany

Client
Bavaria Feuerschutz J. Wannert GmbH
Iserhagen, Germany

Bei Wannert Feuerschutz ist man Feuer und Flamme für die Entwicklung von Sicherheitskonzepten für unterschiedliche Gebäudetypen. Die neue Broschüre im handlichen DIN A6-Format vereint die Komponenten des aktualisierten Corporate Designs: die Bildmarke als Symbiose aus Schutzengel und Schutzschild, die plakative Farbgebung, die inspirierende Fotografie namhafter Referenzen.

People at Wannert Feuerschutz are inflamed with passion for developing safety concepts for all types of buildings. The brand new pocket-sized company's brochure combines all elements of the refreshed corporate design: the logo – created as a composition of a guardian angel and a shield, the striking colors, the inspiring photography of famous references.

WANNERT *feuerschutz*

Project
Erste Hilfe für ein frohes Fest
Buch
Book

Design
büro diffus GmbH
Stuttgart, Germany

Client
büro diffus GmbH
Stuttgart, Germany

büro diffus hat aus eigener Erfahrung heraus die Notwendigkeit erkannt und mit Idee, Witz und Charme ein Tool erstellt, das durch die meist nicht ganz stressfreie Vorweihnachtszeit begleitet und „Weihnachtskatastrophen" vermeiden helfen soll. Das kleine Buch bietet Tipps und Hilfestellungen zur Planung und Vorbereitung mit Checklisten, Geschenkideen, Geschenkpapier und Karten zum Heraustrennen, Geschenkanhängern und Klebestreifen sowie Einkaufstipps, Plätzchenrezepte und sogar Weihnachtsorigami.

büro diffus recognized the necessity and created a witty and charming tool ("First aid kit for a merry Christmas") to help its users navigate the somewhat stressful Christmas season. The stylish booklet offers valuable tips for planning and preparation, providing checklists, gift ideas, wrapping paper, tear-out greeting cards, gift tags, stickers as well as shopping tips, cookie recipes and even Christmas origami.

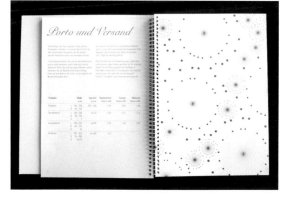

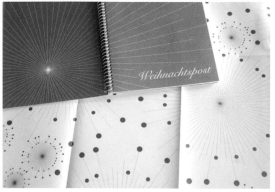

Project
Loewe Imagebroschüre
Printunterlage
Print document

Design
Brandoffice GmbH
Heiko Dertinger, Michael Noli
München, Germany

Client
Loewe AG
Kronach, Germany

Die Loewe Imagebroschüre mit dem Markenthema „Nach allen Regeln gegen die Regeln" verdeutlicht in mehreren Abschnitten zwei gegensätzliche Strategien – und damit den Wettbewerb zwischen Loewe als Premiummarke auf der einen Seite, und preis-/mengenorientierten Volumenmarken auf der anderen Seite. Auf den Kapiteltrennseiten „Die Regel" finden sich Aussagen zu Volumen-Grundprinzipien, von denen sich Loewe differenziert. Auf den Kapiteltrennseiten „Gegen die Regeln" kennzeichnen Stil, Haltung und Leistungsfähigkeit Loewe als qualitätsorientierte Marke. Innerhalb der Kapitel laden wertvolle Angebots- und Technologie-Höhepunkte die Marke Loewe auf.

The Loewe Image brochure, with the brand's central theme "The only rule is that there are no rules", is divided into different sections symbolically representing the competition between the quality-oriented premium Loewe brand and the price/volume-oriented mass market brands. The chapter "The rules" describe basic principles of these latter brands, which Loewe aims to set its brand personality apart from. The chapter "Against the rules" highlights how Loewe's style, poise and performance set it apart as a quality-oriented brand. The chapters themselves delve into valuable product and technology highlights offered by the Loewe brand.

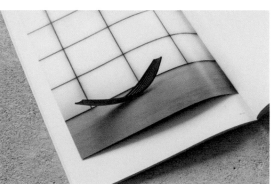

Project
RSL Resort
Darstellung
Image

Design
Proad Identity
Jennifer Tsai, Brenda Chang
Taipei, Taiwan

Client
RSL Enterprise Co., Ltd.
Taipei, Taiwan

Die kalten Quellen von Suao sind eine seltene natürliche Ressource. RSL Construction errichtet in dem weltweit einzigen Gebiet mit Heiß- und Kaltquellen ein Fünf-Sterne-Hotel. Suaos Feuchtgebiete – Refugien für Wasservögel – beherbergen jeden Winter 3.000 Krickenten, weshalb dieser Vogel zum Maskottchen des Hotels erkoren wurde. Wasserblasen rufen die Kälte der Quellen ins Bewusstsein. Farn, Dunst und stille alte Eichen stehen für Suaos ruhige Umwelt. Minimalistische Kannen und Tassen verheißen ebenso wie einfache Krüge, dass ZEN an diesem Ort erreichbar ist. Die Bilder geben den traumhaften Kurort perfekt wieder.

Suao has a rare natural resource, its cold springs. Therefore, RSL Construction is developing a five-star hotel; the only resort in the world to offer both hot and cold springs. Suao's wetland and waterfowl refuge shelters 3,000 teals each winter, so the teal is the hotel's mascot. Bubbles and water beads emphasize the cold spring's coolness. The thriving fern, misty ambience, and silent old tree grain represent Suao's, tranquil, natural environment. The minimalist pots and cups, and simple stones tell the state of Zen attainable at this place. These images present a perfect interpretation of this heavenly spa.

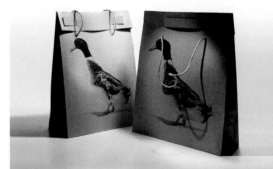

Project
Celebrate Together
Buch
Book

Design
AUFBRUCH
Agentur für neue Kommunikation GmbH
Andreas Fußhöller, Stefanie Froh, Helen Otte,
Andrè Hein, Simone Buch, Liliane Lerch
Düsseldorf, Germany

Client
Esprit Europe GmbH
Ratingen, Germany

Ausgehend von der Frage „What does ESPRIT mean to you" will das Buch den Lifestyle der ESPRIT-Welt vermitteln. Herausgekommen ist ein Feuerwerk an Ideen, Engagement, Humor und Liebe, das klar macht, wie ESPRIT zu der erfolgreichen Marke werden konnte, die sie heute ist. Es ist ein Dankeschön vom Unternehmen an seine Mitarbeiter und soll dazu beitragen, die weltweite ESPRIT-Familie noch enger zusammenrücken zu lassen. Zielgruppe: Die Menschen, die hinter der Marke ESPRIT stehen. Alle Mitarbeiter, Partner und Freunde der Marke und der Firma.

Based on the question "What does ESPRIT mean to you", this book conveys the lifestyle of the ESPRIT world. The result is a firework of ideas, commitment, humor and love that shows why ESPRIT is the successful brand it is today. The book was planned as a thank-you to all employees and contributes to bring the worldwide ESPRIT family even closer. Target group: The people that are connected to the brand ESPRIT. All employees, partners and friends of the brand and company.

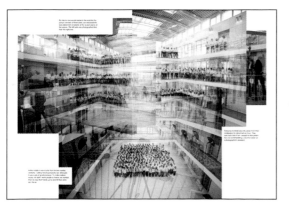

print media image

Project
NRW-Tag 2008
Logo

Design
KOEMMET Agentur für Kommunikation
Jan Koemmet, Stefan Kalscheid
Wuppertal, Germany

Client
Wuppertal Marketing GmbH
Wuppertal, Germany

Zum Nordrhein-Westfalen-Tag 2008 in Wuppertal wurde KOEMMET beauftragt, ein Logo zu konzipieren. Gewünscht war dabei eine Umsetzung unter Verwendung der berühmten Schwebebahn passend zum Thema „Wuppertal bewegt". Ergebnis ist ein dynamischer Fächer, der die Schwebebahn in abstrahierter Form darstellt. Die Farbwahl ist bunt und laut und steht für das Fest, aber auch für Wuppertal: Hell- und Dunkelblau für den Himmel, Gelb, Orange und Rot für die Schwebebahn, Hell- und Dunkelgrün für das Schwebebahngerüst. Das Logo ist so konzipiert, dass es auch in Ausschnitten auf verschiedenen Formaten funktioniert.

Within the event of the NRW Day 2008, KOEMMET was in charge of designing a logo. A concept was required that would emphasize the importance of Wuppertal's suspension railway and its connection to the campaign's theme "Wuppertal moves". The result is the image of a dynamic fan, abstractly representing the suspension railway. The colors range from iridescent to energetic. They directly refer to the festival and the city of Wuppertal: light and dark blue to the sky, yellow, orange and red to the railway, and shades of green to the scaffold of the famous vehicle. The nature of the logo provides the option of applying it to any kind of format.

NRW-TAG 2008
Wuppertal bewegt
29. bis 31. August

Project
Power of The Book
Plakat
Poster

Design
Leslie Chan Design Co., Ltd.
Leslie Chan Wing Kei
Taipei, Taiwan

Client
Taiwan Poster Design Association
Kaohsiung, Taiwan

Stille und Geräuschlosigkeit sind die Eigenschaften von Büchern, deren Seiten endlose Gedanken und Möglichkeiten bereithalten. Der explosive Moment, in dem die Leserin oder der Leser ein Buch versteht, ist so machtig als hebe sich ein schwerer Stein. Das Plakat vermittelt eine eindrückliche Vorstellung von der Art und Weise, wie ein Buch seine Macht entfaltet, und überträgt diese ihrerseits in eine machtvolle Vision.

Silence and noiselessness are the features of the books. There are endless thoughts and possibilities within them as well. The sudden explosive strength right after the readers understand the books is as strong as the power when lifting a heavy stone. The poster gives a shocking impression of how book releases its strength, and transmits it into a powerful vision out of imagination likewise.

Project
via roeper Expedition
Buch
Book

Design
via roeper Erfolgskommunikation GmbH
Almut Röper (Creative Direction)
Aenne Storm (Design, Illustration)
Thorben Flügger (Design)
Guido Strotkötter (Text)
Kristina Jacobs (Produktion)
Bremen, Germany

Client
via roeper Erfolgskommunikation GmbH
Bremen, Germany

Das Geheimnis einer guten Agentur ist erfolgreiche Kommunikation. Das Geheimnis von Erfolgskommunikation ist persönlichster Kundenkontakt. Da nichts so persönlich ist wie eigene, heimliche, handgeschriebene Notizen, ist unsere Imagebroschüre ein fiktives Tagebuch. Dieses dokumentiert den Weg eines Kunden zum Gipfel des Erfolgs – begleitet durch seine Agentur, via roeper. Im ersten Schritt erhält der potenzielle Neukunde ein mit Texten, Illustrationen und Artefakten gefülltes Tagebuch. Im zweiten Schritt (bei Beginn des ersten gemeinsamen Projekts) erhält er ein leeres Tagebuch, das es mit eigenen Erfolgsgeschichten zu befüllen gilt.

The secret of a successful agency is good communication. The secret of good communication is close and individual contact with our clients. Because nothing is as personal, as private, handwritten notes our image brochure is a fictitious diary. It records the road to success of a client – accompanied by his agency, via roeper. So a potential new client gets firstly a diary, filled with texts, illustrations and artefacts. At the beginning of a new project the client gets an empty diary, to fill it with his or her own success story.

Project
into…
Corporate Design

Design
Jäger & Jäger
Olaf Jäger, Regina Jäger
Überlingen, Germany

Client
Siemens Arts Program
Ensemble Modern
München, Germany

Sechzehn herausragende Komponisten und vier internationale Metropolen stehen im Mittelpunkt des gemeinsamen Projekts von „Ensemble Modern" und „Siemens Arts Program", das zwischen 2008 und 2010 realisiert wird: „into…". Jeweils vier Komponisten leben einen Monat lang in einer der vier Megastädte Istanbul, Dubai, Johannesburg oder im Pearl River Delta und komponieren in der Begegnung mit diesen Städten ein Werk. Die Gestaltung des Signets wird aus den Namen der vier Städte abgeleitet. „i" für Dubai, „n" für Istanbul, „t" für Pearl River Delta, „o" für Johannesburg. Als Typogramm steht es so für das Ergebnis, die Essenz, das gesamte Projekt, die Musik.

Sixteen outstanding composers and four international metropolises are the focus of a joint project of the "Ensemble Modern" and the "Siemens Arts Program" to be realized between 2008 and 2010: "into…". Four sets of four composers will each stay in one of the four megacities – Istanbul, Dubai, Johannesburg or Pearl River Delta – and compose a piece inspired by their encounters with these cities. The logotype is taken from the names of the four cities: "i" for Dubai, "n" for Istanbul, "t" for Pearl River Delta, "o" for Johannesburg. As such the logotype embodies the core, the entire project, the music.

Project
Sagrotan „OP"
Anzeige
Advertisement

Design
Euro RSCG Düsseldorf
Felix Glauner, Ralph Aichem, Oliver Hilbring,
Alexandros Antoniadis, Stefan Muhl, André Bastian
Düsseldorf, Germany

Client
Reckitt Benckiser Deutschland GmbH
Mannheim, Germany

Kreative Zielsetzung:
Entwicklung einer Anzeige, die den Produktvorteil
des Sagrotan-Hygienespülers überraschend und un-
terhaltsam kommuniziert.
Idee:
Wir dramatisieren, dass Sagrotan selbst schmutzigste
Wäsche komplett von Keimen und Bakterien befreit.
Und zwar so gründlich, dass man sie in extremsten
Situationen problemlos zweckentfremden könnte.

Creative goal:
Create an ad that communicates the product benefit
of "Sagrotan- Hygienespüler" in a surprising and entertaining way.
Idea:
We dramatise that Sagrotan, a hygienic washing ad-
ditive, makes even the dirtiest laundry completely
germ-free. This is so effective that the laundry could
easily be diverted from its intended use in most extreme situations.

Project
World Games
Plakat
Poster

Design
Leslie Chan Design Co., Ltd.
Chan Wing Kei, Leslie
Taipei, Taiwan

Client
Leslie Chan Design Co., Ltd.
Taipei, Taiwan

Die Weltspiele 2009 werden in Kaohsiung abgehalten. Das Design basiert auf dem Konzept, das im „Malereihandbuch des Senfkorngartens" beschrieben ist. Dabei handelt es sich um eine chinesische Technik der Tuschemalerei. Sie drückt den Sportgeist des Orients und den Geist des modernen Sports mittels zeltnaher geometrischer Bilder aus. Der Kontrast und die Kraft aus der Vermischung von orientalischer Klassik und modernen Formen erzeugen eine besondere Symbolhaftigkeit. Sie zieht die Aufmerksamkeit ausländischer Teilnehmer auf sich.

The 2009 World Games will be held in Kaohsiung. The design is based on the concept of the "Mustard Seed Garden Manual" style of Chinese painting techniques and expresses the sportsmanship of the orient and the spirit of modern sports through contemporary geometric images. The contrast and power of the mix of the oriental classics and modern styles will create special imagery interest to attract the attention of foreign participants.

Project
Das Buch der Zahlen / The Book of Numbers
Imagebroschüre
Image brochure

Design
Beaufort 8
Philipp Heimsch, Jonas Ruch (CD)
Philipp Heimsch, José A. Diego Ferreiro (Text)
Sonja Schuberth (Art Direction)
Christine Hebrank, Ninja Krause (Grafik)
Stuttgart, Germany

Client
HHS Hellinger Hahnemann Schulte-Gross
Stuttgart, Germany

Aufgabe: HHS ist eine Wirtschaftsprüfungsgesellschaft, die sich tagtäglich mit Zahlen auseinander-
setzt. Eine Imagebroschüre soll das Leistungsspek-
trum von HHS vor allem für Laien und potenzielle
Kunden ansprechend darstellen.
Umsetzung: Auf den 32 Seiten der Hardcover-Image-
broschüre „Das Buch der Zahlen" werden die Arbeit
und die Philosophie von HHS illustrativ mit über-
raschenden Details über Zahlen verflochten. Durch
das Zusammenspiel dieser beiden Aspekte entsteht
eine kurzweilige Lektüre über die faszinierende Welt
von Ziffern und deren Bedeutung, die gleichzeitig
die Kompetenz der Wirtschaftsprüfungsgesellschaft
zeigt.

Task: HHS is an auditing company dealing with figures
and numbers on a daily basis. An image brochure
is supposed to present the services and business
activities of HHS especially for laymen and potential
clients.
Realization: The hardcover image brochure "The Book
of Numbers" interlaces work and philosophy of HHS
in an illustrative way with surprising details about
numbers on 32 pages. The interaction between these
two aspects builds up an interesting, entertaining
reading about figures and their meaning, simultaneously demonstrating the competence of the auditing company.

Project
EcoCraft
Imagebroschüre
Corporate brochure

Design
BRANDIT GmbH
Peter Specht, Sabine Nacken, Irene Mohr
Köln, Germany

Client
EcoCraft Automotive GmbH & Co. KG
Wunstorf, Germany

EcoCraft hat den ersten Elektrokleinlaster vom Entwurf bis zur Serienproduktion entwickelt. Damit wird in der Nutzfahrzeugindustrie eine neue Ära eingeleitet. Entsprechend dieser Vorreiterrolle entwickelt BRANDIT die strategische Kommunikationsplattform „Willkommen im Eco-Zeitalter". Das Design greift konsequent das Konstruktionsprinzip des „EcoCarrier" auf: Keine aufwändige Inszenierung, sondern das neue Bild zukunftsweisender Leistungen steht dabei im Vordergrund. In allen Basismedien, vom CD-Manual über den Internetauftritt bis zu Broschüren und dem Messeauftritt wird so die neue Nutzfahrzeug-Philosophie spürbar.

From initial design to production line, EcoCraft has developed the first electric lightweight truck, introducing a new era for the commercial vehicle industry. To complement this pioneering task, BRANDIT created the strategic communications platform "Welcome to the Age of Eco". The design reflects the construction principles of "EcoCarrier": it is not a complex orchestration, but rather focuses on images of its future-oriented features. Whether CD manual or website, brochure or trade-fair appearance, every medium gives a sense of this new philosophy for utility vehicles.

Ein Transportweg, der sich lohnt?
Lassen Sie Schnickschnack hinter sich
und Tankstellen einfach links liegen.
EcoCarrier.

Der perfekte Rahmen
für eine Premiere.
EcoCarrier.

Project
Motiv-ator 03
Magazin
Magazine

Design
New Cat Orange
Gestaltung und Kommunikation
HP Becker (CD)
Julia Maria Depis (Grafik)
Josef Hoelzl (Foto)
Cordula Becker (Text)
Wiesbaden, Germany

Client
New Cat Orange
Gestaltung und Kommunikation
Wiesbaden, Germany

Neben freien redaktionellen Beiträgen zum Thema „Das Glück ist mit den Motivierten" war es diesmal wichtig, dass die neue Kollektion besonders in den Fokus gerückt wird. Das Magazin soll daher den Leitspruch „Motiv-ier Dich!" genauso wie die Kollektion direkt umsetzen – und ganz konventionell das Medium „Print" zum Spielen und Motivieren nutzen. Hintergrund: Die Kollektion nimmt das Motto diesmal wörtlich. Die Shirts bleiben unbedruckt. Dafür ist jedes Shirt mit einem Klettkreuz und einem Set aus je drei Motiven ausgestattet. So kann man sich jeden Tag aufs Neue motivieren. Genau dieses spielerische Element greift das Magazin auf.

Apart from editorial elements surrounding the subject "luck comes to those who are motivated", it was important to this issue to highlight the new collection in a special way. Thus, the magazine needed to both bring the motto "motiv-ate yourself" and the new collection to life. Background: This time, the new collection is taking the motto literally: The shirts are left without a print motif – instead, a Velcro cross is applied, along with three different motifs. Consequently, you get a new chance to motivate yourself every day. And this playful element is also the main subject in the editorial elements.

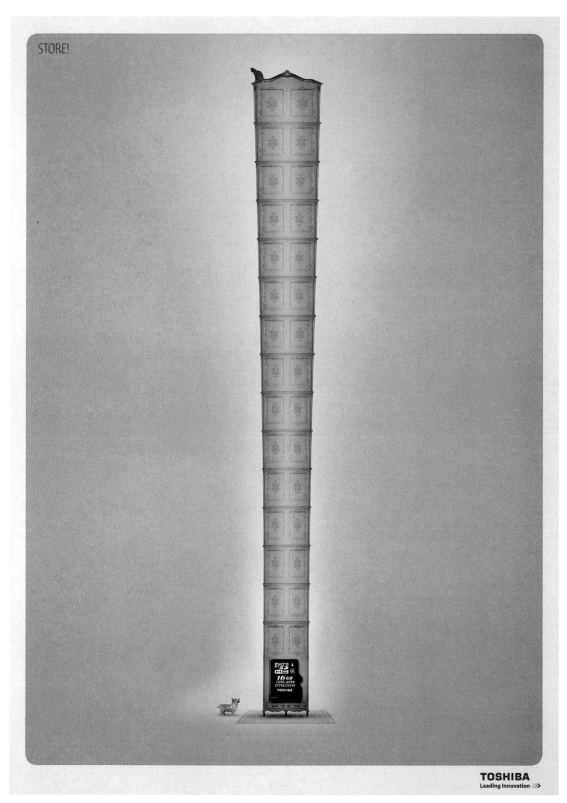

STORE!

TOSHIBA
Leading Innovation >>>

Project
Toshiba "Commode"
Anzeige
Advertisement

Design
Euro RSCG München
München, Germany
Euro RSCG Düsseldorf
Felix Glauner, Oliver Hilbring, Ralph Aichem,
Alexandros Antoniadis, Frank Eickelmann,
Jochen Kirchhof, Sigi Zwar
Düsseldorf, Germany

Client
Toshiba Europe GmbH
Neuss, Germany

Kreative Zielsetzung:
Entwicklung einer Anzeige, die den großen Spei
cherplatz der „Toshiba Micro Memory Card" überraschend kommuniziert. Neue Kunden sollen gewonnen werden.
Idee.
Wir stellen die Speicherkarte als Tür und Zugang zu
endlosem Speicherplatz dar.

Creative Goal:
Communicate the storage capacity of the "Toshiba
micro memory card" in an impressive way in order to
generate new customers.
Idea:
We created the idea directly out of the product and
its benefit. Our campaign dramatises the Toshiba
micro memory card like a magic door to unlimited
storage space.

Project
12mal K wie Köln
Kalender zur Eigenwerbung
Calendar for self-promotion

Design
vierviertel –
Agentur für Kommunikationsdesign GmbH
Judith Schäffer, Jan Wohlenberg
Köln, Germany

Client
vierviertel –
Agentur für Kommunikationsdesign GmbH
Köln, Germany

Jedes Jahr – Anfang Januar – verschickt die Agentur vierviertel einen Kalender an alle Kunden, Geschäftspartner und Freunde. Er soll das Miteinander über das ganze Jahr hinweg positiv begleiten. Gestalterisch stellt der diesjährige Kalender eine Hommage an den Standort der Agentur dar: die Stadt Köln. Auf jedem einzelnen Monatsblatt wird das „kölsche Lebensgefühl" mittels Illustrationen umgesetzt: sei es durch ein Kölner Wahrzeichen, den Kölner Dom, oder durch das Maskottchen des Kölner FC, den Geißbock. Die Motive zeigen „Kölner Spezialitäten" – immer in ironischer, dokumentarischer oder witziger Weise.

Every year – at the beginning of January – the agency vierviertel sends a calendar to all clients, business partners and friends. It is supposed to positively accompany cooperation over the entire year. Creatively, this year's calendar represents homage to the agency's location: the city of Cologne. On each month's page, the "Kölsche attitude to life" is implemented by way of illustrations: be it through Cologne's landmark, the Cathedral, or through the Cologne FC mascot, the billy goat. The motives show "Cologne's specialities" – always in an ironic, documentary or funny way.

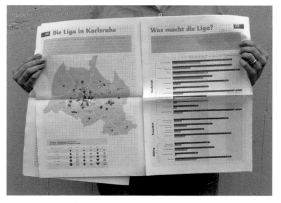

Project
LIGAzette
Zeitung
Gazette

Design
Special Machine
Grafikbüro
Evamaria Judkins, Nelly Brunkow,
Masa Busic (Gestaltung)
Ekart Kinkel (Texte)
Karlsruhe, Germany

Client
LIGA der freien Wohlfahrtspflege
Karlsruhe, Germany

Aufgabe war es, eine Imagekampagne für die LIGA der Freien Wohlfahrtspflege in Karlsruhe mit einem Budget von nur 9.000 Euro zu entwickeln. Immer mehr private Anbieter drängen auf den Markt, jedoch nur in lukrative Bereiche. Ohne die LIGA-Verbände würden viele sozial schwache Menschen keine Unterstützung erfahren. Die Größe und Wichtigkeit der LIGA haben wir mit Diagrammen dargestellt. Die Qualität der Arbeit von LIGA in Form von Interviews mit Menschen, denen von der LIGA geholfen wurde. Um dies vielen Menschen zu vermitteln, wurden 50.000 Zeitungen gedruckt und an Karlsruher Haushalte verteilt. Der Titel ähnelt einer Gleichung: Für Karlsruhe geht diese Rechnung auf!

It was our task to develop an image campaign for the "LIGA der freien Wohlfahrtspflege" in Karlsruhe with a budget of only 9,000 Euro. More and more private suppliers are entering the market but only occupy the profitable sections. Without the league a lot of deprived people would not get support. We captured the size and importance of the league by diagrams. To show the quality of their work we interviewed people who received support. To bring this information to as many people as possible we printed 50,000 newspapers and delivered them to every household in Karlsruhe. The title page looks like a math equation: for Karlsruhe this works out good!

print media image

Project
Secret Talents Award
Anzeigen
Advertisments

Design
Kolle Rebbe / KOREFE
Katrin Oeding (Creative Director)
Reginald Wagner (Art Director)
Jan Simmerl (Grafik)
Sebastian Oehme (Text)
Hamburg, Germany

Client
Google Germany GmbH
Hamburg, Germany

Durch YouTube kann man schon mit einem Video berühmt werden. Zumindest da, wo es heute jeder sein will: Im Internet.
In den Anzeigen für YouTube benutzen wir deshalb „Google Insights for Search", ein Tool mit dem man sehen kann, wie oft bei Google nach einem Begriff gesucht wird. Und vergleichen hier echte YouTube-Nutzer mit berühmten Persönlichkeiten.
„Google Insights for Search" spuckt dabei eine Kurvengrafik aus. Diese bildet auch das Zentrum der Anzeigen. Wir haben die Darstellung von Google für die Darstellung in den Anzeigen von allem Unnützen befreit. Reduziert auf das, was wirklich zählt: die Kurve.

Thanks to YouTube you can become famous with a video. At least where everyone wants to be today: in the internet.
That is why we use "Google Insights for Search", a tool which allows you to see how many times a certain term was searched for on Google, for our YouTube advertisements. Here we compare real YouTube users with famous people. "Google Insights for Search" spits out a curve graphic which presents the centre of the advertisements. For print, we removed all unnecessary features from the Google diagram. Reduced to what really counts: the curve.

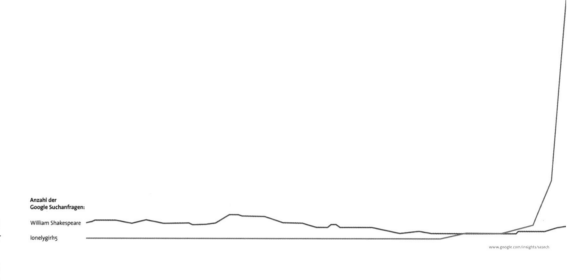

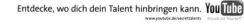

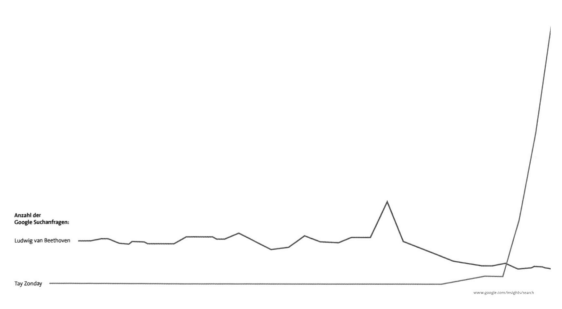

184

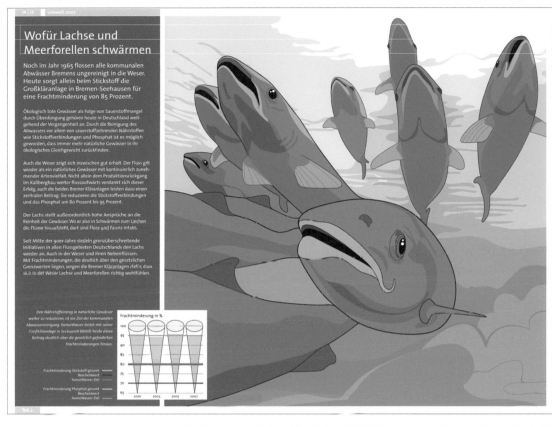

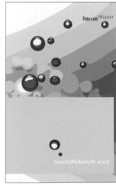

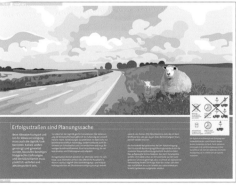

Project
hanseWasser 2007
Geschäftsbericht
Annual report

Design
kleiner und bold GmbH
Antje Kaiser-Deeken, Linda Rothbart
Berlin, Germany

Client
hanseWasser Bremen GmbH
Bremen, Germany

Die hanseWasser Bremen bildet Allianzen, betreibt eine angemessene B-to-B-Kommunikation und knüpft und pflegt Kontakte zu Kommunen und Verbänden. Um das komplexe Beziehungsmanagement der hanse-Wasser Bremen darzustellen, wird für den jährlichen Geschäftsbericht jeweils ein eigener Illustrationsstil entwickelt, der das Engagement und die Leistungen des Unternehmens ansprechend visualisiert. Auf diese Weise kommt dem Geschäftsbericht – neben Zahlen und Fakten – auch eine „unterhaltsame" Rolle mit ungewöhnlichen Blickwinkeln zu.

hanseWasser Bremen forms alliances, conducts appropriate B-to-B communications while at the same time establishing and maintaining contacts with municipalities and associations. To portray hanse-Wasser Bremen's complex relationship management, a unique illustrative style is being developed for the annual report which attractively depicts the commitment and services of the company. In this way, the annual report is being made entertaining and provides unusual perspectives – along with the facts and figures.

Project
Imagemappe
Image folder

Design
Novamondo Design
Christian Schlimok, Bastian Köhler
Berlin, Germany

Client
Akademie der bildenden Künste
Wien, Austria

Die Imagemappe ermöglicht es der Akademie, die komplexe Institution nach außen darzustellen. Gleichzeitig wird den einzelnen Instituten und Einrichtungen (Bibliothek, Gemäldegalerie und Kupferstichkabinett) eine Präsentationsmöglichkeit über integrierte Informationsordner geboten, die einen individuellen und eigenständigen Auftritt im Rahmen des Erscheinungsbildes zulässt.

The image folder enables the academy the opportunity to represent its complex institution. A central component of the complete layout is one Image brochure, reflecting the history as well as the contemporary present of this established training center. Simultaneously the integrated information folders allow a context for the individual institutes and facilities (library, picture gallery, and copperplate engravings) to independently appear and individually present themselves.

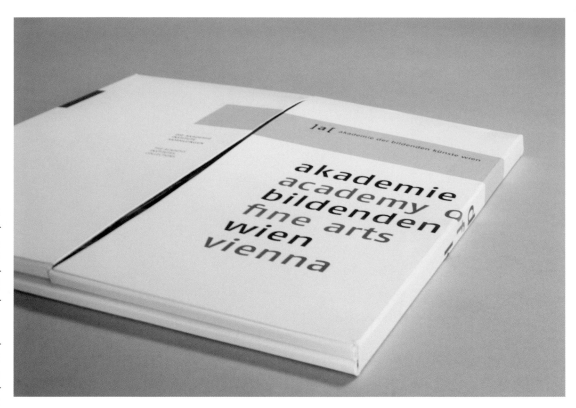

Project
Imagebroschüre
Image brochure

Design
Novamondo Design
Bastian Köhler, Christian Schlimok, Sina Schwarz
Berlin, Germany

Client
Kulturkreis der deutschen Wirtschaft
Berlin, Germany

Für den Kulturkreis der deutschen Wirtschaft entwickelt Novamondo Design ein Printprodukt der besonderen Art. Die neue Imagebroschüre arbeitet mit zwei unterschiedlichen Seitenformaten. Eines beinhaltet den Mantel der Broschüre mit den wichtigsten Informationen zur traditionsreichen Förderinstitution. Das andere im Zentrum der Broschüre befindliche Format illustriert über 50 Jahre Kulturkreisgeschichte in einer plakativen Bildstrecke. Im Rahmen eines ganzheitlichen Konzepts kann die Broschüre in eine Präsentationsmappe eingebunden werden, die auch Informationsordner zu allen Gremien und Arbeitskreisen des Kulturkreises beinhaltet.

Novamondo Design has contrived an out of the ordinary product, for the "Kulturkreis der deutschen Wirtschaft". The new image brochure contains two different page layouts, one being the cover of the brochure, which comprises the most important information referring to the institutions funding tradition and the other being in the center of the brochure, where over 50 years of the "Kulturkreis der deutschen Wirtschaft" is illustrated via a spectacular picture series. In the context this holistic idea, the brochure can be merged into one presentation portfolio which consists of information folders.

Project
Design Walk 2008
Ausstellungskatalog
Exhibition catalog

Design
pi6 communication design
Rena Chrysikopoulou, Michael David Ochs
Athens, Greece

Client
DESIGN WALK
Athens, Greece

Der Design Walk ist eine jährlich stattfindende Ausstellung im Athener Stadtteil Psyrri. Dort ansässige Gestaltungsbüros konzipieren und realisieren jeweils individuelle Ausstellungen in ihren Arbeitsräumen und zeigen diese an drei Tagen dem Publikum. Der Katalog zum Design Walk ist eine visuelle Dokumentation der Ausstellungen in englischer und griechischer Sprache. Der Umschlag, in dessen Klappseiten sich ein Lageplan befindet, zeigt eine stilisierte Luftaufnahme des Stadtteils in die der Schriftzug eingebunden ist. Bestehend aus miteinander verbundenen Punkten thematisiert dieser das Sujet „Kollaboration" der diesjährigen Ausstellungen.

Design Walk is an annual exhibition in the Psyrri area of Athens. Creative studios design and implement individual exhibitions in their workspaces. The exhibitions are open to the public for three days. The Design Walk catalog is a visual documentation of the exhibitions in English and Greek. The cover shows a stylized aerial photo of the Psyrri district in which the lettering of the title is embedded. The lettering consists of dots that are connected to each other thus broaching the issue of "collaboration", which was the main theme of this year's Design Walk. A map is located on the inside of the fold-out cover pages.

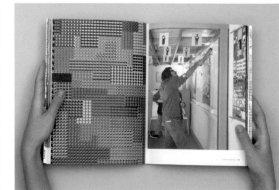

Project
Movie Ticket
Eintittskarte

Design
TED Brand design lab
Graduate School of Techno Design Kookmin University
Hong ji Kim, Seung woo Kang, Se Woong Kim
Seoul, South Korea

Client
CGV
CJ Entertainment
Seoul, South Korea

Leuchtende Sterne im dunklen Nachthimmel sind Wegweiser für verlorene Seelen. Im Dunkel dieses Filmtheaters wird Ihre Eintrittskarte Sie leiten. Informationen wie die Platznummer werden manuell durch das Lochen der Karte eingefügt. Die Karten müssen nicht bedruckt werden, was zur Reduzierung der Herstellungskosten beiträgt. Darüber hinaus bestehen sie aus recyceltem, umweltfreundlichem Papier.

Glittering stars in the opaque night sky are the guide for the lost souls. In this dark theater, the ticket will guide you to find the missing information. Informations like seat numbers will be created manually by punching the holes on the ticket. It will lower the total cost down, considering that there will be no actual printing process involved. Also, tickets will be made out of recycled papers for the preserving the environment purposes.

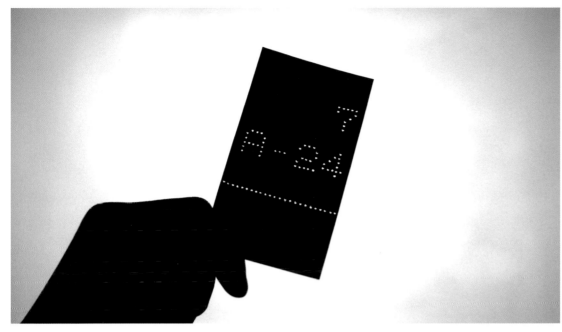

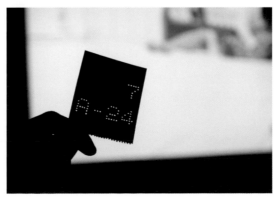

Project
Solid Coded
Ausstellungskatalog
Exhibition catalog

Design
KW Neun Grafikagentur
Daniel Schäfer, Tobias Sommer, Christoph Sauter,
Artur Gulbicki, Michael Stalze (Text)
Marion Ludwig (Fotografie)
Augsburg, Germany

Client
Fachhochschule Augsburg
Fakultät für Gestaltung
Augsburg, Germany

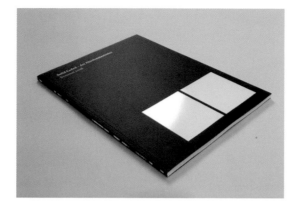

Im Absolventenindex steht die Persönlichkeit der Jung-Designer im Mittelpunkt. Grundelemente sind ein Foto, ein Statement zur Gestaltungsphilosophie und eine individuell ausgewählte Sonderfarbe. Der Seitenaufbau wurde über eine Formel aus dem Pantone-Farbcode jedes Einzelnen abgeleitet. Damit enthielten sich die Projektleiter selbst jeder Wertung und gaben nur einen Raster vor. Sowohl die Platzierung der Seiten im Buch als auch der Seitenaufbau wird allein über die Farbwahl der Studenten bestimmt. Mit diesem Konzept wird auf experimentelle Weise höchste Wertschätzung gegenüber den Studenten zum Ausdruck gebracht – gedruckt in 43 Sonderfarben.

In the index of graduates the focus is on the personality of the young designers. The elements are a photo, a statement on design philosophy and a spot color, individually selected. The page layout is derived from the Pantone color code, using a formula. This meant that the project leaders themselves refrained from making any assessment of the work, providing only a grid for the design. Both the placing of the page in the book and the page layout are determined only by the specific colors chosen by the students. With this experimental concept, a high level of appreciation is expressed towards the students – printed in 43 spot colors.

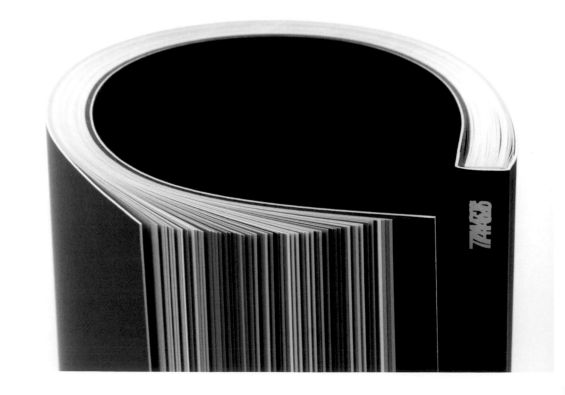

Project
sushi 11
Buch
Book

Design
Susanne Beck, Anne Julia Nowitzki
Mainhausen, Germany

Client
Art Directors Club für Deutschland (ADC)
Berlin, Germany

Liest doch eh keiner. Dem Beruf gewidmet, der nur ein einziges Programm braucht: Word. Der erste Schritt zum Multimillionär? Vor allem – rät Oliver Voss – analytisch denken lernen! Als Texter. Ist übrigens auch der sichere Weg zum Agenturchef. Was nicht dasselbe ist wie Multimillionär. Was sonst dafür spricht, Texter zu werden, Liebesbriefe zu schreiben, Blindtexte zu lesen, Worte auf die Waage zu legen, mehr als nur die Muttersprache zu beherrschen, von Politikern zu lernen – zumindest das Sprechen – und Text eben doch zu lesen, das findet sich neben den prämierten Arbeiten des ADC-Nachwuchswettbewerbs in sushi 11, diesmal angenehm textlastig.

Nobody reads it – anyway. The Swiss marketing specialist and essayist Robert Stalder says: "Writing can be learned, but only by writing." For Dr. Stephan Vogel "the writing will only be a temporary phenomenon in the cultural history of humans". Hans Peter Albrecht knows the answer to the question why "learning to write if no one reads" – is still useful. "I was young and needed the money" – counters top seller author Jan Weiler. Ralf Zilligen reminds of Heinrich Böll: "Thinking humans are not the most obedient ones, writing humans are not at all." In sushi 11 the pure text comes to word for the first time.

Project
Rail & Subway Map of Central Tokyo
Kombinierter Stadtplan mit Liniennetz-Übersicht für
Kurzzeitbesucher
A hybrid route and city map for short-term visitors

Design
Vollmer Design
Yoshiko Tajima, Ansgar Vollmer
Tokyo, Japan

Client
Vollmer Design
Tokyo, Japan

Die R&S Map Central Tokyo bietet insbesondere
Kurzzeitbesuchern einen schnellen Zugang zu dieser
komplexen Stadt.
Im Gegensatz zu konventionellen Liniennetzkarten,
die nur zur Routenfindung dienen und auf Grund
heutiger digitaler Infosysteme bereits überholt sind,
bietet die R&S Map lokale Orientierungshilfen und
ein Vorstellungsmodell der Stadt. Da man sich in
Tokyo eher an Bahnhöfen als an Straßen orientiert
und die R&S Map die Stationen und Linien sowie
die geographischen Gegebenheiten wiedergibt –
z.B. Parks, Inseln, etc. entsprechend ihrer jeweiligen
Lage zueinander – dient die R&S Map zugleich auch
als schematisierter Stadtplan.

The R&S Map provides quick access to this complex
city, and is of particular use to short-term visitors.
Conventional route maps function only as route-
finders and have been made obsolete by today's
digital information systems. The R&S Map, on the
other hand, serves as an orientation guide and gives
a good conceptual view of the city. Tokyo's train stations, rather than its streets, are the important feature of the city. For this reason, because the R&S
Map shows all lines and stations as well as geographic
information, such as parks, islands, etc. in relative
position to each other, it is possible to get the idea
of a schematized city map.

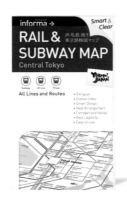

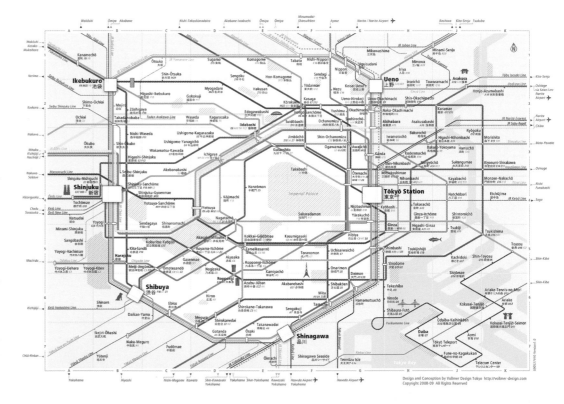

Project
Wohnen auf dem Dorf
Broschüre
Brochure

Design
Special Machine
Grafikbüro
Evamaria Judkins, Nelly Brunkow, Masa Busic
Karlsruhe, Germany

Client
Kreisverwaltung Germersheim
Bereich Bauen und Kreisentwicklung
Germersheim, Germany

Der demografische Wandel betrifft vor allem den ländlichen Raum. Werden jetzt nicht Maßnahmen ergriffen, werden viele Dörfer verwaisen. Ein erster Schritt gegen das Szenario ist dieser Leitfaden, der an die Bürgermeister des Landkreises Germersheim verteilt wird. Wie kann das Wohnen auf dem Dorf wieder attraktiver werden? Ideen hierzu haben wir mit „Playmobil"-Figuren und -Zubehör veranschaulicht. Dieser betont spielerische Ansatz macht Laune, sich mit dem trocken wirkenden und durchaus ernsten Thema auseinanderzusetzen. Auf dem Titel sind im Baukastenprinzip die einzelnen Bestandteile eines Durchschnittsdorfes im Landkreis Germersheim abgebildet.

The demographic shift affects mainly the rural areas. Many villages will become abandoned without action taken now. A first step is this brochure which is distributed to the mayors of the county of Germersheim. How could "Living in a village" become more attractive again? Some of those ideas we visualized with "Playmobil" figures and accessories. This deliberately playful approach to this otherwise serious subject makes it more fun to find interest in the matter. On the title page, mayors will find a list of the constituent parts of an average village in the county. Their village becomes a building block set they are encouraged to play with.

Project
Siemens Industrial Design
Buch
Book

Design
Baumann & Baumann
Barbara Baumann, Gerd Baumann
Schwäbisch Gmünd, Germany

Client
Designzentrum München
München, Germany

Dieses Buch geht der Frage nach der Besonderheit der „sachlich" technisch bestimmten Gestaltungskultur in einem der ältesten Elektrotechnikunternehmen der Welt nach. Es werden die wichtigsten Gestaltungsbereiche exemplarischer Produkte vorgestellt, die für die Designentwicklung im Unternehmen Siemens bezeichnend waren: die „Schnittstellen zwischen Mensch und elektrischer Technik", „Investitionsgüter" und die für die Siemens-Designentwicklung entscheidenden Bereiche „Haushaltsgeräte", „Medizin-" und „Kommunikationstechnik".

This book has taken it upon itself to explore the specific nature of the "objective", technically determined culture of design at one of the oldest electrical engineering company in the world. The most important subfields of Siemens Design are examined with reference to developments in design at Siemens: "interfaces between people and electrical technology", "investment goods", "household appliance", "medical" and "communication technology" segments that have played a crucial role in the history of Siemens Design.

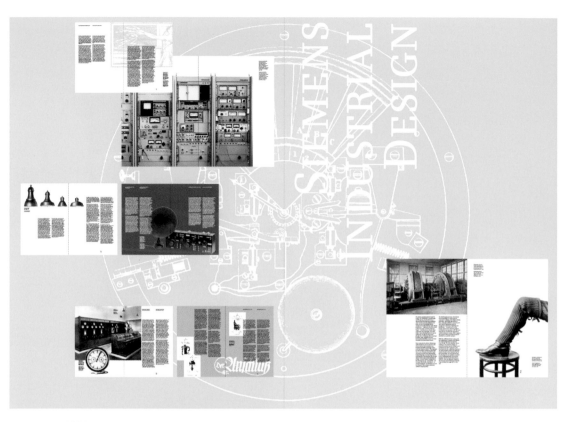

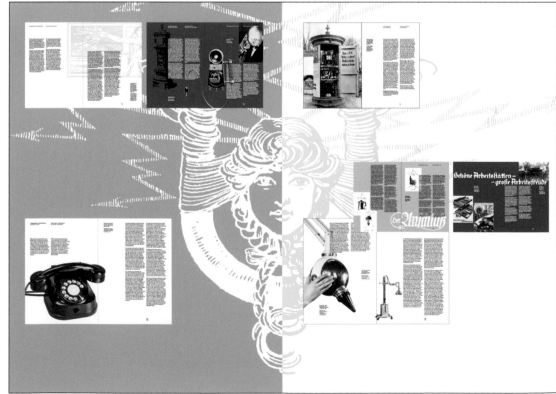

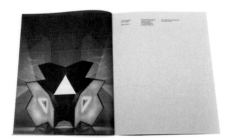
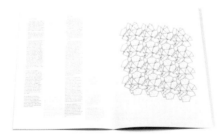

Project
Starbrick O. Eliasson
Produkteinführung
Product launch

Design
BOROS GmbH
Christian Boros, Ingo Maak, Yi-Yeun Youn
Wuppertal, Germany

Client
Zumtobel Lighting Group
Dornbirn, Austria

Starbrick, ein innovatives modulares Leuchtkörpersystem, wurde vom Künstler Olafur Eliasson entworfen und von Zumtobel vermarktet. Eliasson beschreibt Starbrick als „ein Experiment aus Lichtmodulation und Raum". Einzelne Module lassen sich zu Gruppen beliebiger Größe zusammenfügen, die sich entlang verschiedener Vektoren im Raum weiterentwickeln können. Zur Markteinführung wurde ein Kommunikationspaket (Mappe und viersprachige Broschüre) entwickelt. Auf den Titelseiten ist das Drahtmodell des Leuchtkörpers geprägt. Die Hochprägung und das Spiel mit verschiedenen Papiersorten machen das Kommunikationspaket zu einer haptisch und visuell reizvollen Erfahrung.

Starbrick, an innovative modular luminary system, was designed by the artist Olafur Eliasson and marketed by Zumtobel. Eliasson describes Starbrick as "an experiment of light modulation and space". Individual modules may be connected to groups of any size which can further develop alongside various vectors in the room. For the market launch, a communication package (folder and a brochure in four languages) was devised. On the cover pages a wiremodel of the luminary is coined. The embossing and the play of various paper grades turn the communication package into an experience when it comes to the surface feel and visual appealing.

Project
Staatsoper Hannover
Spielzeitheft 09/10
Program of the season 09/10

Design
Aquilanti & Schmidt
Staatsoper Hannover
María José Aquilanti, Birgit Schmidt
Hannover, Germany

Client
Staatsoper Hannover
Hannover, Germany

Im Zuge der Neuentwicklung des Corporate Designs der Staatsoper Hannover entstand als erste Publikation das Spielzeitheft 2009/2010. Es gibt einen Überblick über den Spielplan der kommenden Saison: die Premieren und die Wiederaufnahmen in Oper und Ballett, die Konzerte, das Kinder- und Jugendprogramm, das Ensemble und Service-Informationen (Abonnements, Kasseninformationen, Kontakte etc.). Zu acht Premieren gestaltete die in Berlin lebende französische Künstlerin Cécile Belmont künstlerische Statements, die poetisch und verspielt die Themen des jeweiligen Werkes aufgreifen.

The first publication produced in the course of the new development of the State Opera Hannover's corporate design was the brochure presenting the season 2009/2010. The brochure offers an overview of the season: the premieres, the standing repertoire and the concerts, as well as the program for children and young people, information about the ensemble and service (subscriptions, box office hours, contacts etc.). Individual artistic statements accompany eight premieres. Designed by the French graphic artist Cécile Belmont, currently living in Berlin, these statements poetically and playfully pick up the themes of the productions.

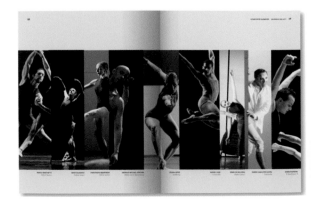

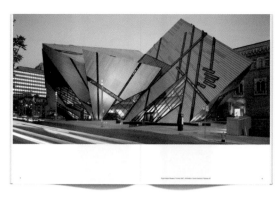

Project
Stabalux
Produktbroschüre
Product brochure

Design
großgestalten GbR
Tobias Groß, Dominik Kirgus
Köln, Germany

Client
Stabalux
Bonn, Germany

Stabalux. Die Idee von Klarheit. Die Stabalux-Produktbroschüre zum Thema „Glasfassadensysteme, Stahl" setzt auf eine klare Struktur, ein strenges rasterorientiertes Layout, präzise Explosionszeichnungen der Systeme, fotorealistische Renderings der Produkte und hochwertige Fotografie von herausragender Architektur. Sie präsentiert die komplexen Themen auf verständliche und leicht nachvollziehbare Weise. Die spiegelnde Heißfolienprägung des Titels deutet auf reduzierte Weise Architektur und Fassade an und vermittelt im Kontrast zu dem matten, offenen Naturpapier Präzision, Hochwertigkeit und Einzigartigkeit.

Stabalux. The Idea of Clarity. The Stabalux product brochure on the topic "Glass Facade Systems, Steel" works with a clear structure, a strict raster-oriented layout, precise sketches of the systems, photorealistic renderings of the products and high-quality photographs of exceptional architecture. The brochure presents complex themes in a coherent and easily understandable manner. It coveys professionalism and trustworthiness. The cover's reflective hot foil embossing suggests the product in a reduced manner and – in contrast to the matt, uncoated paper – communicates precision, high quality and uniqueness.

Glasfassadensysteme
Stahl

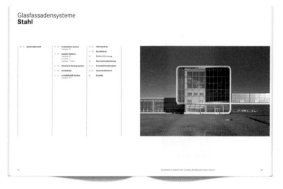

Schraubrohr
System

Schönheit: Extreme Spannweiten mit Glas problemlos möglich. **Patentiert:** Dank innenliegendem Schraubkanal erfolgt die Verschraubung ohne zusätzlichen Aufwand: Zeiteinsatz- und Personalaufwand werden minimiert. **Wirtschaftlichkeit:** Niedrige Materialkosten und minimaler Verarbeitungsaufwand für kostengünstige Realisierung. **Sicherheit:** Beste geprüfte Werte - für unterschiedliche Anforderungen. **Energieeffizienz:** Beste U$_f$-Werte – bis hin zur Passivhaustauglichkeit. **Schnell:** Permanente Verfügbarkeit aller Produkte.

Stabalux SOL

 **print media information**

Project
Faltschachteln / Folding Boxes
Plakat
Poster

Design
Hesse Design GmbH
Klaus Hesse (Gestaltung und Illustration)
Düsseldorf, Germany

Client
Hochschule für Gestaltung
Offenbach a. M., Germany

Das Plakat machte auf einen Vortrag von Andreas Schwindt aufmerksam zum Thema „Faltschachteln – Herstellung, Arten, Anwendungen, Normen und Richtlinien". Zielgruppe: Studierende und Designer im Rhein-Main-Gebiet.

The poster draws attention to the lecture "Folding Boxes – making, types, uses, standards and guidelines" given by Andreas Schwindt. Target group: students and designers from the Rhein-Main area.

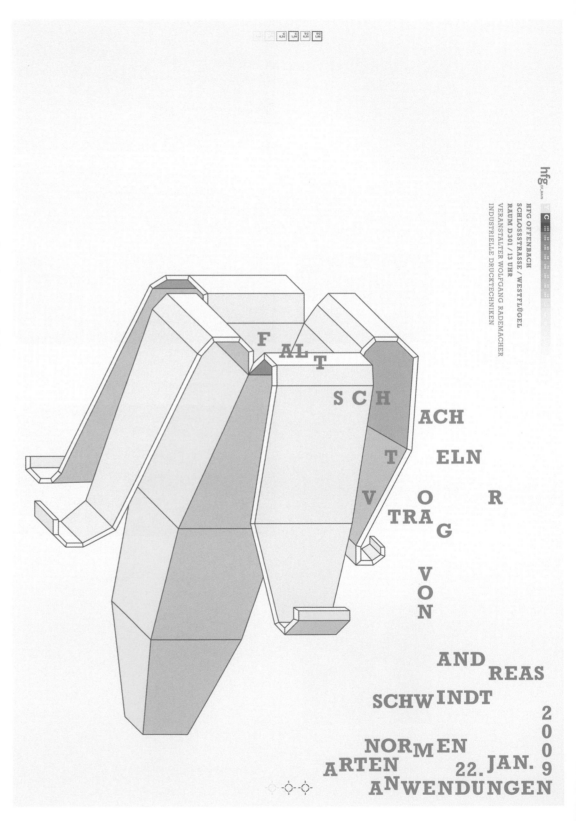

Project
LINDBERG Precious Book
Buch zur Edelmetallkollektion
Book for precious metal collection

Design
LINDBERG
Desk Top Department
Aabyhoj, Denmark

Client
LINDBERG
Aabyhoj, Denmark

Die hochwertige LINDBERG-Edelmetallkollektion „Precious" wird aus 18-karätigem massivem Gold hand gefertigt. Zu den verwendeten Materialien gehören unter anderem auch Platin und Wasserbüffelhorn, Horn von Moschusochsen und Mammuts. Deshalb gehört die LINDBERG-Kollektion zu den exklusivsten und prestigeträchtigsten Kollektionen des Optikerhandwerks. Jede Brille ist einzigartig, da es unendlich viele Kombinationsmöglichkeiten des Designs gibt, sowohl was die Oberflächen des Materials, der Farben als auch das Bügeldesign betrifft. Das Konzept wird in seiner Gesamtheit im LINDBERG Precious Book präsentiert.

LINDBERG's top collection – LINDBERG Precious – consists of handmade frames in 18 carat solid gold, platinum, water buffalo horn, musk-ox horn and mammoth tooth. It is one of the most exclusive and prestigious eyewear collections in the optical industry. The many options available regarding surfaces, materials and temple designs make each frame completely unique. The entire concept is presented in a single publication – the LINDBERG Precious Book.

Project
wobmag
Magazin
Magazine

Design
wob AG
Jonas Glaubitz, Steffen Herbold, Klaus Rausch,
Nathalie Rogowski, Annette Schönleber,
Matthias Schöpflin, Julie Schubert, Steffi Schwing
Viernheim, Germany

Client
wob AG
Viernheim, Germany

wobmag ist das zwei- bis dreimal jährlich erschei-
nende Magazin der B-to-B-Werbeagentur wob AG.
Es beinhaltet eine vielfältige Themenmischung aus
Eigendarstellung, News, Case-Studies, Personality-
Stories und Geschichten aus der Welt der B-to-B-
Kommunikation, die einem festgelegten redaktionel-
len Raster folgt.

wobmag is the corporate magazine of B-to-B advertising agency wob AG that is published periodically
two or three times a year. Following a fixed basic
layout and content-structure each volume covers services and concepts of wob AG as well as general
B-to-B- and branding-topics, news, case-studies,
background-reports, and interviews.

Project
B-Boy Poster
Plakat
Poster

Design
601bisang
Park Kum-jun (Creative Director, Art Director, Designer)
Kang Byung-in (Art Director)
Park Jae-min (Illustrator)
Seoul, South Korea

Client
601bisang
Seoul, South Korea

Dies ist das Plakat mit einer wortlosen Darstellung: „Ballerina who loves B-Boyz" (Ballerina, die einen B-Boy liebt). Die Liebe zwischen einem dynamischen B-Boy und einer wunderschönen Ballerina wurde durch aussagekräftige Pinselstriche und filigrane Feinzeichnungen ausgedrückt. Die Verwendung der Typographie ist auch ein Symbol ihrer Liebe. Die verschieden großen Löcher sind eines der formalen Elemente und dienen dazu, den umliegenden Raum in das Bild aufzunehmen. Wenn das Plakat auf einer Straßenwand voller Graffitis aufgehängt wird, können die Graffitis durch die Löcher Teil des Szenarios werden.

This is a poster for a non-verbal dance performance "Ballerina who loves B-Boyz". The love between a dynamic B-boy and a beautiful ballerina was expressed by powerful brush strokes and delicate fine lines. The use of typography is also symbol of their love. The different size holes are one of the formal elements and were intended to invite surrounding space into the poster. When the poster is put up on the street wall full of graffiti, the holes will reveal graffiti underneath which makes the posters a part of the scene.

Project
Zan – Die Frau/Zan – the Woman
Buch
Book

Design
Peymaneh Luckow
Bochum, Germany

Client
Peymaneh Luckow
Bochum, Germany

„Zan – Die Frau" besteht aus freien Illustrationen und Collagen. Zur Realisierung reiste ich an meinen Geburtsort nach Teheran. Ich entschloss mich zu dieser Reise, um dem Zerrbild, das aus weltpolitischen Gründen vom Iran gezeichnet wird, eine subjektiv gefärbte Innenansicht entgegenzusetzen. Als Muttersprachlerin (Farsi) habe ich andere Zugangsmöglichkeiten als jemand, der von außen auf die iranische Gesellschaft blickt. Das Ergebnis meiner Arbeit ist das Aufzeigen einer femininen Kraft, mit der sich Perserinnen ihre Freiräume im Alltag schaffen und mutig versuchen, die Verhältnisse zu unterlaufen – und zu überwandern.

"Zan – the Woman" consists of free illustrations and collages. For its realization I travelled to my place of birth, Teheran. I decided to go on this journey to contrast a subjectively influenced view from the inside to the distorted picture, which is drawn of Iran because of global political reasons. As a native speaker (Farsi) I have different possibilities of access than someone who looks on the Iranian society from outside. The result of my work is the demonstration of a feminine strength, with the help of which Persian women establish pieces of freedom in every day life and courageously try to oppose and overcome the circumstances.

Project
Die Macht der Zahl / The Power of Numbers
Buch
Book

Design
Yellow Tree Kommunikationsdesign
Andreas Utsch
Freudenberg, Germany

Client
Yellow Tree Kommunikationsdesign
Freudenberg, Germany

„Die Macht der Zahl" ist ein Buch über die Faszination des Numerischen. Es ist mal humorvoll, mal sozialkritisch und oft einfach nur unglaublich. „Die Macht der Zahl" ist eine Zahlensammlung, die nicht den Anspruch auf Vollständigkeit erhebt, sondern als Streifzug durch die Welt der Zahlen zu verstehen ist. Durch den stringenten Stil und die Betrachtung der Zahlenwelt aus der Vogelperspektive zeigt „Die Macht der Zahl" Fakten auf, überlässt es aber dem Betrachter, sie zu bewerten. Die Kombinationen aus Zahlen und Infografiken vermitteln in jedem betrachteten Thema den Eindruck, dem Kern der Wahrheit näherzukommen.

"Die Macht der Zahl" (The Power of Numbers) is a book about numeric fascination. It is sometimes humorous, at times socially critical and often simply incredible. "Die Macht der Zahl" is a collection of numbers that does not claim to be comprehensive but should be viewed as a foray through the numeric world. With its stringent style and bird's eye view of the numeric world, "Die Macht der Zahl" presents facts but leaves their evaluation to the reader. The combination of numbers and informative graphics imparts the impression of coming closer to the ultimate truth in each covered topic.

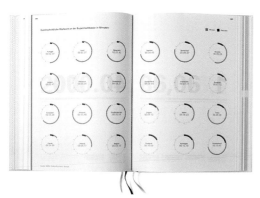

Project
x/u
Plakat
Poster

Design
büro uebele visuelle kommunikation
Andreas Uebele
Stuttgart, Germany

Client
Fachhochschule Düsseldorf
Fachbereich Design
Düsseldorf, Germany

Wenn jemand einem „ein × für ein u vormacht", dann lügt er. Die zwei Buchstaben können nichts dafür, denn Schrift lässt alles zu: Geschichte und Geschichten, aber die Wahrheit ist: es gibt keine Wahrheit. Denn Schriften und Geschichten ändern sich im Laufe der Zeit und die Wahrheit von heute ist morgen vielleicht schon Geschichte. Hier handelt es sich um ein Plakat zur Präsentation der Arbeiten aus der Lehrveranstaltung „die 100 besten Schriften" an der Fachhochschule Düsseldorf.

"Selling someone an × for a u" is German for pulling the wool over someone's eyes. The two letters themselves can't help it – typefaces can't distinguish between fact and fiction, between story and history. But the truth is: there is no truth. Because like typefaces, history is refashioned by time. And today's story could well be tomorrow's history. This is a poster for display the works from the "100 best typefaces" course at Düsseldorf University of applied sciences.

Project
Fierce Conversations
Buch
Book

Design
Found
Cecil Juanarena
Seattle, WA, United States of America

Client
Fierce, Inc.
Bellevue, WA, United States of America

Der Workshop „Fierce Conversations" (auf Deutsch etwa: Harte Gespräche) soll allen Teams oder Abteilungen innerhalb eines Unternehmens Erfolg auf dem Weg zu gemeinsamen Zielen garantieren. Im Laufe des Workshops werden die Teilnehmerinnen und Teilnehmer verschiedene Gesprächssituationen meistern, die ausschlaggebend für den beruflichen Erfolg sind: von Team-Gesprächen über Coaching und Delegieren bis hin zu Konfrontationen. Das Fierce-Conversations-Toolkit stellt den Beteiligten die notwendigen Mittel zum erfolgreichen Gesprächsabschluss zur Verfügung, z. B. Arbeitsblätter, Gesprächsrichtlinien und ein Tagebuch, in dem sie ihre zukünftigen Gespräche und ihren Fortschritt festhalten können.

The "Fierce Conversations" workshop is designed to ensure the success of any team or division within an organization working towards a common objective. Throughout the workshop, participants will master team conversations, coaching conversations, delegation conversations, and confrontation conversations – essential conversations to their success. The submitted Fierce Conversations toolkit provides participants with the tools necessary to succeed in these conversations. Some of these tools include worksheets, conversational model guidelines, and a journal where participants can record their future conversations and track their progress.

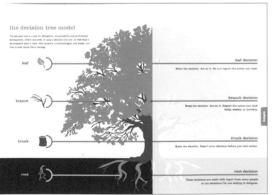

Project
Olympia Express Corporate Design
Besitzerbuch
Owner's book

Design
hpunkt2 gestaltung
Christian Hanke (Art Direction)
Hanna Hildenbrand (Illustration)
Felix Wey (Fotografie)
Berlin, Germany
Klenk & Hoursch GmbH & Co. KG
(Konzept und Text)
Frankfurt a. M., Germany

Client
Olympia Express SA
Mendrisio, Switzerland

Olympia Express ist seit 1928 eine Manufaktur feinster Espressomaschinen und Mühlen. Die Aufgabe bestand darin, der Traditionsmarke durch einen fokussierten Markenauftritt – von der Maschinenbeschriftung bis zur Website und Broschüren – neues Leben als Premium-Hersteller außergewöhnlicher Maschinen für Genießer einzuhauchen. Beim Kauf eines so fantastischen Objekts möchten die Käufer nun aber alles andere als mit unattraktiven Anleitungen gelangweilt werden. So gehört zu jeder Maschine ein „Besitzerbuch", welches Markenhistorie, Espressorezepte und technische Anleitungen enthält, um von Beginn an ein einzigartiges Markenerlebnis zu schaffen.

Olympia Express (Switzerland, est. 1928) is a manufacturer of exclusive espresso machines and grinders. The brief was to revitalise and focus the complete brand appearance. From machine lettering to corporate website and brochures, everything was carefully redesigned reflecting a premium manufacturer of outstanding machines for connoisseurs. When you purchase such a great object, you do certainly not want to read a boring, unattractive technical manual. This "Owner's Book" combines brand history, espresso recipes and technical manuals to create a delighting brand experience from the very first moment on.

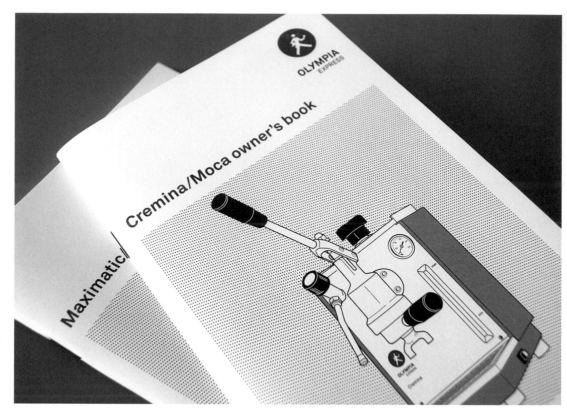

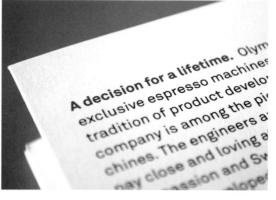

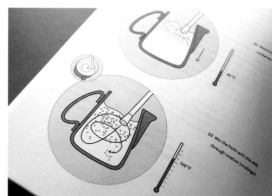

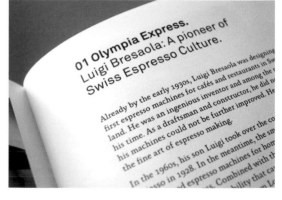

Project
CARE affair
Magazin
Magazine

Design
adams & evas design
Jens Mennicke, Yvonne Adams
Köln, Germany

Client
CARE Deutschland-Luxemburg e. V.
Bonn, Germany

„CARE affair" ist ein zweimal im Jahr erscheinendes Magazin der Hilfsorganisation CARE Deutschland-Luxemburg. Jede Ausgabe thematisiert einen Schwerpunkt der internationalen Entwicklungszusammenarbeit mittels Hintergrundberichten und Länderreportagen. Charakteristisch für CARE affair ist seine unkonventionelle Gestaltung, die vor allem bei der Kernansprechgruppe, den Schülerinnen und Schülern, ein nachhaltiges Bewusstsein für die Arbeit von CARE schafft.

"CARE affair" is a magazine published twice a year by the humanitarian organization CARE Germany-Luxembourg. Each edition focuses on international development cooperation by means of background information and national reports. CARE affair is distinctive due to its unconventional design, which primarily creates lasting awareness of CARE's activities amongst the key target group – school-age girls and boys.

Project
Enriching
Buch
Book

Design
Fabrique Communications and Design
Joana Mühlenbrock, Jeroen van Erp
Delft, The Netherlands

Client
Design & Emotion Society
Delft, The Netherlands

Dieses Buch entstand im Zuge des Workshops „Das Empfinden von Reisenden auf Flughäfen bereichert durch das Design von Eingriffen mit einem gewollt-emotionalen Effekt". Nicht nur die Endergebnisse werden sichtbar, sondern auch der strukturierte Designprozess und die Anwendung der Emotions-theorie. Skizzen sind genau so abgebildet, wie sie während des Workshops an der Wand hingen. Die auftauchenden Post-it-Kärtchen wurden direkt über-nommen, während die grell-fluoreszierend-orange-farbigen Aufkleber an verschiedenen Stellen im Buch die Emotionen ansprechen. „Enriching" macht dabei den Eindruck eines regelrechten Skizzenbuches.

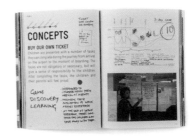

This book is the report on the workshop "Enrich the experience of travellers at airports by designing in-terventions with a conscious emotional effect". Not only the results of the workshop at the end made it visible, but also the structured design process and the application of the emotion theory. Sketches are shown as they hung on the wall during the workshop. The used Post-its have been incorporated directly, while bright, fluorescent orange stickers highlight the emotions in the book at various laces. "Enriching" looks like a real sketchbook: raw and unfinished, but visibly made with great care and love.

Project
TNT Annual Report 2008
Geschäftsbericht
Annual report

Design
Fabrique Communications and Design
Jari Versteegen (Art Direction)
Nils Mengedoht, Joana Mühlenbrock, Martijn Maas
(Design)
Tim de Jong (DTP)
Anton Corbijn (Photography)
Delft, The Netherlands

Client
TNT
Amsterdam, The Netherlands

Das Thema „Sure we can" symbolisiert, dass TNT bei
der Dienstleistung gegenüber seinen Kunden keine
Kompromisse macht und bis zum Äußersten geht.
Bei der Unternehmensbroschüre entschied man sich
daher dafür, die Triebfedern, die hinter den menschlichen Leistungen stecken, in Worte zu fassen und
bildlich darzustellen. Unterstützt wird dies durch
Fotos von Anton Corbijn. In der Ausführung des Geschäftsberichtes wurde bis ins letzte Detail darauf
geachtet, wie man es noch intelligenter und ausge-
feilter angehen kann, um das Thema besser zur Gel-
tung zu bringen. Vom Daumenindex über den mit
Lasertechnik gestalteten Umschlag bis zu den Illustrationen.

This year's theme for TNT's reports, "Sure we can",
shows us how far TNT is willing to go for its clients. In
the corporate brochure this is highlighted by focusing
on the drivers of twelve employees, both visually and
in text, aided by Anton Corbijn's photography. To
fulfill this year's theme, we have continuously looked
for smarter and also better ways to make the reports.
Ranging from an easy way to find the most important chapter in the annual report; a laser cover of the
corporate brochure; to the illustrations inside the corporate responsibility report.

Project
Hering Berlin Corporate Design
Broschüre/Katalog
Brochure/catalog

Design
Edenspiekermann
Ralf Weissmantel, Eva Schekorr, Christian Hanke
Berlin, Germany

Client
Hering Berlin
Berlin, Germany

Porzellan ist nicht gleich Porzellan – dafür steht Hering Berlin: Denn mit der puristischen Formsprache und der ganz individuell kombinierbaren Kollektion setzt die Marke international neue Maßstäbe. Es gilt, die Marke Hering beschreib- und erlebbar zu machen. In der Imagebroschüre wird das Hering-Porzellan sinnlich erfahrbar: Prägungen, Stanzungen, Lack und Metallfarben sind dem Eindruck des Porzellans so nahe, wie es ein Objekt aus Papier nur kann. Und der 700 Seiten starke Gesamtkatalog setzt in Hinsicht Übersichtlichkeit und Gestaltung Maßstäbe. Kein Wunder, dass dieser neue Auftritt in der Branche für Furore sorgte.

Porcelain is not just porcelain – that's what Hering Berlin stands for. Its purist form together with the highly individual combinable collection sets a new international standard. Hering needed a brand strategy and a communication concept. The complex shapes and decorations of Hering porcelain come to life in the image brochure; blind embossing, die cuts, metallic paints and spot varnishes make the porcelain look as lifelike as objects can possibly get in print. There's also the 700-page general catalog with the highest standard of clarity and design. No wonder then that the company's appearance has caused such a stir in the industry.

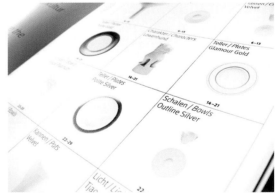

Project
Lacalut Toothpaste Hell
Anzeige
Advertisement

Design
Interone Worldwide GmbH
Georg Warga, Kathrin Guethoff,
Alex Jiang, Frank Neidhardt
Beijing, China

Client
Dr. Theiss Naturwaren GmbH
Homburg, Germany

Zahnfleischbluten und -entzündungen – ein in China weit verbreitetes Problem. Lacalut, eine medizinische Zahnpasta aus Deutschland, verspricht Heilung. Zur Einführung der Zahnpasta auf dem chinesischen Markt wurde eine aufmerksamkeitsstarke Umsetzung realisiert, die sich visuell deutlich von der üblichen Produktkommunikation in diesem Segment abhebt und die „Hölle" im Mund sichtbar und spürbar macht. So don't let your teeth rot in hell.

Bleeding, inflamed gums – a very common problem in China. Lacalut, medical toothpaste from Germany, promises a cure for these ailments. The market launch of the toothpaste in China was accompanied by a high-attention campaign with visuals which are distinctly different to those normally used in product communication in this sector and which graphically depict "inside-the-mouth agony". So don't let your teeth rot in hell.

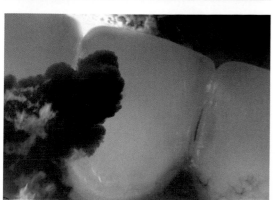

Project
Inspiration
Veredelungskatalog
Finishing techniques catalog

Design
Vitamin 2 AG
Jan Hasler
St. Gallen, Switzerland

Client
Limmatdruck/Zeiler (COPACO)
Koeniz, Switzerland

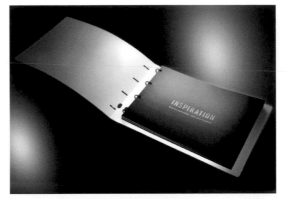
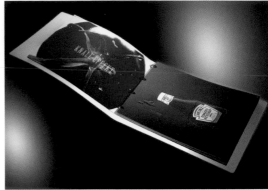

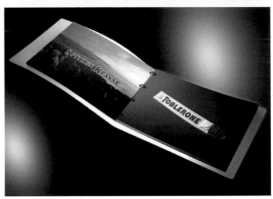

Eine gut präsentierende Verpackung überzeugt am POS. Durch tolle Veredelungen wird das Produkt zum Blickfang. Anhand „Inspiration" wird aufgezeigt, was mit Karton alles möglich ist. Dabei werden nicht nur schöne Sujets gezeigt, sondern mit passenden Bildern auch der Link zur Verpackungswelt geschaffen. Und dies nicht nur zu Kartonverpackungen, sondern auch zu Glas, Metall etc. Zu sehen sind Druckveredelungen sowie verschiedenste Prägungen. Die Anwendung von Veredelungen wird im Faltschachtelsektor immer wichtiger. Neben hochwertigen Produkten werden immer öfter auch Bonbons oder Kaugummis in veredelten Verpackungen angeboten.

A well presenting packaging fully convinces on the POS. Thanks to fantastic finishing techniques the product becomes an eye-catcher. "Inspiration" shows the possibilities cardboard offers. Not only beautiful landscapes are shown but the appropriate pictures make the link to the world of packaging. And this not only to fold cartons but also glass, metal etc. Print finishing and embossing techniques are presented. The use of finishing techniques becomes more and more important in the cardboard sector. Besides first class products, more and more often also candy and chewing gums are packed in finished boxes.

Project
Maximilian 35
Imagebuch
Image book

Design
kloetzldesign
Anja Schieber, Harald Klötzl
München, Germany

Client
W2005/2007 VERNAL ASSET 1 B.V.
Amsterdam, The Netherlands

Image- und Vermietungsbuch für eine markante Büro-Immobilie in Münchens Prachtstraße, der Maximilianstraße. Das Buch dient gleichzeitig als exklusive Vermarktungsmaßnahme und als hochwertiges Give-Away an bestehende Mieter. Ein aufwändig gestaltetes Buchcover aus echtem Nussbaum-Holzfurnier, harmonische Typografie, edles Design und stilvolle Fotos zeichnen das Buch aus.

Image book showcasing an outstanding office building situated in the distinguished "Maximilianstraße" in the heart of Munich. The book is an exclusive marketing tool and premium gift for existing tenants. The cover of the book is finished with a walnut veneer. Outstanding design, harmonious layout and high-end photography impress at first glance.

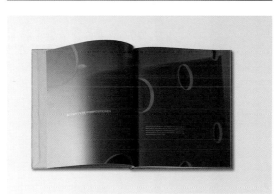

Project
Kaugirls
Kalender
Calender

Design
VIER FÜR TEXAS
Sonja Weber, Elisabeth Esselborn,
Philipp Erlach, Frank Röhrig
Marc Wuchner (Fotografie)
Frankfurt a. M., Germany

Client
123 Nährmittel GmbH
Idstein, Germany

„Essknete" ist die erste essbare Knete der Welt. Mit dem limitierten Kaugirls-Kalender haben wir Einkäufer in den Bereichen „Spielzeug" und „Lebensmittel" verführt. Jede Figur, jedes Detail ist zu 100 % handgemacht – mit „Essknete" und viel Geduld …

"Essknete" is the first edible plasticine in the world. With the limited Kaugirls Calendar (sounds like "cowgirls" but means "chewgirls"), we seduced buyers in the "cake mix" and "toy" segments. Every figure, every detail is 100 % handmade – with "Essknete" and a lot of patience …

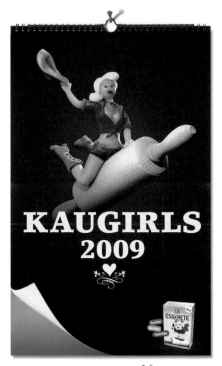

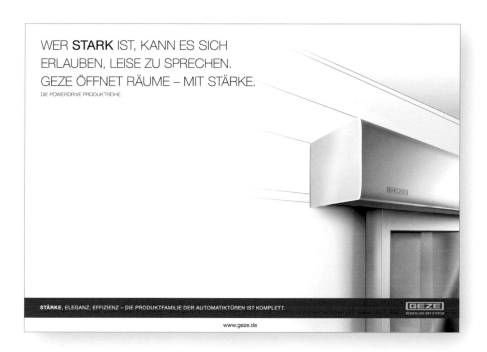

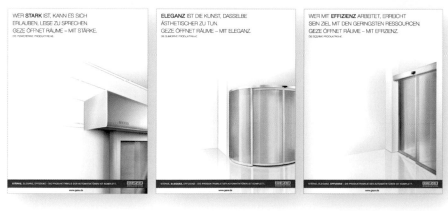

Project
GEZE öffnet Räume
Mailing für eine Kampagne
Campaign mailing

Design
pulsmacher
Gesellschaft für Kommunikationsdesign mbH
Jens Kenserski (Creative Direction)
Rebecca Ulmer (Art Direction)
Ludwigsburg, Germany

Client
GEZE GmbH
Leonberg, Germany

GEZE öffnet Räume – mit Stärke. Mit dem „Power-drive-Antrieb" für hochfrequentierte schwere Türen ist das Portfolio der Automatiktüren von GEZE komplett. Die minimalistische Gestaltung der Kampagne mit Zielgruppe „Architekten" löst das Produkt aus der klassischen Einbausituation im Gebäude heraus. Kampagnenelemente sind Anzeigen in Fachmagazinen und ein Mailing mit „Powerdrive-Türschablone". Der Architekt hat den (Frei)Raum, Ideen im Kopf wachsen zu lassen. Auf Copy und Produktinformation wird bewusst verzichtet. Die konzipierte Schablone ermöglicht es dem Architekten, auf einfachem Weg die perfekte GEZE-Tür für seinen Entwurf zu finden.

GEZE opens rooms – with power. The new "Power-drive" drive train for highly frequented and heavy doors completes the portfolio of automatic doors made by GEZE. The minimalist design of the campaign for the target group of architects unhinges the product out of the classic installation situation in the building. Elements of the campaign are adverts in specialist magazines and a mailing with a "Powerdrive door template". The architect has (free)-space to let ideas grow. Copy and product information are consciously abandoned. The conceived template helps the architect to easily find the perfect door, made by GEZE, for his draft.

Project
Porsche Ärztemailing
Direct mail "X-ray"

Design
Chromedia Dialogmarketing GmbH
Gunnar Hartmann, Andreas Fölkl, Philipp Fürst,
Thomas Mugele, Susanne Zimmermann,
Götz v. Bechtolsheim
München, Germany

Client
Porsche Deutschland GmbH
Bietigheim-Bissingen, Germany

Zur Ansprache der Zielgruppe „Ärzte" wurde ein
„Röntgen-Mailing" kreiert. Dabei handelte es sich
um ein Mäppchen mit fünf eingelegten Modell-
karten, die die aktuellen Fahrzeuge als Röntgenbild
zeigen sowie einem weiteren Röntgenbild mit den
Kontaktdaten von Porsche Deutschland. Das bei-
liegende Anschreiben lud den Mediziner ein, sich
mittels der zugesandten Unterlagen oder direkt im
Porsche Zentrum mit den bemerkenswerten Symp-
tomen – glänzende Augen und eine erhöhte Puls-
frequenz – auseinanderzusetzen. Über ein ebenfalls
beiliegendes Antwortfax konnte der Arzt sich direkt
zu einem Untersuchungstermin anmelden.

To target doctors and medical professionals, an X-Ray
mailing was created. It consisted of a paper folder
carrying five X-Rays of the current Porsche models
plus an extra X-Ray with Porsche's contact details.
The cover letter invited the doctor to further investi-
gate the "symptoms", e. g. eyes lighting up, pulse rate
rising. Furthermore, a reply card offered the direct
option to arrange for an examination date.

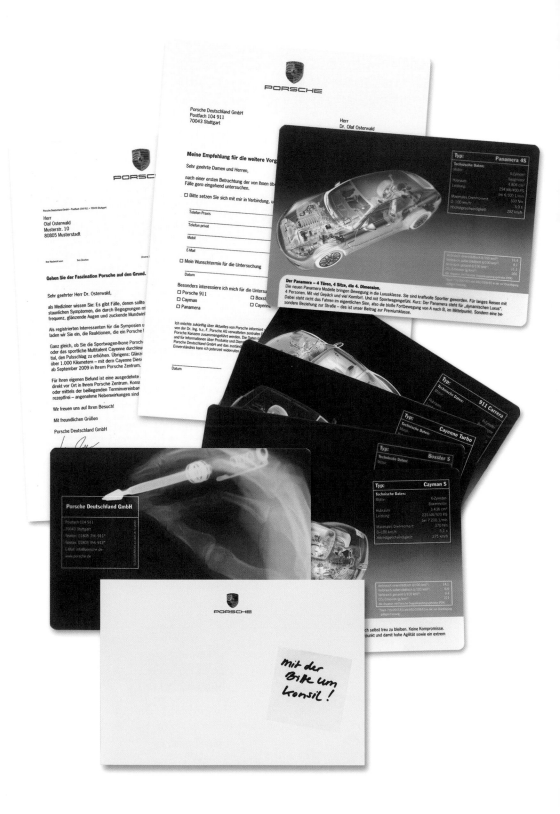

Project
Quirin Bank „Versteckspielbuch"
Buch
Book

Design
Euro RSCG Düsseldorf
Felix Glauner, Martin Breuer, Martin Venn,
Harald Linsenmeier, Yasemin Heimann
Düsseldorf, Germany

Client
Quirin Bank AG
Berlin, Germany

Aufgabe:
Viele Banken täuschen ihre Kunden, wenn es um die eigene Vergütung geht. Sie verstecken Gebühren und Provisionen im Kleingedruckten oder zahlen sogenannte „Kick-Backs" einfach nicht an ihre Kunden zurück. Weil dies bei der Quirin Bank nicht so ist, wurde die Agentur aufgefordert, die fragwürdigen Praktiken im Bankengeschäft ironisch-unterhaltsam aufzudecken.
Lösung:
Um die Kunden über die üblichen Tricks der Banker aufzuklären, kreierte die Agentur ein Büchlein mit den beliebtesten Versteckspielen im Private Banking – samt Spielanleitungen für Banker sowie der finalen Aufforderung an den Kunden, zum Spielverderber zu werden.

Brief:
Many banks keep their clients in the dark about their own allowances. They hide due charges and commissions in the fine prints or do not repay so-called "kickbacks".
To show that the Quirin Bank is different, the agency was asked to unveil questionable methods in the banking sector in an ironic and entertaining way.
Solution:
To explain the banks' common tricks to the clients, the agency created a booklet containing the most popular hide-and-seek games in private banking – completed with instructions for bankers and a request asking the client to become a spoilsport.

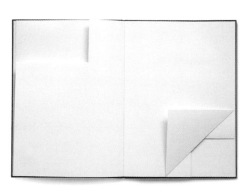

Project
365 calendar
Kalender
Calendar

Design
Park Kum-jun
(Creative Director, Art Director, Designer, Illustrator)
Kim Jung-ran (Designer)
Seoul, South Korea

Client
601bisang
Seoul, South Korea

Als limitierte Auflage mit nur 601 Exemplaren produziert, wurde dieser Kalender zwischen 2005 und 2009 recycelt. Der erste 365-Tage-Kalender diente dazu, Farben und Schlüsselwörter, die der Wendung „Kommunikationsdesign" entspringen, jeden Monat zu entdecken. Die Schlüsselwörter waren die Mitteilung, die die Gestaltungsherkunft hinterfragen und die Emotionen und Gefühle ausfindig machen sollten. Die Kalender, die 2009 hergestellt wurden, werden mit einer Hülle geliefert, welche die Lösungen und Gefühle jedes Nutzers enthält. Dies wird zu einem Werkzeug für die Erinnerungen, die es ermöglichen, auf die letzten fünf Jahre zurückzublicken.

Produced as the limited edition of 601 copies, this calendar has been recycled between 2005 and 2009. The first 365-day-Calendar was made to help the user discover colors and keywords originated from the phrase "Communication Design" unique to each of the 12 months. The keywords were the message meant to question the design identity and seek emotions and feelings unique to each person. The calendars produced for 2009, marking the end of this project, also comes with an envelope to hold each user's resolutions and feelings. It will become a valuable tool for the most cherished memories that will help the users look back to the past five years.

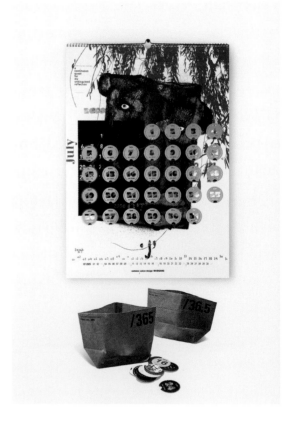

SKIN CARE FOR MEN
LIERAC
HOMME

SKIN CARE FOR MEN
LIERAC
HOMME

Project
Renovation
Plakat
Poster

Design
Kolle Rebbe
Ulrich Zünkeler (Creative Direction)
Jörg Dittmann (Art Direction)
Florian Ludwig (Text)
Hamburg, Germany

Client
Ales Groupe Cosmetic
Deutschland GmbH
Frankfurt a. M., Germany

Echte Männer pflegen ihren Körper nicht, sie reno-
vieren ihn. Dieser Gedanke liegt der Kampagne für
„LIERAC Homme" zugrunde. Sie soll echten Männern
zeigen, wie sie ihr Aussehen professionell instand
halten.

Real men don't groom their bodies. They refurbish
them. This idea is the basis of a campaign for the
"LIERAC Homme" skincare range. It shows how men
can stay good-looking – professionally.

Project
I love Chinese Characters
Plakate
Poster

Design
SenseTeam
Hei Yiyang
Shenzhen, China

Client
SenseTeam
Shenzhen, China

Das Konzept dieser Plakatserie beruht auf zwei chinesischen Schriftzeichen: „xue" und „xi" (die zusammen „lernen" bedeuten). Wir haben ein traditionelles chinesisches Spiel – ein Denksportpuzzle aus Holz mit zwölf Blöcken – in die Form der zwei Schriftzeichen gebracht, um die Idee des gemeinsamen Lernens und Spielens geschickt miteinander zu kombinieren. Darüber hinaus verweisen sie auf Traditionen und auf Aktivitäten, die gut für die geistige Entwicklung sind. Die beiden schlichten Schriftzeichen und die holzartige Textur vermitteln ein Gefühl der Reinheit und Einfachheit und ermöglichen so die volle Konzentration auf das Lernerlebnis. Die Plakate dieser Serie wirken oberflächlich ruhig und sind doch voller Bedeutung.

The concept for this series of posters comes from the two Chinese characters "xue" and "xi" (when combined, they mean "learning"). We took a traditional Chinese game – a wooden brain teaser puzzle with twelve blocks – and put it into the shape of these two characters to adroitly combine the concepts of learning and playing. They also refer to traditions and activities that promote mental development. The two simple characters and the wooden texture impart a sense of purity and simplicity, allowing a complete focus on the learning experience. This series of posters appears calm on the surface but is full of meaning within.

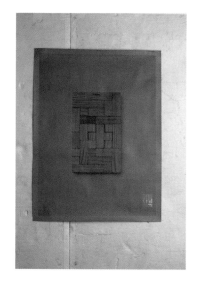

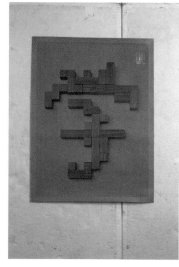

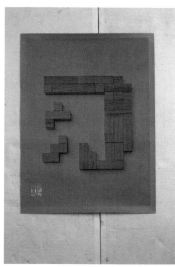

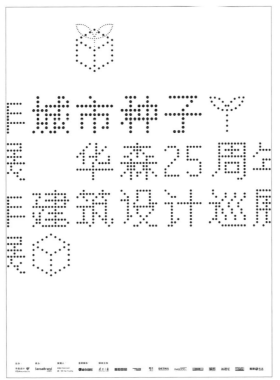

Project
Seeds of the Cities
Plakat
Poster

Design
SenseTeam
Hei Yiyang, Li Junrong
Shenzhen, China

Client
HSA
Shenzhen, China

Diese Plakatserie wurde für die Wanderausstellung der Huasen Architecture Company entwickelt. Die eingestanzten Buchstaben stehen für die in den LED-Anzeigen der Ausstellung zu sehenden Zeichen, deren Inhalt und Erscheinungsbild wir auf die Plakate übertragen haben. Die Plakate sind zusammensetzbar, so dass die Wörter – wie in einer LED-Anzeige – endlos durchlaufen können.

This series of posters is designed for the tour exhibition of Huasen Architecture Company. The slotting letters are the characters which display on the LED indicator system in the exhibition. We applied the idea into the posters. This posters can be put together and the idea (the words) could go on and on like what we see on the LED display.

Project
Projekt 68/89
Vier Buch-Journale
Four book-journals

Design
formdusche
Büro für Gestaltung
Svenja von Döhlen, Tim Finke, Timo Hummel,
Steffen Wierer (Designer)
Sebastian Vollmar, Frederic Groß (Assistenten)
Berlin, Germany

Client
ZZF – Zentrum für zeithistorische Forschung
Potsdam, Germany

Die vier Buch-Journale für das deutsch-tschechische „Projekt 68/89" widmen sich einerseits dem 40. Jubiläum (2008) der 68er Studentenrevolution (West) und dem „Prager Frühling" (Ost) und andererseits dem 20. Jubiläum (2009) des Mauerfalls 1989. Die Deutsch-Tschechischen Beziehungen werden aufgezeigt, erklärt und verknüpft zu den vier Themen/Titeln: „crossing 68/89", „misunderstanding 68/89", „performing 68/89", „transforming 68/89". Für alle Bücher wurde eine 60/70er-Jahre-Ästhetik aufgegriffen und mit moderner, zeitgemäßer Gestaltung kombiniert. Es wurden passende typografische Prinzipien für jedes Buch-Journal/Thema entwickelt.

The four book-journals (german-czech-english) of the "Project 68/89" are dedicated to the 40th annual (2008) of the german student revolution in '68 (West) and the "Prague Spring" (East) and the 20th annual (2009) of the fall of the Berlin Wall in '89. The German and Czech relationship is shown, explained and connected under the four topics/titles: "crossing 68/89", "misunderstanding 68/89", "performing 68/89", "transforming 68/89". All books use the aesthetics of the 1960's/70's in combination with contemporary design. There were used special typographic principles for every book-journal and topic.

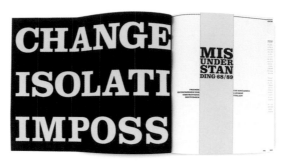

Project
„Wurzeln und Triebe"
Einladungskarte
Invitation card

Design
häfelinger + wagner design
Frank Wagner, Veronika Kinczli
München, Germany

Client
Typographische Gesellschaft München
Gauting, Germany

„Wurzeln und Triebe" ist der Titel einer Vortragsreihe der Typografische Gesellschaft München, zu der pro Abend und Vortrag ein Designer, Typograf oder Gestalter eingeladen wurde, um über seinen Werdegang zu erzählen. Die Einladungen setzen den Titel des jeweiligen Vortrages auf typografisch experimentelle Weise um, indem die Lettern horizontal getrennt und durch Zusammenfügen zweier verschiedener Schrifttypen erneut erzeugt werden. Ein spezielles Rasterverhalten sorgt dafür, dass die gewählten Farben und Schrifttypen das Thema des Vortrags sowie den Redner interpretieren. Durch partiell eingesetzte Lacke wird die Karte zusätzlich veredelt.

In 2007, the "Typografische Gesellschaft München" launched a series of talks titled "Roots and Motivations". For each evening and talk, a designer or typographer was invited to speak about their career choice and their professional path. The accompanying invitations incorporate the title of that particular talk and implement it in a typographically experimental way by splitting the letters horizontally and creating them anew by combining two different fonts. Special halftone properties and the selected colors and fonts reflect the subject of the talk and the speaker. Partial use of lacquers refines the invitation even more.

Project
8 New Fonts on the Block
Buch der Schriftentwicklung
Typeface development book

Design
DAREZ
Jiwon Park, Jaedeok Yun
Seoul, South Korea

Client
DAREZ
Seoul, South Korea

Entwicklung neuer Schriften mit Hilfe der Netze und Module von Bürgersteigen in Seoul:
Steine und Blöcke bauen verschiedene Muster, indem sie eine schlichte regelmäßige Anordnung wiederholen. Diese Muster auf dem Bürgersteig schaffen Netze in der Stadt.
Wir haben verschiedene Designs der Bürgersteige in Seoul recherchiert und acht repräsentative Muster ausgewählt. Wenn Netze und Module von Bürgersteigen in Seoul vielfältig kombiniert werden, kann das kulturelle Bild als Schriftart, d. h. als Kommunikationsmedium, ausgebreitet werden.

Designing new typefaces using the grids and modules of Seoul pavements:
Bricks and blocks build up various patterns by repeating simple periodic arrays. These patterns in the pavements create grids in the city. In the process of collecting actual design of sidewalks, eight representative grids of Seoul have been selected. By combining modules and grids of blocks, Seoul's cultural images can be spread as fonts, a meaning of communication.

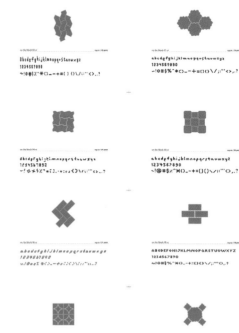

Project
Kafka (Werke)
Buchcover
Book cover

Design
VIER FÜR TEXAS
Philipp Erlach, Sven Kils, Sonja Weber
Frankfurt a. M., Germany

Client
S. Fischer Verlage
Frankfurt a. M., Germany

Die Umsetzung der Coverreihe betont mit Kafkas Unterschrift den Zusammenhang der Reihe, zitiert die Basis des Handschriftlichen und interpretiert das Fragmentarische.

We chose to use Kafka's signature to tie the whole series together, quoting not only the handwriting but also the fragmental character by the sections on each cover.

Project
Typomap
Poster

Design
DS nulldrei
Dirk Schächter
Bonn, Germany

Client
DS nulldrei
Bonn, Germany

Geografie trifft Typografie: The world in words. Aus einem Experiment wurde ein aufregendes Produkt. Mehr unter: www.typomaps.net.

Geography meets typography: The world in words. Started as an experiment, it turned out to be an exciting product. Details at: www.typomaps.net.

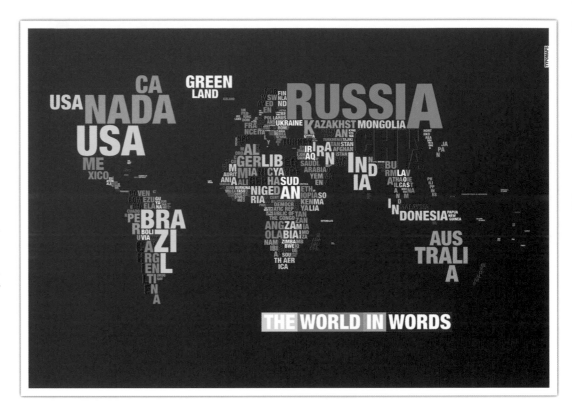

Project
Giesecke & Devrient „Kunstkalender 2009"
Kalender
Calendar

Design
Euro RSCG München
Frank Lübke, Michael Brepohl, Andrea Zeiller,
Alexandra Spitalny, Gerhard Sterr
München, Germany

Client
Giesecke & Devrient GmbH
München, Germany

Der Faszination des Geldes kann sich niemand entziehen. Das gilt auch für berühmte Autoren wie Herman Melville oder Fjodor Dostojewski. Ihre Zitate sind Thema des Giesecke & Devrient Banknotenkalenders 2009. Das Unternehmen druckt Geld für über 80 Länder in der Welt. Zwölf echte Banknoten aus dem Hause G&D finden sich im Kalender. Sie sind jeweils mit einem kunstvoll typographierten Zitat versehen.

No one can resist the fascination of money, not even famous authors like Herman Melville or Fyodor M. Dostoevsky. Their quotations are the subject of the Giesecke & Devrient Banknote Calendar 2009. The company prints banknotes for over 80 countries around the globe. The calendar features twelve genuine banknotes from the house of G&D, each of which is accompanied by a quotation in an artistic script.

Project
Die Kinderbuchbrücke
Plakat
Poster

Design
Büro Alba – Kommunikationsdesign
Tina M. Strobel, Christian Rother,
Andreas Pischetsrieder, Daniela Rudolf
München, Germany

Client
Internationale Jugendbibliothek (IJB)
International Youth Library (IYL)
München, Germany

Mit Hilfe von Buchspenden aus der ganzen Welt gründete die jüdische Journalistin Jella Lepman kurz nach dem 2. Weltkrieg, 1946, die erste Freihandbibliothek Deutschlands. Ihr Anliegen war es, Versöhnung und Verständnis für andere Kulturen mit Hilfe von internationalen Kinder- und Jugendbüchern zu fördern. Das Plakatmotiv für die Ausstellung über die Gründungsgeschichte der IJB greift inhaltlich das Motiv der „Luftbrücke" auf, um einen Hinweis auf die Zeit wie auch auf die Notwendigkeit dieser Buchspenden für die Kinder zu geben. Motiv und Typografie sind frei illustriert und visualisieren den Freiheitsgedanken der IJB.

The Jewish journalist Jella Lepman founded 1946, shortly after World War II, the first open access library in Germany, based on book donations from all over the world. She saw this as an opportunity to find new hope and values after the years of Nazi terror and to awaken a new understanding for other people and nations with books for children. The motive of the poster for the exhibition about the history of foundation of the IYL symbolises the historical term "Luftbrücke". The parachute with the book links to the post-war period and the importance of books. Motive and typography visualise the concept of freedom of the IYL.

Project
Siemens – Our typefaces
Schriftenkompendium
Compendium of lettering systems

Design
MetaDesign AG
Uli Mayer-Johanssen (Chief Design Officer)
Martin Steinacker (Creative Director)
Stefanie Reeb (Senior Designer)
Bernhard Dusch (Designer)
Berlin, Germany
(URW)++
Peter Rosenfeld
Volker Schnebel (Siemens Sans Global)
Hamburg, Germany

Client
Siemens AG
München, Germany

Um sich als internationales Unternehmen auch im Schriftbild weltweit einheitlich zu präsentieren, erweiterte Siemens gemeinsam mit dem Schriftenhersteller (URW)++ die hauseigene Schriftenfamilie „Siemens" um alle bedeutenden Schriftensysteme der Welt. MetaDesign gestaltete dazu das aus zwei CD-Roms und einem Booklet bestehende Kompendium „Our typefaces", das die Schriftenerweiterung umfassend und übersichtlich vorstellt. In der Verarbeitung erstklassig, in der Gestaltung zurückhaltend, aber bestimmt, getreu dem Corporate Design von Siemens, bereitet das Kompendium der Internationalisierung der Siemens-Schrift souverän den Weg.

In order to present itself as an international corporation with a uniform typeface across the globe, Siemens joined forces with the typeface developer (URW)++ to expand its proprietary typeface family "Siemens" to include all the world's major lettering systems. MetaDesign created "Our typefaces", a compendium of two CD-ROMs and a booklet giving a comprehensive description and visual portrayal of the new typefaces. With top-notch production quality and a precise, understated look true to the Siemens corporate design, the compendium confidently prepares the way for the globalization of the Siemens typeface.

Project
2 × 2 m Typografie
Typografie-Zollstock
Typography folding rule

Design
804© GRAPHIC DESIGN
Helge Rieder, Oliver Henn,
Carsten Prenger, Vanessa Poscher
Düsseldorf, Germany

Client
804© GRAPHIC DESIGN
Düsseldorf, Germany

4 m Schrift und Typografie – als „Giveaway" für
Kommunikationsdesigner und Liebhaber der Typografie. Auf der einen Seite Informationen und Hin-
weise zur Verwendung von Schriften in Displaygröße
(z.B. für Leit- und Orientierungssysteme), auf der
anderen Seite mehr als 5.000 Jahre Schriftgeschichte
in kompakter Form. Für uns vor allem die Realisation
einer vor über sieben Jahren geborenen Projektidee.

4 m fonts and typography – as a "promotional" gift
for communication designer, font enthusiasts and
typographers. On one side hints and basic information about the application of fonts in display size (e. g.
for signage systems), on the other side more than
5,000 years history of type. But first and foremost
the realisation of a seven years old project idea.

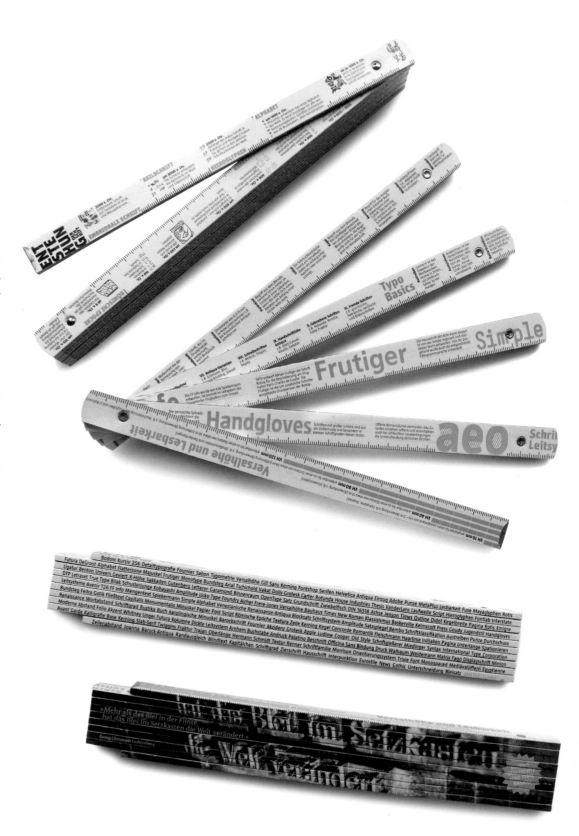

Project
MINI Cabrio Flyer
Verkaufs-Flyer
Sales flyer

Design
Interone Worldwide GmbH
Martin Pahl, Silke Gottschalck,
Matthias Kern, Matthias Kern, Svein Olsen,
Henning Beck, Britta Kussin,
Simon Puschmann, Peter Hetzmannseder
Hamburg, Germany

Client
BMW AG
München, Germany

Der MINI Cabrio Flyer ist Spiegelbild des überarbei-
teten MINI Cabrios. Kompromisslose Offenheit trifft
auf radikalen Fahrspaß. Durch den gezielten Einsatz
von Verzerrungen weitwinkliger Optiken macht der
Fotolook des Flyers das sichtbar, was man sonst nur
fühlen kann: Das typische MINI-Gokart-Feeling, mit
dem sich jede Kurve wie eine „Halfpipe" anfühlt, dem
unmittelbaren, unverstellten Blick aus einem Cabrio
auf alles, was die Straße an Erlebnis zu bieten hat. In
alle Richtungen, in jedem Moment und vor allem in
einem Bild!

The MINI Cabrio Flyer is a reflection of the redesigned
MINI Cabrio. Uncompromising openness meets radical driving fun. Thanks to the targeted use of distor-
tion in extremely wide-angled views, the design of
the flyer makes MINI go-kart feeling almost tangible.
Every bend becomes a "halfpipe". The view of the
street and what it has to offer is direct and unob-
structed. In all directions. At all times. And, above all,
in one single image.

Project
Mirage 01
Magazin
Magazine

Design
Mirage Magazin
Frank Rocholl, Henrik Purienne, Gunter Gebauhr
Frankfurt a. M., Germany

Client
Mirage Magazin
Frankfurt a. M., Germany

Entwicklung eines neuen Fashion-Magazins bzw. eines Fashion-Buch-Objektes. Die USP's (Unique Selling Propositions) sind: Darstellung einer jüngeren Generation von Mode-Fotografen, Interviews mit internationalen Imagemakern, Integration von Fundstücken aus dem Retrobereich (Dreamcars, Jetset der 60er/70er Jahre).

Development of a new fashion magazine respectively fashion book object. The USP's (Unique Selling Propositions) are: Presentation of a new wave of fashion photographers, interviews with international image makers, integration of retro worlds (dreamcars, jetset of the sixties and seventies).

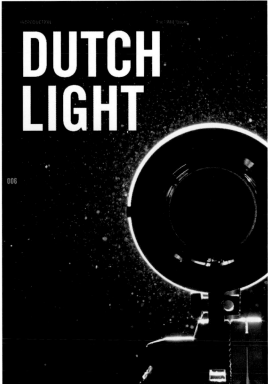

Project
PANL
Buch
Book

Design
Mattmo concept I design
Monique Mulder, Paul van Ravestein, Karen Rosink
Amsterdam, The Netherlands

Client
Mattmo concept I design
Amsterdam, The Netherlands

Mattmo stand dem Fotografenverband der Niederlande, PANL, strategisch und gestalterisch zur Seite, um die niederländische Fotografie international zu fördern. Kreiert wurden drei Bildbände in Rot, Weiß und Blau sowie eine Werbe-Webseite. Das weiße, im Dunkeln leuchtende Buch wurde bei den 18. jährlich stattfindenden PANL-Awards vorgestellt. Mattmo kümmerte sich darüber hinaus um das Kampagnenmaterial für die Preisverleihung: Plakate, Banner und eine audiovisuelle Präsentation. Wir betrachten dieses Projekt als Beweis für den Erfolg von Cross-Media-Kampagnen.

Mattmo sponsored PANL Photographers Association of the Netherlands by supporting them in strategy development and design. To promote Dutch Photography internationally a series of three coffee-table books in red, white and blue plus a promotional website were created. The white "glow in the dark" book was presented during the 18th annual PANL Awards. Mattmo also took care of the campaign materials for the awards night: posters, banners and the audio visual presentation. In our view this project shows the power of cross media.

Project
„schleierhaft"
Fotobuch
Photobook

Design
Peymaneh Luckow
Bochum, Germany

Client
Peymaneh Luckow
Bochum, Germany

Das Adjektiv „schleierhaft" steht im deutschen Sprachgebrauch für ein Rätsel, das bei jemandem Unverständnis über einen bestimmten Sachverhalt hervorruft. Im Kontext meiner Arbeit ist der Fokus auf die Lebenssituation von Frauen in der islamischen Republik Iran gerichtet. Dabei handelt es sich um eine fotografische Arbeit, deren inhaltliche Brisanz in zweiter Lesung im Detail steckt, und aus einem eurozentrischen Blickwinkel betrachtet zwangläufig zu Irritationen führen muss. Zur Realisierung reiste ich zurück zu meinen iranischen Wurzeln nach Tehe-ran, der 14-Millionen-Einwohner-Metropole, in der ich mehr als die Hälfte meines Lebens verbracht habe.

In German the adjective "cryptic" stands for a riddle, which arouses incomprehension in someone about a certain issue. In the context of my work the focus lies on the living conditions of women in the Islamic republic of Iran. It is a photographic work and the explosiveness of the issue can be depicted in details with the help of a second reading. From a Eurocentric point of view it inevitably leads to irritations. For the realization of it I travelled back to my Iranian roots to Teheran, the 14 million habitant metropolis, in which I had spent more than half of my life.

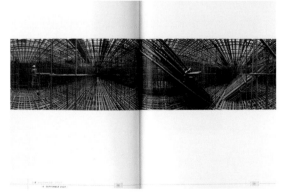

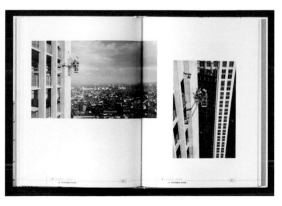

Project
OpernTurm Gesichter
Fotobuch
Photobook

Design
Activ Consult Real Estate GmbH
Sandra Breidbach (AD)
Stefan Rosenberger (Grafik)
Maren Heldt-Klötzke (Text)
Klaus Helbig (Foto)
Ute Kelety (Produktion)
Yvonne Liebherr (Beratung)
Frankfurt a. M., Germany

Client
Tishman Speyer
Frankfurt a. M., Germany

Das Buch „OpernTurm Gesichter" ist eine Hommage des Bauherrn Tishman Speyer an alle Menschen, die den OpernTurm in Frankfurt zum Meisterwerk gemacht haben. Jeder von ihnen hat mit seiner Handschrift dazu beigetragen, ein ganz besonderes Bauwerk zu schaffen. Die Bilder des Fotografen Klaus Helbig dokumentieren den Baufortschritt und machen den Geist und die verborgene Ästhetik der Bauarbeiten sichtbar. Zum Richtfest im Februar 2009 erhielten Gäste und Bauarbeiter das Fotobuch als Präsent. Eine Ausstellung im Rohbau zeigte Original-Fotografien im Großformat.

The book titled "OpernTurm Gesichter" is a homage of the developer Tishman Speyer to all people involved in turning the OpernTurm in Frankfurt into a masterpiece. Every one of them has contributed with their individual skills in order to create a very special building. The images of the photographer Klaus Helbig document the construction progress and make the spirit and hidden aesthetics of the construction work visible. Guests and builders received the photo book as a present upon the occasion of the topping-out ceremony in February of 2009. An exhibition inside the building shell featured original pictures in large scale.

Project
Domfenster
Dokumentation
Documentation

Design
Simon & Goetz Design GmbH & Co. KG
Bernd Vollmöller (Creative Direction, Art Direction)
Christina Schirm, Bernd Vollmöller (Design)
Frankfurt a. M., Germany

Client
Sal. Oppenheim jr. & Cie.
Köln, Germany

Sal. Oppenheim ist eine der größten unabhängigen Privatbanken Europas. Die Familie Oppenheim hat im Jahr 2008 die Finanzierung der Rekonstruktion des Apokalypse-Fensters des Kölner Doms übernommen und knüpft damit an ihre Stiftertradition seit dem 19. Jahrhundert an. Zur Einweihungsfeier des neuen rekonstruierten Glasfensters im Kölner Dom sollte eine repräsentative Broschüre entwickelt werden, die die Bankiersfamilie sowohl als Mäzen, Stifter und Förderer vorstellt, vor allem aber die Entstehungsgeschichte des Glasfensters, die Geschichte des Kölner Doms und die exzellente Handwerkskunst der dazugehörigen Dombauhütte präsentiert.

Sal. Oppenheim is one of the largest independent private banks in Europe. In 2008, following a tradition of benefaction dating back to the 19th century, the Oppenheim family sponsored the reconstruction of the Apocalypse window in the Cologne Cathedral. A representative brochure for the ceremony at which the new, reconstructed stained glass window in the Cologne Cathedral will be unveiled would be appropriate. The brochure should present the Oppenheim family as patron and benefactor, but above all the story behind the stained glass window, the history of the Cologne Cathedral and the outstanding craftsmanship of the Cathedral's build.

 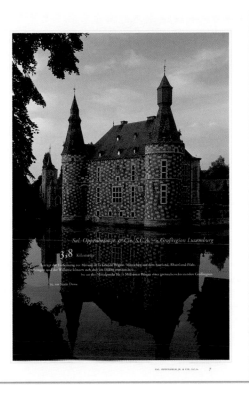

Project
Broschüre Luxemburg
Unternehmensbroschüre
Corporate brochure

Design
Simon & Goetz Design GmbH & Co. KG
Bernd Vollmöller (Creative Direction, Art Direction)
Frankfurt a. M., Germany

Client
Sal. Oppenheim jr. & Cie. S.C.A.
Luxemburg, Luxembourg

Sal. Oppenheim ist eine der größten unabhängigen Privatbanken Europas. Unter dem Titel „Entdecken Sie Europas kurze Wege" präsentiert die Bank den Standort Luxemburg – einen der bedeutendsten europäischen Finanzplätze – als idealen Ausgangspunkt für ihre neue internationale Ausrichtung. Die überraschend geringen Entfernungsangaben zu anderen europäischen Ländern zeigen, dass in Luxemburg das vereinte Europa nicht nur Symbolcharakter hat, sondern tagtäglich gelebte Realität ist. Diesen strategischen Standortvorteil zum Wohle seiner Kunden zu nutzen, ist das Ziel des Bankhauses Sal. Oppenheim.

Sal. Oppenheim is one of the largest independent private banks in Europe. In its image brochure "Discover Europe's short distances" the bank presents Luxembourg, the new location of its headquarters and one of the most important European financial centres, as an ideal starting point for their new international alignment. The astonishing short distances towards other European countries are showing that in Luxembourg the European Union has not only symbolic aspects, but is everyday lived reality. To use this strategic advantage of the location for the benefit of his client's, is the goal of the bank.

Project
360°
Magazin
Magazine

Design
Büro4
Gestaltung + Kommunikation
(Master Design)
Zürich, Switzerland
Open Systems AG
(Layout, Editorial Work)
Zürich, Switzerland
Noë Flum (Photography)
Zürich, Switzerland

Client
Open Systems AG
Zürich, Switzerland

Das Kundenmagazin „360°" der Open Systems AG zeigt vierteljährlich Produktneuheiten, Client-Cases und Blicke hinter die Kulissen des führenden Schweizer IT-Sicherheitsanbieters.

Büro4 konzipierte eine Zeitschrift, welche mit starken Bildern des Schweizer Fotografen Noë Flum, auf die Themen von Open Systems fokussiert: Risiko und Sicherheit in allen Erscheinungsformen. Dazu gut aufbereitete Inhouse-News, Referenz-Projekte und Mitarbeiter-Portraits. Markant ist auch das neue Cover-Konzept: Das Titelbild bleibt unangetastet – Informationen sind auf der verkürzten Umschlag-Klappe untergebracht.

Open Systems' customers magazine "360°" provides a view on specific product news, client cases and looks behind the window blinds of the leading IT-security consultant in Switzerland. Büro4 created a magazine supported by big sized expressive pictures of the Swiss Photographer Noë Flum. A magazine that contents all the basic topics of Open Systems' daily business: Themes like risk and security visualised in different featured forms. And in addition: In-house news, references and portraits of the employees. The new cover idea shows a high quality full-sized and "untouched" photograph only covered by a shorter flap for index and editorial.

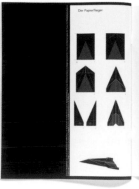

Project
Programmbilanz 2008
Geschäftsbericht
Annual report

Design
Büro4
Gestaltung + Kommunikation
Zürich, Switzerland
Schweizer Fernsehen
Gestaltung
Cordula Gieriet
Zürich, Switzerland
Schweizer Fernsehen
Media und Public Relations
Regula Weber, Urs Durrer, Heidi Stöckli
(Editorial Work)
Kata Rodriguez-Pongrac, Roberto Crevatin,
Eva Nussbaumer (Photographic Editorial Work)
Zürich, Switzerland

Client
Schweizer Fernsehen
Zürich, Switzerland

Prägnanz durch Authentizität – Die Programmbilanz des Schweizer Fernsehens bedient sich dieses Ansatzes auf eine sehr persönliche Art und Weise. In einer 18-seitigen Einführungsstrecke porträtiert sie neun Mitarbeiter des Senders in ganzseitigen Aufnahmen. Darunter sind vertraute, vom Bildschirm bekannte, Gesichter und solche, die im Hintergrund arbeiten. Ihre Zitate bilden den Auftakt des Jahresberichts. Der Geschäftsbericht selbst wird im Kontext der einzelnen Sparten auf Ausklappseiten präsentiert und mit Bildern der Produktionen illustriert. Diese geben Einblick hinter die Kulissen und vermitteln das sympathische und anspruchsvolle Image des Senders.

Conciseness through authenticity – The annual report avails itself of this approach in a highly personal manner. In an 18-page introduction it portrays nine employees in full-page photographs, including familiar faces from the screen, as well as others working backstage. Their statements mark the prelude to the annual report. The financial statements themselves are each presented in the context of individual sectors on fold-out charts and illustrated by photographs of different TV productions. These provide a glimpse behind the scenes and through their aesthetic, clearly-structured appearance communicate the friendly and sophisticated image of the broadcaster.

Project
BayWa 2008
Geschäftsbericht
Annual report

Design
Peter Schmidt Group
München, Germany

Client
BayWa AG
München, Germany

Anlässlich des Wechsels im Vorstandsvorsitz soll ein optisches Signal für einen Neubeginn gesetzt werden. Das Konzernjubiläum gibt das Thema vor: „Zukunft braucht Herkunft." Erstmals wird eine Trennung in Finanzbericht und Konzernprofil vorgenommen. Ein Schuber bildet hierbei die Klammer um beide Printmedien. Der Finanzbericht zeigt pure Information, die durch Farbunterlegung gegliedert ist. Die Leitidee des Konzernprofils ist der Dialog, ein Erfolgsfaktor der BayWa. Kernthemen werden mit Fragen und Antworten eingeleitet, die durch überraschende Bildmetaphern interpretiert werden. Der plakative Einsatz der Markenfarben verkörpert Herkunft und Zukunft.

A change in the managing directorship of BayWa was used as an opportunity to introduce a new optical signal and "new beginning". A new corporate claim was developed for the corporation's anniversary: "Future requires Heritage." For the first time ever the financial report and corporate profile were separated from one another, yet still joined by one common report case. The information within the financial report was color coded according the respective topics. The underlying idea of the corporate profile was dialog, which is one of BayWa's primary success factors. Core themes were introduced with question and answers, and visualized using striking metaphorical interpretations of images. The striking use of the brand's colors represents both "Heritage" and "Future".

Project
The Linde Group 2008
Geschäftsbericht
Annual report

Design
Peter Schmidt Group
Hamburg, Germany

Client
Linde AG
München, Germany

Der Linde Geschäftsbericht 2008 transportiert im Einklang mit der „Linde Equity Story" die beiden derzeit wichtigsten Botschaften: Stabilität und Vertrauen. Der Titel „Kurs halten" steht für das solide Geschäftsmodell der Linde Group. Der Linde Geschäftsbericht zeigt anhand von fünf zentralen Themen wie Linde auch in konjunkturell schwierigen Zeiten erfolgreich bleiben kann. Bildstrecken im Reportagestil belegen anhand eines konkreten Projektes jeweils eines von fünf Stabilitätsargumenten. Auf die Bildstrecken folgen relevante Entwicklungen oder Ereignisse des Jahres 2008 bei Linde, die das jeweilige Thema stützen.

The Linde 2008 annual report, consistent with the "Linde Equity Story", focuses on the two core messages of current times: Stability and Trust. The report is titled, "Staying on Track", which stands for the solid business model of Linde Group. It is based on five central themes such as Linde's continued success even during the difficult economic conditions. The visual journey takes on a "reportage-style", and follows relevant developments and events of 2008 from Linde, with each project and development supporting one of the five central themes.

Project
Elephant Print #2
Kundenmagazin
Consumer magazine

Design
Peter Schmidt Group
Hamburg, Germany

Client
Peter Schmidt Group
Hamburg, Germany

Mit dem Kundenmagazin „Elephant Print" berichtet die Peter Schmidt Group regelmäßig über aktuelle Projekte. In dieser Ausgabe stehen die Arbeiten im Mittelpunkt, mit denen Awards gewonnen wurden. Die „Elephant Print" – erschienen im Dezember 2008 als Weihnachtsausgabe – feiert unter dem Motto „Stars" Bescherung und überbringt den Kunden gleichzeitig die Weihnachtswünsche der Peter Schmidt Group.

With its personalized magazine, "Elephant Print", Peter Schmidt Group regularly updates interested parties and clients about actual projects, focusing on the recognized award-winning work of Peter Schmidt Group. The Christmas edition of "Elephant Print" celebrates the motto "Stars", and sends out Christmas Greetings to all of Peter Schmidt Group's clients.

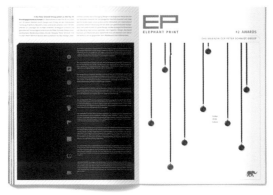

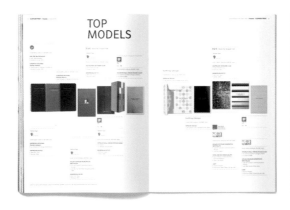

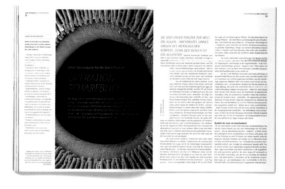

Project
Linde Technology 2008
Kundenmagazin
Consumer magazine

Design
Peter Schmidt Group
Hamburg, Germany

Client
Linde AG
München, Germany

„Linde Technology" ist das Kundenmagazin der Linde AG und richtet sich an Geschäftspartner, Kunden und Medienvertreter. Mehrmals im Jahr berichtet die Publikation wissenschaftlich fundiert und gleichzeitig verständlich aufbereitet über Innovationen aus den Bereichen Industriegase, medizinische und therapeutische Gase, über neue Erkenntnisse zu Wasserstoff-Technologien und aktuelle Entwicklungen im Anlagenbau. Jede Ausgabe hat einen Themenschwerpunkt, über den umfassend mit flankierenden Infografiken und Interviews berichtet wird. Die Linde Technology erscheint in Deutsch und Englisch und hat eine Auflage von 10.000 Exemplaren.

"Linde Technology" is the consumer magazine of Linde AG, and addresses business partners, customers and media. Throughout the year the magazine reports about innovations in the gases industry, medical and therapeutic gases, new expertise in the field of hydrogen technology and developments in plant engineering and construction. Every issue concentrates on one core theme and presents comprehensive information in various formats (e. g. charts, diagrams, interviews, etc.). It is published in both German and English and has a circulation of over 10,000 persons.

Project
D. Logistics AG
Geschäftsbericht 2008
Annual report 2008

Design
First Rabbit GmbH
Brigitte Läpper-Röhricht, Jens Tappe
Köln, Germany

Client
D. Logistics AG
Hofheim/Wallau, Germany

Der Geschäftsbericht der D. Logistics AG wurde analog dem Unternehmensschwerpunkt „Verpackung" mit einem Schaumstoffumschlag gestaltet, der gestanzt, hinterdruckt und kaschiert wurde. Die Titelgrafik zeigt eine Abwicklung eines Kartons. Das erweiterte Vorwort wurde durch ein abweichendes Format und in einer anderen Farbigkeit vom Bericht abgesetzt und korrespondiert mit dem Jahresabschluss. Ein formularartiger Charakter, der sich an der grafischen Sprache von Lieferscheinen oder Ähnlichem orientiert, zeigt sich in Typographie und Seitenaufbau. Farbige Trenner als Register mit eigener Symbolik sind stilgebende Elemente und strukturieren den Bericht.

In accordance with the company's key business field of packaging, the annual report of D. Logistics AG is designed with a cover made from foam material. The material is punched, relief printed and laminated. The title graphics show the development of a cardboard box. The extended foreword differs from the management report in format and in color, and corresponds with the financial statements. Typography and layout are reminiscent of printed forms, taking up the graphic language of delivery notes and similar items. Colorful dividers employed as registers with specific symbolism provide structure and style to the entire report.

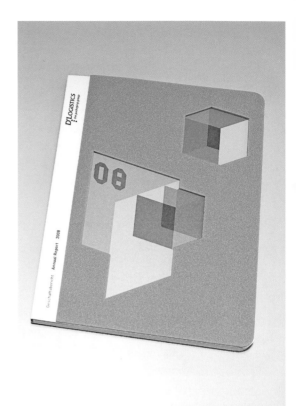

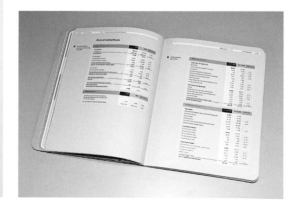

Project
SKW Schwarz Rechtsanwälte
Corporate Design

Design
hauser lacour kommunikationsgestaltung GmbH
Stefan Hauser, Elena Reiniger, Sabrina Köhler
Frankfurt a. M., Germany

Client
SKW Schwarz Rechtsanwälte
München, Germany

Einheit in der Vielfalt – dieses Motto transportiert das für die Sozietät neu entwickelte Erscheinungsbild. Die fünf Standorte der Partnergesellschaft forderten einen einheitlichen Auftritt, ohne dabei ihr Gesicht zu verlieren. Gestaltungsstil und Bildwelt des Corporate Design verbinden hierfür die stärksten Eigenschaften der Sozietät: Effizienz und Menschlichkeit. Die gradlinig kühle Gestaltung vermittelt fachliche Kompetenz und Einheit, kombiniert mit einer Bildsprache, die eine persönliche Darstellung jedes Anwalts und Standorts leistet. Der Name „SKW Schwarz" fließt in die Farbwelt ein und schafft so eine besondere Prägnanz der Marke.

Unity in diversity – this motto conveys the newly created corporate identity for the legal practice. The partner company's five offices required a uniform appearance, without sacrificing their individuality. To this end, the style and visual elements of the corporate design combine the practice's strongest qualities, namely, efficiency and humanity. The cool, linear design communicates specialist competence and unity, combined with a visual language which personally represents each lawyer and branch. The name "SKW Schwarz" will be adequately rendered in color and thus will create an especial conciseness for the brand.

Project
Sun at Work
Geschäftsbericht 2008
Annual report 2008

Design
Strichpunkt GmbH
strichpunkt design
Stuttgart, Germany
Sandra Schuck (Fotografie)
Berlin, Germany
Graphische Betriebe Eberl GmbH (Druck)
Immenstadt im Allgäu, Germany

Client
SolarWorld AG
Bonn, Germany

Sun at Work – Der Bericht des führenden Solarkonzerns nimmt die Leser mit auf eine Reise rund um die Welt. Bildreportagen aus sechs Ländern zeigen wie SolarWorld das unerschöpfliche Potenzial der Sonne nutzbar macht – für Menschen in Entwicklungsländern, für Eigenheimbesitzer, für Arbeitnehmer und nicht zuletzt für die Aktionäre des im deutschen TecDAX notierten Unternehmens. Der Schwerpunkt des Berichts liegt auf der umfassenden Darstellung nachhaltiger Aspekte und in der Verzahnung ökonomischer, ökologischer und sozialer Themen. Ein auf dem Umschlag platzierter Sticker und die beigelegte „Solare Weltkarte" ergänzen den Bericht.

Sun at Work – the report by this leading solar company takes readers on a round-the-world journey. Picture reports from six countries show how SolarWorld utilises the never-ending potential of the sun – for people in developing countries, home-owners, people at work and – not least – for shareholders in the company, which is listed on Germany's TecDAX. The report focuses on the comprehensive representation of sustainable aspects and the dovetailing of economical, ecological and social topics. A sticker on the envelope and the enclosed "Solar map of the world" complete the report.

Project
Standfest seit 1894.
Geschäftsbericht
Annual report

Design
dietrabanten
Büro für Kommunikationsdesign
Friederike Hujer (CD)
Claudia Wanke, Andreja Medved,
Lothar Reusch (Konzept und Text)
München, Germany

Client
Raiffeisenbank Kleinwalsertal AG
Riezlern, Austria

Die Raiffeisenbank Kleinwalsertal rückt organisches Wachstum in den Fokus ihres Geschäftsberichts 2008. Anhand eines Baumstamms visualisiert er auf anschauliche Weise die historisch gewachsene Vielfalt einer alpenländisch verankerten Bankenge-schichte. Wachsende Kreisstanzungen, die sich Seite für Seite durch den Bericht ziehen, simulieren Jah-resringe. So werden auf haptisch nachvollziehbare Weise Wachstum und stetige Veränderung der einzel-nen Geschäftsfelder transparent. Die zeitlos warme Bildsprache unterstreicht den Gesamteindruck einer Bank, die traditionelle Verwurzelung und globale Verantwortung über den schnellen Erfolg stellt.

The Raiffeisenbank Kleinwalsertal AG's annual re-port 2008 draws attention to organic growth. In a simple and vivid way it visualizes the bank's alpine-anchored history using the example of a tree trunk: punched holes, that run through the reports pages, simulate increasing annual rings. Thus growth and constant change of single business units in the stress field between nature and modern imperatives be-come touchable transparent. The reports warm and organic appearance underlines the overall impression of a bank that prefers local tradition and global re-sponsibility to fast success.

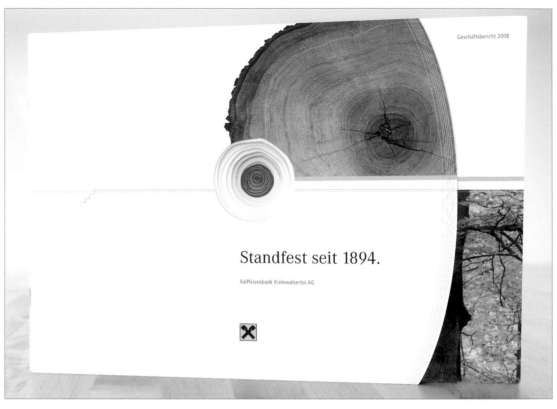

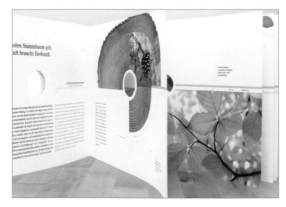

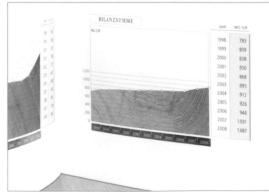

Project
4010 – Die Marke in Bewegung
Corporate Identity

Design
Mutabor Design GmbH
Heinrich Paravicini (CD)
Axel Domke (AD)
Nils Zimmermann (Designer)
Thomas Manig (Künstler)
Mate Steinforth, Timo Schädel, Jaquement Baptiste,
Rimantas Kukavicius (Filmanimation)
Ian Pooley (Musik)
Krieger des Lichts (Programmierung)
Susanne Weber (Reinzeichnung)
Hamburg, Germany

Client
Deutsche Telekom AG
Bonn, Germany

4010 ist der neue Concept-Store der Deutschen Telekom in Berlin Mitte. Der Name leitet sich aus dem Telekom-Magenta Farbwert RAL4010 ab. Die Idee: Eine Shop-Identität, die ständig in Bewegung ist für eine Zielgruppe, die niemals schläft. Die Lösung: Eine fortwährende gestalterische Weiterentwicklung der Ziffern 4010 – permanente Veränderung als einzige Konstante. Internationale Künstler und Designer aus der Zielgruppe werden eingeladen, an der Inszenierung der Videos, Wände und Schriftzüge mitzuwirken. Die Ergebnisse laufen in einem kontinuierlich wachsenden Medien-Loop zusammen. Ein neuer Aspekt des Telekom Markenbildes: „Erleben was verbindet."

4010 is the new Deutsche Telekom concept store in Central Berlin. The name comes from the RAL color code for Telekom's magenta brand color. The idea: A shop identity that never looks the same – for an audience that never acts the same. The solution: An ongoing typographic interpretation of the numbers 4010, permanent change is the only constant. International artists and designers were commissioned to contribute their interpretation to a constantly growing media loop. The result is sharpening up Telekom's brand image from within the target group itself: "Life's for Sharing."

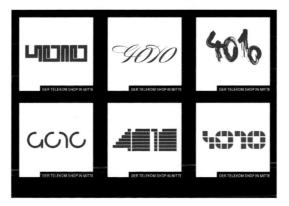

Project
zu tisch / à la carte
Kundenmagazin
Customer magazine

Design
G+J Corporate Media GmbH
Regine Smith-Thyme
Hamburg, Germany

Client
Miele & Cie. KG
Gütersloh, Germany

Um bei Haushaltsgeräten Emotionen auszulösen, bedarf es einer Inszenierung, die den aus der Technik entstehenden Nutzen dramatisiert. Das Miele-Kundenmagazin „zu tisch" und die internationale Ausgabe „à la carte" werden diesem Anspruch gerecht, indem sie die Begriffe Genuss, Ernährung und Lebensart für eine anspruchsvolle Leserschaft mit Leben füllen. Im Fokus beider Magazine stehen Speisen, die mit Liebe zubereitet und mit Genuss verzehrt werden. Miele-Produkte sind da ganz souverän funktionales wie formschönes Mittel zum Zweck. Der Mantelteil ist inhaltlich breit gefächert – mit Themen rund ums Kochen, um Reise und Kultur. Als Heft-im-Heft informiert die „Miele Welt" über Aktuelles aus dem Unternehmen. Durch diese – inhaltlich wie optisch – deutliche Trennung erhält das Magazin eine klar definierte Struktur. „zu tisch/á la carte" sind Kundenmagazine voller Unterhaltungswert und hohem Serviceanspruch, die dank der exklusiven Inhalte einen adäquaten Rahmen bieten, um das herausragende Image von Miele überzeugend zu vermitteln. Die internationale Ausgabe erscheint z. Zt. in Russland, Tschechien, Spanien, Mexiko und Chile.

Triggering emotions for home appliances requires a production that dramatises the benefits arising from technology. The Miele "zu tisch" customer magazine and the international "à la carte" edition meet this requirement by filling the concepts of pleasure, nutrition and lifestyle with life for a discerning readership. The focus of the magazines is on food prepared with loving care and eaten with pleasure. Here Miele products are a very masterfully functional and elegant means to the end. The front section offers a wide spectrum of content – with topics dealing with cooking, travel and culture. As an insert in the magazine "The World of Miele" provides news from the company. Through this clear separation of content and appearance the magazine achieves a clearly defined structure. "zu tisch/à la carte" are customer magazines full of entertainment value and high service standards that due to the exclusive content provide an appropriate framework for convincingly communicating the out standing image of Miele. The international edition is currently published in Russia, the Czech Republic, Spain, Mexico and Chile.

НЕБЕСА ПОДОЖДУТ!

С научной точки зрения, Средиземное море – это водная поверхность площадью в 2,5 млн кв.км, обеспечивающая окружающим ее территориям жаркое сухое лето и мягкую зиму. Благоприятный климат приносит замечательные плоды.

Project
zeroninezero
Buch zur Imagebildung der Agentur
Corporate image book

Design
admembers advertising
Hushang Omidizadeh, Anne Christine Petruck
Düsseldorf, Germany

Client
admembers advertising
Düsseldorf, Germany

Das Buch „zeroninezero" entstand als Imagebroschüre für admembers advertising, entwickelte sich aber rasch auch zu einem künstlerisch-philosophischen Werk. Dessen ungeachtet wurde entschieden, es in unveränderter Form herauszugeben. Das Ziel des Buches ist es zu demonstrieren, wie weit man in der Mode-Bildgestaltung gehen kann, ohne das eigentliche Ziel aus den Augen zu verlieren. Die Story, eine locker erzählte Agenten-Geschichte, dient zur Unterstützung der Bilder und gibt ihnen den nötigen Rahmen. Die fantastischen Bilder machte der renommierte Modefotograf Michael Reh. Die Resonanz auf dieses ungewöhnliche Mailing war überwältigend.

Created as an image book for admembers advertising, the book "zeroninezero" expended itself very fast, also with the artistic-philosophic artwork. Nevertheless the admembers decided to send an unchanged form out. The intention of zeroninezero is to demonstrate how far you can get in the fashion-artwork, without losing the sight of real purpose. The storyline, a funny secret-agent-story, is benefit of the pictures and gives them the necessary coverage. The fantastic pictures were taken by the well-known fashion-photographer Michael Reh. The feedback of this, in fashion work exceptional, mailings was very satisfying.

Project
zvbn Leitbild
Broschüre
Brochure

Design
via roeper Erfolgskommunikation GmbH
Almut Röper (Creative Direction)
Aenne Storm (Design, Illustration)
Holger Sinn (Projekt Management)
Guido Strotkötter (Text)
Thorsten Breyer (Produktion)
Bremen, Germany

Client
zvbn
zweckverband verkehrsverbund bremen/
niedersachsen
Bremen, Germany

Wie macht man Unternehmensgrundsätze anfassbar? Mit knappen Texten und einfachen Illustrationen verdeutlicht diese Broschüre einprägsam das Leitbild eines im Verkehrsbereich tätigen Verbands. Der Original-Bushandgriff, der die gefächerte Broschüre zusammenhält, stimmt schon beim ersten Anblick auf das Thema ein und lässt den Empfänger sofort „begreifen".

How do you approach to business values?
By using short texts and simple illustrations this brochure points out the mission statement of an association mediating in traffic business. The original handle of a bus which keeps the pages together gives an idea of the topic immediately.

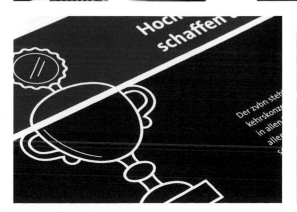

Project
Designreisen
Geschäftsausstattung
Office equipment

Design
Martin et Karczinski GmbH
Peter Martin, Nadine Arau Mussons,
Hélène Kratz, Rafael Dietzel
München, Germany

Client
Designreisen GmbH
München, Germany

Die Designreisen-Geschäftsausstattung vermittelt Perfektion und Leidenschaft. Dieser exklusive Markencharakter wird mittels Wort-Bildmarke, Typografie und Farbwahl transportiert. So bringt edles Schwarz, Weiß und Bronze die besondere Eleganz und den Premiumcharakter von Designreisen zum Ausdruck – zusätzlich betont durch produktionstechnische Veredelungen wie Heißfolienprägung und Siebdruck. Individuell wirkt die Marke auch durch das einprägsame Typografiekonzept. Einen hohen Wiedererkennungswert haben zudem die beiden Paradiesvögel, die das Logo prägen und im übertragenen Sinne den Weg in die schönsten Paradiese dieser Erde weisen.

The Designreisen office equipment offers a convincing impression of the perfection and passion. The exclusive character of the brand is conveyed through the word and figurative mark, typography and the selection of colors. Thus noble black, white and bronze express the special elegance and the premium character of Designreisen – additionally emphasised by production technique finishing such as hot foil stamping and screen printing. The brand has an individual appearance due to its expressive typography concept. The latter is characterised by two birds of paradise that metaphorically show the way to the most beautiful paradises on earth.

Project
Amnesty International
Broschüre
Brochure

Design
Scholz & Friends Identify
Wolf Schneider (Creative Direction)
Kathrin Wetzel, Olivier Nowak,
Maria-Michaela Tonn, Vera Müller (Art Direction)
Anna Kubitza (Beratung)
Berlin, Germany

Client
Amnesty International
Berlin, Germany

Mehr Wirkung für die Menschenrechte durch ein neues internationales Erscheinungsbild für Amnesty International. Die neue Identität ist geprägt durch ein Symbol für Unterdrückung und Hoffnung, eine Farbwelt für Aufmerksamkeit und Dringlichkeit, eine authentische und dokumentarische Bildsprache, eine Typographie für Fakten und Aktionen – für eine weltweite Wiedererkennbarkeit und einfache Anwendbarkeit. Allein im Rahmen des Einführungsprozesses für Deutschland wurden die Markenarchitektur und alle Kommunikationsmittel überarbeitet. Die mehr als 20.000 Mitglieder erhielten ein einfaches „Toolkit" mit allen Werkzeugen für die tägliche Arbeit.

More effectiveness in the battle for human rights through a new international visual profile of the world's largest human rights organization – Amnesty International. The new international visual identity is marked by a symbol of suppression and hope, a color world that draws attention and expresses urgency, an authentic and documentary-style visual language, and a typeface that is suitable for conveying facts and for campaigns – promoting global recognizability and easy applicability. During the launch process in Germany alone the brand architecture and all communication media were revised. The more than 20,000 members got an easy toolkit with all tools for the daily work.

Project
K-ARTS
Broschüre
Brochure

Design
InterGram
Dan Ahn, Eun-Hee Ko, Gap-Sik Jang,
Inoh Ryu, Son Injong
Seoul, South Korea

Client
Korea National University of Arts
Seoul, South Korea

K-ARTS unterscheidet sich deutlich von den Broschüren anderer Universitäten. Statt trockene Fakten zu präsentieren, spricht sie von der Leidenschaft für Kunst und die durch diese geschaffenen Werte. Sie gleicht einem Tempel, einem Ort für ein Miteinander von Kreativität und Kontemplation. Beim Lesen wandelt man gewissermaßen durch eine Kultstätte, mit einem Gedicht des Universitätspräsidenten Ji-woo Hwang als Höhepunkt. So werden unveränderliche Werte und der Respekt vor dem Lernen vermittelt. Recycling-Papier symbolisiert, dass sich Kunst in einem Spannungsfeld zwischen Konflikt und Eintracht mit der Welt bewegt.

The K-ARTS brochure is intrinsically different from those of other universities. Rather than dryly providing academic information, it conveys the school's passion for art and the social value it creates. In design terms, the brochure resembles a temple, a place where creativity and contemplation coexist. The contents are presented to mimic the experience of walking through a temple, highlighted by a poem from eminent poet and University President Ji-woo Hwang. The effect is one of appreciating intangible values and respect for learning. Recycled paper symbolizes the way in which art can exist in both conflict and harmony with the world.

Project
Messekommunikation
Einladung und Broschüre
Invitation and brochure

Design
Jäger & Jäger
Olaf Jäger, Regina Jäger
Überlingen, Germany

Client
Nils Holger Moormann GmbH
Aschau im Chiemgau, Germany

Die Nils Holger Moormann GmbH stellt auf der diesjährigen Mailänder Möbelmesse sechs Neuheiten vor: „Mobel am Rande der Verkäutlichkeit". In Einladung und Messebroschüre werden die Möbel als Scherenschnitte gezeigt. Mit Hilfe der Transparenz des Dünndruckpapiers entsteht in der Broschüre ein Dialog zwischen dem Möbelstück und seinem wesentlichen Merkmal.

The Nils Holger Moormann GmbH presents six new products at the 2009 Milan Furniture Fair. "Furniture on the brink of saleability". In invitations and brochures, the new products are shown as silhouettes. By means of the transparency of the brochure paper a dialogue is created between the new product and its central feature.

Project
Audi magazin
Automobilmagazin
Automotive magazine

Design
loved gmbh
Sabine Cole, Phillip Bittner, Jan-Christoph Prilop,
Mieke Haase, Peter Matz,
Sandra Rehder, Penelope Toro
Hamburg, Germany

Client
AUDI AG
Ingolstadt, Germany

Das Audi magazin versteht sich als Premium-Automobilmagazin und orientiert sich an klassischen Publikumstiteln aus den Bereichen Automobil, Sport und Lifestyle. In den Kapiteln „drive", „move", und „inspire" gibt das Audi magazin in Form von Reportagen, Features und Interviews Einblicke in Produkt, Unternehmen und Markenwelt. Bekannte Journalisten und Fotografen aus dem Magazinbereich garantieren höchste Qualität, außergewöhnliche Ideen und eine professionelle Umsetzung. Weltweit hat das Audi magazin eine Auflage von neun Millionen Exemplaren und erscheint in 34 Sprachen.

The Audi magazin is a premium automobile magazine. The editorial and visual concept is inspired by leading lifestyle, automotive and sports magazines. The Audi magazin gives insights of the brand, products and the world of Audi to the readership in its new created chapters "drive", "move" and "inspire". Well-known photographers and writers guarantee high quality, surprising ideas and professional implementation. The worldwide coverage is up to nine million and translated in 34 languages.

Project
TATENDRANG
Magazin
Magazine

Design
LIQUID Agentur für Gestaltung GbR
Martin Stich (Art Direction)
Carina Orschulko, Ilja Sallacz (Creative Direction)
Augsburg, Germany

Client
LIQUID | Presse & mehr | Druckerei
Joh. Walch | MS Marketing ServiceS
Augsburg, Germany

TATENDRANG ist ein von vier Augsburger Unternehmen herausgegebenes, kostenloses Magazin von Un-
ternehmern für Unternehmer. TATENDRANG richtet
sich mit vier Themenheften im Jahr an Marketing-
spezialisten und Führungskräfte. Ausgabe 15 hat den
Themenschwerpunkt „Werbung". Das Bildkonzept
dieses Heftes ist auffallend und bleibt im Gedächtnis.
Neonfarbe auf den Bildern markiert Werbeflächen
und macht die Intensität deutlich, mit der uns Werbung „draußen" begegnet. Im redaktionellen Teil er-
fährt der Leser, wie man sich mit kreativen Ideen und
konsequenten Strategien gezielt in Szene setzt.

TATENDRANG is a free-of-charge magazine published by four Augsburg based entrepreneurs for
entrepreneurs. With four issues a year, TATENDRANG
is addressed to marketing specialists and executive
managers. Issue 15 has its focus on advertisement.
The style of the pictures in this issue is eye-catching
and leaves a lasting impression on the viewer. Neon-
colored fields in the pictures flag advertising space
and reveal the intensity with which advertisement
hits us out there. The editorial section explains how
to play to the gallery with creative ideas and a consistent strategy.

Project
impact
Unternehmensmagazin
Corporate magazine

Design
BurdaYukom Publishing GmbH
Kim Kranz, Markus Czeslik, Thomas Escher,
Dr. Christian Fill, Alexander Gutzmer,
Blasius Thätter, Olaf Puppe, Sabine Skrobek,
Beate Blank, Michelle Otto
München, Germany

Client
Fujitsu Siemens Computers
München, Germany

Fujitsu Siemens Computers gelingt mit seinem IT-Executive-Magazin „impact" europaweit einmalig die Kombination aus strategischen IT-, Management- und exklusiven Lifestyle-Themen. In den Fokus rücken erfolgreiche CIOs, die in ihren Unternehmen europaweit Benchmarks setzen und nicht nur trockene Theorien verkünden sowie renommierte Entrepreneure, die neue Wege in der Unternehmensführung gehen. Jede Ausgabe fächert ein Schwerpunktthema unter völlig neuen Gesichtspunkten auf, wobei Fujitsu Siemens Computers als Unternehmen dezent im Hintergrund bleibt. Die Bildsprache ist klar, modern und ausdrucksstark.

With its European IT executive magazine "impact", Fujitsu Siemens Computers has succeeded at uniquely combining strategic IT and management topics with exclusive lifestyle themes. The focus is placed on successful CIOs who, in their own companies, set benchmarks throughout Europe. These are people who do not merely recite dry theories – rather, they are renowned entrepreneurs who forge new paths in business management. Each issue explores a particular topic from completely new viewpoints, while Fujitsu Siemens Computers as a company remains unobtrusively in the background. The picture language is clear, modern and expressive.

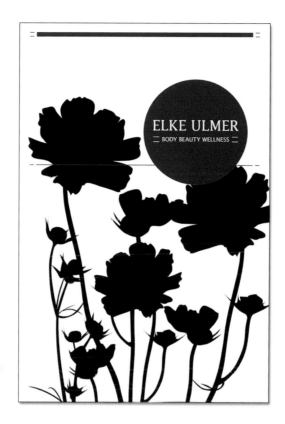

Project
Elke Ulmer
Corporate Design

Design
RD STUDIO
Frank Rösner, Rebecca Ulmer
Stuttgart, Germany

Client
Elke Ulmer
Body Beauty Wellness
Schömberg, Germany

„Elke Ulmer – Body Beauty Wellness" ist ein Institut für Kosmetik- und Wellnessanwendungen. Ziel des Gestaltungsauftrags war die Entwicklung eines klaren sympathischen Erscheinungsbildes, das auf gängige Wellness-Stereotypen verzichtet. Das Konzept behandelt die Verbindung von natürlicher Schönheit und biologischen Produkten. Dieses Thema wird ganzheitlich über die Visualisierung verschiedener Pflanzenformen transportiert. Der im Logo verankerte Beeren-Farbton und die grafische Darstellung der Pflanzen schlagen die Brücke zwischen der Natürlichkeit der Wirkstoffe und der Innovation, der vom Institut praktizierten Behandlungen.

"Elke Ulmer – Beauty Body Wellness" is an institute for cosmetics and wellness treatments. The design task was to develop a clear and friendly appearance – doing without the common wellness stereotypes. The concept embraces the connection of natural beauty and organic products. This issue is conveyed holistically by using the illustration of numerous types of plants. Furthermore the berry colors used in the logo and the graphic illustration of the plants build a bridge to the organic substances and the innovation used in the institute's treatments.

Project
Bayer-Geschäftsbericht
Geschäftsbericht 2008
Annual report 2008

Design
Bayer AG
Leverkusen, Germany

Client
Bayer AG
Leverkusen, Germany

Der Magazinteil vermittelt mit Text und Fotos die „Faszination Bayer" emotional und authentisch. Eingeleitet wird er mit dem Konzernartikel „Welt im Wandel", gefolgt von Forschungsberichten aus den Teilkonzernen „HealthCare", „CropScience" und „MaterialScience". Die Neukonzeption von Farben, Grafiken und Tabellen sowie eine klare Gliederung erhöhen die Funktionalität und Attraktivität. Eine Stanzung erlaubt den direkten Zugriff auf Lagebericht und Konzernabschluss. Es wurden lösemittelarme Farben und wasserbasierende Lacke eingesetzt. Die CO_2-Emissionen wurden durch den „Klimaneutralen Druck" kompensiert. Das Papier ist nach FSC zertifiziert.

The magazine section uses text and photos to communicate the fascination of Bayer in an emotional and authentic way. It starts with the Bayer Group article entitled "A Changing World". This is followed by reports detailing the research activities of our "HealthCare", "CropScience" and "MaterialScience" subgroups. The newly designed colors, graphics and tables coupled with a clear structure enhance the annual report's attractiveness and readability. A thumb tab provides direct access to the management report and consolidated financial statements. Solvent-free inks and waterborne coatings were used in producing the annual report. CO_2 emissions were compensated via "climate neutral print". The paper is FSC certified.

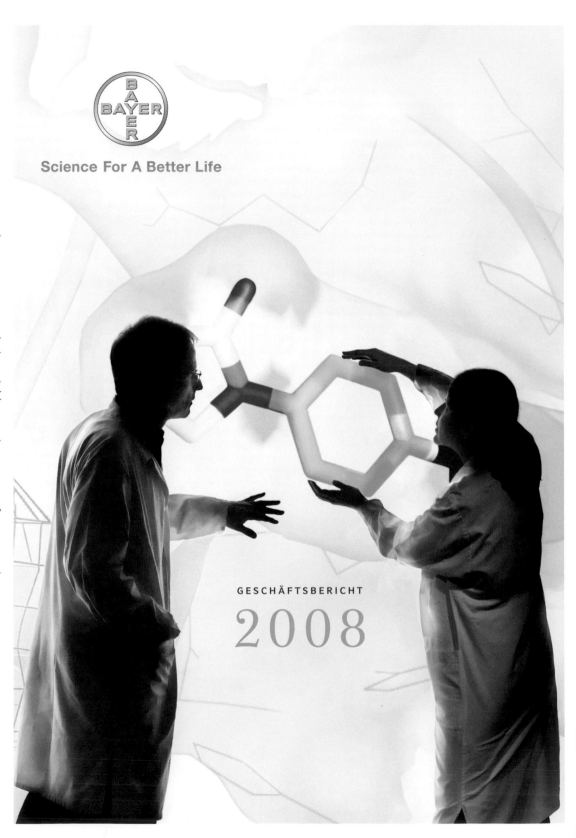

Science For A Better Life

GESCHÄFTSBERICHT
2008

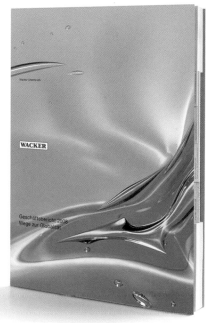

Project
WACKER Chemie – „Wege zur Globalität"
Geschäftsbericht 2008
Annual report 2008

Design
häfelinger + wagner design
Frank Wagner, Sandra Gieseler
München, Germany

Client
Wacker Chemie AG
München, Germany

Der Geschäftsbericht unter dem Motto „Wege zur Globalität" ist zweiter Teil einer Trilogie. Er fokussiert das Unternehmen als global agierenden Partner mit starkem lokalem Bezug zu Kunde und Kultur, der „Globalität" im täglichen Unternehmensalltag begreift und umsetzt. Die Umsetzung des Themas Globalität wird anhand von vier Reportagen mit je zwei Kommunikationsebenen – eine global-kulturelle Ebene und eine produkt- und unternehmensspezifische Ebene – anschaulich dokumentiert. Gestärkt wird die produktspezifische Ebene durch die Abbildung eines Wacker-Grundstoffes und einer jeweiligen Anwendung auf dem Titel und den Kapiteltrennseiten.

The annual report with the slogan "Paths to Globalism" is the second part in a trilogy. It focuses on the company as a global partner with strong local relationships to clients and culture, which understands and implements "globality" in day-to-day business. The realisation of the subject of globality is clearly documented through four reports, each with two communication levels – a global-cultural level and a product and company-specific level. The product-specific level is strengthened through the image of a Wacker raw material and a related use on the title and chapter separation pages.

Project
Fresenius Medical Care – „Innovationen zum Leben"
Geschäftsbericht 2007
Annual report 2007

Design
häfelinger + wagner design
Frank Wagner, Christopher Biel
München, Germany

Client
Fresenius Medical Care AG & Co. KGaA
Bad Homburg, Germany

Der Geschäftsbericht zeigt die Innovationsführerschaft der Fresenius Medical Care, indem anhand weltweit durchgeführter Reportagen von verschiedenen – die Innovationskraft bestätigenden – Aspekten berichtet wird. Im zweiten Teil jeder Reportage werden die technisch-medizinischen Zusammenhänge nochmals erläutert. Somit beinhaltet der Geschäftsbericht nicht nur eine Darstellung der Unternehmensstärken, sondern auch einen Imageteil, der das individuelle Wissen vertieft: Das Vorwort ist in einem speziellen Briefformat und in Teilen handgeschrieben, was den persönlichen Bezug unterstreicht.

The annual report demonstrates the innovative leadership of Fresenius Medical Care by means of five different reports carried out worldwide, dealing with various aspects which confirm this innovation. In the second part of one report in particular, the technical and medical connections are commented on again. Thus, the company report does not just comprise an account of the strengths of the company, but also broadens your own horizons. The foreword is in a special letter format and is partly handwritten, thus underlining the personal significance.

Project
Fresenius Medical Care – „VERTRAUEN leben"
Geschäftsbericht 2008
Annual report 2008

Design
häfelinger + wagner design
Frank Wagner, Sandra Gieseler
München, Germany

Client
Fresenius Medical Care AG & Co. KGaA
Bad Homburg, Germany

Im Fokus des Geschäftsberichts „VERTRAUEN leben"
steht die Dimension des Themenschwerpunkts „Qualität für ein Gesundheitsunternehmen". Das Motto
vermittelt den Anspruch, Qualität im gesamten Unternehmen zu leben, und so dem Patientenbedürfnis
optimal gerecht werden zu können. Den Kerngedan-
ken setzt die Imagestrecke auf zwei Erzählebenen
um. Auf der Hauptebene über ein Interview zu unterschiedlichen Qualitätsaspekten des Unternehmens
zwischen dem Vorstandsvorsitzenden und einer Ne-
phrologin. Die zweite Erzählebene ist die Themen-
ebene, die in das Interview eingestreut ist. Vertreten
durch vier Mitarbeiter beinhaltet sie vier vertiefende
Stories zu verschiedenen Qualitätsaspekten.

The annual report "living CONFIDENCE" focuses on
the meaning of quality for a health organisation. The
slogan delivers the message of implementing quality
throughout the whole company, thus meeting pa-
tient needs in the best possible way. The image gallery materialises the main idea on two narrative levels.
On the main level it uses an interview on various
company quality aspects between the CEO and a
nephrologist; on the subject level – interspersed with
the interview – it offers more details through four
stories on different quality aspects illustrated by four
employees.

Project
TyssenKrupp –
„Einblicke. Unsere Mitarbeiter. Unsere Zukunft."
Geschäftsbericht 2007–2008
Annual report 2007–2008

Design
häfelinger + wagner design
Annette Häfelinger-Wagner, Nils Jaedicke,
Sascha Obermüller
München, Germany

Client
ThyssenKrupp AG
Düsseldorf, Germany

Fokus des ThyssenKrupp-Geschäftsberichts sind die
Mitarbeiterqualifikation und -förderung als Schlüssel
zum Unternehmenserfolg. Die Idee ist, einen Blick in
die Unternehmenskultur zu vermitteln, die wie ein
„Treibhaus" Engagement und Kreativität fördert. Ein
herausnehmbares Magazin zeigt selektive „Einblicke"
in Förderprogramme als repräsentative Bandbreite
quer durch Hierarchien, Länder und Kulturen. Sieben
Reportagen stellen, als journalistischer und gestal-
terischer „Potpourri", bemerkenswerte Lebens- und
Berufswege von Mitarbeitern vor. Jedes dieser Beispiele steht für eine Konzernhaltung bezogen auf
seine Mitarbeiterkultur.

The focus of the ThyssenKrupp annual report is
employee qualification and promotion as the key to
company success. The idea is to allow a glimpse
into the company culture which cultivates commitment and creativity like a "greenhouse". A detach-
able magazine shows selective "insights" into support programs as a representative spectrum across
hierarchies, cultures and countries. Seven reports present remarkable life and career paths of employees
as a journalistic and creative "potpourri". Each one of
these examples represents a company attitude relating to its employees.

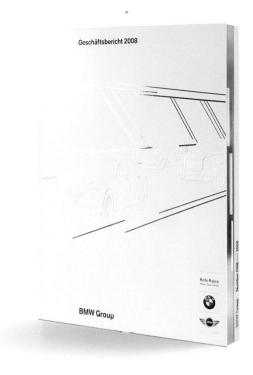

Project
BMW Group –
„Number One. Herausforderung Zukunft"
Geschäftsbericht 2008
Annual report 2008

Design
häfelinger + wagner design
Frank Wagner, Stefan Kaderka, Manuel Rigel
München, Germany

Client
BMW AG
München, Germany

Mit dem Geschäftsbericht 2008 wurde eine neue Trilogie eingeleitet, die den Geschäftsbericht der BMW Group von Grund auf neu definiert. Die im Vorjahr eingeführte strategische Neuausrichtung ist Metathema des 90-seitigen Imageteils. Das kreative Leitthema „Balance" interpretiert die strategische Neuausrichtung auf fast jeder Seite in innovativer Weise neu. Der Bericht unterstreicht damit den kreativen Ingenieursgeist sowie die Strategie des Unternehmens. Die BMW Group erfindet sich neu. Das ist die Grundaussage dieses Geschäftsberichtes. Das den Leser spüren zu lassen, war oberstes Anliegen bei der Entwicklung dieser herausragenden Konzeption.

The 2008 annual report introduced a new trilogy that radically redefines the BMW Group annual report. The strategic realignment that was introduced last year is the meta subject of the 90-page image section. The creative lead theme "Balance" innovatively reinterprets the strategic new direction on almost every page. The report thereby emphasizes the creative engineering spirit and the company strategy. The BMW Group is reinventing itself. That is the main message of this annual report. Allowing the reader to sense this was the main priority in the development of this outstanding design.

Project
adidas Group – „Our game plan"
Geschäftsbericht 2008
Annual report 2008

Design
häfelinger + wagner design
Frank Wagner, Christopher Biel
München, Germany

Client
adidas AG
Herzogenaurach, Germany

Die adidas Group und ihre Marken besitzen eine starke Identifikationskraft, die Sportler weltweit verbindet. Unter dem Motto „Our game plan" macht sich das Unternehmen die zielstrebige Sportlerhaltung zu eigen: Mittels strategischem Spielplan wird absolute Höchstleistung erreicht. Imagestrecke und Kapiteltrenner nehmen diese Leitidee auf, indem sie Ziele und Erfolge weltweiter Spitzenssportler inszenieren und in Beziehung zu den Unternehmenszielen und -erfolgen der adidas Group setzen. Als Ausdruck sportlicher Dynamik und zielorientierten Handelns ist die Pfeilthematik als durchgängiges Gestaltungselement angewendet.

The adidas Group and its brands enjoy strong recognition power, bringing together athletes from around the world. The slogan "Our game plan" allows the company to identify with an athlete's goal: it develops a strategic game plan, enabling it to achieve the best possible performance. An image gallery and chapter dividers incorporate this lead idea by presenting goals and successes of top-class global sports persons, and linking these to the goals/successes of the adidas Group. As an expression of sporting dynamics and goal-orientated action, the arrow theme is used as a universal design feature.

Project
BLKB
Geschäftsbericht 2008
Annual report 2008

Design
Eclat AG
Helm Pfohl (Art Direction)
Diana Sanusi (Design)
Erlenbach/Zürich, Switzerland
Basellandschaftliche Kantonalbank
Liestal, Switzerland

Client
Basellandschaftliche Kantonalbank
Liestal, Switzerland

Gemeinsam kann Außergewöhnliches erreicht werden. Auch Leistungen Einzelner werden oft erst möglich, wenn eine Gemeinschaft stärkend dahinter steht. Im Geschäftsbericht 2008 der Basellandschaftlichen Kantonalbank werden Menschen vorgestellt, die in und mit ihrem Verein Außergewöhnliches erreicht haben. Die leidenschaftlich und engagiert sind; bereit, etwas mehr zu geben. Der Fotograf Yann Gross hat ihre Geschichten eingefangen. Seine Bilder zeigen Menschen, die erfolgreich sind und dabei den Gemeinsinn bewahren. Konzept, Gestaltung, Texte der Bildseiten und redaktionelle Unterstützung kamen von Eclat.

Together, people can achieve extraordinary things. Often, accomplishments by individuals are only possible with the backup of their communities. The annual report of Basellandschaftliche Kantonalbank portrays people who have achieved extraordinary things in and with their clubs or their communities. People who are passionate and dedicated. People who are ready to give more. Photographer Yann Gross captured their stories. His photographies show people who are successful and have maintained their public spirit. Eclat was responsible for the concept, design and copy on the image pages.

Project
BKW FMB Energie AG
Geschäftsbericht 2008
Annual report 2008

Design
Eclat AG
Helm Pfohl (Art Direction)
Roger Mazzucchelli, Margit Feurer (Design)
Erlenbach/Zürich, Switzerland

Client
BKW FMB Energie AG
Bern, Switzerland

Energiequellen: Inspiration und Kraft
Die Alpen bilden ein gewaltiges Energiereservat. Sie
berühren mit ihrer Schönheit und Stille, inspirieren
Künstler und fordern Sportler zu Höchstleistungen
heraus. Und sie speichern riesige Wasservorkommen
zum Trinken, zum Transport und zur Stromgewinnung.
Neben den Bergen gibt es auch persönliche Energiequellen. Sie bringen Ausgleich, erfreuen die Seele
und beflügeln die Schaffenskraft. Die Bildseiten des
Geschäftsberichts 2008 zeigen, was die Herzen der
BKW-Partner höher schlagen lässt. Beat Schweizer
hat fotografiert und Eclat war zuständig für das Konzept, die Gestaltung und Texte der Bildseiten.

Energy Sources: Inspiration and Power
The Alps are a huge reservoir of energy. They touch
us with their beauty and calm, inspire artists and spur
athletes on to achieve peak performance. They also
store enormous amounts of water which we use for
drinking and transportation and to generate electricity. Alongside the mountains there are other, very
personal sources of energy that restore the daily balance of life, calm the spirit and boost our creative
powers. BKW set out to find where its partners draw
their personal energy from. Beat Schweizer took the
photos. Eclat was responsible for the concept, design
and texts on the image pages.

Project
Orell Füssli Holding
Geschäftsbericht 2008
Annual report 2008

Design
Eclat AG
Helm Pfohl (Art Direction)
Roger Mazzucchelli, Diana Sanusi (Design)
Erlenbach/Zürich, Switzerland

Client
Orell Füssli Holding AG
Zürich, Switzerland

Orell Füssli ist seit 1519 am Puls der Zeit. Der Geschäftsbericht 2008 positioniert Orell Füssli als internationales Industrie- und Handelsunternehmen mit den Kerngeschäften „Industriesysteme", „hochwertiger Banknotendruck", „Buchhandel" und „Verlagswesen". Mit einer bronzenen Bildwelt und Statements von Wirtschaftsgrößen zeigt der Bericht den Wert und die hohe Glaubwürdigkeit des Unternehmens Orell Füssli, das Tradition und weltweit führende Spitzentechnologie souverän verbindet. Beat Schweizer und Stephan Knecht haben fotografiert und Eclat war zuständig für das Konzept, die Gestaltung und Texte der Bildseiten.

Since 1519, Orell Füssli keeps up with the times. The 2008 annual report positions Orell Füssli as an international company for industry and commerce with the core businesses "Industrial Systems", "High-Quality Banknote Printing", "Book Trade" and "Publishing". The report with its imagery in bronze demonstrates the values and credibility of Orell Füssli, a company that competently brings together tradition and leading-edge technology. Beat Schweizer and Stephan Knecht were the photographers. Eclat was responsible for the concept, design and texts on the image pages.

Project
Der Mensch
Geschäftsbericht
Annual report

Design
Keim Identity GmbH
Matthias Keim
Zürich, Switzerland

Client
Suva (Unfallversicherung)
Luzern, Switzerland

Keim Identity, Zürich, hat für die Suva ein neues Gestaltungskonzept für den Geschäftsbericht entwickelt. Die Umsetzung für 2007 erfolgte Suva-intern. Thema der Bildgeschichte ist die gesellschaftliche Verantwortung der Suva. Sie zeigt mit großzügigen Bildern und persönlichen Berichten auf, wie die Suva durch ihren Produktemix von „Prävention", „Versicherung" und „Rehabilitation" dazu beiträgt, dass Menschen in ihr berufliches und soziales Umfeld integriert bleiben oder wieder integriert werden. Die Fotos sind von Stefan Minder. Der Berichtsteil macht die interessanten statistischen Zahlen durch Hervorhebungen und Piktogramme leicht zugänglich.

Keim Identity, Zurich, has developed a new design for the Suva annual report. The layout and contents for 2007 were made by Suva internally. The picture story shows the social responsibility of Suva. Impressive picture sceneries and personal stories illustrate how Suva helps to keep people integrated in their social environment or helps to reintegrate them by its mix of prevention, insurance and rehabilitation. The photos are made by Stefan Minder. The report makes interesting statistics easily accessible through typography and pictograms.

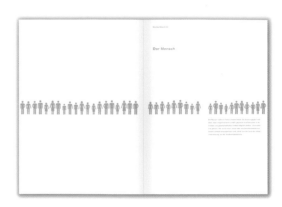

Project
zehn.
Jubiläumsmagazin
Jubilee magazine

Design
Bassier, Bergmann & Kindler
Digital Sales and Brand Specialists GmbH
Thomas Kindler, Marco Meßer, Agnieszka Schejok
Oberhausen, Germany
JOUMI Art & Design
Jochen Zimmer, Miro Delija
Oberhausen, Germany

Client
Bassier, Bergmann & Kindler
Digital Sales and Brand Specialists GmbH
Oberhausen, Germany

Wie vermittelt man zehn Jahre erfolgreiche Agentur-geschichte und macht neugierig auf mehr? Vor dieser Herausforderung stand die New-Media-Agentur Bassier, Bergmann & Kindler anlässlich ihres zehnjährigen Jubiläums. Erwartet wurde wahrscheinlich ein digitales Magazin; BB&K entschied sich jedoch für den analogen Seitensprung und überraschte ihre Zielgruppen mit einer Zeitung. Auf 60 hochwertig und farbig gestalteten Seiten im DIN-A3-Format bietet die Zeitung interessante Best Practices, Interviews und Beiträge. Eine Hommage an die crossmedialen Herausforderungen der Kunden und gleichzeitig an zehn Jahre erfolgreiche Internetgeschichte.

How do you convey ten years of successful agency history and fuel everybody's curiosity for more at the same time? New media agency Bassier, Bergmann & Kindler was facing that particular challenge on the occasion of their 10th anniversary. Expectations for a likely digital magazine were running high; but BB&K decided to step sideways into the analogue world of a newspaper and took their target group by surprise. 60 premium-quality pages in broad sheet format provide appealing best practice examples, interviews and articles and honour clients' current cross-medial challenges while paying tribute to ten years of thriving internet history.

273

Project
804© Portfolio
Booklet

Design
804© GRAPHIC DESIGN
Helge Rieder, Oliver Henn
Düsseldorf, Germany

Client
804© GRAPHIC DESIGN
Düsseldorf, Germany

Agenturselbstdarstellung: Die Verwendung einer (verdeckten) Wire-O-Bindung ermöglicht es uns, das Booklet auch kurzfristig mit aktuellen Arbeiten zu ergänzen. Um einen „industriellen, handwerklichen Look" zu erreichen, haben wir für die Umsetzung des Umschlags rauen Karton, Siebdruck und Sticker eingesetzt.

Agency profile: The choice of the separate, double folded cover and the wire-o-binding offers us the possibility to update the booklet on a short run. To achieve a slightly industrial look we've used rough cardboard, silk-screen printing and a sticker for the production of the cover.

Project
The Slade School of Fine Art
Drei Broschüren
Three brochures

Design
Paarpiloten
Nanni Goebel, Christopher Wiehl, Kathrin Roussel
Düsseldorf, Germany

Client
The Slade School of Fine Art
London, United Kingdom

Die Slade School of Fine Art ist eine international renommierte Kunsthochschule in London. Der visuelle Auftritt der Slade zeichnet sich durch große plakative Typografie aus. Die Besonderheit aller Broschüren ist, dass sich Texte und Bilder fortlaufend durchziehen. Deshalb werden die Broschüren von unten nach oben geblättert. In der Kursbroschüre sind die Informationen über den B. A.-Studiengang (hellgrün) und den M. A.-Studiengang (blau) in kleinen farbigen Heftchen eingebunden und heben sich so vom allgemeinen Teil der Broschüre ab. Die Broschüre für die Sommerkurse benutzt Neonorange und die RDP-Broschüre das Blau der M. A.-Studiengänge.

The Slade School of Fine Art is an internationally renowned art school in London. Large typography and striking colors characterise the visual identity of the Slade. The distinctive feature of all brochures is that text and images are compiled in a continuous format. Therefore the brochure pages are turned from bottom to top. Information on the courses is incorporated in small, colored segments (blue for graduate studies and light green for undergraduate studies) that stand out from the rest of the text in the course brochure. The Summer School brochure uses fluorescent orange, the RDP brochure the blue color of the graduate courses.

Project
MorphoSys Geschäftsbericht
Geschäftsbericht 2008
Annual report 2008

Design
3st kommunikation GmbH
Astrid Baumann, Marcel Teine
Mainz, Germany

Client
MorphoSys AG
Martinsried/Planegg, Germany

Grundlage des Erfolgs von MorphoSys bildet die eigene Antikörperbibliothek „HuCAL GOLD". Die Farbe Gold steht gleichzeitig für den technologischen Führungsanspruch und sorgt für visuelle Eigenständigkeit innerhalb der Branche. Der Weg „Von der Technologie zum Produkt" wird bereits auf dem Titel grafisch illustriert und mit einer Heißfolienprägung veredelt. Das gestanzte „Y" symbolisiert das Zielmolekül des humanen Antikörpers und führt den Leser elegant in den Innenteil des Berichts. Der Einsatz von Farbfläche, Illustration und Fotografie macht die Trennseiten zu einem besonderen Erlebnis und vermittelt das Leitthema auf eigenständige Weise.

MorphoSys owes its success to "HuCAL GOLD", its proprietary antibody library. The color gold represents technological leadership, while at the same time making the report visually unique within the industry. The journey "From technology to product" is impressively illustrated on the cover page with a hot foil stamping finish. The stamped "Y" symbolises the human antibody target molecule and guides the reader elegantly into the report. The use of colored backgrounds, illustrations and photographs gives a special feel to the dividing pages of this report and serves as a unique way of presenting the key topic.

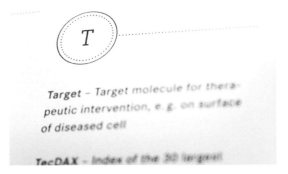

T

Target – Target molecule for therapeutic intervention, e. g. on surface of diseased cell

TecDAX – Index of the 30 largest

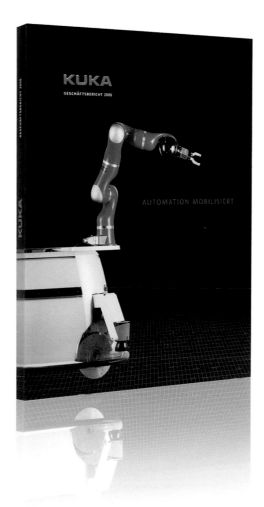

Project
KUKA Geschäftsbericht
Geschäftsbericht 2008
Annual report 2008

Design
3st kommunikation GmbH
Anja Biebl, Florian Heine
Mainz, Germany

Client
KUKA AG
Augsburg, Germany

Die KUKA AG automatisiert Produktionsprozesse. Mit dem KUKA-Roboter entwickelt das Unternehmen Einzelaggregate, Roboterzellen und vollständig roboterbasierte Anlagen. Im Geschäftsbericht sorgt der Einsatz der Farben Orange und Schwarz für visuelle Eigenständigkeit und Dramaturgie, die den Leitgedanken „Automation mobilisiert" optisch in Szene setzt. Die expressiven Trennseiten betonen die Innovationskraft und die Wachstumspotenziale des faszinierenden Unternehmens. Prägung, Farbkontraste und s/w-Fotografie machen diesen Bericht zu einem kraftvollen und eigenständigen Report.

KUKA automates production processes. Using KUKA robots, KUKA develops and markets stand-alone machines, robot cells and entire robotic systems, helping their customers to achieve superior product quality and improve plant productivity. Using the visually dramatic colors of orange and black makes the report stand out and showcases the key message "Automation mobilises". The dividing pages express and accentuate the innovative power and growth potential of this fascinating company. Embossing, contrasting colors and black-and-white photography make this a powerful and unique report.

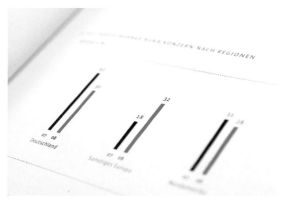

Project
Stihl Geschäftsbericht
Geschäftsbericht 2008
Annual report 2008

Design
3st kommunikation GmbH
Caroline Schmitt, Marcel Teine
Mainz, Germany

Client
Stihl AG & Co. KG
Waiblingen, Germany

Was Stihl antreibt, ist die Leidenschaft für Technik und kompromisslose Qualität. „Von der Idee zum Kunden" ist das Leitthema des Berichts und zeigt auf den Trennseiten Mitarbeiter entlang der Wertschöpfungskette, die sich dieser Philosophie verpflichtet fühlen. Der Umschlag greift das Leitthema subtil auf und zeigt ein Kunststoffmodell, das die „Idee" skizziert, die auf dem Rücktitel bereits ihren Weg zum Kunden gefunden hat. Die gradlinige Typographie spiegelt die Formsprache des modernen Produktdesigns wider. Das Layout sorgt für ein helles, freundliches Klima. Die Trennseiten überzeugen durch die ehrliche, journalistische Stilistik.

Stihl is driven by a passion for technology and for quality without compromise. The central theme of the report is "From concept to customer" and its dividing pages show staff through the value chain committed to this philosophy. The front and back cover also make a subtle reference to the slogan, with the former showing a plastic model drafting the "concept" which, on the back page, has found its way to the customer. The linear typography reflects the clear use of form in modern product design. The layout ensures that the report is lucid and accessible. The journalistic style of the dividing pages is a further winning feature.

Project
Volkswagen Geschäftsbericht
Geschäftsbericht 2008
Annual report 2008

Design
3st kommunikation GmbH
Caroline Schmitt, Florian Heine, Marcel Teine
Mainz, Germany

Client
Volkswagen AG
Konzern Kommunikation
Wolfsburg, Germany

Die Mobilität von morgen verlangt neue und mitreißende Ideen. Mit dem Slogan „Driving ideas" stellt der Geschäftsbericht 2008 die Antworten des größten europäischen Automobilherstellers auf die Herausforderungen der Zukunft in Form eines Magazinteils vor. Die Begriffe „Mensch", „Umwelt" und „Technik" bilden dabei den inhaltlichen Rahmen und geben mit 13 Stories spannende Einblicke in die Welt der Mobilität. Der Titel zeigt das zukunftsweisende Elektro-Fahrzeugkonzept „Space Up! Blue". Um die Abbildung schwebt eine Wort-Wolke mit Schlüsselbegriffen aus den Artikeln des Magazins, die durch einen partiellen UV-Lack hervorgehoben werden.

The mobility of tomorrow demands new and exciting ideas. With the slogan "Driving ideas", the company's annual report for 2008, presents the responses of Europe's largest motor vehicle manufacturer to the challenges of the future in the form of an integrated magazine. 13 stories, whose contents focus on the concepts of "People", "Environment" and "Technology", provide exciting insights into the world of mobility. The cover page shows the futuristic electric vehicle concept "Space Up! Blue". A word cloud floats around the illustration containing key terms taken from articles in the magazine. The words are emphasised by a partial UV lacquer.

Project
Deutsche Telekom
Corporate Fashion

Design
Interbrand
Marc T. Bernauer, Jana Haserodt, Nina Oswald
Köln, Germany
GMK by pepper
Guido Maria Kretschmer, Sabine Hülsbusch
Münster, Germany

Client
Deutsche Telekom AG
Bonn, Germany

Corporate Fashion ist eine ausgezeichnete Grundlage, um den Wandel eines Unternehmens nach innen und außen erlebbar zu machen: 240.000 Mitarbeiter zeigen bei der Deutschen Telekom täglich, für welche Marke sie arbeiten. Im Zuge des neuen Markenauftritts wurde für die Bereiche „Technischer Service", „Shop" und „Messe" eine neue Corporate-Fashion-Linie entwickelt, die Dynamik und Kompetenz mit einem modernen und innovativen Auftritt vereint und für das Markenversprechen „Erleben, was verbindet." steht. Ein „Kleiderschrank-System" ermöglicht es dem Mitarbeiter, aus verschiedenen Kollektionselementen wählen und selbst kombinieren zu können.

Holding a mirror up to corporate fashion is a good way to reflect on a company's experiences as it changes from within and externally. Everyday 240,000 Deutsche Telekom employees wear clothing that sports the brand they work for. In the course of developing a new brand identity, a new corporate fashion line was created for "service technicians", "shop personnel" and "trade fairs". The dynamic and competent profile of the company is portrayed by a modern and innovative CI which supports the brand promise "Life is for sharing". A "wardrobe system" makes it possible for employees to select and combine different pieces of clothing from the collection.

Project
Vogelsang Short Cut Nr. 7
Eigendarstellung
Agency brochure

Design
Vogelsang Konzeptagentur GmbH & Co. KG
Miriam Damati, Adrianna Drzisga,
Christian Schaffrath, Dirk Schalis
Grevenbroich, Germany

Client
Vogelsang Konzeptagentur GmbH & Co. KG
Grevenbroich, Germany

Die Vogelsang Konzeptagentur veröffentlicht für Kunden und Interessenten regelmäßig ihre aktuelle Eigendarstellung, den sogenannten „Short Cut". Mit seiner Hilfe können sie sich ein Bild über Philosophie, Leistungen und die jüngsten Projekte der Agentur machen. Der Short Cut Nr. 7 zeichnet sich durch seine individuelle, personalisierte Umschlaggestaltung aus. Passend zum Titel „Erfolgsrezepte" kann man jeden Short Cut – wie eine Menütafel – mit Kreide beschriften. Möglich wird dies durch den Druck des Umschlags mit Schiefertafelfarbe. Durch Fixierung der Aufschrift ermöglicht man dem Adressaten die problemlose Nutzung seines Unikats.

The Vogelsang Konzeptagentur regularly publishes an image presentation called "Short Cut" for all interested parties. It portrays the philosophy, the achievements and the most recent projects of the agency. The Short Cut No. 7 is characterized by an individual, personalized cover. Matching the title "recipe for success", its unique chalkboard-look and the slate-printed cover allows us to label every Short Cut with chalk. The label fixation enables the addressee to use his own personal edition without difficulty.

Project
Das Futurotop
Kundenmagazin
Customer magazine

Design
großgestalten GbR
Tobias Groß, Dominik Kirgus, Martin Schüngel
Köln, Germany

Client
Z_punkt, The Foresight Company
Köln, Germany

Falschprognosen, Future Charts, Trendvorhersagen, Zukunfts-Quiz, Was ist Zukunft, …
Das Kundenmagazin „Futurotop" von „Z_punkt, The Foresight Company" spielt mit dem Kernthema des Unternehmens: „Zukunft" (Corporate Foresight). Die Gestaltung setzt das Thema durch das große Format (DIN A3), die schwarz-weiße Farbgebung, den extremen Schriftmix, die kraftvolle Typografie, die harten Wechsel von hell-dunkel, groß-klein, laut-leise, das raue Recyclingpapier und die ungebundene Verarbeitung in Szene. So entsteht ein sehr eigenständiger, kreativer und experimentierfreudiger Eindruck und eine spannende, leichte, aber ebenso kurzweilige Lektüre.

False predictions, future charts, future quiz … The client magazine "Futurotop" published by "Z_punkt, The Foresight Company" plays with the company's core issue: "The Future" (Corporate Foresight). The magazine's design underscores the topic through its large standard paper size A3format, a black-and-white color scheme, an extreme mixture of typefaces, strong typography, a severe contrasting of light and dark, large and small, loud and muted, as well as its rough recycled paper and unbound execution. These elements create a quite independent, creative and bold impression and make for a gripping, light and equally entertaining read.

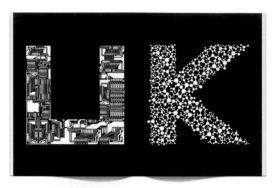
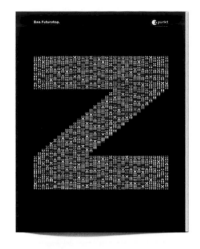

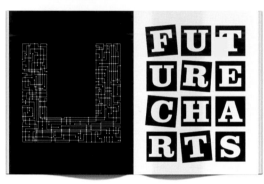

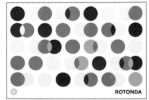

Project
Rotonda
Visuelle Kommunikation
Visual communication

Design
großgestalten GbR
Tobias Groß, Dominik Kirgus, Martin Schüngel
Köln, Germany

Client
Rotonda Business-Club
Köln, Germany

Wie sieht eine zeitgemäße Interpretation eines Business-Clubs aus? Wie tritt er im deutschsprachigen Raum auf? Mit welchen Themen beschäftigt er sich? Wofür steht er? Fragen, die sich der Rotonda Business-Club im zehnten Jahr seines Bestehens erneut gestellt hat. Die Antworten: Offenheit, Vielseitigkeit und Toleranz und gleichzeitig Verantwortung, Eleganz und Exklusivität. Der Auftritt: Auf den ersten Blick modern, stilvoll und elegant durch eine reduzierte Gestaltung, den Einsatz von Heißfolie, edles Naturpapier und viel Weißraum. Auf den zweiten Blick kraftvoll, farbenfroh, dynamisch und voller Symbolkraft.

What characterizes an up-to-date interpretation of a business club? How does the club present itself in the German-speaking region? What topics does it focus on? What does it stand for? In its tenth year of existence, the Rotonda Business-Club once again addressed these questions. The answers: Openness, diversity and tolerance and, at the same time, responsibility, elegance and exclusivity. Its look – at first glance – is modern, stylish and elegant through its reduced design, the use of hot foil embossing, premium uncoated paper and lots of white space. Upon second look: strong, colorful, dynamic and full of symbolic power.

Project
Kulturbericht 2007
CSR-Jahresbericht
Annual CSR report

Design
Milch design GmbH
Anna Döppl, Judith May, Friedel Patzak, Urban Zintl
(Fotografie)
München, Germany

Client
E.ON Energie AG
München, Germany

Die E.ON Energie AG stellt mit den von Milch design konzipierten Kulturberichten seit 2005 ihr kulturelles und soziales Engagement vor. Damit richtet sich die E.ON Energie an Presse, Partner, Öffentlichkeit, aber insbesondere auch an die Mitarbeiter des Konzerns. Der Kulturbericht 2007 ist erstmals als Themenbuch konzipiert, das sich dem Sammeln, einem Aspekt der Kulturarbeit der E.ON Energie, widmet. Ergänzt wird der Thementeil durch einen chronologischen Bericht, der alle kulturellen Aktionen des Jahres dokumentiert. Diese Gliederung erlaubt einen umfassenden Einblick in Motivation und Methodik der Kulturarbeit bei E.ON Energie.

Since 2005 E.ON Energie AG presents its cultural and social activities by publishing an annual cultural report designed by Milch design. The report is targeted to press, partners, public and last but especially to employees. The cultural report of 2007 is focused on one topic of the cultural activities of E.ON Energie for the first time. 2007's topic was collecting; future topics will be sponsoring and exhibiting. The central part is completed by a chronological documentation of all cultural activities. This new concept gives the audience a deeper insight in the motivation and methods of the cultural and social engagements of E.ON Energie.

Lieben

So alt wie die Existenz des
Menschen auf der Erde ist auc...
seine Neigung zu sammeln. I...
den Anfängen wohl eher der
Notwendigkeit geschuldet, de...
Lebensunterhalt zu bestreiten
hat sich diese Neigung aus
der Notwendigkeit in pure Lus...
verwandelt. Ingvild Götz –
Sammlerin zeitgenössischer
Kunst aus besonnener Leiden...
schaft – über ihr besonderes
Verhältnis zum Sammeln...

Project
Perfect Moments
Geschäftsbericht 2008
Annual report 2008

Design
Bueroecco
Kommunikationsdesign GmbH
Stephan Beisser, Julia Hörbrand, Anna Döppl
Augsburg, Germany

Client
Kuoni Reisen Holding AG
Zürich, Switzerland

Der Kuoni-Geschäftsbericht besteht aus drei Teilen und orientiert sich an den neu formulierten Unternehmenswerten: Reliability, Authenticity und Passion. Jeder Teil nimmt zu einem dieser Werte mit einem einleitenden Kurztext Bezug. Der Brand Report greift den Wert „Passion" auf und illustriert im Stile eines Magazins den Re-Brandingprozess von Kuoni. Im Marktbericht werden die Organisation sowie die finanziellen Resultate erläutert, wobei der Begriff „Authenticity" gewählt wurde. Für den Finanzbericht wurde der Begriff „Reliability" verwendet. Alle drei Teile sind in einem Schuber eingebettet, der den Kernwert – Perfect Moments – repräsentiert.

The Kuoni annual report Perfect Moments consists of three parts and is based on the newly defined company values: reliability, authenticity, and passion. On each cover, a short introducing text makes a reference to one value. The Brand Report describes "passion" and presents on the inside the whole re-branding-process of Kuoni in the style of a magazine. The Market Report stands for the value "authenticity" and describes the organisation and also presents the results. The financial Report uses the value "reliability". All three parts are integrated in a slipcase, which represents the core value – Perfect Moments.

286

Project
CR-Report
Broschüre
Brochure

Design
Büroecco
Kommunikationsdesign GmbH
Stephan Beißer, Lucia Götz, Selina Bauer
Augsburg, Germany

Client
Kuoni Travel Holding Ltd.
Zürich, Switzerland

Der Corporate Responsibility-Report von Kuoni stellt solche Projekte aus den Bereichen Umweltschutz und sozialem Engagement vor, für die sich das Reiseunternehmen einsetzt. Dieser Philosophiegedanke spiegelt sich auch in der Gestaltung und Materialauswahl der Broschüre wieder. Inhaltlich wird der CR-Report durch Kurzportraits von Menschen, die in unterschiedlichem Bezug zu Kuoni stehen, in Kapitel eingeteilt. Diese „Short-Stories" verbinden die einzelnen Themenbereiche gestalterisch miteinander und ziehen sich wie ein roter Faden durch die Broschüre.

The Corporate Responsibility-Report of the Kuoni Group presents projects and initiatives that this tour operator implements as part of its endeavours for people and the environment. The philosophical thought of the CR-Report is reflected in the design and also influenced the choice of material on which the brochure is printed. Regarding the content, the CR-Report is divided in different chapters that are underlined by short portraits of people who are somehow interlinked with the company. The design of these "short stories" connects the various chapters in the report and draws a continuous line through the whole brochure.

Project
Handmade Berlin
Corporate Design

Design
PLAYFRAME GmbH
Prof. Volker Pook, Jörg Junghans
Berlin, Germany

Client
Handmade Berlin
Tanja Lay & Michael Schindler GbR
Berlin, Germany

Strategische Markenberatung und Entwicklung des Corporate Designs von Handmade Berlin: Berlin und die Faszination für Wolle und Garne, Stricken und Häkeln soll auf erfrischende und charmante Art kommuniziert werden. PLAYFRAME hat das Corporate Design für Handmade Berlin entwickelt und dabei das Wahrzeichen von Berlin, den Fernsehturm, geschickt mit Garn und Nadel verstrickt.

Strategic branding advice and development of Corporate Design: In its shop in the centre of Berlin the "Handmade Berlin" label combines a fascination for threads from across the world with the latest crochet trends. In the corporate design the capital's most prominent landmark, the Berlin television tower, is reflected in a logo composed of a crochet needle and a ball of wool.

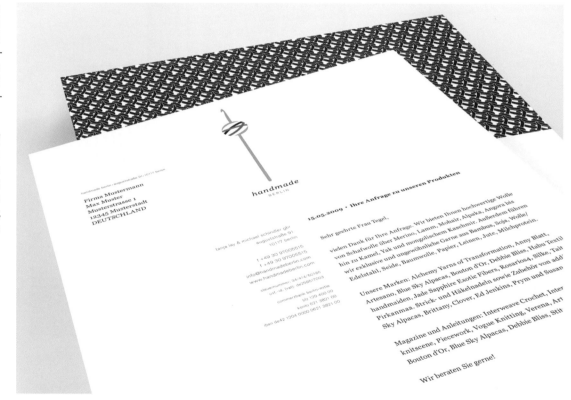

Project
Klartext
Corporate Design

Design
Lockstoff Design
Susannne Coenen, Nicole Slink
Grevenbroich, Germany

Client
Klartext GmbH
Langenfeld, Germany

Neben den Kernkompetenzen „Werbemittelproduk-
tion" und „Logistik" bietet die Klartext GmbH weitere Leistungen an. Das Erscheinungsbild soll diese
unterschiedlichen Leistungen unter einem Dach vereinen und sich von der bunten Konkurrenzwelt der
Werbemittelproduzenten abheben. Das Logo ist dem
Namen entsprechend auf den Punkt gebracht. Typografisch bildet das „X" mit dem „K" eine visuelle
Klammer um die vielen Leistungen des Unternehmens. Die Kommunikation ist schwarz-weiß umgesetzt und besinnt sich auf Kernwerte. Die starke aber
kontrastreiche Reduktion sorgt für eine hohe Prägnanz und Wiedererkennbarkeit. Das Erscheinungsbild spricht Klartext.

The service portfolio offered by Klartext GmbH does
not only include the core competencies "advertising
media production" and "logistics". The corporate design aims at bringing these different services under
one umbrella in order to stand out from the myriad
of competitors. As its German name implies the logo
is plain and cuts right to the chase. As for its typographic design its bracket-shaped letters "X "and "K"
surround the numerous services offered by the company. The communication is implemented in black
and white and focuses on core values. The strong
but contrasty reduction enables a concise design and
allows a high degree of recognition.

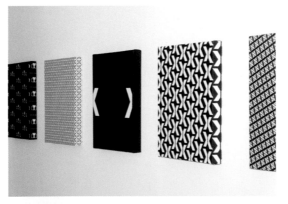

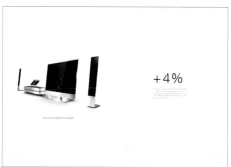

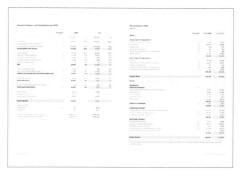

Project
Loewe
Geschäftsbericht 2008
Annual report 2008

Design
Kuhn, Kammann & Kuhn AG
Arne Schmidt (Designer)
Jan-Piet van Endert (Kreativdirektor)
Köln, Germany

Client
Loewe AG
Kronach, Germany

Das Wesentliche.
Loewe setzt gestalterische Maßstäbe, in diesem Jahr auch mit dem Geschäftsbericht. Der Report folgt dem hohen Anspruch der Premiumprodukte des börsennotierten Unternehmens. Sein Titel ist Maxime: „Das Wesentliche." Das von der Kölner Agentur Kuhn, Kammann & Kuhn entwickelte Konzept verbindet Ästhetik und Funktion in bestechender Klarheit. Geprägt ist der Geschäftsbericht von der exklusiven Formensprache der vier Produktlinien und den individuellen Audio-Lösungen sowie signifikanten Kennzahlen – und das nicht allein in Abschluss und Anhang. Dabei geht es um Details und ungewohnte Perspektiven.

The Essential.
Loewe sets new standards in design. This year's annual report continues the trend and follows the superior standard of the premium products of this listed company. The title conveys the maxim: "The Essential." Striking in its clarity, the concept developed by the Cologne agency Kuhn, Kammann & Kuhn combines aesthetics and function. The report is characterized by the exclusive design vocabulary distinguishing the four product lines and customized audio systems, as well as by the relevant key data – and the latter not only in the financial statements and notes. Unusual perspectives and details set the tone.

Project
The Poetry Collection of Agnes Lam
Buch
Book

Design
Joaquim Cheong Design
Kuokwai Cheong (Creative Direction, Graphic Design)
Macau, China

Client
Agnes Lam Iok Fong
Macau, China

Die traurigen Verse in der Lyrik von Agnes Lam bekommen in diesem Buch ihre Gestalt. Das Buch bedient sich der beiden chinesischen Schriftzeichen für „Poesie" und „Denken" in der Hoffnung, die Idee der Gedichte durch die Bedeutung dieser Wörter darzustellen. Ein schwarzer Faden durch das chinesische Schriftzeichen für „Denken" symbolisiert das Bindeglied zwischen Lesern und Autor, um in die profunde Natur der Dinge einzutauchen. Der schwarze Faden steht für das Gefühl der Traurigkeit und verbindet wichtige Zeilen einzelner Gedichte.

Composed by words of sadness and transforming the poetry of Agnes Lam into design, this book uses the two Chinese characters "poetry" and "thinking" and hopes to bring out the conception of the poems using these words' image. A black string through the Chinese character "thinking" symbolises a bridge between the reader and the author to cross into the profound nature of things. The black string represents the sad feeling connecting the important lines of each poem. Space is left on each page for the readers to write down their thoughts and feelings regarding the poems.

USB-Stick im Kreditkartenformat
mit animierter, digitaler Umsetzung des Berichts.
Credit-card-sized USB-stick with an animated
digital version of the annual report.

Project
Bertelsmann AG
Geschäftbericht 2008
Annual report 2008

Design
Red Cell Werbeagentur GmbH
Claudia Weithase
Düsseldorf, Germany
Kirchhoff Consult AG
Thorsten Greinus
Hamburg, Germany

Client
Bertelsmann AG
Gütersloh, Germany

Der Geschäftsbericht der Bertelsmann AG hat die primäre Funktion der Darstellung der Kennzahlen und der finanziellen Situation des Konzerns im zurückliegenden Geschäftsjahr sowie die Vorstellung des Konzerns und der dazu gehörenden Unternehmensbereiche: RTL Group, Random House, Gruner + Jahr, Arvato und Direct Group. Dem Finanzteil steht ein Imageteil voran, der in diesem Jahr unter besonderen Vorzeichen steht: Die in der zweiten Jahreshälfte 2008 einsetzende weltweite Wirtschaftskrise erfordert auch in der Konzeption und Umsetzung eines Geschäftsberichts den „richtigen Ton", nämlich glaubwürdige und aufrichtige Kommunikation mit Augenmaß.

The primary function of Bertelsmann's annual report is to communicate the key financials and financial situation of the group in the business year just past, and to present the group and its corporate divisions: RTL Group, Random House, Gruner + Jahr, Arvato and Direct Group. The financial section is preceded by an image section which this year was shaped by special portents: The onset of the worldwide economic crisis in the second half of 2008 made it necessary to find the "right tone" in designing and implementing an annual report and basically prohibited any exuberant posturing, instead calling for credible, sincere communications.

Project
Auf Hemd reimt sich fremd!
Jahresbericht
Annual report

Design
KOCHAN & PARTNER GmbH
Martin Summ, Dominik Parzinger, Katja Knahn,
Sandra Hachmann, Daniela Gattinger, Robert Iwen,
Gabriele Werner
München, Germany

Client
Studiosus Reisen München GmbH
München, Germany

Reisen. Aufbrechen ins Fremde, Blaue, Unbekannte.
Neue Ein- und Ansichten gewinnen. Sich einlassen auf
Wechselspiele: Was uns fremd ist, ist dem Anderen
Heimat. Dabei ist manchem Fremden Deutschland
längst zum neuen Ankerplatz im Leben geworden.
Was lassen Menschen bei einer Reise in eine neue
Heimat zurück? Was gewinnen sie? Welchen Blick
haben sie, die vormals Fremden, auf unsere alltäg-
liche Lebensart? Welche Brücken finden sie zurück zu
ihrem Herkunftsort? Dazu haben wir 28 Gesprächs-
partner gebeten, aus den Studiosus-Katalogen das
Bild auszuwählen, das am ehesten dem individuellen
Heimatempfinden entspricht.

Travel. Stepping into the unknown, the unfamiliar, the
uncharted. Shifting perspective. Gaining new insights
and new outlooks. Travel invites us to look at the
world through someone else's eyes: what's strange
for us is home for them. People travel to Germany
and some of them decide to stay, to make a new
home. We ask: what do they leave behind? What do
they gain? What is their impression, these who once
were strangers, on the day-to-day life in Germany?
For each of our interviews, we have asked 28 inter-
viewees to identify one image from the Studiosus
catalogs that best depicts their individual sense of
their home.

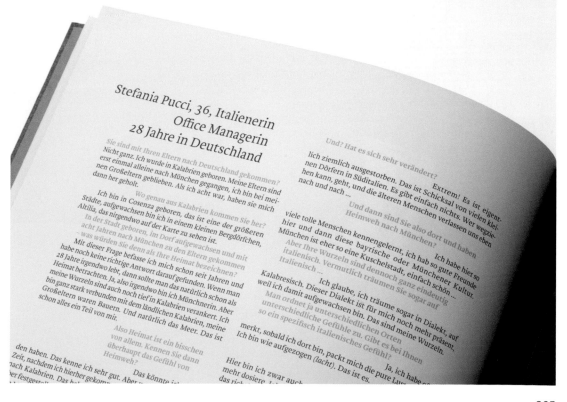

Stefania Pucci, 36, Italienerin
Office Managerin
28 Jahre in Deutschland

Project
Leitbilder
Monografie
Monograph

Design
HPP Hentrich-Petschnigg & Partner GmbH + Co. KG
Düsseldorf, Germany
Heimann und Schwantes (Grafische Gestaltung)
Berlin, Germany

Client
HPP Architekten
Düsseldorf, Germany
Hatje Cantz Verlag
Ostfildern, Germany

Die Architektursprache von HPP wird von einer un-
dogmatischen Auseinandersetzung mit den Inhalten
einer Bauaufgabe bestimmt. Dadurch entstehen un-
terschiedlichste Bauwerke, die nicht über einen formalen Stil, sondern über eine klare Haltung verbunden sind. Diese Haltung sichtbar zu machen, ist das
Kommunikationsziel des Buches. Über die gezeigten
Projekte hinaus ist es Abbild der Arbeitsweise des Büros und thematisiert dabei die Frage nach Leitbildern
und Dualität. Das grafische Konzept visualisiert diesen Anspruch und gibt Raum für das Spannungsfeld,
in dem sich die Arbeit von HPP bewegt: Architektur
zwischen Emotionalität und Rationalität.

HPP's architectural vocabulary is determined through
a non-dogmatic dialogue with the content of a building task. As a result a diversity of buildings emerges,
all combined by a clearly defined approach rather
than by the use of a standard set of design elements.
The book's communicative target is to show this attitude. Beside the presented projects it also functions
as an image of the practice's work approach issuing
guiding principles and its duality. The graphic concept visualizes this demand and at the same time
reveals the field in which the firm works – a field that
strikes a careful balance between emotionality and
rationality.

Konstruktion Arena »AufSchalke«

Hülle
Parkhaus am Zoo

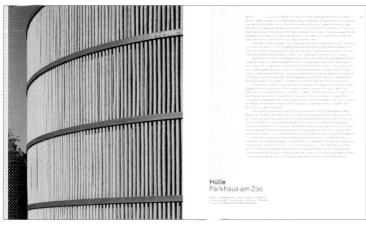

Detail Justizzentrum Wuppertal

Project
Pivot Media
Corporate Design

Design
van Ommen
Visuelle Kommunikation
Carl van Ommen
Hamburg, Germany

Client
Pivot Media GmbH
Hamburg, Germany

Für die junge Filmproduktion, die sich im Modefilmsegment positioniert, entwickelten wir ein neues Erscheinungsbild. Die konzeptionelle und erzählerische Stärke dieser Produktionsfirma sollte transportiert werden. Für Pivot Media kreierten wir ein einprägsames Zeichen, das an eine Sprechblase erinnert und gleichzeitig als „P" zu erkennen ist. Um den Charakter der Bewegtbildkommunikation auf das Medium Papier zu übertragen, sind wechselnde Farben und unterschiedliche Bildausschnitte gewählt worden. Alle Bestandteile des Corporate Designs sind verschieden. Durch den prägnanten Look bilden sie eine klare visuelle Einheit.

We devised the identity for a new film production company engaged in the fashion film sector. With a brief to convey the company's conceptual and narrative strength, we created a memorable logo that alludes to a speech bubble in the shape of the letter "P". Changing colors and imagery sections translate the notion of moving image communication into printed media. Whilst all items of the corporate design are different, the striking identity provides visual consistency throughout.

Project
Netzwerk Zeitung
Zeitung
Newspaper

Design
Novamondo Design
Christian Schlimok, Bastian Köhler, Julia Fuchs
Berlin, Germany

Client
Netzwerk Neue Musik
Berlin, Germany

Mit einer zweimal im Jahr erscheinenden Zeitung will das „Netzwerk Neue Musik" seine Arbeit vorstellen und den Diskurs über Neue Musik einer breiteren Öffentlichkeit zugänglich machen. Der variable Name 1'33' (2'33', 3'33', ...) stellt auf nachdrückliche Art und Weise den Bezug zum Thema „Neue Musik" her, indem er auf ein Hauptwerk von John Cage verweist. Das offene Verständnis von Neuer Musik und ihrer Vermittlung zeigt sich in Cages legendärem Stück 4'33' anhand der freien Entscheidung des Interpreten über die Länge, die Satzdauer sowie das Instrumentarium und stellt so eine Parallele zu den Grundgedanken des „Netzwerks" dar.

With the bi-annually appearing newspaper the "Netzwerk Neue Musik" wants to present its projects and topics. The "Networks" aim is also to encourage public dialogue regarding "New Music" and to support accessible to the broader public. The variable name 1'33' (2'33', 3'33', ...) refers to a main John Cage composition and in a very distinct way makes the connection to "New Music". The appreciation and open-mindedness of "New Music" as well as its general message reveals itself in Cages legendary piece 4'33'. Cage gives the interpreter freedom in decisions pertaining to the movements of duration as well as that of instruments.

Project
Kulturkreis-Brief
Mitteilungsblatt
Newsletter

Design
Novamondo Design
Christian Schlimok, Bastian Köhler,
Sina Schwarz, Julia Fuchs
Berlin, Germany

Client
Kulturkreis der deutschen Wirtschaft
Berlin, Germany

Im Zuge der Einführung des modernisierten Erscheinungsbildes wird auch der Kulturkreis-Brief, das Mitteilungsblatt für Mitglieder und Interessierte, neu gestaltet. Aus einem sechsseitigen unhandlichen Newsletter wird eine kompakte und übersichtliche Zeitung mit zeitgenössischem Anspruch. Das Layout ist von der geometrischen Form des Kreises bestimmt. So setzen sich beispielsweise die Ziffern der Paginierung aus Kreissegmenten zusammen.

During the process of introducing a modernized appearance, the "Kulturkreis-Brief" (not only given to its members but also to people who generally are interested in the cultural undertakings of the "Kulturkreis der deutschen Wirtschaft"), has also taken on a new form. From a six-paged, unmanageable newsletter it has evolved into a compact and clear newspaper, meriting contemporary standards. The geometrical form of the circle defines the layout. Thus for example, segments of a circle determine the numbers of the pagination.

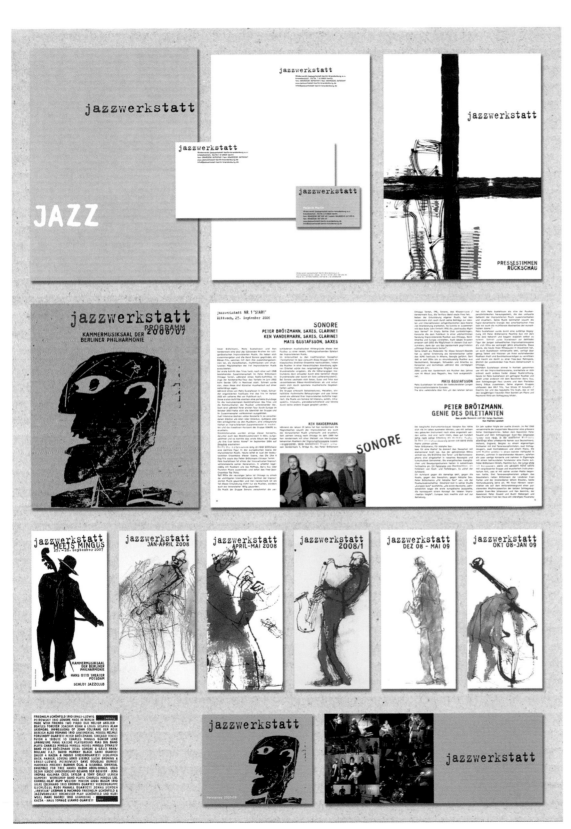

Project
jazzwerkstatt
Corporate Design

Design
wppt:kommunikation GmbH
Klaus Untiet, Rob Fährmann, Süleyman Kayaalp,
Ali Tercan, Beatrix Göge
Wuppertal, Germany

Client
Förderverein jazzwerkstatt
Berlin-Brandenburg e. V.
Berlin, Germany

Unter dem Titel „jazzwerkstatt" finden seit 2006 in Berlin wieder regelmäßig aktuelle Jazzkonzerte statt. Der Förderverein jazzwerkstatt Berlin-Brandenburg e. V. führt damit die Tradition der legendären Festivals „Jazzwerkstatt Peitz" fort. Heute treffen sich die Großen der Szene wie Alexander von Schlippenbach, Peter Brötzmann oder Conny Bauer, um gemeinsam zu improvisieren. Das Logo und die Kommunikationsmedien für den Verein bringen den Werkstattcharakter dieser Musik zum Ausdruck: Alles ist handgemacht, stark und authentisch.

Since 2006, topical jazz concerts under the heading "jazzwerkstatt" have been taking place again at regular intervals in Berlin. Thus, the support association jazzwerkstatt Berlin-Brandenburg e. V. continues the tradition of the legendary "Jazzwerkstatt Peitz" festivals. Today, giants of the scene like Alexander von Schlippenbach, Peter Brötzmann, and Conny Bauer get together to improvise. The association's logo and communication media express the studio character of this kind of music: Everything is handmade, sturdy and genuine.

Project
Pro Asyl e. V.
Willkommen in Deutschland
Welcome in Germany

Design
JWT
Oliver Kessler (CD, Text)
Gordand Erceg, Simone Rohé (Art Direction)
Annette Endrass, Christine Nilges (Art Buying)
Marc Wuchner (Fotografie)
Frankfurt a. M., Germany

Client
Pro Asyl e. V.
– National Working Group for Refugees –
Frankfurt a. M., Germany

Pro Asyl e. V. versucht Menschen die Situation von Flüchtlingen und Asylsuchenden nahezubringen, und zwar auf individueller, gesellschaftlicher und politischer Ebene. Dieser Kalender soll einen Teil dazu beitragen, indem er das Thema aus einer neuen und ungewöhnlichen Perspektive betrachtet. Wenn wir uns umschauen bzw. in den Kalender gucken, stoßen wir auf sehr verschiedene „Immigranten", die unser Leben und unsere Kultur oft seit Jahrhunderten bereichern. Niemals wären wir auf die Idee gekommen, ihnen die Einreise zu verweigern oder sie abzuschieben. Warum tun wir es heute?

Pro Asyl e. V. endeavors to bring home the situation confronting refugees and asylum-seekers to individuals at the personal, social and political levels. This calendar is intended to make its contribution to this overall objective by viewing the topic from a new and unusual perspective. When we take a look around us, or in the calendar, we come across all sorts of "immigrants" – many of whom have enriched our lives and our culture for centuries. We never would have thought of denying them entry or deporting them. So why do we today?

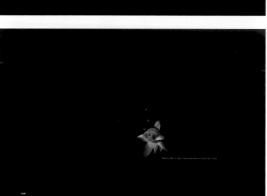

Project
Hot Streets In Taipei
Buch
Book

Design
Right and Left Design Co., Ltd.
Sun Chiu Ping (Art Director)
Taipei City, Taiwan

Project
Taipei City Office of Commerce
Taipei City, Taiwan

„Hot Streets in Taipei" ist ein Handbuch, das zwölf verschiedene Einkaufsstraßen in lockerer Umgangssprache vorstellt. Dieses nützliche und hochwertige Buch stellt Einkaufsstraßen und -viertel vor, die mit Hilfe der Regierung eingerichtet wurden. Die Texte sind in Englisch sowie Chinesisch und reich an Bildern und Fotos. Der Umschlag zeigt im Pop-Art-Stil charakteristische Produkte der jeweiligen Einkaufsstraßen vor einem elegant-violetten Hintergrund in mehreren Bildebenen. Wir verbinden Kunst, Alltag sowie Elemente der Pop-Art, z. B. Jugend, Kreativität, Massenproduktion, Humor und Kommerz.

"Hot Streets in Taipei" is a handbook that introduces twelve different shopping streets with popular slang. This convenient, practical and high-quality handbook introduces shopping streets and districts that were established with assistance from the government. It contains information in both Chinese and English, and also has many illustrations and pictures. The cover, with an elegant purple background, combines images of the characteristic products of each shopping street into layers, pop art style. We incorporate art with daily life with elements of pop art such as youth, creativity, mass-production, humor, and commerce.

Project
Dogon – Portrait einer Kultur
Buch
Book

Design
Schmidt und Weber Konzept-Design
Kerstin Weber, Olaf Schmidt (Fotografie,
Entwicklung der Spannstab-Bindung)
Hauke Olaf Nagel (Fotografie)
Kiel, Germany

Client
Dogon-Schulen e. V.
Hamburg, Germany

Das Buch „Dogon – Portrait einer Kultur" basiert
auf einem visuellen Konzept, das im Bildteil nur
ganzseitige Bilder zeigt. Die Bildzuschriften sind auf
durchsichtigen Layern gedruckt, wodurch eine Transparenz entsteht, die sich in der Umschlaggestaltung
mit einem Acrylglas-Einband fortsetzt. Die innovative Spannstab-Bindung wurde exklusiv für dieses in
der „Edition Satimbe" erschienene Buch entwickelt.
Das Ziel der Edition ist es, hochwertig aufgemachte
Bücher für einen karitativen Zweck zu einem mode-
raten Preis zu verlegen. 20,00 Euro vom Verkaufs-
preis kommen dem Verein „Dogon-Schulen e. V." zu-
gute.

A visual concept has been developed for the book
"Dogon – Portrait einer Kultur" that shows full-page
images in the illustrative part of the book. The text is
printed on translucent layers creating a transparency
that is continued by a perspex binding for the cover
design. The innovative tie rod binding was developed
especially for this book, which is published in the
"Edition Satimbe". It is the aim of this edition to pub-
lish books with high-quality design for a charitable
purpose at a moderate price. A share of 20.00 Euro
of the sales price benefits the association "Dogon-
Schulen e. V.".

Project
HQ – High Quality
Buch
Book

Design
Heine/Lenz/Zizka
Volker Weinmann
Frankfurt a. M., Germany

Client
Edition Braus
Heidelberg, Germany

Heidelberger Druckmaschinen, Günter Braus und HQ: alles Ikonen des bedruckten Papiers. Was liegt hier näher, als ein Bekenntnis zum Buch und dessen Fähigkeit, Gedanken, Ideen und Fantasien real werden zu lassen. Ein interaktiver Kontrapunkt zum Verschwinden in der Flüchtigkeit und Unfassbarkeit der digitalen Zeit. Ein Konglomerat aus richtungsweisender Kreativität gepaart mit einer dezenten Leistungsschau des drucktechnisch machbaren. Selbstreferenzielle Typografie ist da fehl am Platze, eher braucht es einen gestalterischen Rahmen, der die Welt einfasst und das Fragmentale der Wahrnehmung in der Buchform begreifbar macht.

Heidelberger Druckmaschinen, Günter Braus and HQ: all icons of printed paper. What could be more important that declaring our belief in books and their ability to allow thoughts, ideas and fantasies to become real – an interactive counterpoint to disappear into the fleetingness and incomprehensibility of the digital age. A conglomerate of creativity pointing the way ahead, coupled with a subtle display of what is feasible when it comes to printing. Self-referential typography is uncalled for here. It is more about requiring a creative framework that encompasses the world and makes the fragmentary nature of perception comprehensible in book form.

Project
Ralf Ziervogel: Every Adidas Got Its Story
Künstlerbuch
Artist's book

Design
20FIRST
Helder Suffenplan, Ralf Ziervogel
Berlin, Germany

Client
Sammlung Südhausbau
München, Germany

„Every Adidas Got Its Story" zeigt in Originalgröße 100 Arbeiten im FM-Raster, mit offener Bindung im Schuber für ein optimales Aufschlagverhalten. Reduzierte Gestaltung und akribische Ausführung zitieren die objekthafte Form, in der der Künstler seine Arbeiten in Ausstellungen präsentiert. Es gibt zwei Ausführungen:
REGULAR EDITION, Auflage 1.000:
Auf den Seiten des Schubers sind die Namen von Künstler und Verlag geprägt.
ARTIST'S EDITION, Auflage 1:
Die Sonderedition aus 25 Unikaten lässt sich zu einem Gesamtmotiv zusammenfügen und zeigt als Paperlux-Gravur ein Motiv des Buchs. Jeder Schuber trägt einen anderen Ausschnitt des Gesamtmotivs.

"Every Adidas Got Its Story" presents 100 drawings in original size, printed with a FM-raster. The block has an open binding to allow flat opening. The monolithic appearance quotes the minimalist way in which the artist presents his drawings in exhibitions. There are two versions:
REGULAR EDITION, Circulation 1,000:
The slip case's sides carry's the embossing of the names of the artist and the publishing house.
ARTIST'S EDITION, Circulation 1:
The 25 slip cases carry Paperlux laser engraving. Lying next to each other they form a 55 × 120 cm 3-dimensional relief of one of the motives from the book. Each one exists in a circulation of one only.

Project
12 Ideen zur Visuellen Kommunikation
Buch
Book

Design
Waidmann/Post
Visuelle Kommunikation
Mechthild Waidmann, Stefan Waidmann
Braunschweig, Germany

Client
Verlag Niggli AG
Sulgen, Switzerland

Ideen und Werte bilden den Kern von Unternehmen, Institutionen, Aktionen und Produkten. Waidmann/Post analysiert diese Inhalte systematisch und entwickelt daraus Ideen zur Visuellen Kommunikation – in einer hohen und langlebigen Gestaltungsqualität. Der Kern wird sichtbar, erlebbar und spürbar, die Inhalte grundlegend, einzigartig und glaubwürdig auf den Punkt gebracht. Zwölf Ideen von Waidmann/Post sind in diesem Buch dokumentiert: Visuelle Kommunikation als Programm, im Raum und auf Papier.

Ideas and values are the bedrock of companies, institutions, activities and products. Waidmann/Post systematically analyzes content and develops ideas for visual communications – delivering top class quality which will stand the test of time. Ideas and values become visible and a first-hand experience. Content gets to the heart of the matter – clearly, uniquely and authentically. Twelve ideas from Waidmann/Post are represented in this book: Visual Communication as a manifesto, a tangible experience and a written concept.

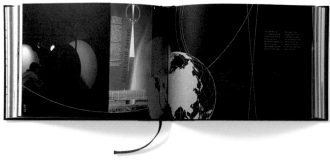

Project
Zhang Huan
Ausstellungskatalog
Exhibition catalog

Design
L2M3 Kommunikationsdesign GmbH
Simon Brenner, Sascha Lobe
Stuttgart, Germany

Client
Deutscher Sparkassen Verlag GmbH
Stuttgart, Germany

Die ganze Wucht der Kunst von Zhang Huan wurde in ein Riesenformat übersetzt. Beginnend auf dem Cover werden die wichtigsten Werke in chronologischer Reihenfolge gezeigt und bekommen wie in einem Portfolio größtmöglichen Platz eingeräumt. Das kraftvolle Layout der Bilder wird durch eine in leichten Schriftschnitten gestaltete Typografie ergänzt. Der Papierwechsel hin zu einer leichteren Grammatur unterstreicht den Kommentarcharakter des Leseteils. Auf der Rückseite des Buchs ist der Künstlername angestanzt. Diese Verletzung ist eine Referenz an die auch körperlich kompromisslose Arbeit Zhang Huans.

The whole weight of Zhang Huan's art has been translated into a giant format. Starting on the cover, the most important works are displayed in chronological order, with maximum space devoted to them, as in a portfolio. The powerful layout of the pictures is backed up by typography in light font weights. The switch to a lighter paper underscores the commentary nature of the text section. The artist's name is punched into the back of the book. This "injury" is a reference to Zhang Huan's physically uncompromising work.

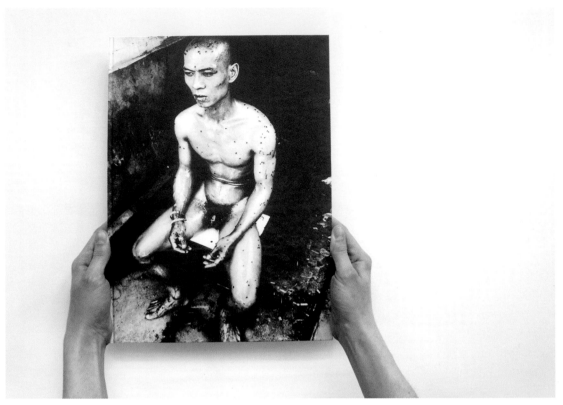

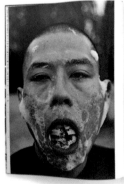

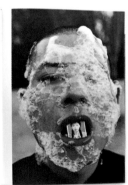

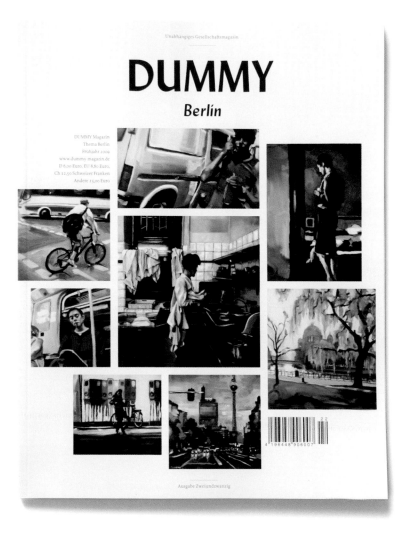

Project
Dummy Berlin
Magazin
Magazine

Design
leomaria
Markus Büsges, Björn Wolf
Berlin, Germany

Client
Dummy Verlag GbR
Berlin, Germany

Jede Ausgabe des unabhängigen Gesellschaftsmagazin „Dummy" ist monothematisch angelegt. Wechselnde Redakteure, Fotografen und Designer gestalten jede Ausgabe neu. Diese Ausgabe wurde ausschließlich mit Ölbildern des Künstlers Edward B. Gordon gelayoutet. Er malt seit Jahren jeden Tag ein Bild von Berlin! Aus diesem umfangreichen Oeuvre und einigen exklusiven, für diese Ausgabe gemalten Bildern, entstand das neue Magazin „Dummy Berlin".

Each issue of the independent society magazine "Dummy" is based around a monothematic concept and created by changing the team of editors, photographers and designers for each new issue. The layout of this issue makes exclusive use of oil paintings by Edward B. Gordon. For a number of years this artist has been doing one painting of Berlin every day! The "Dummy Berlin" magazine selects from this extensive body of work as well as several paintings created exclusively for this issue.

Project
HEAR THE WORLD 9
Magazin
Magazine

Design
SIGN Kommunikation GmbH
Antonia Henschel
Frankfurt a. M., Germany

Client
Hear The World Foundation
Stäfa, Switzerland

HEAR THE WORLD 9 ist das Magazin der gleichnamigen Initiative. Es erscheint vierteljährlich und es gibt eine deutschsprachige und eine englische Fassung. Rubriken gibt es zu zahlreichen Themen von der Kunst über Architektur hin zur Musik. Doch eins haben alle gemeinsam, es wird immer ein Bezug zum Hören hergestellt. Die Titel werden immer von Bryan Adams fotografiert, einem Botschafter der Initiative.

HEAR THE WORLD 9 is the magazine of a foundation of the same name. It is published quarterly in a German and an English issue. Various categories from art and architecture to music have all one thing in common. They are all featured in correlation to sounds and hearing. All covers are photographed by Bryan Adams who is an ambassador of the foundation.

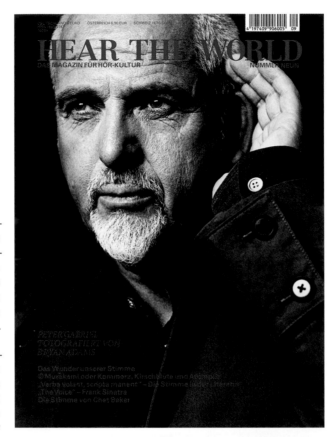

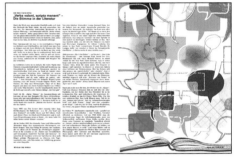

Project
601 Artbook Project 2008
Katalog
Catalog

Design
601bisang
Park Kum-jun (Creative Director, Art Director, Designer, Photographer)
You Na-won (Designer)
Lee Hyun-tae (Illustrator)
Cho Ok-hee (Photographer)
Kim Ki-yeon (Copy)
Jung Jong-in (Publisher)
Seoul, South Korea

Client
601bisang
Seoul, South Korea

Dies ist der Sieger-Katalog des „601 Artbook Project 2008". Der Band beginnt mit 29 „As" und „Bs", die jedes der 29 preisgekrönten Werke anführen. Die Buchstaben stehen jeweils für Kunst bzw. Band und sind entlang der Abbildung eines Waldes angeordnet. In der Mitte sind die preisgekrönten Werke, als ob sie das Thema dieses Jahres – „Kunstband ist Konversation" – aussprechen und die Essenz und Harmonie aufzeigen wollten. Der offene Buchrücken, die einzigartige visuelle Geschichtenerzähltechnik und die Darstellung von Bildern voll kindlicher Unschuld wurden zusammengetragen, um den Band hervorzubringen, der durch einen Vorleser zum Leben erweckt wird.

This is the award catalog of "601 Artbook Project 2008". The book begins with 29 'A's and 'B's heading each of 29 award-winning work. Standing for "Art" and "Book," respectively, these letters are arranged in both beginning and end of the book alongside the image of a forest. In the middle are award-winning works so as to voice out this year's theme "Art Book is Conversation" and illustrate the essence and harmony of art and books. Exposed book spine, unique visual storytelling technique, and illustration images full of childlike innocence are brought together to give birth to this one-of-a-kind art book where you will be inspired alive through the reader.

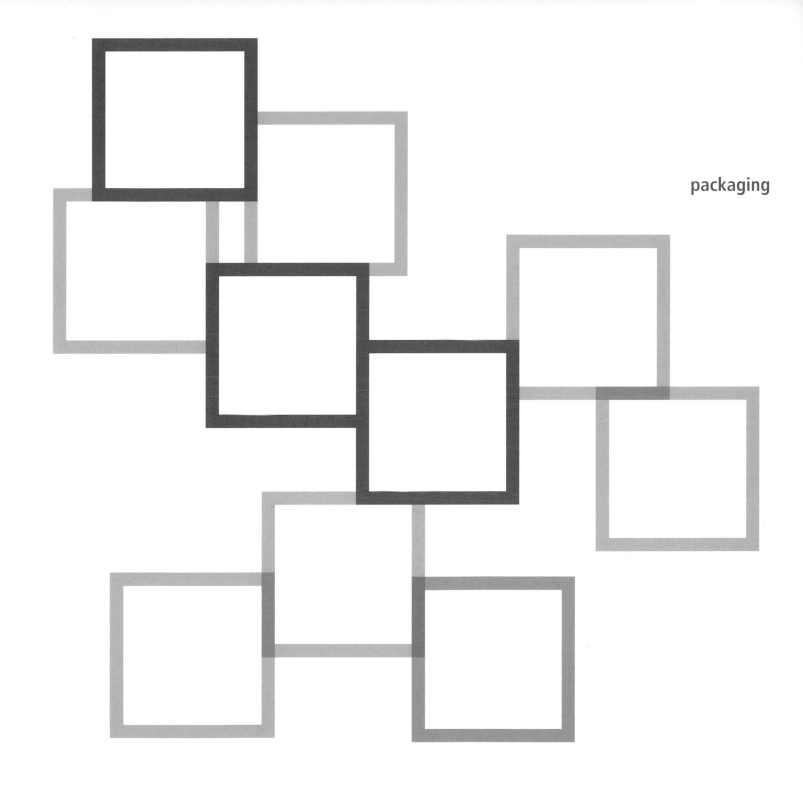

packaging

Verpackungen schaffen vielfältige Begegnungsmomente

Packaging offers numerous opportunities for interaction

Verpackungen sind vielschichtig: Sie sind Hülle und Schutz, Werkzeug und Umgang, Information und Ansprache, Ratgeber und Unterhalter, Markenzeichen und Plakat ...

Eine Verpackung ist Teil des Produkts und Teil der Kommunikation. Sie verbindet beides und trägt damit Attribute aus beiden Genres. Das macht die Arbeit an Verpackungen so anspruchsvoll. Im optimalen Falle funktioniert sie perfekt, informiert umfassend und weckt positive Gefühle.

Das eigentlich geniale an ihrer Konstitution: Sie besetzt auf einzigartige Weise verschiedene Momente der Begegnung mit dem Menschen, der kein anderes Medium nahekommt. Sie wirkt schon in dem Moment der Auswahl des Produktes beim Kauf – sie ist dabei, wenn das Produkt, der Inhalt, benutzt wird und sie kann auch beim Wegwerfen noch überzeugen. Die Verpackung ist ganz nahe dran und beweist ihre Intelligenz und Emotionalität im Moment des Entdeckens, Gebrauchs und Wiedererkennens.

Von den zu jurierenden Arbeiten schöpfte kaum eine die gesamte Kette dieser Begegnungsmomente aus. Zu wünschen wären in der Zukunft mehr Konzepte, die sich der Stärke dieser Nähe zum Menschen bewusst werden und sie in messbare, kommerzielle Erfolge verwandeln.

Packaging is multifaceted: Covering and protection, medium and interaction, information and communication, advice and entertainment, branding and poster ... It combines both and thereby incorporates attributes of both genres. This is what makes packaging projects so demanding. In the ideal case, packaging works perfectly, offers comprehensive information and creates positive feelings.

The true genius of its constitution: In a unique way, it covers various moments of human interaction not approached by any other medium. It has an impact from the moment of product selection when a purchase is made – it is there when the product, the contents, is used and can even prove convincing as it is discarded. Packaging is where the action is, and proves its intelligence and emotional impact at the moment of discovery, product use and subsequent recognition.

Few of the entries submitted for evaluation fully exploit this entire chain of interaction. More concepts that are aware of this proximity to the user and transform it into measurable, commercial success would be desirable.

Arne Schultchen

Project
Ölwechsel/Oil Change
Verpackung für Öl
Packaging for oil

Design
Kolle Rebbe/KOREFE
Katrin Oeding (Creative Direction)
Reginald Wagner (Art Direction)
Jan Simmerl (Grafik)
Katharina Trumbach (Text)
Hamburg, Germany

Client
the garage winery e. k.
Oestrich-Winkel, Germany

Sowohl der Name des Öls als auch die Verpackung passen zu dem industriellen Gefühl der Marke. „Öl-wechsel" beschreibt einen handwerklichen Vorgang und unterstreicht den Werkstatt-Touch genauso wie die Verpackung. Die illustrierten Monster repräsen-tieren jeweils den Inhaltsstoff und die Wirkung, wenn sie auf das Öl treffen.

Both the name of the oil and its packaging match the industrial look and feel of the brand. Called "Oil Change", based on what garages often do, the oil is packaged in high-quality oil cans with a different il-lustration for each type of oil. The monsters represent the three different ingredients and what happens to them, when you combine them with olive oil.

Project
Marxen / Schifftaufchampagner
Verpackung
Packaging

Design
Mutabor Design GmbH
Heinrich Paravicini (Creative Direction)
Axel Domke (Art Direction)
Nils Zimmermann (Illustration)
Luciano Tezzele (Produktion)
Susanne Weber (Reinzeichnung)
Hamburg, Germany

Client
Marxen Wein GmbH & Co. KG
Kiel, Germany

Der Sommelier Jan P. Marxen aus Kiel ist ein Quer-
denker. Er vertritt eine sehr eigene Auffassung was
den Genuss von Wein angeht und stellt klassische
Kriterien in Frage. So verwundert es kaum, dass der
erste Marxen-Champagner einen ebenso hochqua-
litativen wie eigenwilligen Ansatz verfolgt. Das maritime Umfeld Kiels stand Pate für die Edition No. 1 –
den Champagner zum Schiffetaufen. Das Packaging
Design unterstreicht den funktionalen Charakter des
Produktes. Es steht in der Tradition des reduzierten
Corporate Designs der Marke Marxen, welches stets
den Inhalt über die Form erhebt. In letzter Kon-
sequenz liegt dem Champagner nicht nur ein Seil
für den Taufakt, sondern auch ein Beipackzettel mit
Handlungsanweisungen für die Schiffstaufe bei.

Sommelier Jan P. Marxen from Kiel is an unconventional thinker. He has his own very individual views
on the enjoyment of wine and challenges classic criteria. So it is hardly surprising that the first champagne from Marxen takes an approach characterized
as much by idiosyncrasy as it is by quality. Kiel's maritime setting provided the inspiration for Marxen's
first champagne: champagne for naming ships. The
packaging design emphasizes the functional character of the product. It follows the tradition of the
minimalist corporate design of Marxen as a brand,
which always elevates content over form. As a finishing touch, the champagne comes with a rope for the
ship naming, and a leaflet containing directions for
ship-naming ceremonies.

Project
DigiECO-System
Aufbewahrung digitaler Speicherkarten
Storage system for digital media

Design
prausedesign
Philipp Prause
Wien, Austria
Ernst Schausberger & Co. GmbH
Christian Magoc (Produktentwicklung)
Gunskirchen, Austria

Client
Hama GmbH & Co. KG
Monheim, Germany

SD- und andere Speicherkarten erfreuen sich für Fotos, Musik und Videoaufnahmen großer Beliebtheit. Lösungen sind gefragt für Transport, Weitergabe, Archivierung. DigiECO ist ein umfassendes Aufbewahrungssystem für diverse Speichertypen. Im handlichen DVD-Format integriert sind Indexfeld, ausklappbare Abheftlaschen und ein Steckfach für Karten und weitere Unterlagen. Für Hochzeitsfotos empfiehlt sich die DigiECO-Grußkarte mit Bewegungseffekt – aus neutralem Material für kreative Gestaltung. Das „Ass" von DigiECO ist die „Pocket-Card" im Kreditkartenformat: Sie ermöglicht die sichere Aufbewahrung von Speicherkarten, griffbereit in der Brieftasche. 100% Karton, recyclebar.

SD cards and other types of storage media are widely used for photos, music, video recordings – both at home and on the go. Solutions are welcome for carrying, passing-on, archiving. DigiECO is a comprehensive transport/archival system for various types of storage cards. The DVD-sized covers feature index fields and slots for cards or additional papers, and can be filed in ring binders. Send wedding pictures in the animated DigiECO greeting card – its neutral material supports your creative design! Ace of DigiECO is the credit-card-sized "PocketCard", which allows to keep one's storage media in the briefcase, always at hand. 100% cardboard, recyclable.

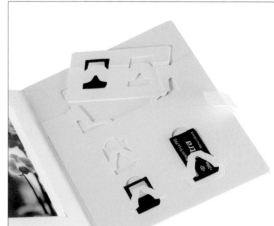

Project
OHui LED Compact – Lumiarte
Kosmetik-Etui
Cosmetics compact case

Design
LG Household & Healthcare
Ji-Hae Kim (Designer)
Jong-il Kim (Design Center Director)
Gok-Mi Kim (Team Manager)
Jong-Kuk Ryu (Engineer)
Seoul, South Korea

Client
LG Household & Healthcare
Seoul, South Korea

Das erste innovative LED-leuchtende Kosmetik-Puder-Etui, das emotionale Eigenarten hat. Mit diesem besonderen Puder-Etui kann man sich im Dunkeln schminken, denn das Licht, das im Spiegel eingebaut ist, leuchtet, wenn das Etui geöffnet wird. Wenn man den Deckel schließt, leuchtet automatisch die versteckte Grafik auf der Vorderseite des Deckels. Das Licht des Spiegels und der LED-Leuchte im Deckel kann auch mittels eines Knopfes an der Seite ein- und ausgeschaltet werden. Die Verpackung hat ein ergonomisches Design, angelehnt an das Design von klappbaren Mobiltelefonen.

World's first innovative cosmetics LED lighting powder case with emotional touch. This phenomenal powder case enables one to put on make-up in the dark as it has lights installed inside the mirror that light up when opened. Once the lid is closed, hidden motion graphics in the upfront lid will automatically light up after one another. Mirror lights and upfront LED lights can also be controlled by button on the left side. The outer package is ergonomically designed based on the folder-type cell-phone concept.

Project
Schokodeern
Verpackungsdesign
Packaging design

Design
deernsundjungs design
Ilka Zentgraf
Hamburg, Germany

Client
deernsundjungs design
Hamburg, Germany

In dem visuellen Auftritt der „Schokodeern" sind alle wichtigen Merkmale der Gourmet-Marke verankert: die hohe Qualität der regionalen Bio-Produkte, die liebevolle Handarbeit sowie der zugleich moderne Charakter. So finden ein lauter Himbeer-Ton und handgeschriebene Schriftzüge zueinander – für jede Sorte aufs Neue. Weiche Linien kontrastieren die kühle Farbigkeit und führen zu einer spannenden Kombination aus Natürlichkeit und Professionalität. Im Mittelpunkt steht die „Schokodeern" selbst – ein Mädchen in traditioneller Kleidung, welches das Logo zusätzlich emotional auflädt.

The visual appearance of the "Schokodeern" includes all important attributes of the gourmet-brand. The high grade of quality of the organic ingredients from regional sources, the loving producing of the hand-crafted candies as well as the modern nature. A blatant, self-confident coloring which supports its autarchy combined with a hand-drawn figure and a handwritten word mark every grade anew. Tender lines contrast the cool coloring and yield to a fascinating combination of naturalness and professionalism. The center of all is the "Schokodeern" herself – a girl wearing traditional clothing who composes the logo in an emotional way.

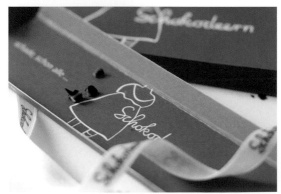

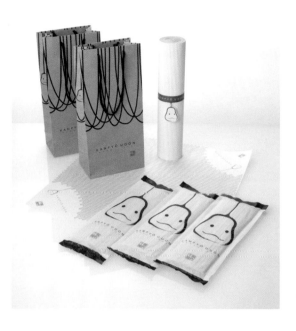

Project
KANPYO UDON
Markenkampagne für ein Nudelprodukt
Branding campaign for noodles

Design
NOSIGNER
Tokyo, Japan

Client
Oyama
Chamber of commerce and industry
Tochigi, Japan

Markenkampagne für das neue „Udon-Nudelpro-
dukt" aus Kürbispulver.
Bei der Gestaltung der neuen Marke habe ich mich
auf zwei Design-Vorgaben konzentriert. Einerseits
sollte das Design freundlich wirken und auf den ersten Blick wiedererkennbar sein. Andererseits sollte
es dem Produkt Niveau verleihen, so dass es mit
anderen traditionellen, hochwertigen Udon-Marken
konkurrieren kann. Um diesen scheinbar gegensätz-
lichen Ansprüchen gerecht zu werden, habe ich den
Charakter „Kanpyo" (Kürbis) entworfen, der an die
japanische Tradition der Kalligrafie erinnert und auf
Japanischem Papier gezeichnet wird.

Branding campaign for the new "Udon noodle"
product composed of gourd powders.
For making the new brand, I focused on two tasks of
design. One was to make the friendly design which
would be remembered at one glance at store. The
other one was to make the high class design which
was able to compete with other traditional high class
Udon brands.
To solve these seemingly-contradict tasks, I made the
new character of Kanpyo(gourd) with the touch of
traditional Japanese calligraphy drawn on Japanese
paper.

Project
Pu tube package
Verkaufsverpackung
Sales packaging

Design
Subkarma International Associates Co., Ltd.
Subkarma Commercial Design Team
Taichung, Taiwan

Client
Shan Hua Plastic Industrial
Tainan, Taiwan

Das Gesicht der SHPI-Marke hat sich verändert. Die neue SHPI-Marke zeigt sich mit ihrem klaren und kontrastreichen Farbdesign professionell und dynamisch. SHPI ist Hersteller für Luftschläuche und Anschlüsse – eine eher „traditionelle" Branche. Die Wiederbelebung zeigt sich im neuen Markenzeichen, im Farbsystem, im Slogan und im Werbematerial. SHPI ist noch einen Schritt weiter gegangen und bietet nun den Endverbrauchern ein umfassendes SHPI-Markenerlebnis mit einer farbkräftigen und unkonventionellen Produktverpackung. SHPI ist ein traditioneller Hersteller mit neuem Markendesign.

SHPI has undergone a tremendous brand face-lift. The new SHPI brand exerts professionalism and dynamism through a clean and color-contrasting visual design expression. SHPI is a manufacturer of air hoses and connectors, an industry categorized as "Traditional". The revitalization is apparent through the new brand trademark, brand color system, brand slogan and other promotional material. SHPI has gone one step further to offer end-users a full SHPI brand experience with vibrant and unconventional product packaging. SHPI is a traditional manufacturer with a brand design twist.

Project
paint container
Verpackung
Packaging

Design
Geckodesign
Ilan Shniezik
Tel Aviv, Israel

Client
Nirlat
Natania, Israel

Dank dieses innovativen Behälters mit integriertem Rührstab im Deckel wird die Farbvorbereitung zum Kinderspiel. Größe, Fassungsvermögen und Form des Behälters sollen den Transport und die Handhabung während eines typischen Streichvorgangs erleichtern. Der Behälter ist stabil, kompakt, einfach zu tragen und so gestaltet, dass er beim Transport nicht umherrollen kann. Er ist mit einem Tragehenkel und einem auf der Unterseite eingelassenen Griff für leichtes Ausgießen ausgestattet. Die Form des Deckels und Bodens lässt einfaches Stapeln beim Transport und im Regal zu, und dank der quadratischen Vorderseite eignet sich das Produkt hervorragend für eine ansprechende Verkaufspräsentation.

Featuring an integrated stirring paddle indented within the lid, this innovative container makes paint preparation convenient and easy. Package size, volume, and shape are designed to facilitate the use, transport, and handling of paint during a typical paint project. The form is stable, compact, easy to carry, and designed to prevent rolling around during transport. The container also includes a carrying handle and a recessed grip on the underside to ease pouring. The container lid and base form are shaped to accommodate stacking for shipping and retail display, and the square shape of the container's front presents neatly on shelves.

Project
Blooming Package
Verpackung
Packaging

Design
LG Electronics, Inc.
Byung Jin Oh, Young Mi Yoon,
Sang Yun Lee, Na Won Lee
Seoul, South Korea

Client
LG Electronics, Inc.
Seoul, South Korea

Das Blooming Package vermittelt ein blumiges Gefühl beim Öffnen, wenn das Telefon unerwartet herausspringt. Die Verpackung ist einfach zu öffnen. Gerät und Zubehör sind leicht zugänglich. Das Paket selbst ist schon ein Blickfang, so dass die Präsentation des Gerätes bereits durch einfaches Öffnen der Verpackung ansprechend ist.

The blooming package gives unexpected fresh delight and impact to a user when the telephone pops out as it is opened. The packaging is easy to open and the product and appendix can easily be taken out. The package itself constitutes an eye-catching element so that the presentation of the product is already appealing when the packaging is simply opened.

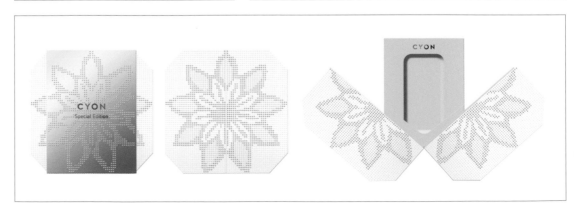

Project
STABILO® GREEN
Verkaufsverpackung
Sales packaging

Design
Ideenhaus
Nürnberg, Germany

Client
STABILO International GmbH
Heroldsberg, Germany

„Farben für eine grünere Welt" ist der Anspruch für das FSC-zertifizierte Sortiment STABILO® GREEN, zu dem Farbstifte, Bleistifte und Trocken-Highlighter gehören. Attraktive Displays überzeugen durch klares Design und plakative Bildsprache. Ein speziell für diese Linie konzipiertes Logo – weißer Schwan auf grünem Hintergrund – dient als Qualitätssiegel und gibt der LOHAS-Zielgruppe (LOHAS Abk. für Lifestyle of Health and Sustainability) ein gutes Gefühl beim Kauf. Die Verpackungen bestehen mindestens zu 80% aus recyceltem Material und stehen ebenfalls für eine klare Linie im Umweltschutz. Die Nachhaltigkeit von STABILO® GREEN-Produkten und -Verpackungen sorgt für ein gutes Gewissen und eine grünere Welt.

"Colors for a greener world" is the claim made by the FSC-certified STABILO® GREEN range, which includes colored pencils, graphite pencils and dry highlighters. Eye-catching displays attract customers with their clear design and striking visuals. A logo created especially for this line – a white swan on a green background – serves as a seal of quality, allowing the "LOHAS" (Lifestyle of Health and Sustainability) to feel good about their purchase. The packaging is made from at least 80% recycled materials and also represents a clear policy of environmental protection. The sustainability of STABILO® GREEN products and their packaging ensures a clear conscience and a greener world.

Project
RP-HJE900 Stereo
Kopfhörer-Verpackung
Earphones packaging

Design
Design Company
Panasonic
Tomohisa Shirosawa
Osaka, Japan

Client
Panasonic
Kadoma, Osaka, Japan

Das Vorbild für diese fortschrittliche Öko-Verpackung ist eine traditionelle japanische Lackkiste mit mehreren Schichten. Auf der ersten Ebene befinden sich die hochentwickelten Kopfhörer, die zweite beinhaltet das Etui für die Kopfhörer. Die Verpackung soll nicht weggeworfen, sondern zur Aufbewahrung des Produkts verwendet werden, wenn dieses nicht gebraucht wird. Auch erhältliches Zubehör wie z. B. ein zusätzliches Hi-Fi-Kabel wird in einer ähnlichen Kiste verkauft, die nahtlos zur Originalverpackung hinzugefügt und so platzsparend aufbewahrt werden kann.

Japanese traditional "multilayered lacquered box" is used as a motive for this premium ECO Package. On the first layer we have the premium earphones and on the second the earphone carrying case. It is designed with the intention that this packaging will not be thrown out after taking the product out of the box, but will be used for storing the product when it is not in use. In addition, when purchasing other related products, such as an extra hi-fi cord, the additional accessories come in a similar box which is designed to fit seamlessly with the original packaging. It easily stacks above the rest to save space.

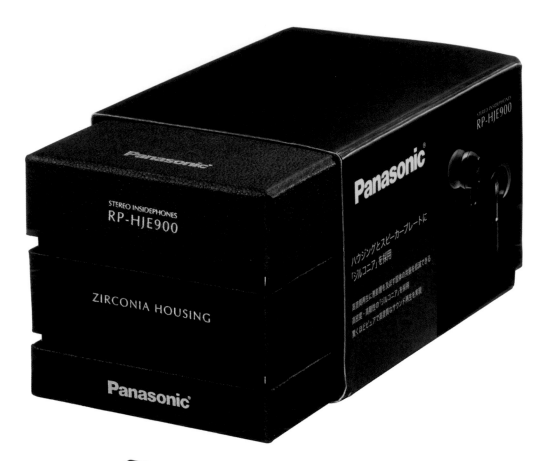

Project
Nespresso Chocolat
Verpackung für Schokoladen-Linie
Packaging for chocolate assortment

Design
FutureBrand Paris
Pierre Abel (Directeur Artistique)
Clichy Cedex, France
Limmatdruck/Zeiler (COPACO)
(Verpackungsdesign)
Koeniz, Switzerland

Client
Nestlé Nespresso SA
Paudex, Switzerland

Ein neuer Trend bringt einen Hauch von Luxus in die Nespresso-Boutiquen: Feine Veredelungseffekte, reduziert eingesetzt und kombiniert mit vornehmen Weißtönen, sorgen für Exklusivität im Regal. Auch die Verpackungen einer neuen stilvollen Nespresso-Schokoladenlinie verführen durch hochklassiges Understatement. Entworfen wurde eine fast durchgängig weiße Verpackung, von deren mattglänzender Oberfläche sich der Nespresso-Schriftzug lediglich durch eine starke Hochprägung abhebt. Feine geprägte Rillen im Hintergrund verstärken den Eindruck zurückhaltender Eleganz.

A new trend is carrying a whiff of luxury in the Nespresso boutiques: fine finishing effects, sparingly deployed in combination with elegant white hues, communicate exclusivity. The packages for a new, stylish Nespresso chocolate line also seduce with aristocratic understatement. An almost completely white package has been created, with the Nespresso logo merely high-embossed on its matte-glossy surface. Fine embossed scoring in the background enhances the impression of subdued elegance.

Project
Herbal Garden
Corporate Communication

Design
Proad Identity
Jennifer Tsai, Chung-Ching Huang
Taipei, Taiwan

Client
Eastern Herbal Garden Bio. Tech. Co.
Yunlin County, Taiwan

Das Symbol von Zhang Zhongjing, dem Großmeister der traditionellen chinesischen Medizin, dient als Logo und Verkörperung des spirituellen Ziels von Eastern Herbal Garden. Der dampfende Kräuterkessel im Hintergrund steht für das Mitgefühl und die Beharrlichkeit, die die Grundlage der medizinischen Versorgung bilden. Der geschmeidige Rangunschlinger und der Portulak verweisen auf die Heilkraft von Mutter Natur – eine vortreffliche Interpretation der Mission von Eastern Herbal Garden. Die Erdfarben im zarten Design des Logos und der Schriftarten lassen an traditionelle chinesische Heilkräuter denken und symbolisieren die Wirkungsweise von Eastern Herbal Garden.

The symbol of Zhang Zhongjing, the Great Master of traditional Chinese medicine, is the logo to represent the spiritual goal of Eastern Herbal Garden. In the background, the steaming herbal cauldron is a token of the compassion and perseverance to provide people with medical care, while the supple Rangoon creeper and the purslane tell the healing power of Mother Nature – a best-suited interpretation of the mission of Eastern Herbal Garden. Earth colors signifying traditional Chinese medicinal herbs are adopted for the delicate design of the logo and the elegant fonts to symbolize the functions of Eastern Herbal Garden.

Project
Rotatable Notebook
Notebook

Design
Proad Identity
Jennifer Tsai, Brenda Chang, Janice Kao
Taipei, Taiwan

Client
Taipei County Goverment
Banciao City, Taiwan

Hier wurde das Konzept von „vier Museen und ein Garten" in Design umgesetzt. Fünf verschiedene Notebooks sind charakteristischen Eigenschaften nachgeahmt. Das drehbare Gehäuse stellt Merkmale des Anwesens und Gartens der Lin-Familie dar. Eine Besonderheit dieses Anwesens kommt in dem fensterartigen Design zum Ausdruck. Dreht man das Gehäuse, öffnet sich gewissermaßen das Tor. Das Notebook ist fadengeheftet, was die Kunstverbundenheit unterstreicht. Die Cover betonen die Merkmale der fünf Strukturen. Die fünf Notebooks in einem Gehäuse repräsentieren die Kultur des Bezirks Taipei – „vier Museen und ein Garten."

The product has integrated the concept of" Four Museums and One Garden" into design. Five different notebooks are made after the main features. The revolving external frame represents special characters of the Lin Family Mansion and Garden. The special window-like design is one of the features of this estate. When the case revolves, it is like opening its gate. Notebook inside the gate is thread-bound to show its artistic nature. Notebook covers focus on the features of these five structures. The five notebooks with one frame completely represent the Taipei county's culture of "Four Museums and One Garden".

Project
Orchid Pattern
Gedeck
Dining ware

Design
Proad Identity
Jennifer Tsai, Brenda Chang, Philips Yeh
Taipei, Taiwan

Client
Cheerful Fashion Goods Co., Ltd.
Taipei, Taiwan

Gedeck im Orchideen-Muster – Orchideenduft verfeinert ein erlesenes Mahl.
Konfuzius sagt: „Orchideen in tiefen Tälern, an denen niemand riecht, duften deshalb nicht weniger gut." Orchideen brauchen kaum Sonnenlicht. Obgleich versteckt, verströmen sie in heiterer Gelassenheit ihren Duft. Um etwas von dieser Gelassenheit und diesem Duft zu vermitteln, haben wir für unser Gedeck das Orchideen-Design gewählt. Deren zurückhaltende heitere Eleganz verzaubert das Essen, ohne ihm etwas von seinem Reiz zu nehmen. So verwebt sich das Speisen auf diesem Gedeck fast unmerklich mit dem vielschichtigen tiefgründigen Wesen der Orchidee.

Orchid Pattern Dining Ware – Fragrance of Orchids to Add to the appeal of Tasteful Food.
Confucius says: "Orchids that grow in deep valleys are not less fragrant because there is no one to smell them." Orchids grow where there is little sunlight. Despite being hidden, they continue to give out their aroma in serenity. To extend this serenity and aroma, we have adopted orchids in the design of dining ware. The restrained and serene elegance of orchids is perfect for adding charm to the food without stealing the appeal. Thus, dining with such utensils is subtly incorporated with the multi-leveled and profound savor the orchids bring.

Project
Blessing cultivated
Geschenkverpackung in Reis-Optik
Rice gift box

Design
Proad Identity
Jennifer Tsai, Brenda Chang, Janice Kao
Taipei, Taiwan

Client
Taiwan Design Center
Taipei, Taiwan

Die Nation Taiwan wurde auf dem Fundament der Landwirtschaft aufgebaut. Der Pflugochse steht für die Tradition der harten Arbeit und des bäuerlichen Metiers. Die Kombination ist ein Ausdruck für die Bewahrung von Taiwans Kultur und Lebensart.
Die schlichte Schönheit von Reiskörnern am Halm wird durch tiefe Erdtöne und umweltfreundliche Materialien vermittelt. Zusammen mit dem Griff aus Jutefäden und Bambus erzielt das Design einen allgemeinen Eindruck rustikaler Einfachheit. Der Artikel wird so zu einem eleganten Erinnerungsstück, das einen Aspekt von Taiwans Reiskultur kommuniziert und das Streben nach Wohlstand durch harte Arbeit symbolisiert.

Taiwan is a nation built on agriculture and the plowing ox stands for the tradition of hard work and industry. The combination expresses the preservation of Taiwan's culture and way of life.
The unadorned beauty of rice grains on the stalk is represented through the use of low chroma earth tone colors and eco-friendly materials. Combined with a handle made of jute strings and bamboo, the design achieves an overall sense of rustic simplicity. This makes the item an elegant souvenir that conveys an aspect of Taiwan's rice culture while symbolizing the cultivation of prosperity through hard work.

Project
The Blue Earth Dream
Ökoverpackung
Eco package

Design
Samsung Electronics
Yoonhee Cho, Nhokyung Hong,
Hyunho Shin, Kayeon Kim
Seoul, South Korea

Client
Samsung Electronics
Suwon-city, South Korea

Diese Ökoverpackung hat einen Herstellungsprozess, der durchweg die Umwelt schützt: vom Verzicht auf Klebstoffe über die handliche Größe und die Verwendung umweltfreundlicher Materialien bis hin zum Recycling und der Entsorgung der Druckerschwärze. Es gibt folgende Verwendungsmöglickeiten: 1. Wiederverwendung – die Handy-„Schale" aus recylingfähiger Riffelpappe kann als Bilderrahmen oder Visitenkartenhalter dienen. 2. Recycling – die Verpackung lässt sich, ähnlich wie eine Dose, flach zusammenlegen und somit leicht entsorgen. 3. 1 : 1-Rücknahmeprogramm – der Nutzer sendet sein altes Handy in der Verpackung mit aufgedruckter Anschrift des Unternehmens ein.

This is an eco package that considers environment-friendly elements throughout the entire creation process, such as non-use of adhesives, smaller size, use of environment-friendly materials, recycling, disposal, and collection of ink. It consists of the following three methods: 1. Reusing Package – The mobile "tray" is made of recyclable fluted paper so that it can be used as a picture frame or business card holder. 2. Recycling Package – It can be made flat, like a can, for easy disposal. 3. 1 : 1 Take Back Program Package – The user places and sends his old mobile phone through the package, on which the address of company is printed.

Project
Genius Mouse Series
Maus-Paket
Mouse package

Design
KYE Systems Corp. (Genius)
Genius Graphic Design Center
Taipei Hsien, Taiwan

Client
KYE Systems Corp. (Genius)
Taipei Hsien, Taiwan

Orientiert am Stil ozeanischer Stämme wie der Bunun und Maori, unterstreichen die Verpackungen das Bewusstsein für Natur und Umwelt. Auf der rechten Verpackung symbolisiert das Rautenmuster eine Schlange, während die Prägung für Hirse steht, das wichtigste Getreide des Bunun-Volkes. Die linke Verpackung zeigt Kunst der Maori und symbolisiert neben der Begrüßung „Kiaora! Kiaora!" auch die traditionelle Gesichtstätowierung „To MoKo". Rot und Schwarz stehen für das CI von Genius. Der goldene Schnitt verleiht der Verpackung eine hohe Ästhetik. Umweltfreundliche Herstellung und Materialien unterstreichen die Werte der Marke Genius.

The design concept reflects the "primitive" and "eco-friendly" culture of the Austronesia tribes (Bunun and Maori). The rhombus pattern and embossing resemble a "Chinese copperhead" and "straw" from the Bunun who respect nature. The left box means "Kiaora! Kiaora!" (nose-bumping ritual) and "To MoKo" (face tattoo) displaying Maori tribal art. The usage of red and black on the package represent the company identity. In addition, the golden ratio of the package emulates visual harmony. By reducing ink, using Kraft paper, and reducing waste, the design is consistent with the spirit of the Genius brand.

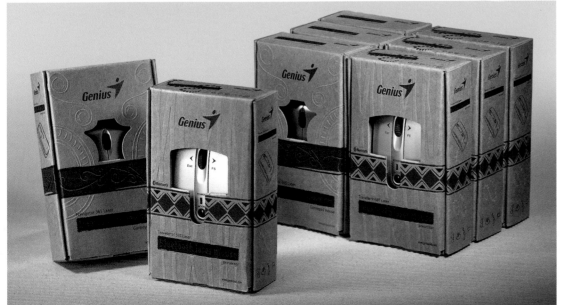

Project
RADO Standard Box
Etui für Uhren
Case for watches

Design
RADO Product Lab
Jasper Morrison
Lengnau, Switzerland

Client
RADO Uhren AG
Lengnau, Switzerland

Das neue – von Jasper Morrison gestaltete – Standardetui für RADO-Uhren ist komplett schwarz. Einfachheit und puristische Linienführung geben den Ton an. Die Oberseite wird im Heißprägeverfahren mit dem RADO-Logo versehen. Eleganz und perfekte Farbharmonie – ein Etui im Dienste des Produktes, zum Bergen und Schützen. Die Uhr liegt in der Box wie am Handgelenk. Das Öffnen und Schließen – als Ritualisierung des Augenblicks der Entdeckung.

The new standard case for RADO watches designed by Jasper Morrison is completely black. Simplicity and purist lines set the tone. The RADO logo is applied to the top using a hot embossing process. Elegance and the perfect harmony of colors – a case that serves the product: guarding, protecting. The watch lies in the box as it does on the wrist.
Opening and closing – as a ritual of the moment of discovery.

Project
Kent Sampling Box
Zigarettenverpackung
Cigarette packet

Design
Burgopak Germany Ltd.
Steven Klett, Jens Striethorst, Daniel Fuchs
Wandlitz, Germany

Client
British American Tobacco GmbH
Hamburg, Germany

Burgopak Germany hat für British American Tobacco, Hamburg, eine spezielle Zigarettenschachtel als Teil einer Marketingkampagne für den österreichischen Markt entwickelt. Die Verpackung lässt sich mit einer Hand öffnen, gleichzeitig wird dabei ein unsichtbarer Magnet entriegelt, der eine Karte auf der Rückseite der Verpackung aufklappen lässt. Beim Öffnen gleiten die Zigaretten verschiedener Geschmacksrichtungen durch einen Schiebemechanismus elegant heraus und sind griffbereit. Beim Schließen bewegen sich die Zigaretten ebenso sanft wieder in die Verpackung zurück, die rückseitige Klappe wird geschlossen und ist wieder eins mit der Schachtel.

Burgopak Germany was designing this give-away cigarette packet especially for British American Tobacco, Hamburg, as part of a marketing campaign for the Austrian market. A smart technical detail is its elegant one hand operated sliding mechanism. When opening, cigarettes of various flavours are lowered out of the top of the packet, ready to hand. Simultaneously, an invisible magnet is releasing a back sided flap that flips open. By closing it, cigarettes are retracted as smoothly as they appeared, the back sided flap is closed and part of the packet again.

Project
Max Factor Mascara
Tasche im Wimpern-Look
Lash look bag

Design
Leo Burnett GmbH
Benjamin Merkel (Copywriter)
Daniela Ewald (Art Director)
Tom Ungemach (Illustrator)
Ulf Henninger von Wallersbrunn (CD)
Andreas Stalder (CD)
Andreas Pauli (CCO)
Kerrin Nausch (AECD)
Frankfurt a. M., Germany

Client
Procter & Gamble
P&G International Operations SA
Petit Lancy, Switzerland

Mit der Wimpern-Tasche demonstrieren wir auf ver-
blüffende Art und Weise den „False Lash Effect" des
neuen Max Factor Mascara. Die Wimpern des aufge-
druckten Auges sind dank des Mascaras so volumi-
nös und lang, dass sie über den Taschenrand hinaus
wachsen und als Henkel zum absoluten Blickfang
werden. Die Wimpern-Tasche wurde in ausgewählten
Kaufhäusern an Kunden verteilt.

With the Max Factor eye bag, we deliver a surprising
and tangible product experience.
The handles of the bag show what happens when
using the "False Lash Effect" Mascara – your lashes
get longer, fuller and more voluminous than ever. The
bag not only shows the product's benefit in an outstanding way, but also gains attention among other
women who see the bag. It is distributed to customers as a free sample at selected department stores.

Project
S Beer
Markenidentität
Brand identity

Design
IDnComm Inc.
Seung-Bum Kim, Heung-Ki Kim, Seon-Ah Ahn
Seoul, South Korea

Client
Hite Brewery Co., Ltd.
Seoul, South Korea

Hite ist die größte Bierbrauerei Koreas.
S Beer, eine der Marken von Hite, enthält als erstes Premium-Bier in Korea Ballaststoffe. Es wendet sich an junge Frauen und spricht den Verbraucher eher emotional als rational an. Das große, auf der Vorderseite des Etiketts zu sehende „S" steht für stylisch, speziell, S-Linie … eben ein Bier mit Stil für junge Leute, das sich von gewöhnlichen Biermarken abhebt. Der starke Kontrast zwischen Dunkel- und Hellgrün weckt die Neugier und macht Lust auf mehr.

Hite brewery is the biggest beer industry in Korea.
S Beer is one of Brands in Hite and it is the first premium beer in Korea to contain fiber. It tries to approach consumers emotionally rather than rationally because it's for young women. Accordingly, "S" which means Stylish, Something Special, S-line, etc is showed in front of the brand. It tries to emphasize "style beer" for young people by putting S that presents the story of beer in front of a beer bottle, different from general beer designs with remarkable products. In addition, the strong color contrast between dark green and light green stimulates your curiosity and taste.

Project
Tomax Seasoning
Verpackung
Packaging

Design
Chart Design
Taipei City, Taiwan

Client
Tomax Enterprises Co.,Ltd.
Taichung, Taiwan

Verpackung für die exotische Gewürzserie der Marke „Why for you". Der neue Entwurf lässt die herkömmliche Gestaltung von Gewürzbehältern weit hinter sich. Der Markenname „Why for you" verbreitet einen Hauch von Spannung – hiervon inspiriert, trotz der geringen Größe des Behälters strebt das Design danach, optisch so ansprechend wie möglich zu sein. Die brillanten Farben der Gewürzgefäße sind mit Sicherheit ein starker Blickfang, ganz anders als die herkömmlichen, neutralen Farben anderer Gewürzmarken.

Packaging for the exotic seasoning series of the brand "Why for you". The new design is a breakaway from the conventional seasoning container design. Inspired by the brand name "Why for you" which gives a sense of suspense, the design strives to maximize visual pleasure within the limited space on the container. Sitting on the racks, the brilliant colors of the design will surely catch eyes, as they are a strong contrast to the conventional neutral colors used by other seasoning brands.

Project
Weißenhorner Milch Manufaktur
Relaunch

Design
Eberle Brand Design
Jochen Eberle (Creative Director)
Katja Schmid (Art Director)
VISCOM (Fotografie)
Schwäbisch Gmünd, Germany

Client
Weißenhorner Molkerei GmbH
Weißenhorn, Germany

Die Eberle GmbH Werbeagentur GWA in Schwäbisch Gmünd verleiht der Weißenhorner Molkerei
ein neues Gesicht. Neben einem neuen Logo erhält
der Hersteller von Molkereiprodukten in Bio-Qualität
nun einen komplett neuen Look, der dem Gourmet-
Anspruch der Produkte gerecht wird. Eberle gestaltet
neben dem ca. 40 Produkte umfassenden Sortiment
auch Image-Kampagne, Messestand, Geschäftsausstattung, Internet und Imageflyer neu.

Eberle GmbH Werbeagentur GWA in Schwäbisch
Gmünd is attributing the Weißenhorner Molkerei a
new image. Apart from a new logo, the manufacturer
of organic dairy products is now also receiving an entire makeover in line with the gourmet demand of its
products. Eberle is redesigning the range comprising
approx. 40 products as well as an image campaign,
the trade fair stand, business equipment, internet and
image flyers.

Project
Humidifier packaging
Verpackung für Luftbefeuchter

Design
HANIL Electric
Du Han Kim
Seoul, South Korea

Client
HANIL Electric
Seoul, South Korea

Das Design unterstreicht die Optik des Produkts. Die Papierverpackung betont mit ihrem innovativen Konzept die kleinkonische Form und ist damit bestens geeignet, die Neugier des Verbrauchers zu wecken. Auf schwarzem Grund wurde neben einer Darstellung des Produkts der Markenname in Silberfolie aufgebracht – das erzeugt ein Gefühl von Klasse und Anspruch. Die Verpackung aus recyclebarer, umweltfreundlicher Wellpappe ist in einem Stück gefertigt, was die Produktivität erhöht.

Through the design emphasizing the visual aspect of the product, the concept of mini cone was innovately applied in the package paper structure of the humidifier, maximizing the curiosity of the consumers regarding the form. The color black was used, and in order to express the feeling of high-class and sophistication, the product shape and the brand was processed in silver foil. Corrugated cardboard, which is recyclable, was used for environment-friendly production.

Project
TCHO Corporate Design
Schokoladenverpackungen
Chocolate packaging

Design
Edenspiekermann
Susanna Dulkinys, Tobias Trost, Robert Stulle,
Marcus Scheller, Francesca Bolognini
Berlin, Germany

Client
TCHO Ventures, Inc.
San Francisco, CA, United States of America

TCHO – das ist Schokolade in bester Qualität und aus fairem Handel, hergestellt mit modernster Technik in einer gigantischen Lagerhalle im Hafen von San Francisco. Diesem Premium-Genuss ein Gesicht zu geben, ist die Herausforderung. TCHO-Schokoladentafeln sind mit feinen Guillochenmustern überzogen und muten wie eine neue Währung an. Diese Gestaltungsmetapher prägt das Erscheinungsbild der Marke. Ein Auftritt mit einem Paukenschlag, der weder in der Presse, im Web noch in der Blogsphäre zu überhören ist.

TCHO stands for the highest quality fair trade chocolate manufactured using the most modern technology in a gigantic warehouse in the San Francisco docks. The challenge was to give this gourmet's experience a face. A TCHO Chocolate bar, with its algorithmic guilloche patterns, looks like a modern form of currency. This design metaphor is carried out through the whole brand appearance. Identity couldn't be any clearer or more emphatic. TCHO is boldly positioning itself as a brand of high quality chocolate, self assured and modern.

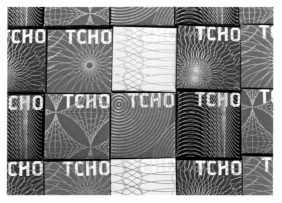

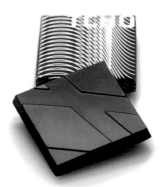

Project
Black Forest Still – PETCYCLE
Flasche
Bottle

Design
Scholz & Friends Identify
Wolf Schneider (Creative Direction)
Maria-Michaela Tonn, Nicole Algieri, Kathrin Wetzel,
Olivier Nowak, Jürgen Krugsperger, Thomas Helzle
(Art Direction)
Berlin, Germany

Client
Peterstaler Mineralquellen GmbH
Bad Peterstal, Germany

Wie schafft man Aufmerksamkeit für ein stilles Mineralwasser aus dem Schwarzwald auf einem hart umkämpften internationalen Markt? Das Geheimnis liegt in der Stille. Das Produkt-Design greift diese Leitidee auf und gibt den Markenattributen Natürlichkeit, Mythos und Frische eine Gestalt. Wie ein Tropfen, der in stilles Wasser fällt, präsentiert sich die neu entwickelte PETCYCLE-Flasche. Das CD stellt eine moderne Interpretation des märchenhaften Schwarzwaldes dar. Die Kombination aus einem Scherenschnitt und dem Schriftzug „Black Forest" verleiht der Marke ihren Charakter. Entwickelt wurde ein emotionales und identifizierbares Design.

How do you draw attention to a still mineral water from the Black Forest amidst a vigorously contested international market? The secret is in stillness. The product design takes up this core idea and incorporates the lead brand properties of naturalness, myth, and freshness. The PETCYCLE bottle we developed is shaped like a drop falling into still water, creating concentric ripples undulating outward and downward from the top towards the base. The corporate design represents a modern interpretation of the fairytale Black Forest. The brand is given its character by a combination of a silhouette and the "Black Forest" lettering.

Project
Again, New Beginning
Geschenkverpackung
Gift box

Design
G-idea Group
David Pan (Creative Director)
Tainan City, Taiwan

Client
Jiu Zhen Nan Taiwan Pastry
Kaohsiung, Taiwan

Geschenkkarton zum Beginn des neuen Mondjahres, hergestellt für Jiu Zhen Nan (gegr. 1890), eine der ältesten und beliebtesten Gebäckmarken Taiwans. Inspiriert von den Präsentiertabletts, die es in beinahe jedem Haushalt gibt und auf denen Besuchern eine Auswahl an Süßigkeiten und Keksen angeboten wird. Wir wollten schon das Öffnen des Kartons zum Erlebnis machen, bei dem sich dem Beschenkten eine wunderbare Welt der Näschereien darbietet. Darüber hinaus sollte der Inhalt so „essfertig" wie möglich sein. Die vier schwarzen Kästchen stehen auch für die vier Jahreszeiten, und die Goldbox in der Mitte repräsentiert die aufgehende Sonne, ein Symbol für einen guten Jahresanfang – daher der Name: „Again, New Beginning" (Wieder ein neuer Anfang).

Created for Jiu Zhen Nan (est. 1890), one of the oldest and most beloved pastry brand in Taiwan as a lunar new year gift box. Inspired by candy trays found in almost all homes, which holds an assortment of candies and cookies for visiting family and friends. We wanted to create an unique "opening" experience, where the user sees a wonderful world of treats revealed upon opening, and also make the process as "ready to eat" as possible. The Four Black Boxes also represent the four seasons, and the Gold boxes in the middle represent the rising sun, which signal a grand beginning to the new year, hence the name "Again, New Beginning".

Project
APEX-i
Kosmetik
Cosmetics

Design
POLA CHEMICAL INDUSTRIES, Inc.
POLA Design Laboratories
Takeshi Usui (Creative Director)
Takashi Matsui (Art Director)
Yushi Watanabe, Haruyo Eto, Kentaro Ito (Designer)
Tokyo, Japan

Client
POLA COSMETICS, Inc.
Nishi Gotanda, Shinagawa-ku, Tokyo, Japan

Das „ultimative persönliche Hautpflegesystem"
APEX-i analysiert die Hautzellschicht einer jeden Be-
nutzerin, wodurch die bestmögliche Produktlösung
erarbeitet wird. Den wissenschaftlichen Ansatz hinter diesen jeweils nach den Ansprüchen der Kundin-
nen angefertigten Artikeln spiegelt das kegelförmige
Flaschendesign wider. Der Flakon symbolisiert das
Verlangen und die Sehnsucht nach weiblicher Schönheit und ihre Erfüllung mithilfe der Wissenschaft.

APEX-i, engineered as the "ultimate personal skin
cosmetic", marshals precision cell level analysis of
each user's skin to propose the best possible product solutions. To manifest the order-made sensation of every item being expressly blended, a scientific touch is embraced for the bottle designs in the
image of a conical flask motif. Conveying, symbolically, the yearning, and the aspiration, for female
beauty fulfilled through the powers of science.

Project
Early Taiwan Scenes
Verpackung mit traditionellen Szenen
Agricultural packings

Design
Good Studio Innovation Co., Ltd.
Van Chen
Taipei City, Taiwan

Client
TTSHOE (NGO)
Nantou County, Taiwan

TTSHOE ist eine NGO (Non-Governmental Organization), die sich mit der Lehre und mit traditionellen Tätigkeiten, wie dem Weben, beschäftigt. Mit
Unterstützung des Good Studios in Fragen der Ästhetik und der Organisation wurden ökologische Verpackungen, die taiwanesische Eigenarten zum Ausdruck bringen, hergestellt. Es handelt sich dabei zum
Beispiel um die einheimische Schiffform für den Pilz,
die Heubälle für die Teedose, Omas Tüte für die Va-
kuum-Reispackung und die Stirnbänder der Arbeiter
für den Reisschnaps. Das sind ländliche Symbole aus
der frühen Zeit in Taiwan. Die Verpackung wird bei
TTSHOE hergestellt.

TTSHOE is a NGO (Non-Governmental Organization)
skilled in traditional straw weaving and teaching.
With the help of Good Studio in aesthetics and process, they develop such packing with Taiwan characteristics and ecological concept. Wisely, aboriginal
boat shape for the mushrooms, hay bale for tea
can, grandma's wrap bag for vacuum rice pack, and
worker's head band for the rice wine are the early
year farm scenes of Taiwan. The manufacturer of the
packing is TTSHOE, directed by Ms. Bi-Hsia, Lin.

Project
L & M NIGHT
Zigaretten-Verpackung
Cigarettes packaging

Design
The Brand Union
Norman Quadflieg, Kai Koltermann,
Elke Pietzsch, Christiane Kleinschmidt
Hamburg, Germany

Client
Philip Morris GmbH
München, Germany

Für die Marke L & M wurde ein völlig neuartiges Konzept entwickelt: Eine Marke, die sich an erwachsene Nachtschwärmer richtet. Dabei wartet das Design mit einigen innovativen Features auf: das schwarze Soft Pack, das die Nacht visualisiert, ein schwarzes Lack-Logo auf schwarzem Grund und als Höhepunkt ein Ausstattungsdetail, das es in diesem Genussmittel-segment noch nie gab – eine rote metallisierte Innen-folie. Als Gesamtkonzept (schwarzes Ton-in-Ton-Au-ßenkleid, rote Metallic-Innenfolie) steht die Packung für den Glamour und das Ambiente der aktuellen Nightlife-Szene, ein Statement und Understatement zugleich.

A completely unconventional concept was developed for the brand L & M: A cigarette which is focused on adult night owls. Several innovative features accentu-ate the design: the black soft pack which envisages the night-time atmosphere, a black colored high gloss logo on a matte black background underlined by an added highlight, as yet unprecedented in the tobacco market – the unique red metallised inner foil. As a holistic concept (exterior in shades of black plus red metallised inner foil) the brand design represents the glamour and ambience of the urban nightlife-scene – a statement and understatement at the same time.

Fruit Ice Tea

Matcha au lait

Project
Tale of Desserts Bag
Verkaufsverpackung
Marketing package

Design
MOS BURGER
Kin Lin
Taipei City, Taiwan

Client
MOS BURGER
Taipei City, Taiwan

Unsere Handytaschen wollten wir in Form von Socken gestalten, die sich als besondere und praktische Weihnachtsgeschenke eignen würden. Doch welches Design und welche Farben sollten wir nehmen? Mir kamen die Desserts und Soft-Drinks von MOS Burger in den Sinn, deren Verpackungen äußerst attraktiv sind und daher ausgezeichnete Modelle für dieses Projekt darstellten. Der fruchtige Eistee und der Matcha au Lait wurden zu Streifen, die Broccolisuppe und der Erdbeerkäsekuchen zu Tupfen und Karos. Jede Handytasche trägt den Namen unserer Produkte, so dass die Designelemente die Esswaren und damit auch das Unternehmen verkörpern. Diese Handytaschen sind die beste Reklame für unsere Esswaren.

Broccoli

Strawberry Cheese

We decided our cell phone bags to have the form of socks, that would be suitable as special and practical Christmas gifts. But what design and colors should we use? I thought of the MOS Burger desserts and soft drinks with their extremely attractive packaging which makes them outstanding models for this project. The fruity iced tea and the matcha au lait were transformed into the gradient stripes; the broccoli soup and the strawberry cheese cake converted into dots and diamonds. Each cell phone bag bears the name of our products so that the design elements embody the foods and therefore also the company. These cell phone bags are ideal promotional tools for our food.

Project
Kraftstoff/Powerfuel
Wodka
Vodka

Design
Kolle Rebbe/KOREFE
Katrin Oeding (Creative Direction)
Reginald Wagner (Art Direction)
Jan Simmerl (Grafik)
Heiko Windisch (Illustration)
Katharina Trumbach (Text)
Hamburg, Germany

Client
The DeliGarage
Hamburg, Germany

The DeliGarage soll als Kooperative verstanden werden, die kleine ortsansässige Hersteller von Delikatessen mit ästhetischen Verpackungen, liebevollen Designs und außergewöhnlichen Ideen bei einem erfolgreichen Markteintritt unterstützt. Die Verpackungsidee und das Design sind immer eine Mischung aus hochwertigem Design und einem Hauch „Garage". „Kraftstoff" ist ein Wodka mit dem unkonventionellen Geschmack von Melone und Minze, Ingwer und Koriander und Espresso.

The DeliGarage shall be understood as a cooperative that supports little, local manufacturers of delicacies with aesthetic packaging, loving designs and exceptional ideas for a successful market entry. The packaging idea and design are always a mix between high standard design and a taste of garage. "Powerfuel" is vodka with the unconventional taste of melon and mint, ginger and coriander and espresso.

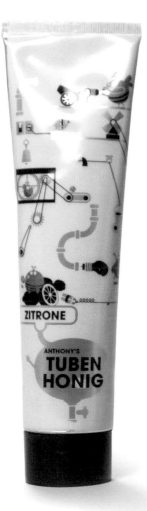

Project
Tubenhonig
Honig-Verpackung
Honey packaging

Design
Kolle Rebbe / KOREFE
Katrin Oeding (CD)
Reginald Wagner (AD)
Jan Simmerl (Illustration)
Santa Gustina (Illustration)
Katharina Trumbach (Text)
Madelen Gwosdz (Text)
Hamburg, Germany

Client
the garage winery e. k.
Oestrich-Winkel, Germany

Da der Winzer Anthony Hammond seine Delikatessen in einer alten Traktoren-Werkstatt herstellt, haben all seine Produkte einen industriellen Touch. Auch der Honig ist in einer werkstatttypischen Verpackung abgefüllt – in Tuben. Jede Sorte ist durch ein hochwertiges Design mit Illustrationen passend zur jeweiligen Geschmacksrichtung gestaltet.

Since winemaker Anthony Hammond produces his delicatessen foods in a former tractor repair shop, all of the products from his label have an industrial look and feel. The honey comes in packaging similar to that found in garages; in this case, in tubes. Obviously, all sorts are presented in high quality designs with different illustrations for each type of honey.

Project
GROHE Rainshower
Verpackungen
Packaging

Design
Grohe AG
In-House Design Team
Düsseldorf, Germany

Client
Grohe AG
Düsseldorf, Germany

Die neue Generation der GROHE Rainshowers – „Icon", „Eco" und „Solo" verbindet das optimale Duscherlebnis mit einem geringen Wasserverbrauch sowie ressourcenschonender Herstellung, Verpackung und Logistik. Jede Seite der Verpackungseinheit liefert eine eindeutige Botschaft – von der Produkt-Technologie bis hin zu den Vorteilen für den Nutzer. Dabei wurde das Verpackungsvolumen gegenüber der Vorgängergeneration um fast 50% reduziert. So passen mehr Packungen auf eine Versandpalette – ein weiterer Beitrag zur CO_2-Einsparung.

The next generation of GROHE Rainshowers, "Icon", "Eco" and "Solo" have been created to fuse the optimum showering experience with the assurance that they significantly reduce consumption of water and resource to make, package and ship. Each side of the package delivers a clear and concise message from the technology within the product to the benefits for the user. The package is almost 50% less in volume than its predecessor which means significantly more packages fit onto a pallet for shipping; substantially reducing the overall carbon footprint of the product.

Project
Eins, Zwei, Dry
Etikett und Kartonage
Label and container

Design
Fuenfwerken Design AG
Wiesbaden, Germany

Client
Weingut Josef Leitz
Rüdesheim am Rhein, Germany

Als Anspielung auf Billy Wilders (fast) gleichnamige Cold-War-Komödie kommt mit „Eins, Zwei, Dry" keine amerikanische Brause ins Nachkriegsdeutschland, sondern ein trockener deutscher Riesling in die „lieblichen" USA. Bei „Eins, Zwei, Dry" gingen die Entwicklung des Weins und dessen Verpackungsdesigns Hand in Hand, um ein Produkt zu schaffen, das perfekt auf den amerikanischen Markt abgestimmt ist. Das klassische Erscheinungsbild von Leitz wurde durch die forschen handgezeichneten Lettern sowie die grob gehaltene Ziffer gezielt aufgeraut. Der Schriftzug verläuft bruchlos über die Flaschenkartons hinweg, wenn diese versetzt gestellt werden.

As an allusion to Billy Wilder's Cold War movie comedy of almost the same name, "Eins, Zwei, Dry" is not an American carbonated beverage coming to postwar Germany but a dry German Riesling they're getting sweet on in the USA. With "Eins, Zwei, Dry" the development of the wine and its pack design went hand in hand to create a product that is perfectly tuned to the American market. The classic Leitz look was roughed up a bit with bold hand-drawn letters and the crudely presented number. The logotype runs seamlessly across the bottle cartons when they are arranged in a staggered formation.

Project
PowerShot E1
Kamera-Verkaufsverpackung
Camera packaging

Design
Canon Inc.
Osami Matsuda, Chieko Shimotsu, Yuuka Fujii
Tokyo, Japan

Client
Canon Inc.
Tokyo, Japan

PowerShot E1 wurde für Frauen entwickelt, die die Kamera jederzeit leger benutzen – drinnen und draußen. Eine solche intuitive Ausstrahlung war Entwurfschwerpunkt. Um Frauen Vertrautheit zu vermitteln, wurde das Kamerafoto mit einem Bild für Wärme überlegt. Der Eindruck ist entspannt. Das Innere ist übersichtlich und schön, mit gleichfarbigem Papier und kompakter Dokumentierung. Das Design ist umweltfreundlich: Die kleine Kamera und digitalisierte Dokumente verkleinerten den Karton um ca. 48% im Vergleich zu vorher. Dies spart Wertstoffe und CO_2. Eine Designherausforderung, die das neue Wesen von Digitalkameras berührt.

The PowerShot E1 is oriented as a camera that women can grab on their way out and use casually on a daily basis. This concept was kept in mind when designing the package. To have women identify with the PowerShot E1, the package was designed to give a warm, relaxed impression. Ingenuity was also used to make the inside of the box appear simple and clean when it is first opened, by combining the manuals together and by using the same color for the backing paper. The box was also made 48% smaller than regular digital camera boxes, and also enables for environmental-consciousness through resource saving and reduction of CO_2 emissions.

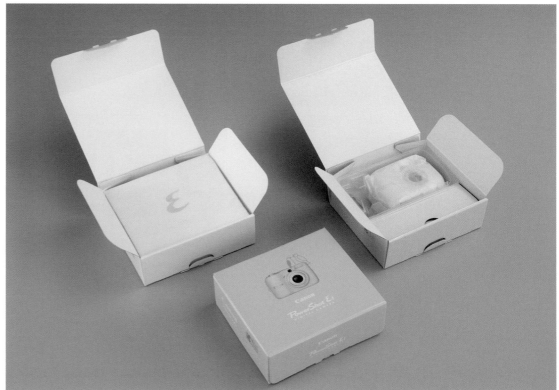

Project
EVE
Alkoholhaltiges Getränk
Alcoholic drink

Design
feldmann+schultchen design studios
Julia Otten, Ursula Eisen, Stephan Kremerskothen,
André Feldmann, Arne Schultchen
Hamburg, Germany

Client
Carlsberg Deutschland
Hamburg, Germany

Ein prickelndes Erlebnis elegant verpackt – das ist Eve,
ein spritziges, fruchtiges Getränk für die Frau. Das aus
natürlichen Zutaten hergestellte, leicht alkoholische
Getränk präsentiert sich für die Einführung auf dem
deutschen Markt in einer femininen Flasche mit ele-
ganter Silhouette und macht durch sein ansprechen-
des Äußeres Lust auf das leichte, fruchtige Innen-
leben. Am Flaschenhals fühlbar erhabene Glasperlen
machen das Prickeln in der Flasche auch von außen
erlebbar. Am nach oben strebenden Flaschenhals ver-
dichten sich die Perlen, die die Flasche markieren und
ihr die individuelle Gestalt geben.

A sparkling experience packed in elegance – this is
Eve, a tingly, fruity drink for women. The light alcoholic drink, produced from natural ingredients, en-
ters the German market in a novel, feminine-shaped
bottle with elegant silhouette that creates desire for
the light, fruity content through its attractive appearance. Embossed glass beads around the bottle
neck make the tingly experience within the bottle
perceptible from outside. The glass beads gradually
intensify up the bottle neck to designate and endow
the bottle its characteristic shape.

Project
P7 Packaging
Verkaufsverpackung
Sales packaging

Design
iriver Ltd.
YeongKyu Yoo,GoEun Han,
SangHyun Jeong, JinYoung Park
Seoul, South Korea

Client
iriver Ltd.
Seoul, South Korea

Die transparente Verpackung lässt das Produkt sichtbar werden, sodass die Verpackung selbst ein großartiges Medium ist. Das Design des mittleren Verpackungsteils vermittelt den Eindruck, das Produkt sei auf einer Platte angerichtet und serviert und der Inhalt fließe in das Loch, das wie ein „R" geformt ist. Außer als Produktverpackung kann P7 nach Entnahme des Produkts als Behälter benutzt werden. Die Designer von iriver gestalteten P7 so, dass die Verpackung wieder verwendbar ist, bevor sie endgültig recycelt wird.

The transparent plastic exterior makes the inside product visible, so the package itself serves a great display tool. The design of the middle part delivers the sensation that the product is "served" on a dish, and the hole in the middle is "R" shaped so it looks as if the inside contents flows into the hole. Besides serving its purpose as a product package, after the product is taken out of the box it becomes a container. The iriver designers made it so that the package is re-usable and recycled for real-life application, before it's recycled for good.

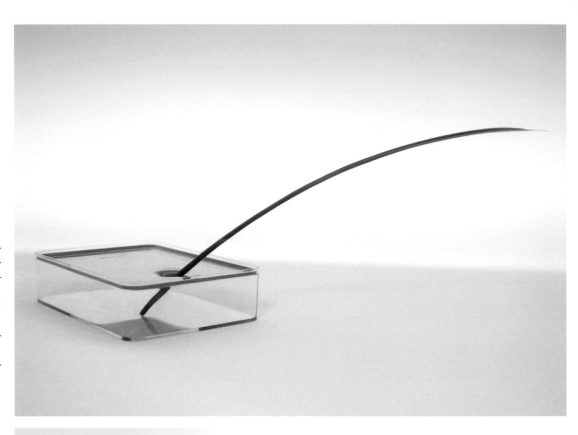

Project
Systemkofferserie
Systemkoffer für professionelles Malerwerkzeug
Case system for professional tools for painters

Design
stotz-design.com GmbH & Co. KG
Oliver Stotz, Oliver Gehrmann, Andrea Kroos,
Cornelia Schütte, Frank Thiemann
Wuppertal, Germany

Client
STORCH
Malerwerkzeuge & Profigeräte GmbH
Wuppertal, Germany

Die Systemlösung für die „Werkzeugkiste" im täglichen Einsatz – ressourcenfreundlich, langlebig, prozessorientiert. Der Grundkörper greift die traditionelle Malerkoffer-Konzeption aus Holz auf und wird je nach Anwendungsfall mit weiteren Haltesystemen, Auszügen und Schubfächern ausgestattet. Die „blue box" gibt es in zehn verschiedenen Ausführungen. Die perfekte Kombination von Arbeiten, Lagern und Transportieren wird durch individuelle Flexibilität ermöglicht. Die Dynamik im System, durch übersichtliche, produktspezifische Lagerung gewährleistet, bietet sichere Aufbewahrung, Transport von Werkzeug und Zubehör sowie einen optimalen Arbeitsablauf.

The system solution for the "tool box" in daily use – resource-friendly, long-lasting, process-oriented. The base body picks up the traditional concept of the wooden painter's tool case and can be equipped with further storage systems, extracts and drawers depending on the area of performance. The "blue box" comes in ten different designs. The perfect combination of working, save-keeping and transporting – a dynamic system made possible by clearly arranged and product-specific storage provides save-keeping, transport of tools, accessories and consumables as well as an optimal work flow.

Project
White Cases
Kofferserie
Case series

Design
Wahrheitdesign GmbH
Katrin Becker, Carina Roth, Gabriele Ruf,
Heike Wahrheit, Michael Wahrheit
Remshalden, Germany

Client
Licefa GmbH & Co. KG
Bad Salzuflen, Germany

White Cases bietet Lösungen für die attraktive Verpackung und Präsentation individueller, kundenspezifischer Inhalte. Mit ihrer klaren und leichten Formensprache und mit ihrem glänzenden Finish eignen die Koffer sich ideal für vielfältige Aufgaben. Wertvolle Produkte und Ideen lassen sich eindrucksvoll in Szene setzen. Die exklusive Kofferserie zeigt sich sehr flexibel in Sachen Größe, Stückzahl und Ausstattung. Jetzt werden hochwertige Verpackungslösungen möglich, die sinnvoll Ordnung schaffen und durch ihre Eleganz bestechen. Packaging-Design und ergänzende Kommunikationsmittel sind optimal aufeinander abgestimmt und sprechen neue Zielgruppen an.

White Cases offers solutions for the attractive packaging and presentation of individual, customer-specific contents. With their clear, light style and high-gloss finish, the cases are ideal for a wide variety of tasks. High-end products and ideas can be presented in an impressive manner. The exclusive series of cases is very flexible in terms of size, quantity and layout. Now you can obtain high-end packaging solutions that create meaningful order as well as appealing through their elegance. Packaging design and supplemental communication media are optimally harmonized and address new target groups.

Project
customized calendar
Werbeartikel
Promotional

Design
THIMM Verpackung GmbH & Co. KG
Florens Lau
Northeim, Germany

Client
THIMM Verpackung GmbH & Co. KG
Northeim, Germany

Dieser Wand-Kalender ist als ein außergewöhnliches Werbegeschenk in der Adventszeit für Mitarbeiter, Geschäftspartner oder Freunde konzipiert. Er unterscheidet sich von herkömmlichen Standard-Kalendern durch seine auffällige Form und Funktion sowie durch individualisierbares Design. Hergestellt aus umweltfreundlicher Wellpappe, wird der Kalender im hochwertigen Digitaldruck individuell mit firmenspezifischem Logo, Produkten oder persönlichen Bildern gestaltet. Der Versender kann sich auf diese Weise mit einer individuellen Erscheinung und Befüllung des Kalenders bei Freunden oder Geschäftspartnern täglich in Erinnerung bringen.

This wall-calendar is designed as a special promotional gift during Christmas time for employees, business partners or friends. The calendar differs substantially from standard calendars due to an eye-catching form and function as well as its potential for customization. It is made of corrugated board as an environmentalfriendly material and can be individually designed by digital printing with specific company logos, products as well as personalized images. As a result, the sender creates a frequent reminder for friends or business partners with its customized design of the calendar including individual gifts for every day.

Project
LägereBräu
Bierflaschen und Träger
Beer bottles and carriers

Design
LIMA-KILO-WHISKEY
Thomas Lehner, Jacob Kadrmas, Oliver Wehn
Basel, Switzerland

Client
LägereBräu AG
Bierspezialitäten
Wettingen, Switzerland

Die LägereBräu AG, eine Kleinbrauerei in Wettingen (Schweiz), produziert seit 2008 Spezialbiere für den regionalen Markt. Das Produkt LägereBräu ist ein besonderes Bier für die speziellen Momente des Miteinanders. Die visuelle Identität bringt die geteilte Begeisterung für das traditionelle Produkt Bier mit dem Leben der jungen Zielgruppe zusammen. Wichtiger Teil des Gestaltungskonzepts ist ein ehrlicher und bewusster Umgang mit Materialität im Kontext des Produkts. Dadurch werden Natürlichkeit und selbstbewusste Bescheidenheit der Marke vermittelt. Kostengünstige Standardmaterialien werden dezent veredelt oder ungewöhnlich verwendet.

LägereBräu AG, a small beer brewing company located in Wettingen (Switzerland), has been producing special beers for a regional market since 2008. LägereBräu is an outstanding beer for memorable moments spent with others. The visual identity expresses the shared enthusiasm for beer as a traditional product within the lives of a young target audience. An important aspect of the design concept is the conscious handling of materials in relation to the product: it expresses the brand's natural quality and its confident modesty. Inexpensive and readily available materials are modestly refined or used in surprising ways.

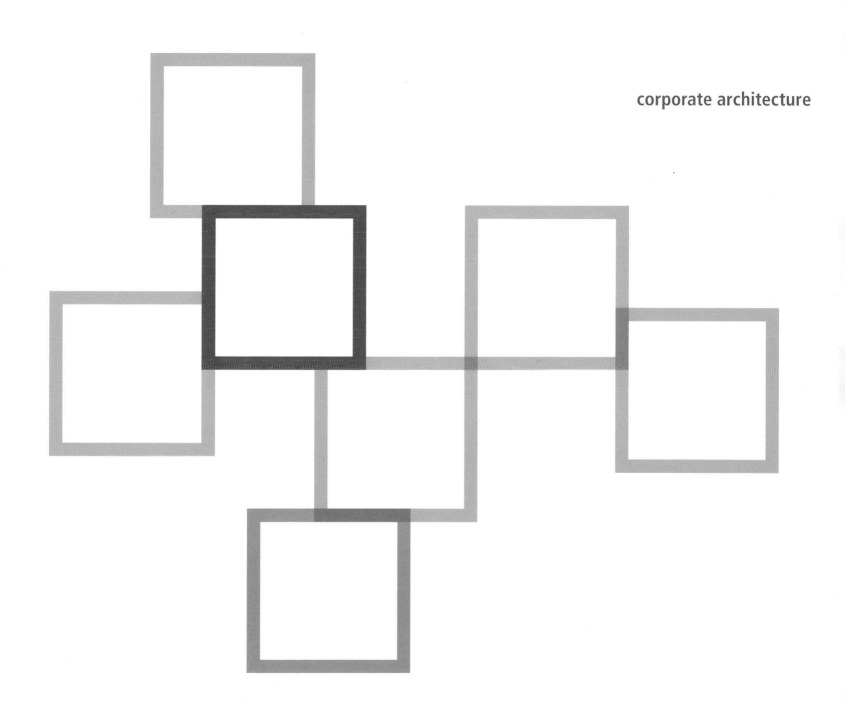

corporate architecture

Ein eindeutiges „corporate architecture" ist in den Köpfen der Verantwortlichen fest verankert

Die diesjährige Prämierung in der Kategorie corporate architecture hat mich sehr begeistert, da das Thema nun eindeutig am Markt angekommen ist.

Wenn es früher nur große Industrieunternehmen und Marken waren, die darauf sehr viel Wert gelegt haben, sind es jetzt auch Mittelständler und Kleinunternehmen, die mit einer eindeutigen corporate architecture auftreten.

Das zeigt, dass dieses Thema fest in den Köpfen der Verantwortlichen verankert ist.

Dies ist auch anhand der Briefings festzustellen; die Dokumente sind nicht mehr seitenlang mit CD und CI Informationen gefüllt. Es geht viel mehr darum, die Zielgruppe zu identifizieren und ein Konzept zu entwickeln, das darauf abzielt, die Zielgruppe für das Unternehmen zu begeistern und die Produkte auf emotionale Weise erlebbar zu machen.

Hierfür braucht es mehr als ein drehendes Würfellogo und die Logofarbe als Vorlage für die Farbe der Wandabwicklung. Bei den Einreichungen, die die Jury mit einem gold award ausgezeichnet hat, ist diese Tendenz und Qualitätssteigerung der Kommunikation und Interaktion deutlich zu erkennen.

Die Bedürfnisse der Zielgruppe wurden bei den ausgezeichneten Projekten sehr genau analysiert und auf sehr beeindruckende Weise in die Architektur und in die unterschiedlichen Flächenbespielungen übertragen.

Insgesamt ist bei allen Einreichungen eine eindeutige Tendenz zu erkennen. Die Zukunft der corporate architecture wird nicht in überdimensionierten „Brand Tempeln" liegen, sondern viel mehr in der Gestaltung und intelligenten Inszenierung von Räumen und Flächen, in denen sich die Zielgruppe heimisch und verstanden fühlt.

A well-defined "corporate architecture" is firmly rooted in the minds of those responsible

I was very excited about this year's awards in the corporate architecture category because the topic has now clearly reached the market.

Where only large industrial enterprises and major brands used to place a lot of emphasis on this, SMEs and small companies are now also appearing with their own distinct corporate architectures.

This indicates that the topic has become firmly entrenched in the minds of those responsible.

The briefings also confirm this; no longer are the documents filled with pages of CD and CI information. Instead, the objective is to identify the target group and develop a concept aimed at attracting the target group to the company and allowing the products to be experienced emotionally.

This requires more than a rotating cube logo and the logo colors as a template for the color of the wall drawings. Among the entries selected by the jury for a gold award, this trend and improvement in the quality of communication and interaction is clearly evident.

In the selected projects, the needs of the target group were analyzed quite precisely and transferred to the architecture and various surface designs in a very impressive manner.

A clear trend is recognizable among all of the entries. The future of corporate architecture does not lie in oversized "brand temples" but rather in the design and intelligent presentation of spaces and surfaces in which the target group feels at home and understood.

Hubert Grothaus

Project
Carpetecture
Messestand
Trade fair stand

Design
TULP Products GmbH
Maik Schober, Alexander Striegl,
Michael Zanin
München, Germany

Client
DESSO
PA Waalwijk, The Netherlands

Die Carpetecture-Produktlinie des Teppichherstellers DESSO, inspiriert von zeitgenössischer Architektur, steht im Mittelpunkt des 64 m² großen Messestands, entworfen für die „Interieur08" in Belgien. Ausgehend von der Idee, die Verbindung von Teppich und Architektur (carpetecture) zu nutzen, entsteht aus dem Produkt heraus ein architektonisches Objekt mit haptischem Erlebnisfaktor. Durch die Anhebung und Verkippung des Bodens wird die Teppichfläche raumbildend und es entsteht eine großzügige Fläche zur Produktpräsentation. Darunter, von der Seite aus sichtbar, befinden sich – in weiß gehalten – der Empfang sowie der Besprechungs- und Funktionsbereich.

The product line Carpetecture by carpet manufacturer DESSO, drawing its inspiration from contemporary architecture, is the focus of the trade fair stand (64 m²) designed for the "Interieur08" in Belgium. Based on the concept of a combination of carpets and architecture (carpetecture), the product itself is the source of inspiration for an architectural structure that offers tactile experiences. By means of lifted and tilted floor sections, the carpeted area defines the space while offering generous product displays. Underneath, just visible from the side, are the reception, meeting and functional areas, all of them white.

Project
4010 Der Telekom Shop in Mitte
Shop

Design
Mutabor Design GmbH
Heinrich Paravicini (CD)
Axel Domke (AD)
Thomas Huth (Architektur)
Holger Schardt (Innenarchitektur)
Nils Zimmermann (Design)
Mate Steinforth, Timo Schädel,
Jaquement Baptiste,
Rimantas Lukavicius (Filmanimation)
Thomas Manig (Künstler)
forose humanactive spaces (Media)
Ian Pooley (Musik)
Krieger des Lichts (Programmierung)
Hamburg, Germany

Client
Deutsche Telekom AG
Bonn, Germany

4010 ist der neue Concept-Store der Deutschen Telekom in Berlin Mitte. Der Name leitet sich aus dem Telekom-Magenta Farbwert RAL 4010 ab. Das neuartige Konzept ist mehr Galerie als Shop, mehr Erlebnis als Verkauf – und doch findet alles zusammen. Zielvorgabe des neuen 200-m²-Stores war, der urbanen Jugend ein Telekom-Angebot auf Augenhöhe zu machen. Das Ergebnis ist eine Dialog-Plattform, welche die Themen „Community" und „Shopping" miteinander verwebt und eine Anlaufstelle zum Verweilen und Entdecken bietet.

4010 is the new Deutsche Telekom concept store in Central Berlin. The name comes from the RAL color code for Telekom's magenta brand color. The novel concept is more gallery than shop, more experience than sales – and yet everything fits together. Describe how you arrived at the final design. The aim of the new 200 m² store was to offer urban young people Telekom products and services at street eye level. The result is a dialog platform where "community" and "shopping" merge, a place for lingering and exploring. Another unique feature of the store is its chameleon-like nature. All the products disappear quickly into custom-made furniture.

Project
AMBIENT GEM
Messearchitektur
Trade show architecture

Design
Veech Media Architecture (VMA)
Stuart A. Veech,
Mascha Veech-Kosmatschof,
Peter Mitterer, Utku Mutlu
(Project Team)
Wien, Austria

Client
D. Swarovski & Co
Wattens, Austria

Das Architektur- und Designstudio VMA übernahm sowohl Konzeption und Design als auch die Umsetzung des 400 m² großen Swarovski-Messestandes für die „BASELWORLD Watch and Jewellery Messe 2008". Das Designkonzept dieses ambitionierten und innovativen Projektes basiert auf der Übersetzung der Markenidentität von Swarovski und im Speziellen der neuen Gemstone-Produktlinie „ENLIGHT-ENED TM". Swarovski-Elemente präsentieren sich in einem raumgreifenden visuellen, akustischen und haptischen Gesamterlebnis. Die Raumform folgt der Logik einer gefalteten Struktur. Der kristalline Kern aus einer multimedial-bespielbaren facettierten, pneumatischen Membran reflektiert die Magie eines Kristalls.

The architecture and design studio VMA conceived designed and managed the production of the 400 m² Swarovski stand at the "BASELWORLD Watch and Jewellery Fair 2008". The design concept of this ambitious and innovative project was focused on translating the Swarovski brand identity and staging the launch of the new gemstone product line "ENLIGHT-ENED TM". Swarovski Elements are presented as a vibrant three-dimensional ambient environment. The form of the spaces follows the logic of a folded structure. The crystalline core materialized as a pneumatic faceted membrane was enhanced by animated lighting / video projections reflecting the magic of the gemstone.

Project
Sparkasse Berchtesgadener Land
Haupt- und Geschäftsstelle
Central office and branch

Design
Bolwin Wulf
Architekten Partnerschaft
Thomas Bolwin, Hanns-Peter Wulf,
Tobias Rotermund, Kristin Schott,
Dagmara Kaczmarczyk,
Christina Krüger
Berlin, Germany
Kunst am Bau und Leitsystem
Ingeborg Kumpfmüller
Wien, Austria

Client
Sparkasse Berchtesgadener Land
Bad Reichenhall, Germany

Die Haupt- und Geschäftsstelle der Sparkasse Berchtesgadener Land in Bad Reichenhall wurde inhaltlich und baulich umfassend neu konzipiert. Trotz Verwendung der sparkassentypischen Elemente der Corporate Identity sollte ein unverwechselbares Haus entstehen, welches sich in höchstem Maße zum Standort bekennt. Die Region um Bad Reichenhall verdankt ihren Aufstieg dem Salz (Hall = Saline, Salz). Das gesamte Gestaltungskonzept des Hauses basiert daher auf dem natürlichen Farbspektrum des Salzes, von hellrosa bis dunkelviolett. Die Farben finden sich im gesamten Haus in ausgewählten Tönen und Helligkeiten in Material und Licht wieder.

The central office and branch of the Sparkasse Berchtesgadener Land in Bad Reichenhall was comprehensively redesigned in terms of content and structure. Notwithstanding the corporate identity elements typical for the savings bank, the intent was to create a unique facility with a clear local commitment. The region around Bad Reichenhall owes its importance to salt (Hall = salt mine, salt). As a result, the overall design concept for the building is based on the natural color spectrum of salt from light pink to dark purple. Throughout the facility, the colors are found in select shades and brightness levels of material and light.

Project
Der IDEENPOOL
Messestand
Exhibition stand

Design
wirDesign communications AG
Michael Rösch (Konzept)
Jan Straßenburg (Text)
Malte Honecker (Design)
Karsten Müller (Animation)
Braunschweig, Germany
Fricke inszeniert.
Dreidimensionale
Kommunikation GmbH
Karsten Fricke (Konzept)
Melanie Bugge (Planung)
André Brandes (Design)
Börßum, Germany

Client
wirDesign communications AG
Braunschweig, Germany
Fricke inszeniert.
Dreidimensionale
Kommunikation GmbH
Börßum, Germany

Am Anfang stand eine zentrale Frage: Wie können Marketing- und Messeverantwortliche heute noch für außergewöhnliche Messeerlebnisse interessiert werden? Die Antwort: Mit einer klaren Kernidee, die über alle Sinne begreifbar und erlebbar gemacht wird – umgesetzt in unserem Gemeinschaftsprojekt „Der IDEENPOOL", den wir 2008 auf der „MX Messe-Expo" in Stuttgart präsentierten. Der Stand war ein sinnliches Erlebnis von nur 24 m² Größe. Die zentrale Botschaft: „Wagen Sie den Sprung in einen Pool frischer Ideen!" – optisch wie haptisch übersetzt mit einem Swimmingpool, gefüllt mit 14.000 Bällen. Alle Elemente des IDEENPOOLs formten die Kernidee: Transparente Standwände mit badenden Kindern und Markenbotschaften, Startblöcke mit unseren Kompetenzen und eine Poolbar, an der ein Imagefilm zeigte, wie Cocktails für erfolgreiche Kommunikationsprojekte richtig gemixt werden. Im Zuge der Messenachbereitung bekamen Besucher des Stands eine kleine transparente Kiste mit Pool-Bällen zugeschickt. Unter dem Label „OFFICE-EDITION 1.0" konnten sie so noch einmal den IDEENPOOL erleben. Die Botschaft des beiliegenden Booklets: „Wagen Sie den Sprung in den Pool der Ideen. Wir reichen Ihnen die Hand."

It started with a central question: How can one get today's marketing and trade show decision-makers interested in unusual trade show experiences? The answer: With a clear basic concept that can be grasped and experienced with all the senses – implemented in our joint project "Der IDEENPOOL" (The IDEA POOL) presented at the 2008 "MX Messe-Expo" (MX Trade Show Expo) in Stuttgart. The booth was a sensual experience, only 24 m² in size. The central message: "Take the plunge into a pool of fresh ideas!" – visually and tactilely translated into a swimming pool filled with 14,000 balls. All elements of the IDEA POOL formed the core concept: Transparent walls with bathing children and brand messages, starting blocks with our expertise and a pool bar where an image film showed how to correctly mix cocktails for successful communication projects. In the course of trade show follow-up, booth visitors received a small transparent box of pool balls. Under the label "OFFICE EDITION 1.0", this allowed them to once again experience the IDEA POOL. The message of the enclosed booklet: "Take the plunge into the pool of ideas. We're ready for you."

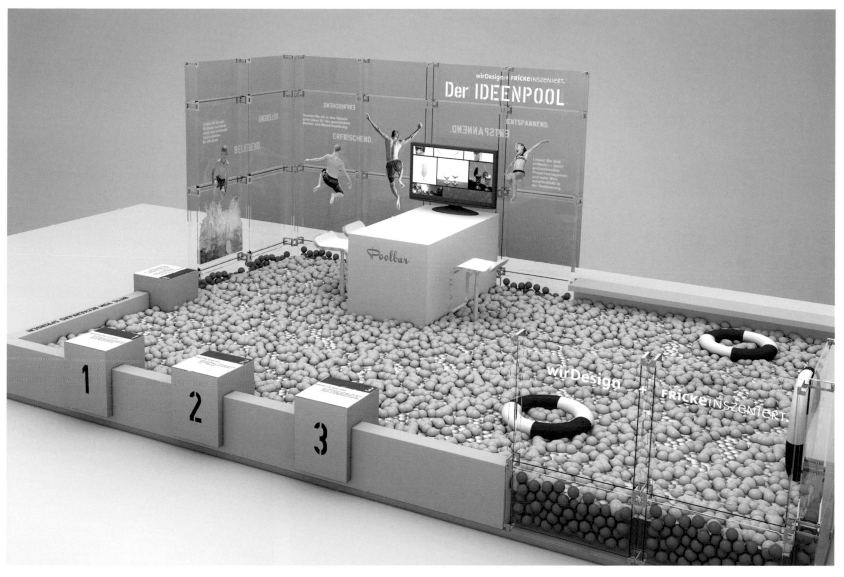

Project
Kinetische Skulptur
Mechatronische Installation
Mechatronical installation

Design
ART + COM
Prof. Joachim Sauter, Patrick Kochlik,
Petra Trefzger, Susanne Traeger
Berlin, Germany

Client
BMW Group
München, Germany

Die „Kinetische Skulptur" übersetzt den Prozess der Formfindung im Design metaphorisch in den Raum. 714 Metallkugeln bewegen sich im Zusammenspiel aus Mechanik, Elektronik und Code durch eine siebenminütige Erzählung. Auf einer Fläche von sechs Quadratmetern an feinen Stahlseilen hängend, werden sie einzeln über computergesteuerte Schrittmotoren bewegt. Anfangs bildet die Installation einen chaotischen Zustand ab, dann miteinander im Wettstreit liegende Formen, bis diese schließlich zu einem finalen Objekt werden. Dabei werden historische und aktuelle BMW-Fahrzeugformen abgebildet.

The "Kinetische Skulptur" is a metaphorical translation of the form-finding process in design. The installation consists of 714 metal spheres hanging from thin steel wires attached to individually controlled stepper motors. Covering a six-square-metre area, the spheres enact a seven-minute long mechatronic narrative, creating a representation of the form-finding process in different variations. Moving chaotically at first, the sculpture evolves through several competing forms and eventually resolves into a final shape whose profile hints at one of many well-known, historic and current, BMW automobiles.

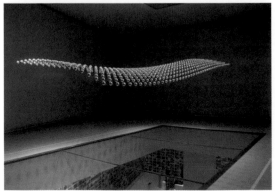

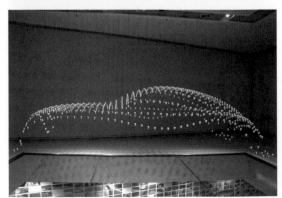

Project
smart lane
Messekonzept
Exhibition concept

Design
BRAUNWAGNER
Aachen, Germany

Client
Daimler AG
Stuttgart, Germany

BRAUNWAGNER, strategischer Partner der Daimler AG, entwickelte das Messekonzept „smart lane", welches über die Form einer architektonischen Spur – der smart lane – eine Metapher für die urbane Heimat des „smart fortwo" bildet. Als führende Agentur für Architektur und Kommunikation haben wir ein Konzept geschaffen, das urbane Komplexität und innovative Technologien mit Lebensfreude und Kreativität vereint. Die Marken- und Produktwerte wie Funktionalität, Innovation, Emotion, Ästhetik und Eigenständigkeit werden in ein nachhaltiges Messeerlebnis übersetzt. Das modulare skalierbare System ermöglicht eine Nutzung für weltweite A-Messen bis 2010.

BRAUNWAGNER, strategic partner of Daimler AG, developed the exhibition concept „smart lane", which consists of an architectural lane – the smart lane. It is a metaphor for urbanity, the home of the "smart fortwo". As a lead agency for architecture and communication we have created a concept that combines urban complexity and innovative technologies with joy of life and creativity. The brand and product values like functionality, innovation, emotion, aesthetics and independence are translated into a lasting exhibition experience. The modular scalable system will be used at international A-Shows until 2010.

Project
Dräger Safety Projektarium
Ausstellungsraum
Exhibition room

Design
diekoordinaten
Ulrich Bähr, Miriam von Bogen, Karen Kubbutat,
Pepe Lange, Nick Müller, Sven Sonne, Wilm Ihlenfeld
Kiel, Germany
Dräger Marketing Communications
Lübeck, Germany

Client
Dräger AG & Co. KGaA
Lübeck, Germany

Aufgabe:
Für Dräger soll als permanente Ausstellung auf be-
schränktem Raum das Thema Sicherheitsdienstleis-
tungen interaktiv erlebbar gemacht werden.
Idee:
Ein neuartiges räumliches Interface macht unsicht-
bare Gefahren sichtbar und präsentiert Lösungen.
Umsetzung:
Die Innenwand des runden Raumes zeigt den Umriss
eines Rundum-Panoramas. Davor kann ein hochkant
hängender Monitor bewegt werden. Wie ein Rönt-
genschirm zeigt er immer den aktuellen Ausschnitt
als Realbild. An vier Stationen kann innegehalten
werden, um eine audiovisuelle Animation anzusehen,
die über ein Thema in Wort und Bild informiert.

Challenge:
As a permanent showroom for Dräger the topic safety
services is to be presented within a limited space – to
be experienced interactively.
Idea:
A new spatial interface uncovers invisible hazards and
presents solutions.
Realization:
The inner walls of the rotund room show the out-
line of a 360° panorama. An upright monitor can be
moved in front of it. Like an X-Ray screen it shows the
respective detail as a real image. There is a chance to
hold and listen to an audio-visual animation, which
informs of a topic in sound and vision, at four positions.

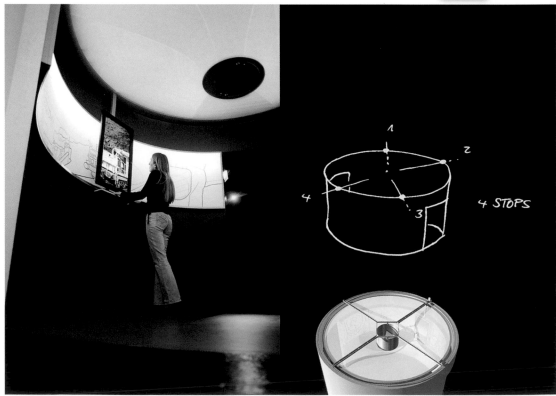

Project
Loewe Messestand IFA
Präsentationspappe
Presentation board

Design
Brandoffice GmbH
Heiko Dertinger, Michael Noli, Georg Dejung
München, Germany

Client
Loewe AG
Kronach, Germany

Im Zentrum des Loewe-Messeauftritts auf der IFA 2008 stand die erstmalige Positionierung der Marke im Home Entertainment-Luxussegment mit dem Launch des neuen „Loewe Reference". Dazu wurde die Weltneuheit umrahmt von einem 6 × 4 × 3 m großen Kubus, dessen Glasoberfläche alternierend von opak auf transparent umstellte. In einem Moment verbarg sich das TV-System hinter der undurchsichtigen Fassade, während es im nächsten Augenblick – begleitet von kraftvoller Musik – spektakulär in Erscheinung trat. Dadurch veränderte sich die audiovisuelle Atmosphäre des gesamten Standes im steten Wechsel zwischen konzentrierter Ruhe und fokussierter Dramatik.

Focus of the brand presentation at the IFA 2008 was the world premiere of the new "Loewe Reference System", marking the Kronach-based company's entry into the luxury segment of the consumer electronics industry. For this purpose the new top system was framed in a 6 × 4 × 3 m big glass cube whose surface alternated from opaque to transparent. It was hidden one moment behind an impenetrable facade, only to reappear spectacularly the next moment to the accompaniment of dramatic music. The stand's simple yet effective staging constantly changed the visual and auditory atmosphere at it altogether, alternating between focused calm and intense drama.

Project
gebautes Licht
Messestand
Exhibition stand

Design
bachmann. kern & partner
Dirk Bachmann-Kern,
design team bachmann. kern & partner
Solingen, Germany

Client
Osram Opto Semiconductors
Regensburg, Germany

Die Analyse der LED-Technologie im Bereich der Sensorik, insbesondere die technische Fähigkeit, Gegensätze zu erkennen, bildete für bachmann. kern & partner die Konzeptgrundlage für die gestalterische Umsetzung des Messestandes. Eine schwarze, sechs Meter hohe Hülle umgab den 180 m² großen Kopfstand und ließ somit das weiße Interieur noch heller leuchten. Ellipsenförmige Öffnungen gewährten hierbei Ein- und Ausblicke. Sie erweckten die Assoziation an Lichtkegel, die auf eine Fläche auftreffen und diese durchbrechen. Im Inneren wurde der Stand in den zwei Hausfarben von Osram, Orange und Weiß, gestaltet, um kommunikative und informative Zonen optisch voneinander zu trennen. Orangefarbene Kreise am Boden unterstützten hierbei den Effekt von innen und außen und definierten die Bereiche. Ein sechs Meter langer orangefarbener Tresen war zentrales Element der Standfläche. Parallel vor der Rückwand angeordnet, war er optischer Anziehungspunkt und Bewirtungsbereich für den Besucher. Eigens für die Präsentation von Leuchten für den Außenbereich integrierten die Architekten einen „grünen Hügel" in den Messestand. Ein von Echtrasen umgebener Baum diente hierbei als Beleuchtungsobjekt.

Architects bachmann. kern & partner took the conceptual inspiration for the booth's design realization from the LED technology analysis in the field of sensor systems, especially the technical ability to recognize opposites. A black, six meter high shell enclosed the booth and made the white interior shine even brighter. Openings in the shape of ellipses in the shell granted a glance into and out of the booth. Those shapes created an association of light cones bursting through a surface. The booth's interior is designed in the Osram's two corporate colors, orange and white, to separate communicative and informative zones visually. Orange circles on the floor supported the effect of inside and outside and defined the areas. A six meter long, orange colored bar was the main feature of the booth. The bar, located parallel to the back wall, was the visual attraction and hospitality area for visitors. The architects integrated a "green hill" into the booth especially for the presentation of outdoor lights. A tree surrounded by real lawn was the illuminated object.

Project
Audi Paris 2008
Messestand
Trade fair stand

Design
Schmidhuber + Partner
(Konzept und Architektur)
München, Germany
Mutabor Design GmbH
(Konzept und Kommunikation)
Hamburg, Germany

Client
AUDI AG
Ingolstadt, Germany

Audi öffnet sein Herz und präsentiert seinen Vorsprung im Bereich Technologie auf emotionale Weise. Zentrum des Standes ist das rote Herz. Sein rotes Pulsieren zieht sich über den Stand. Jedes Medium, ob Licht oder Ton, ist auf den Puls getaktet. Angelehnt an die Terminalarchitektur der Audi-Showrooms umspielt den Stand ein umlaufendes Band. Es definiert den räumlichen und visuellen Rahmen, öffnet sich und gibt den Weg frei in die Audi-Markenwelt. Zwei Straßen führen den Gast entlang der Fahrzeuge zum Herzen der Audi-Welt. Die kontrastreiche klare Form- und Farbsprache spiegelt die Klarheit und Präzision der hochwertigen sportiven Fahrzeuge wider.

Audi opened up its heart and presented its technological origins in an emotional manner. The center of the stand was the red heart. Its red beat extended across the booth. Every medium, whether light or sound, followed the same beat. Inspired by the terminal architecture of the Audi showrooms a ribbon swirled around the booth. It defined the spatial and visual framework, opened up and led the way into the Audi brand world. Two roads lead the guest past the vehicles to the heart of the Audi world. The highly contrasting, clear formal and color language reflected the clarity and precision of the high-quality sporting vehicles.

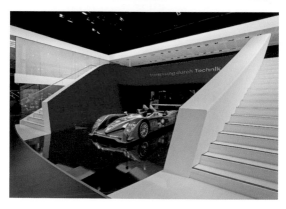

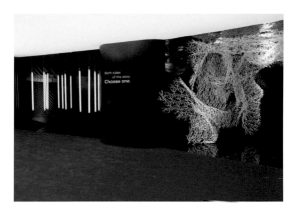

Project
Audi Q5, Lissabon 08
Ausstellung und Show
Exhibition and show

Design
Schmidhuber + Partner
(Konzept und Architektur)
München, Germany
tischdreizehn GmbH
(Kommunikation)
München, Germany

Client
AUDI AG
Ingolstadt, Germany

Zur weltweiten Einführung des Audi Q5 im Oktober 2008 waren ca. 3.000 Händler zu Gast in der Ausstellung und Show in Lissabons „Pavillon Atlantico". Im Foyer trifft der Händler auf zwei Gänge, verbunden mit der Aufforderung: „Both sides of the story. Choose one." Durch eine Installation („outdoor" / „urban") betritt er die jeweilige Erlebniswelt und trifft dann auf den Q5, den idealen Begleiter für ein Leben in Bewegung, in Natur oder in der Stadt. Entlang einer weißen Bodenspur wird der Besucher dann durch die Stationen der Ausstellung geführt. Von der in einem Tunnel inszenierten Performance des Q5 wird der Besucher schließlich in das Showtheater gezogen.

Some 3,000 dealers attended the exhibition and show in Lisbon's "Atlantico Pavilion" for the global launch of the Audi Q5 in October 2008. In the foyer the dealer encountered two corridors and the invitation: "Both sides of the story. Choose one." Passing through an installation ("outdoor"/"urban") they entered the respective event world and then encountered the Q5, the ideal companion for a life on the go, in the country or city. Following a white line on the floor visitors were then led through the sections of the exhibition. Having experienced a performance featuring the Q5 in a tunnel visitors were finally guided into the show theatre.

Project
Experience T
Messeauftritt IFA 2008
Exhibition stand at IFA 2008

Design
q-bus Mediatektur GmbH
Berlin, Germany

Client
Deutsche Telekom AG
Bonn, Germany

Auftritt eines Marktführers, der Wert legt auf Nahbarkeit und Erlebniswert – der IFA-Stand der Deutschen Telekom setzt die Marke „T" dreidimensional und interaktiv in Szene. Eine frei geformte, dramatisierende Architektur schafft Inszenierungsräume für die Präsentationsschwerpunkte zuhause, unterwegs sowie für ihr Zusammenspiel und bringt die Marke auf die Höhe ihrer Kunden, getreu dem Selbstverständnis eines dienstbaren Mittlers. Weiterer Präsentationskern ist eine 18 m-Multitouch-Installation: Eine beliebig große Zahl von Messegästen kann zugleich auf multimediale Inhalte und Gewinnspiele zugreifen. „Experience T" mit hohem Erinnerungswert.

A market leader presentation emphasizing virtues such as proximity and experience value – Deutsche Telekom's IFA stand sets the stage for a three-dimensional, interactive experience of the T-brand. A freely formed, dramatizing architecture creates spaces for the topical focus points home and mobile, as well as their combination. It levels the brand to customers' height, true to the self-conception of a subservient enabler. A multi-touch installation 18 m in width acts as yet another presentational core: It guarantees access to multi-media contents and competitions for unlimited numbers of visitors at a time. A highly memorable "Experience T".

Project
Urban Topography
Messeauftritt ISH 2009
Exhibition stand at ISH 2009

Design
Totems | Communication & Architecture
Frank C. Ulrich (Creative Director)
Cüneyit Akcakoça (Architekt)
Ulrich Henzler (Ausführung)
Lilian Fitch (Exponate und Grafik)
Birgit Lorinser (Grafik)
Stuttgart, Germany
Hospes Team GmbH
Leinfelden-Echterdingen, Germany
P3 Photo Production Pool
Düsseldorf, Germany

Client
Eczacibaşi Yapi Gereçleri
Levent – Istanbul, Turkey

„VitrA", der weltweit einzige Komplettanbieter im Bad- und Sanitärsektor, entwickelt und gestaltet Produkte mit hohem Designanspruch, bei denen das Wohl des Menschen im Vordergrund steht. Die Reduktion auf große, den Raum definierende Projektionselemente und eine sehr gradlinige Architektur machen den Reiz dieses Entwurfes aus. Die Produkte werden auf den erhöhten, von allen Seiten erschließbaren Ebenen präsentiert, die sich um den „Hospitality-Bereich" gruppieren – dem Zentrum der Begegnung mit dem Kunden. Die Kommunikationsebenen sind sehr klar getrennt: Die raumbildenden Projektionskuben zeigen VitrA und seine Markenwerte in der Fernwirkung.

"VitrA", the only international full-range supplier in the bath and sanitary sector, creates and develops products with a high design standard where user well-being is of utmost importance. The reduction to large, space-defining projection elements and a pronounced linear architecture make this design so appealing. The products are presented on raised levels, accessible from all sides, arranged around the hospitality area – the point of encounter with the customer. The communication levels are very clearly separated. The space-creating projection cubes show VitrA and its brand value at a distance.

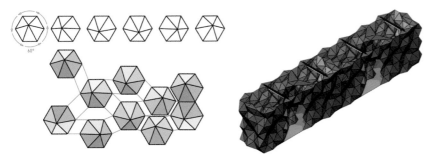

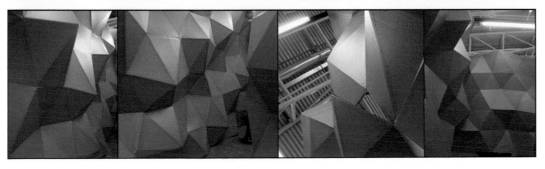

Project
Messestand opti 2009
Messestand
Exhibition stand

Design
WHITEOUT & GLARE
Fabian Hofmann, Thomas Bischoff
Berlin, Germany

Client
WHITEOUT & GLARE
Berlin, Germany

Ein Messestand, der mit einem minimalen Budget umgesetzt werden musste, aber dennoch dem Anspruch an Design und Wertigkeit des Labels W & G gerecht werden konnte. Nach ersten Tests an Modellen im Maßstab 1 : 10 war klar: Es ist möglich, einen freitragenden Messestand aus Wellkarton ohne jegliche unterstützende Träger aufzubauen. Die einzelnen Segmente wurden nach komplexen Plänen in Berlin vorgefertigt, aus nur 6 mm Doppelwelle und Gafferband. Die Elemente konnten vor Ort zusammengebaut werden und erhielten durch einen einheitlichen Brandschutzanstrich das Finish. Der Abbau erfolgte in nur 20 Minuten; der gesamte Stand wurde dem Recycling zugeführt.

In this case the booth had to follow a restricted budget, but at the same time had to maintain the high standards of design and quality of the label W & G. After first tests it was verified, a self-supporting cardboard booth could be built without the aid of additional girders. The segments were preassembled using corrugated board and gaffer band only. On site assembly was finished with a colored fire protection layer. Disassembly took 20 minutes; the whole booth was completely recycled.

Project
Doosan Art Square
Corporate Achitecture

Design
Hanyang University
Soon Gak Jang
Doosan Housing Design Team + JIW Co., Ltd.
Soongak Jang, Haejin Choi, Seyoung Lee
Seoul, South Korea

Client
Doosan Engineering & Construction
Seoul, South Korea

Der Doosan Art Square ist die fortschrittliche Ausgestaltung eines traditionellen Modellhauses und vereint ein beispielhaftes Bauwerk mit seinem ganz eigenen Markenimage zu einer Synergie aus modernem Wohnen, Kunst, Kultur und Kommunikation. Der Architekt Jang Soon Gak arbeitete mit einem Keramikkünstler zusammen und verwendete weißes Porzellan als Außenmaterial, um kulturelle Verbindungen herzustellen und das Gebäude als Wahrzeichen der Gegend zu etablieren. Es spricht von traditioneller koreanischer Schönheit und ist gleichzeitig Teil der urbanen Kunst. Der Art Square ist in zwei Bereiche unterteilt. Eine „gebogene Wand" bedeckt die „Box", das Äußere des Gebäudes, und ist mit LED-Lichtern ausgestattet. Motion-Graphics und Text können auf die Wand projiziert werden. Die „gebogene Wand" durchbricht die „Box" und stellt im Inneren eine direkte Verbindung zur holzverkleideten Konzerthalle her. Auch die Innenwände der „Box" sind aus Holz, was ihr eine sanfte, gemütliche Atmosphäre verleiht.

Art Square is an advanced configuration of traditional model houses. It displays not only a sample of a house, but also the brand image of itself by representing the modern residential culture with art, culture, and corporate communication spaces. Architect Jang Soon Gak collaborated with a pottery artist and used white porcelain as an exterior material to create cultural elements, and estabilish itself as a landmark. It shows Korean traditional beauty, and also takes place as an urban art. Art Square is divided into two parts and the "bending wall" covers the box figure of the building. Filled with LED lights, motion graphics and messages can be exhibited on "bending walls". It chrashes the box and leads via a stairway directly to the concert hall, which is the inside of the building with wooden panel materials. It also covers the inside walls which defines a mild, cosy atmosphere.

Project
Goodbye & Hello: Im Dialog mit dem Jenseits
Ausstellungsgestaltung
Exhibition design

Design
gewerk design
Jens Imig, Birgit Schlegel,
Rita Rentzsch, Susanne Kluge
Berlin, Germany

Client
Museum für Kommunikation
Bern, Switzerland

Die Ausstellung „Goodbye & Hello: Im Dialog mit dem Jenseits" präsentiert Begegnungen mit dem Jenseits in einem imaginären Raum, konstruiert aus schwarzen Streifenrastern auf weißem Grund. Diese künstlichen Perspektiven erzeugen Raumillusionen. Gleichzeitig entstehen durch Überlagerung zahlreicher Ebenen Interferenzerscheinungen, die Raumgrenzen auflösen und den Raum bewegt erscheinen lassen. Die kontrastreichen optischen Illusionen der Raumgestaltung stören Wahrnehmung und Raumgefühl der Besucher als Vorbereitung auf die Fremdartigkeit der Geschichten und Objekte der Ausstellung, die aus einem ungewohnten und unbekannten Raum stammen – dem Jenseits.

The exhibition "Goodbye & Hello: In a dialogue with the hereafter" presents encounters with the afterlife in an imaginary space designed via black on white strip patterns. These artificial perspectives create spatial illusions. Simultaneously, the overlap of several levels generates an interference creating the illusion of dissolving spatial borders and shifting spaces. The stark contrasts and visual phenomena of the spatial design influence and disturb the exhibition visitor's sense of perception and orientation as a preparation for the stories and objects from an unknown and foreign area, the hereafter.

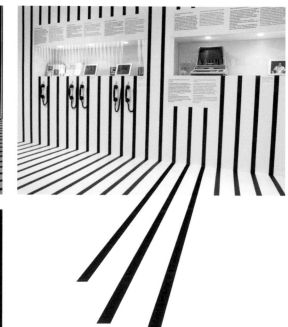

Project
Ozeaneum Stralsund
Ausstellung
Exhibition

Design
Atelier Lohrer
Stuttgart, Germany
Atelier Lohrer (Ausstellung)
Leitfaden-Design (Grafik)
Fassbender / Heppert (Aquarien)
Behnisch Architekten (Gebäude)
Schlorke (Fotos)

Client
Deutsches Meeresmuseum
Stralsund, Germany

Das Ozeaneum soll zukünftig weltweit mit seinem Inhalt zu den Top Ten der Meeresmuseen gehören. Einen Beitrag dazu leistet diese Dauer-Ausstellung: Der Besucher begibt sich auf die Reise von den unendlichen Tiefen des „Weltmeeres" über die „Ostsee" und die „Erforschung und Nutzung der Meere" bis hin zu den „1 : 1 Riesen der Meere". Jeder Raum wird durch ein unverwechselbares Raumbild geprägt (Bild 1: Weltmeer = Unendlichkeit / Bild 2: 1 : 1 Riesen der Meere = bühnenbildartige Großinszenierung). Die Formensprache der Ausstellungsarchitektur ist aus dem Inhalt heraus begründet und soll langfristig überzeugen. Raumbild und Information bilden eine einheitliche visuelle Erscheinung.

The Ozeaneum is intended to rank among the Top Ten aquatic museums worldwide. The following permanent exhibitions are on display: A journey from the infinite depths of the "ocean", across the "Baltic", "The Exploration and Use of the Oceans" to "1 : 1 Giants of the Oceans". The individual exhibition rooms are deliberately different from each other in terms of atmosphere and content. Each room is dominated by an unmistakable impact. The formal language of the exhibition architecture is in each case based on its contents. The room, its impact and the information provided all boast a uniform look.

Project
Borusseum
Museum

Design
Facts + fiction GmbH
Robert Müller, Patrizia Widrizki, Martin Sinken,
Gunnar Weber, Dirk Mailänder
Köln, Germany

Client
Borussia Dortmund GmbH & Co. KGaA
Dortmund, Germany

Das Borusseum – ein Museum, das die Geschichte des Fußballvereins BVB Dortmund erlebbar macht. Ein Zweiklang aus Fußballhistorie und Fankultur wurde zum Grundgerüst der Dauerausstellung. Die Konzeption besteht aus zwei wesentlichen Elementen: das eines klassischen Museums, in dem sich Besucher ausgewählten Exponaten gegenübersehen, sowie interaktiven Stationen, die zur Teilnahme und Mit-Gestaltung des Museums einladen. Die „Gelbe Wand" mit ihren rundum platzierten Fanstationen bildet inhaltlich und räumlich das Rückgrat des Museums. Sechs Ausstellungsinseln erzählen die sportliche Entwicklung des Vereins von der Gründung bis in die Gegenwart.

The Borusseum is a museum that brings the fabled history of FC BVB Dortmund 09 to life. The permanent exhibition is based on intertwining football history with fan culture. The concept consists of two main ideas: that of a traditional museum where visitors can view select exhibits and interactive stations that invite them to get involved and even help refine the Borusseum. The "Yellow Wall", with its fan stations in front, on top and behind, forms the foundation for the museum's content and layout. Six exhibit islands relate the sporting development of the club, from its founding up to the present day.

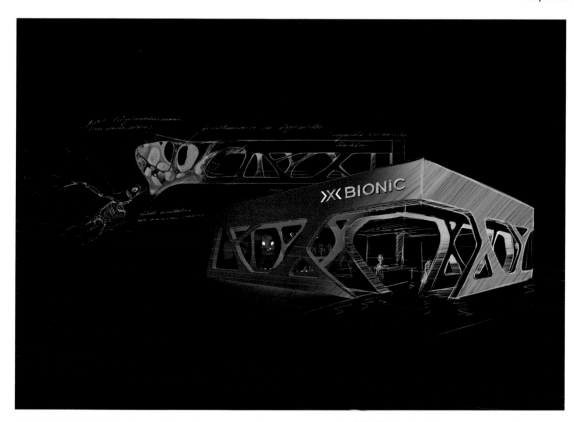

Project
X-Technology
Messeauftritt nach dem Vorbild der Natur
Exhibition stand modelled upon nature

Design
Andreas Messerli AG
Christian Streng
Wetzikon, Switzerland

Client
X-Technology Swiss R&D AG
Wollerau, Switzerland

Der Messeauftritt der Kultmarke „X-BIONIC" spiegelt ihren bionischen Ansatz klar wider und ist in seiner Art einmalig. Das Design wurde von Knochenstrukturen inspiriert und fließt mit der Farbwelt von X-BIONIC in die gesamte Architektur des Standes ein. Der Besucher wird dramaturgisch durch die Mehrschichtigkeit geleitet: Über die Außenhülle in den Zwischenraum als Informationszone bis ins Innere mit großzügiger Ausstellungsfläche. Entsprechend dem Premium-Anspruch der Marke ist die Detailqualität. Der geplante mehrjährige Einsatz stärkt den Wiedererkennungseffekt und trägt der Ökologie Rechnung.

The trade-fair appearance of the classic brand "X-BIONIC" clearly reflects its bionic approach and is unique in its way. The design is inspired by bone structures and the colors of X-BIONIC which flow into the stand architecture. In a dramaturgical way, the visitor is being led through the different layers: starting at the outer shell to the interspace – an information zone – into the center where a generous exhibition space unfolds. Corresponding to the premium positioning of the label the quality of the details is high. X-BIONIC plans to reuse the stand for several years which increases the brand recognition and is ecologically sensitive.

Project
Volkswagen zur Autoshow Paris 2008
Messeauftritt
Exhibition stand

Design
cebra GmbH
Kommunikation & Design
Zeina Mawlawi, Knuth Kripke
Wolfsburg, Germany

Client
Volkswagen AG
Forum für Marketing & Kommunikation
Wolfsburg, Germany

Zur Weltpremiere des neuen Golf auf dem Automobilsalon in Paris wurde für die Volkswagen AG eine neue Markenarchitektur für internationale Automobilmessen entwickelt. Aufgabenstellung war die Entwicklung einer neuen Gestaltungslinie, welche die wesentlichen Merkmale des Fahrzeugdesigns in sehr moderner und dynamischer Form interpretiert. Auf Grundlage der Vorgaben und der hohen Ansprüche an Design und Materialität wurde ein Konzept entwickelt, das durch seine klare Linienführung und seine reduzierte Formensprache die besonderen Qualitätsanforderungen an die Markenarchitektur der Volkswagen AG unterstreicht.

A new brand image design to be used at international motor shows was developed for Volkswagen AG for the world premiere of the new Golf at the Paris Motor Show.
The task was to develop a new design series that interprets the essential characteristics of the car in a highly modern and dynamic way. A concept was devised based on the specifications and high demands for design and materials used which showcases the unique quality standards and brand image of Volkswagen using clear contours and minimalist form.

Project
AUDI Coastline Marina
Messeauftritt
Exhibition stand

Design
Mutabor Design GmbH
Johannes Plass (CD)
Jessica Hoppe, Frederike Putz, Paul Neulinger (AD)
Maxie Pantel, Holger Schardt, Tobias Huber,
Jürgen Kloster (Designer)
Stefan Bräutigam, Andrea Lüders (Illustrator)
Job Wouters, a. k. a. Letman (Künstler)
Hamburg, Germany

Client
AUDI AG
Ingolstadt, Germany

Mit der „AUDI Coastline Marina" bringt AUDI die Ästhetik einer klassischen Yacht und das Ambiente der Küste auf die Designplanken der „Design Miami". Die AUDI Coastline Marina, gestaltet als riesiges Lounge-Objekt in Steg- und Marine-Optik, ist der Rahmen für den „AUDI Q7 Coastline". Auf der Vernissage und zu den Öffnungszeiten signiert der Kalligraph Letman die Vornamen der Gäste auf die Holzbalken der Lounge. Mit einem Booklet, gestaltet als Logbuch, führt AUDI die Gäste zu den Hotspots der City und versorgt sie zudem mit Tipps und Terminen rund um die „Design Miami" und die „Art Basel Miami".

The "AUDI Coastline Marina" brings the aesthetics of a classical yacht and the ambience of the coast to the design boards of "Design Miami". The AUDI Coastline Marina, designed as a huge lounge with landing stage and maritime visuals, makes up the backdrop for the "AUDI Q7 coastline". During vernissage and opening hours, the calligrapher Letman writes the guest's first names onto the wooden marina in order to accomplish the growing artwork "Inscriptions" within five days. AUDI guides their guests to the hotspots of the city with a special designed brochure including useful tips and dates around the "Design Miami" and the "Art Basel Miami".

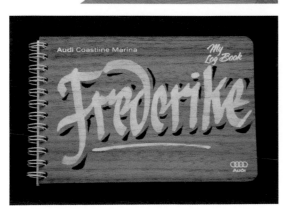

Project
Bundesdruckerei GmbH
Messeauftritt CeBIT 2009
Trade fair CeBIT 2009

Design
Office for spatial identity. GmbH
OFSI CeBIT Team 09
Zürich, Switzerland

Client
Bundesdruckerei GmbH
Berlin, Germany

„The Home of Identification – Trust I Security I Lifestyle."
Wir machen Sicherheit erfahrbar.
Die Bundesdruckerei ist ein weltweit führender Dienstleister für sichere Identifikation. Für den Einzelnen kaum wahrnehmbar, gewährleisten Hochsicherheitstechnologien den Schutz unserer Identität in einer immer stärker digitalisierten Welt. Auf der CeBIT 2009 wurde dieses zentrale Thema anhand vieler Praxisbeispiele für die Bereiche „eGoverment", „eBusiness", „eAdministration" und „Secure Transaction" „greifbar" gemacht. Ein zylinderförmiger „Data-Lock" und die konzentrische Organisation der Themen und Bereiche waren das Leitbild für die Gestaltung der Standarchitektur, der Kommunikation und der medialen Präsentationen.

"The Home of Identification – Trust I Security I Lifestyle."
Welcome to the security experience!
Bundesdruckerei is one of the world's leading service providers in the field of secure ID. Although hardly perceivable, high-security technologies guarantee identity protection in an increasingly digitised world. At CeBIT 2009, many practical and easy to understand examples were presented for "eGovernment", "eBusiness", "eAdministration" and "Secure Transactions". A cylindrical "Data Lock" and the concentric organisation of the topics and areas formed the basis for the design of the booth architecture, communication and media presentations.

CONSULTING POINT

VISOCORE® INSPECT WITH
VISOTEC® EXPERT 300

▶ Reliable verification of
authenticity

▶ Hardware-independent software
for the automated verification of
document and data authenticity

Project
Heinrich Berndes Haushaltstechnik
Messestand
Exhibiton stand

Design
ippolito fleitz group
Peter Ippolito, Gunter Fleitz, Sherief Sabet,
Axel Knapp, Frank Fassmer, Yuan Peng,
Daniel Unger
Stuttgart, Germany
Skalecki Marketing & Kommunikation
Jörg Skalecki
Frankfurt a. M., Germany

Client
Heinrich Berndes Haushaltstechnik
Arnsberg, Germany

„Was ist Dein Rezept im Leben?", fragt Berndes und meint damit Einstellungen und Themen, die die Menschen beschäftigen. Die Antworten auf diese Frage können dabei eng am Kochen liegen, aber genauso aus assoziativen Lebensbereichen stammen. Den Messestand für die „Ambiente" formulieren asymmetrische Holzkörper aus Seekiefer. Durch ihre gebrochene Geometrie stehen sie dafür, dass es auf komplexe Herausforderungen wie Nachhaltigkeit und gesellschaftliche Verantwortung keine einfachen, also gradlinigen Wege gibt. Der Kommunikation mit dem Kunden wird der Stand durch eine lange Sitzbank gerecht, die sich fast über dessen gesamte Länge erstreckt.

"What is Your Recipe in Life?" is the question posed by Berndes; thereby addressing attitudes and themes that preoccupy people. The answers to this question may well be closely connected with cooking, but could also come from associated areas of life. The exhibition stand for the "Ambiente" is provided by asymmetrical structures made of maritime pine. The contours and forms are in fact as diverse as the approaches and answers that concern Berndes when it poses its question of a recipe in life. The stand fulfills the requirement of communicating with its customers through a long seating element that runs almost the entire length of the stand.

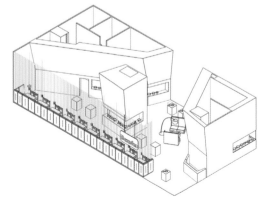

Project
Hong Kong's Participation in World Expo 2010
Shanghai
Ausstellung
Exhibition

Design
Oval Design Limited
Dennis Wong
Hong Kong

Client
Information Services Department
Hong Kong SAR Government
Hong Kong

Im Auftrag der Regierung von Hong Kong hat Oval Design eine Ausstellung gestaltet, die Hong Kongs Teilnahme an der Weltausstellung 2010 in Shanghai unter zwei Gesichtspunkten veranschaulicht: „Hong Kong – eine Stadt mit unbegrenzten Möglichkeiten" und Smartcard-Anwendungen. Die Ausstellung sollte Hong Kongs Markenpositionierung als Stadt von Weltklasse und ihr kontinuierliches Streben nach innovativen und kreativen Lösungen für mehr Qualität und Effizienz im urbanen Alltag, bessere Verbindungen innerhalb der Stadt und zu anderen Teilen der Welt promoten.

Oval Design was commissioned by the Hong Kong SAR Government to design and produce an exhibition publicising Hong Kong's participation in World Expo 2010 Shanghai under two themes: "Hong Kong – A City with Unlimited Potential" and Smart Card Applications. The exhibition's goal was to promote Hong Kong's brand position as a world-class city which continuously adopts innovative and creative ways to improve the quality and efficiency in the city's everyday life and connectivity within the city and with other parts of the world.

Project
Bundesarchitektenkammer e. V.
Messestand
Exhibition stand

Design
ippolito fleitz group
Peter Ippolito, Gunter Fleitz, Tim Lessmann,
Anne Lambert, Christian Kirschenmann,
Kirill Gagarin
Bruce B.
Stuttgart, Germany
Thomas Elser, Thomas Waschke
Stuttgart, Germany

Client
Bundesarchitektenkammer e. V.
Berlin, Germany

Die Bundesarchitektenkammer wünschte sich für ihren Messeauftritt auf der „Expo Real 2008" einen Messestand, der das Thema „Nachhaltigkeit" konsequent umsetzt. Die Elemente des Messestandes stammen mehrheitlich aus dem „Wegwerf-Lager" eines Messebauers mit ausgemusterten Resten unterschiedlicher Messestände. Die einzelnen Bauelemente wurden entsprechend der Standabmessungen und der vorgegebenen Funktionszonen in einer Art 3-D-Puzzle kombiniert und mit ökologisch zulässigen Farben homogenisiert. Der collagenartige Charakter des Messestandes sollte sichtbar bleiben, um den Recycling-Gedanken deutlich wahrnehmbar zu präsentieren.

The German Federal Chamber of Architects asked us to design an exhibition stand for the "Expo Real 2008" that consistently embodied the concept of "sustainability". A large number of the elements making up the stand originate from an exhibition builder's "reject warehouse", and are basically offcuts from different exhibition stands. The individual parts were combined in line with the stand dimensions and predefined function zones into a kind of 3D puzzle and then homogenised using ecologically viable paints. The stand's collagen-like character remains deliberately visible in order to present the concept of recycling as a tangible presence.

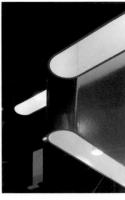

Project
AstraZeneca Messe
Messestand
Exhibition stand

Design
hartmannvonsiebenthal GmbH
corporate architecture
Ralph Hartmann, Viktoria Schulze,
Verena Wolz, Armin Treptau
Berlin, Germany

Client
AstraZeneca GmbH
Wedel, Germany

Unbegrenzte Variationen - Unverkennbarer Markenauftritt.
Auch auf kleinstem Raum steht die Kommunikation
im Vordergrund. Die Variabilität des neuen innovativen Messesystems entwickelt sich aus modularen
Bausteinen, deren unzählige Kombinationsmöglichkeiten individuelle Markenauftritte für das Pharma-
zeutikunternehmen AstraZeneca gestalten. Markante
Module vereinen sich zu maßgeschneiderten Kom-
munikationsräumen mit hohem Wiedererkennungswert. So entstehen Messestände mit schonendem
Ressourceneinsatz und nachhaltiger Markenwirkung,
die weitreichende Fernkommunikation ermöglichen
und den passenden Rahmen für persönliche Gespräche bieten.

Unlimited variations – unmistakable brand image.
Even in the smallest space, communication is at the
forefront. The variability of the innovative new trade
show system is based on modular components, whose
countless combination options are used to design
individual brand presentations for the AstraZeneca
pharmaceutical company. Striking modules blend
into tailor-made communication spaces with high
recognition value. The resulting trade show booths
conserve resources and have a lasting brand impact,
facilitate far-reaching remote communication and
offer the proper setting for personal discussions.

Project
Tomato Flash Computex 2008
Ausstellung
Exhibition

Design
DesignHouse Co., Ltd.
Aswan Yang
Taipei, Taiwan

Client
Incito Technology Co., Ltd.
Taipei, Taiwan

Das frische Image der Speicherkarte fordert einen auf, seine Gedanken aufzubewahren, Musik abzuspeichern und Fotos zu teilen. Der Editor der Serie „Tomato Flash" wurde erweitert, um das dreidimensionale Erscheinungsbild Wirklichkeit werden zu lassen. Der farbenfrohe Tomatenstielansatz ist der optische Hingucker. Die Zelle mit dem geschwungenen, springenden, glücklichen Stielansatz soll die Magie einer Speicherkarte symbolisieren und angenehm überraschen. Eine große Anzahl schwammiger Tomaten ist ein weiterer Hingucker, der einerseits als Geschenk für eine lebhafte Beschäftigung weitergegeben werden kann oder für den „Tomato-Vergnügungspark" steht. Durch das Überreichen von „Tomato"-Geschenkartikeln soll das Markenzeichen mit dem Image im Gedächtnis des Besuchers bleiben.

The flash card was used to record memory, storage music, share happiness photos, as many joyous and fresh image were jumped from the card. We extend VI of "Tomato Flash" to realize image three dimensional. Colorful Tomato stalks are visual point of all, the booth, curve iron line to leap happy stalk, to symbolize flash card as magic, play pleasant amazement. A great quantity of sponge tomato, to be another visual point, in one-side can be given away of alive activity, in the other side, present stand as a "tomato amusement park". Through give visitors Tomato gift away, to deeply root brand image in visitors' brain.

Project
Siemens – New Blue
Messestand
Trade fair stand

Design
Franken Architekten GmbH
Frank Brammer, Bernhard Franken
Hauser Lacour Kommunikationsgestaltung GmbH
Laurent Lacour
Meso Digital Interiors GmbH
Frankfurt a. M., Germany

Client
Siemens Elektrogeräte GmbH
München, Germany

Siemens – die Zukunft zieht ein. Mittelpunkt ist die Neueinführung der „IC5-Einbaugeräteserie". Ein futuristischer Baukörper liegt gleich einem großen gelandeten Meteoriten im Zentrum des Messeauftritts. Für die Premieren-Präsentation wurde eine räumliche Inszenierung geschaffen, die sich am Ritualraum von Tempelanlagen orientiert. Vom öffentlichen äußeren Publikumsbereich aus führen Einblicke in ein inneres, dunkleres „Allerheiligstes", dem Händlerbereich mit „LifeKochArena". Die Architektur bildet eine transitorische Zone, die einen Zugang von weißer minimalistischer Gegenwart in die blau erleuchtete Zukunft des monolithischen Baukörpers ermöglicht.

Siemens – The future is here. Focus is on the "IC5 built-in appliance series" launch. A futuristic structure lies at the center of the presentation like a meteorite that has just landed. An architecture was created which is inspired by the ritual room of temple complexes. There is an outer public area from which you can look into the darker "inner sanctum" with "LifeKochArena" of the retailer area. The architecture creates a transitory zone as you move from the outside – the white outer appearance as well as the minimalist architecture cites classic Modernism, the blue lit interior of the monolithic building could be read as a projection into the future.

Project
Live the Future
Unternehmensauftritt auf der Cityscape Dubai 2008
Company presentation at Cityscape Dubai 2008

Design
Atelier Markgraph GmbH
Frankfurt a. M., Germany

Client
Omniyat Properties
Dubai, United Arab Emirates

Auf der Cityscape Dubai 2008, der weltweit größten Immobilien-Fachmesse, zeigt Omniyat Properties, dass es sich erfolgreich den Herausforderungen der modernen Stadtentwicklung stellt – „Live the Future". Im Zentrum des Auftritts rotiert vor einer hochauflösenden Medienfläche eine futuristische Skulptur. Sie besteht aus vier dynamisch geschwungenen Segmenten. Diese dienen als Exponat-Träger für jeweils ein Architekturmodell und einen Screen mit Informationen zum jeweiligen Bauvorhaben. Kommt ein Segment gegenüber der zentralen Medienfläche zum Stehen, wird von diesem ein Lichtimpuls ausgelöst, der den Projektfilm auf der Medienfläche startet.

At Cityscape Dubai 2008, the world's biggest trade show for real estate planners, Omniyat Properties displayed their ability to address the challenges of modern urban development – "Live the Future". The centerpiece of the exhibition was a futuristic, revolving sculpture in front of a high-resolution media zone. It consisted of four dynamically curved segments. These served as display stations containing an architectural model and a screen with information on the planned construction in question. When a station stopped opposite the surrounding media zone, a light signal ran out to the media zone, starting the main film about the project.

Project
Effiziente Stadt
Messeauftritt ISH 2009
Exhibition stand at ISH 2009

Design
Atelier Markgraph GmbH
(Konzept, Gestaltung, Durchführung)
Frankfurt a. M., Germany
Grosse 8
(Motion Graphics)
Köln, Germany
Floridan Studios
(Musik / Ambient Sound)
Stuttgart, Germany

Client
Viessmann Werke GmbH & Co. KG
Allendorf / Eder, Germany

Auf der ISH nutzt Viessmann das Bild einer „effizienten Stadt", um Heizsysteme für alle Anwendungsbereiche zu präsentieren. Über den Köpfen der Besucher sorgt ein 50 Meter breites, vertikales Stadtmodell für Aufmerksamkeit. Vollformatige Projektionen machen es zur dreidimensionalen Leinwand. Immer wieder überraschend, tauchen aus dem skulpturalen Weiß Gebäude auf – und signalisieren plakativ, dass Viessmann für alle Anwendungen die maßgeschneiderte Systemlösung anbietet: vom Einfamilien- über Mehrfamilienhäuser, Industriegebäude bis hin zu Nahwärmenetzen. Zum „Leben erweckt" wird die Stadt durch Panoramainszenierungen der fünf Energieträger.

At the ISH, Viessmann uses the image of an "efficient city" to present heating systems for all applications. Above the heads of the visitors, a 50 m wide vertical model of a city attracts attention. Full-format projections turn it into a three-dimensional canvas. Surprising the viewer time and again, buildings appear from the sculptural white – and strikingly illustrate that Viessmann offers tailor-made system solutions for any application: From single-family to multi-family dwellings, industrial buildings to local heat networks. The city is "brought to life" by panorama productions of the five energy sources.

Project
Faszination Holz
Messeauftritt
Trade fair appearance

Design
jürgensarchitekten
soloTM
Kommunikationsdesign
Stuttgart, Germany

Client
Pfleiderer AG
Business Center Westeuropa
Neumarkt, Germany

Das Kommunikationskonzept für den Messeauftritt der Pfleiderer AG in Westeuropa stellt den Nutzen für den Kunden in den Mittelpunkt: „more than competence". Diese Botschaft wird grafisch und architektonisch aufgegriffen und emotional auf dem Messestand erlebbar gemacht. Die dynamische Linienführung auf den gekippten Flächen steht für die Offenheit und Lebendigkeit des Unternehmens und repräsentiert die Synergien zwischen den Marken unter dem Dach der Aktiengesellschaft. Die Belegung der Monolithen wurde so detailliert, dass die Holzwerkstoffplatte – das Kernprodukt aller Pfleiderer-Marken – in ihrer Charakteristik erkennbar wird.

The communications concept for Pfleiderer AG's trade fair presentation places central emphasis on the value-added for the customer: "more than competence". The message is communicated visually and architecturally and is brought to life in a surprising manner at the trade fair stand. The dynamic design on the inclined surface stands for the company's openness and liveliness and shows the synergies between the various brand names marketed by Pfleiderer AG. The layout of the monoliths is so detailed that the quality of the wood panels – the core product of all Pfleiderer brands – is clearly recognizable.

Project
Fraunhofer-Jahrestagung 2008 –
Zukunft braucht Forschung
Event

Design
Multitask Gesellschaft für Eventmarketing mbH
Thomas Peters, Sascha Wolf
(Beratung und Konzeption)
Frauke Harnack (Projektmanagement)
Berlin, Germany
Brandatmosphere
Medienkommunikation und Architekturdesign
Tobias Mund, Maximilian Quast
(Architektur und Design)
Sebastian Bach (Mediendesign)
Berlin, Germany

Client
Fraunhofer-Gesellschaft zur Förderung
der angewandten Forschung
München, Germany

Berlin, 28.05.2008. 650 hochrangige Gäste verfolgen die Verleihung der „Joseph-von-Fraunhofer-Preise". Zentrales Element der Veranstaltung ist ein fünf Meter breites und 30 Meter langes, komplett bespielbares Medienband durch den gesamten Raum – die Fraunhofer-Zukunftsbahn. Diese nimmt im Auditorium Forschungsimpulse auf, führt diese auf der Bühne zu einer konkreten Innovation zusammen und zeigt schließlich auf einer sieben Meter hohen Rückwand die weiteren Potenziale auf. Die Preisträger selbst betreten jeweils zum Ende eines Intro-Trailers die Zukunftsbahn und nutzen diese, um das Projekt mit Hilfe von Einspielern detailliert vorzustellen.

Berlin 28 May 2008. 650 high-ranking guests attended the award ceremony for the "Joseph-von-Fraunhofer-Prize". The central element of the protocol event was a five by thirty meter projector screen surface that crossed the entire room – the Fraunhofer Runway of the Future. It collected research impulses from the auditorium, merging them into a concrete project as they crossed the stage, before finally depicting the potential of the innovation on a seven-meter tall screen. At the end of each of these trailers, the prize winners stepped onto the runway, using it as a tool to illustrate details of their specific venture by means of film-clips.

Project
Migros Familypark

Design
Bellprat Associates AG
Philipp Anderegg, Fabienne Barras,
Xavier Bellprat, Janina Rinne
Zürich, Switzerland

Client
Genossenschaft Migros Zürich
Zürich, Switzerland

Anlässlich der EM '08 hat Bellprat Associates für die Migros an der Züricher Fanmeile einen Familypark konzipiert. Der über 5.000 m² große Themenpark stand im Zeichen des „Public Doing" und überzeugte mit vielen Attraktionen und einer einzigartigen Optik. Die Besonderheit bestand in der Verbindung aus ökologischer Bauweise und Architektursprache. Das Designkonzept war mit über 8.000 Holzpaletten stark auf das Thema Nachhaltigkeit ausgerichtet. Die Paletten wurden später in der Logistik der Migros wieder verwendet. Das Naturmaterial erzeugte eine freundliche Atmosphäre und wirkte durch das klare Design der Gebäude sehr einladend.

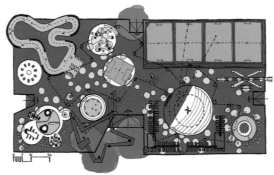

During the 2008 European Football Championships, Migros Zurich built and ran the Family Park, a leisure and entertainment platform displaying a unique architectural language, designed by Bellprat Associates AG. When almost all other corporate offerings during these championships meant public viewing, the Family Park offered public doing! The area which covered 5,000 m² was conceived as a theme park, offering sports and fun activities for the young and their parents alike. 8,000 wooden transport pallets were used to create a unique and ephemeral setting, only to be taken down after the one month event and be put back to use as everyday transport tool.

Project
FanWalk 2008
Event

Design
Serviceplan BRANDEVENT GmbH & Co. KG
München, Germany

Client
Sony Ericsson Mobile Communications
International AB
München, Germany

Sony Ericsson war Sponsor der 15. MTV Europe Music Awards in Liverpool. Im Sponsorenpaket waren 100 VIP-Tickets, die durch eine Promotion medienwirksam vergeben werden sollten. Idee: Der Sony Ericsson-FanWalk. Wir schickten die 100 besten Musikfans aus 20 Ländern auf Tour – von London nach Liverpool, zu den MTV EMAs. Free VIP-Tickets waren wohl der beste Grund, sich zu Fuß aufzumachen. Wer seinem Star als „Award Presenter" ganz nahe kommen wollte, musste sich in verschiedenen musikbezogenen Aufgaben selbst als Star unter 100 „FanWalkern" beweisen.

Sony Ericsson sponsored the 15th MTV Europe Music Awards in Liverpool. The sponsorship included 100 VIP tickets which should be given away through a promotion that creates media attention. Concept: The Sony Ericsson FanWalk. We sent 100 top music fans from 20 countries on tour – from London to Liverpool, to the MTV EMAs. And this was the best reason to set off by foot: free VIP tickets! To get even closer to their favorite star as the "Award Presenter", the die-hards had to prove themselves as a true star among 100 "FanWalkers" in music related contests.

Project
Qatar Railways
Event- und Ausstellungskonzept
Event and exhibition concept

Design
:: dan pearlman markenarchitektur gmbh
Marcus Fischer, Daniel Weidler, Sebastian Stottele,
Sebastian Lange, Julia Bindseil, Kay Guth,
Rocco Kruse, Esther Perbandt, Steffen Armbruster,
Katharina Maurer, Markus Hofmeister, Roger Nientiet
Berlin, Germany

Client
Atkon AG
Berlin, Germany

Qatar Railways: Inszenierung des Verkehrssystems
der Zukunft für das Emirat Qatar
Wie schafft man es, in 60 Minuten dem Emir von
Qatar die Ergebnisse einer sechsmonatigen Mach-
barkeitsstudie für ein Verkehrssystem zu vermitteln?
Im Auftrag der Atkon AG entwickelte dan pearlman
für die Deutsche Bahn AG in nur drei Monaten eine
Markenwelt vom CI bis hin zur architektonischen Gestaltung eines 1.300 m² großen Showrooms. Leitidee
für diese interaktive Erlebniswelt bestehend aus
„Bahnhofshalle", „Schaltzentrale" und „VIP-Lounge"
ist die Welt der Verkehrs- und Menschenströme.
Aufgrund großer Begeisterung des Emirs wird diese
virtuelle Vision ab 2016 Realität.

Qatar Railways: Presentation of the transportation
system of the future for the emirate of Qatar
How do you convey to the Emir of Qatar the results
of a 6-months feasibility study for a transportation
system within 60 minutes? On behalf of Atkon AG,
dan pearlman developed an entire brand world –
from the CI to the architectural design of a 1,300 m²
showroom – for Deutsche Bahn AG within just three
months. With its "Station Hall", "Control Centre" and
"VIP Lounge", the concept for this interactive world
was based on the flow of traffic and people. The Emir
was so enthusiastic about this virtual vision that it
will become a reality from 2016.

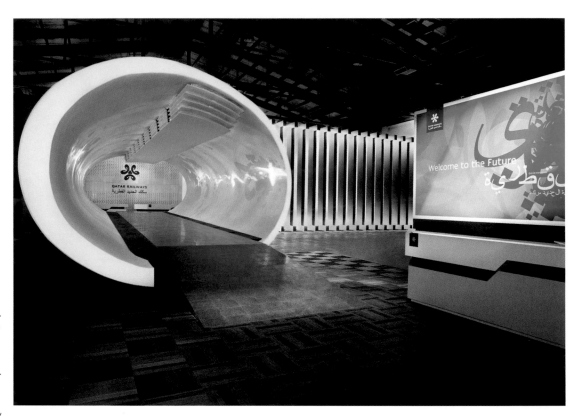

Project
NESPRESSO Citiz Trade Event
Launch der Citiz-Produktlinie
Launch of Citiz product range

Design
VOK DAMS GRUPPE
Gesellschaft für Kommunikation mbH
Wuppertal, Germany

Client
NESPRESSO Deutschland GmbH
Düsseldorf, Germany

Das Launch-Event der neuen NESPRESSO Citiz vereinte für rund 250 Gäste erlebbare Perfektion mit
relaxter Atmosphäre. Skylines weltweit standen Pate
für das innovative Citiz-Design und die neue Kampagne. Im 28. Stock des Westhafentowers mit Blick
über Frankfurt gestaltete VOK DAMS eine künstlerisch
inszenierte Skyline-Welt aus weißen Kuben: die Citiz-
Sky-Lounge. Hochhäuser und Straßenschluchten entwickelt aus dem Markensignet, verliehen urbanes
Flair. Eine transparente interaktive Hologramm-Prä-
sentation stellte die Geräte vor. Zunächst in Kuben
versteckt, waren die Maschinen nach der Enthüllung
harmonisch in die Skyline-Landschaft integriert.

At the Launch Event of the new NESPRESSO Citiz
around 250 guests were able to experience perfection in a relaxed atmosphere. Skylines worldwide inspired the innovative Citiz design and the new campaign. VOK DAMS created a skyline scenery made of
white cubes on the 28th floor of the Westhafentower
over the rooftops of Frankfurt: the Citiz Sky Lounge.
Skyscrapers and street canyons made up of the brand
icon provided an urban atmosphere. The machines
were launched in a transparent, interactive hologram
presentation. First they hid in the cubes. And after
being revealed, the machines merged perfectly with
the skyline scenery.

Project
Nouvelle Image
Architektonisches Licht Design
Architecture light design

Design
EONSLD. Co.,Ltd
Mee Jeong (Director)
UCLD (Concept)
Sound Design JAPAN, Inc. (Sound)
Ushio Lighting (Contents)
Seoul, South Korea

Client
Konkuk AMC
Konkuk University Foundation
Seoul, South Korea

Das „Starcity", Wahrzeichen von Seoul, ist der imposanteste Wohn- und Gewerbebau der Stadt. Der Komplex enthält eine Passage, die als Haupteingang zu dem Areal dient. Eine der hier verwirklichten Ideen bestand darin, urbanen Gewerberaum zu einer Kunstgalerie umzufunktionieren und dadurch die Öffentlichkeit Kunst und Kultur hautnah erleben zu lassen. Im Mittelpunkt steht „Gatharia." Dieses Wort, zusammengesetzt aus „gather" (erfassen) und „area" (Bereich), bezeichnet den „Raum, der alle Schönheiten der Natur in sich birgt." Sechzehn bewegliche, in der Wand installierte Beamer projizieren sehr realistische, dreidimensionale Bilder an die gegenüberliegende Wand. Auf dem Fußboden erzeugen die je nach Bodenmaterial zu unterschiedlichen Zeiten installierten LED-Leuchten organische Formen: Über 3.000 LEDs stellen verschiedene, zu den Themen an der Wand passende Motive dar. Multidirektionale Lautsprechersysteme sind unsichtbar in der Wand, im Fußboden und in der Decke des Raumes untergebracht. Jedes Thema wird von realistischen, in der Natur aufgenommenen Klängen untermalt, was den Raum im Verein mit der Lichtpräsentation zu einem aufregenden, dynamischen Erlebnis macht.

The starcity, the landmark of Seoul, is the best and biggest residential-commercial building. The pathway which is a part of Starcity is the very important main entrance for people visiting this area. Another purpose is to make the public experience art and culture more closely by converting the commercial space of a big city into an art gallery. The main concept is "Gatharia". This is a compound word coming from "gather" and "area", which means "The space that encompasses all beautiful scenes of nature". Sixteen moving image lighting equipments which are installed on the wall display three-dimensional images on the opposite wall. This performance gives the observer a more realistic feeling. On the floor, the LED lightings display an organic shape, which are installed at different intervals depending on the finishing material of the floor. More than 3,000 LEDs perform various themes linked with the same theme of the wall. Multi-directional system speakers are installed invisibly inside the wall, floor, and ceiling of the architecture. The real sound recorded on the spot according to each theme makes the space more rhythmical and dynamic along with the lightning performance.

Project
Wie viel Benz steckt in Dir?
Kommunikationskampagne
Communication campaign

Design
CB. e Clausecker | Bingel. Ereigniss
Gunnar Kavermann, Ralph Schollähn, Trixi Stumpe
Stuttgart, Germany

Client
Mercedes-Benz Werk Mannheim
Daimler AG
Mannheim, Germany

Das Mercedes-Benz Werk Mannheim feiert 2008 sein 100-jähriges Jubiläum. Eine interne Kommunikationskampagne begleitet das Jubiläumsjahr, um Motivation und emotionale Bindung der 10.000 „Benzler" zu festigen. Die Werksleitung sagt „Danke!" und macht ihre Wertschätzung so für alle erlebbar. Dabei entsteht ein Jubiläums-Key-Visual ganz im Zeichen des Werkes: von oben aus betrachtet ergeben die drei Werksbereiche das Bild eines Herzens. Unter dem Slogan „Wie viel Benz steckt in Dir?" erzählen die „Benzler" CB. e außergewöhnliche Geschichten – gesammelt im Benz-Buch und in verkürzter Form als Brandings täglich im Werk sichtbar.

The Mercedes-Benz plant Mannheim is celebrating its 100th anniversary in 2008. An internal communication campaign is accompanying the anniversary year, in order to strengthen motivation and emotional ties of the 10,000 Benz employees. The plant management would like to make its appreciation a true experience for everyone. In this context, an anniversary key visual is developed: seen from above the three plant areas have the shape of a heart. Under the slogan "How much Benz is there in you?", the Benz employees tell unusual stories – collected in the Benz book. Abbreviated versions are visible in the plant every day as brandings.

Project
Dead or Alive
Künstler-Turnier
Poetry slam

Design
Kolle Rebbe
Jakob Kriwat (Creative Direction)
Till Heumann (Creative Direction)
Jan Brandes (Grafik)
Moritz Preißer (Grafik)
Tobias Wortmann (Text)
Hamburg, Germany

Client
Kampf der Künste
Hamburg, Germany

Bei Poetry-Slams blieb die junge Autoren-Szene jahrelang praktisch unter sich. Für den Veranstalter „Kampf der Künste" gestalteten wir deshalb eine Event-Reihe, die ein breites Publikum begeistern sollte: Dead or Alive. Tote Dichter und junge „Poetry-Slammer" tragen abwechselnd ihre Werke vor – und das Publikum wählt den Gewinner. Dead or Alive gilt inzwischen als größte europäische Poetry-Slam-Reihe und findet regelmäßig in ausverkauften Theatern statt.

For many years, poetry slams only attracted small audiences. This is why we created a series of events for the poetry slam organizer "Battle of the Arts" to grab the attention of the general public: Dead or Alive. Dead poets and young poetry slammers take turns in reciting their literary creations – and the audience elects the winner. Dead or alive is now the largest European poetry slam series. It regularly takes place in sold-out theatres.

Project
CENTRAL Rat Race
Event

Design
Oval Design Limited
Dennis Wong
Hong Kong

Client
Hongkong Land
Hong Kong

CENTRAL Rat Race ist eine Fundraising-Aktion, die von unserem Kunden Hongkong Land organisiert wurde. Die Aufgabe von Oval Design war es, ein Aufsehen erregendes Event zu gestalten, mit dem die Markenpositionierung des Kunden als Hongkongs führendes Unternehmen für Immobilien-Entwicklung und -Management mit Spitzenportfolio im Stadtzentrum (CBD) weiter gestärkt werden sollte. Zu diesem Zweck haben wir den Aufstieg eines Anzugträgers auf der Karriereleiter vom Universitätsabgänger bis zum Senior Executive in Form eines Hindernisparcours nachgestellt. Als Spielfläche dienten die exklusiven Bürogebäude des Kunden und die Hauptverkehrsstraßen des Stadtzentrums.

CENTRAL Rat Race is a fundraising event organised by our client, Hongkong Land. Oval Design's task was to design and produce an exciting event aiming at further strengthening client's brand position as Hong Kong's leading property development/management company with a top-notch portfolio in the city's Central Business District (CBD). In fulfilling this mandate, we designed the race as a mini-scene re-creation of a white collar's climb up the corporate ladder from graduate to senior executive in the form of an obstacle-ridden course, using as race track client's top grade office buildings and major roads in the CBD.

Project
RAEMIAN STYLE HOUSE
Marken-Ausstellungsraum
Brand showroom

Design
Samsung C & T
Seoul, South Korea

Client
Samsung C & T
Seoul, South Korea

Dieser Ausstellungsraum ist im Informationszentrum der Wohnungsmarke RAEMIAN errichtet worden. Er stellt das Designkonzept des Jahres in seiner tatsächlichen Größe dar. Für die Kunden direkt erlebbar – ein so genannter Ort für Markenkommunikation. Der Raum besteht aus drei Zonen. Eine „Interiorzone", die das Wohnzimmer, Küche, Arbeitszimmer und Badezimmer enthält, die „reflektierende Umweltzone", und als letztes die Naturenergie nutzende „technische Zone". Der Ausstellungsraum ist quadratisch angelegt. In jedem Raum befindet sich eine Treppe. Das erleichtert die Orientierung und macht den Gang durch die Räume angenehm.

This showroom was raised in the information center of the housing brand RAEMIAN. It exhibits this year's design concept in its actual size and makes it a real experience – a spot for brand communication. The room is divided into three zones: "the interior zone" including the living room, the kitchen, the study, and the bathroom, the "reflective environmental zone", and the "technical zone" showing natural energy recycling. The showroom has quadratic shape. Stairs are located in every room. This facilitates orientation and makes for a comfortable passing through the rooms.

Project
POP Fashion Store

Design
EXPOLAB GmbH
advanced communication and design
München, Germany

Client
Excited GmbH
München, Germany

Klare Oberflächen, grafische Kontraste, bewusster Einsatz von Farben und schräge Details kennzeichnen den eigenständigen Charakter des Fashion Stores. Hier werden Pop Art, Comics und Oberflächen zeitgemäß interpretiert und umgesetzt. Der Shop bietet ein Feuerwerk an Überraschungen und besonderen Features. In Clubatmosphäre treffen schwarze Elemente auf weiße Flächen, neongelbe Akzente verstärken den grafischen Eindruck und bieten eine starke Präsentationsfläche für stylishe Labels. An der Decke scheint sich die speziell für den Shop konzipierte Lichtinstallation „Rush of Lights" durch Spiegel in die Unendlichkeit zu verlängern.

Clean surfaces, graphic contrasts, deliberate use of color and quirky details demonstrate the idiosyncratic character of POP. Here Pop Art, comics and surface design come together in a very contemporary interpretation. The shop is organised on two levels and offers a firework of visual surprises and special features. In a clubby atmosphere black elements meet arctic white surfaces. Bright yellow accents underline the graphic impressions and present a strong backdrop for stylish labels. On the ceiling, the exclusive custom-made light installation, "Rush of Lights", appears to extend infinitely with the use of mirrors.

Project
Canyon.Home
Showroom

Design
KMS TEAM GmbH
Knut Maierhofer (Creative Director)
Sandra Ehm (Account Director)
Simon Betsch (Brand Strategy)
Patrick Märki (Design Director)
May Kato, Christian Hartig, (Designer)
München, Germany

Client
Canyon Bicycles
Koblenz, Germany

Auf 1.300 m² Fläche hat sich der auf Internetvertrieb spezialisierte, technologisch führende Fahrradhersteller Canyon in Koblenz eine attraktive Markenheimat geschaffen. Das „Canyon.Home" ist Unternehmenszentrale, Entwicklungszentrum, Produktionsstandort, Reparaturwerkstatt, Auslieferungszentrum und „Flagshipstore" in einem. Die Grundidee für das „Canyon.Home" ist die räumliche Interpretation des Canyon-Erscheinungsbilds. Die kursive Dynamik des Namenszugs wurde zum Formprinzip des Raumes, der durch einzelne monolithische Elemente strukturiert ist. Daraus ergibt sich ein stilisierter Canyon, der sowohl formal als auch semantisch auf die Marke verweist.

Canyon, the leading-technology bicycle manufacturer in Koblenz specializing in internet distribution, has created an attractive brand presence on 1,300 m² of floor space. "Canyon.Home" is the company headquarters, development center, production facility, repair workshop, logistics center and flagship store all in one. The basic concept for "Canyon.Home" is the spatial interpretation of the Canyon image. With its cursive dynamics, the company name is the principle behind the layout which is structured by individual monolithic elements. This results in a stylized canyon which refers to the brand both formally and through semantics.

Project
Highly Adaptable
Produkt-Erlebniscenter
Product Experience Center

Design
Atelier Markgraph GmbH
(Konzept, Gestaltung, Durchführung)
Frankfurt a. M., Germany
Zum Kuckuck
(Erstellung Software)
Würzburg, Germany
Meso Digital Interiors
(Erstellung Software)
Frankfurt a. M., Germany

Client
Deutsche Telekom AG
Bonn, Germany

Das 300 m² große Product Experience Center ermöglicht es Mitarbeitern und Besuchern, aktuelle Highlight-Produkte des Konzerns in ihrer Funktionsvielfalt an 25 interaktiven Exponatstationen zu erleben. Touchgesteuerte Infosysteme bieten neben Produktinformationen multimedial aufbereitete Anwendungsbeispiele, die der Besucher parallel mit dem realen Produkt nachvollziehen kann. Ein mit der Produktentwicklung gekoppeltes integriertes Feedbacksystem fördert den unternehmensinternen Dialog. Die Leistungsfähigkeit der Netzinfrastruktur der Deutschen Telekom wird mit der Visualisierung von Datenströmen und Informationen in Echtzeitgrafiken erlebbar.

The 300 m² Product Experience Center allows employees and visitors to experience the variety of functions of current group product highlights at 25 interactive exhibit stations. In addition to product information, touch-controlled information systems offer visitors multimedia application examples of the actual product. An integrated feedback system linked to product development promotes internal company dialog. The capacity of the network infrastructure of Deutsche Telekom is experienced with the display of data streams and information in real-time graphics.

Project
Mercedes-Benz Gallery München
Showroom

Design
Atelier Markgraph GmbH
(Kommunikation, Ausstellungs- und Mediendesign)
Frankfurt a. M., Germany
Kauffmann Theilig & Partner
(Architektur)
Ostfildern, Germany
FOUR TO ONE: scale design
(Lichtdesign)
Hürth, Germany

Client
Daimler AG
Stuttgart, Germany

Ab 2009 eröffnet Mercedes-Benz in den Metropolen Europas eine neue Generation von Showrooms. Die Mercedes-Benz Galerien sind als Botschafter der Marke im urbanen Umfeld konzipiert. Auf 400 bis 1.200 m² Ausstellungsfläche bieten sie einen lebendigen, atmenden Raum für die Begegnung von Marke und Besucher. Im Zentrum steht das ganzheitliche Markenerlebnis in persönlicher Atmosphäre. Prägendes gestalterisches Element ist eine „intelligente" skulpturale Wand. Sie kann sich mittels medialer Bespielung jederzeit Raum und Anlass anpassen. Wechselnde Inszenierungen und Ausstellungen verwandeln die Galerien in dynamische Orte des Stadtlebens.

In 2009, Mercedes-Benz begins to open a new generation of showrooms in major European cities. The Mercedes-Benz galleries are designed as brand ambassadors in urban environments. On 400 to 1,200 m² of exhibition space, they offer a living, breathing venue for the meeting between brand and visitor. The focus is on the integrated brand experience in a personal atmosphere. An "intelligent" sculptural wall is the defining design element. With media displays, it can adapt to the space and occasion at any time. Alternating presentations and exhibitions transform the galleries into dynamic sites of urban living.

Project
BMW Museum
Dauerausstellung
Permanent exhibition

Design
ATELIER BRÜCKNER
Prof. Uwe R. Brückner, Eberhard Schlag,
Michel Casertano, Dominik Hegemann,
Alexandra Vassilakou, Marietta Fischer,
Bernita Le Gerette, Gesa Dörfler, Maria Millan
Stuttgart, Germany
ART+COM (Mediale Inszenierungen)
Prof. Joachim Sauter, Gert Monath
Berlin, Germany
Integral Ruedi Baur (Grafik Design)
Prof. Ruedi Baur, Axel Steinberger
Zürich, Switzerland

Client
BMW AG
München, Germany

Das BMW Museum wurde als wirkungsvoll strukturierte Raumlandschaft konzipiert, die – analog zur
Marke BMW – Dynamik und Innovation zum Ausdruck bringt. Es geht neue Wege bei der integrativen
Verbindung von Architektur, Ausstellungsgestaltung
und kommunikativen Medien. Ein Rampensystem,
ausgebildet als Straße mit Plätzen und Brücken, lässt
den Besucher in ein urbanes, großzügiges Ambiente
eintauchen. Hell leuchtende Ausstellungshäuser mit
dynamisch bespielten Medienfassaden bieten Zugang zu Geschichte und Herkunft der Marke BMW.
Raum und Exponate scheinen in Bewegung zu ge-
raten.
Fotos:
Marcus Meyer, Bremen
Marcus Buck, München (links oben)

Corresponding to the brand, the BMW Museum
was conceived as a strikingly structured urban space,
which expresses dynamic and innovation. It takes
new approaches by intertwining architecture, exhibition design and communicative media. A system
of ramps designed like a street with squares and
bridges immerses the visitor in a broad urban ambience. Bright luminescent exhibition houses with
dynamic media-facades provide access to the history
and origins of the BMW brand. Space and exhibits
seem starting to move.
Photos:
Marcus Meyer, Bremen
Marcus Buck, Munich (above left)

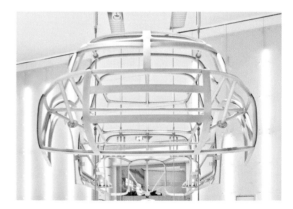

Project
feldmilla
Hotel

Design
herzogenrathsaxler design
Margarethe Saxler, Matthias Herzogenrath
Düsseldorf, Germany

Client
feldmilla. designhotel
Campo Tures, Italy

„Gegenwärtige Natur" ist das Leitmotiv für die architektonische und innenarchitektonische Neugestaltung des Hotels. Die Kulisse der Südtiroler Alpen wird zum integrierten Bestandteil der Innenraumgestaltung. Die Einfachheit traditioneller Möbel war Vorlage für das formale Konzept der Möbelentwürfe, bis hin zu den Badewannen und Waschbecken. Die klare Linienführung der Möbel trennt Gestaltetes und Natur. Das Raumkonzept, Farben und Materialien schaffen einen entspannten und fließenden Übergang zwischen innen und außen, zwischen Konstruktion und Natur.

"The Presence of Nature" is the guiding theme for the hotel's architectural and interior redesign. The backdrop of the South Tyrol Alps becomes an integrated component of the interior design. The simplicity of traditional furniture was the guiding principle for the formal concept of the furniture designs, down to the bathtubs and basins. The clear lines of the furniture separate design and nature. The spatial concept, colors and materials create a relaxed and flowing transition between interior and exterior, between structure and nature.

Project
MAHLE INSIDE
Unternehmensausstellung
Showroom building

Design
Heinisch . Lembach . Huber Architekten BDA
Ltg. R. Fischer, D. Steenfatt | MAHLE GmbH,
Ltg. B. Albrecht, M. Sieder | design hoch drei
GmbH & Co. KG | Jean-Louis Vidiere |
zooey braun fotografie (Abbildungen)
Stuttgart, Germany

Client
MAHLE International GmbH
Stuttgart, Germany

Auf vier Etagen bietet MAHLE in seiner Ausstellung
Mitarbeitern, Kunden und Besuchern Einblicke in
das Unternehmen. Der schlichte Baukörper bildet
die Hülle für ein komplexes, durch Lufträume und
Sichtbezüge verbundenes System von Räumen unterschiedlicher Proportion und Anmutung. Das räumliche Konzept des Hauses bildet so die komplexen
Beziehungen der Ausstellungsthemen untereinander
ab. Neben einer Präsentation der Produktlinien werden Historie, Unternehmens-Philosophie, Methoden
und Ziele in Forschung und Entwicklung dargestellt –
und in einen räumlichen Zusammenhang gebracht,
welcher vom Besucher auf vielfältige Weise gelesen
werden kann.

By its exhibition on four floors MAHLE provides staff,
clients and visitors insights into the company, its
know-how, products and history. The plain building
forms the shell for a complex system of rooms with
differing proportions and impressions which are af-
filiated to each other by plenums and visible relations. A floating, natural sequence of rooms allows
the visitor to experience the building in its entirety.
Thus the special conception of the house illustrates
comprehensibly the sophisticated relations between
the exhibition subjects: the inextricable interplay of
research, development and production.

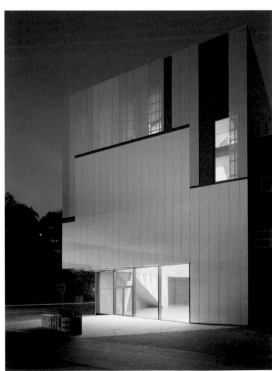

Project
Infusion Lounge
Lounge-Bar

Design
Kinney Chan and Associates
Kinney Chan
Hong Kong, China

Client
Hotel Fusion
San Francisco, CA,United States of America

Die Infusion Lounge ist eine gehobene Lounge-Bar mit asiatischen Einflüssen. Der 600 m² große Raum besteht aus einem Hauptbereich mit Bar, VIP-Terrasse und eindrucksvollen Gittersäulen, die auf chinesische Architektur und Fensterdekorationen zurückgehen. Der zweite Raum mit DJ-Bühne steht für Bankette und Modenschauen zur Verfügung. Ein programmierbares LED-System beleuchtet die Säulen aus gebeiztem Glas. Die kurvigen Wände um die Waschbecken und Kabinen in den Unisex-Toiletten sind mit Mosaikfliesen bedeckt. Eine Kombination aus extravagantem Ambiente und schickem, innovativem Design: Die Infusion Lounge ist ein unbedingtes Muss.

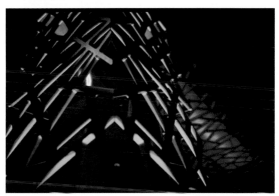

Infusion Lounge is an Asian-inspired upscale lounge bar. The 600 m² space features a main room with a full bar, an elevated VIP terrace and striking latticed columns based on Chinese architecture and window decorations. The second room features a DJ stage and is available for banquets and fashion shows. A programmable LED lighting system illuminates the etched-glass columns. The curved walls around the sinks and stalls in the unisex restrooms are covered in mosaic tiles. A combination of an extravagant ambiance with a chic, innovative design, Infusion Lounge is a must-see destination.

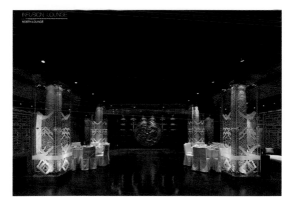

Project
Karo 5
Eingangsgebäude
Entry

Design
Fuenfwerken Design AG
Wiesbaden, Germany

Client
Technische Universität Darmstadt
Darmstadt, Germany

Information und Kommunikation sollen im neuen Eingangsgebäude der TU Darmstadt im Fokus stehen. Zusammen mit dem Architekten Martin Schmitt entwickelten wir dafür multifunktionale Raum-Licht-Objekte, die architektonische Anforderungen und Kommunikationsziele mit Forschung und Lehre verbinden. Quer durch das Foyer erstreckt sich ein LED-Display mit eigenem Pixel-Font als interaktive Informationsplattform und technischem Experimentierfeld für einzelne Fachbereiche. Im Galeriegeschoss schweben drei überdimensionale „Lampenschirme" mit beleuchtungs- und medientechnischen Funktionen – in ihrer Formgebung eine augenzwinkernde Reminiszenz an das Credo „Tradition und Fortschritt".

Information and communication are to be the focus of attention in the new foyer of Darmstadt University of Technology. For this purpose we designed in co-operation with the architect Martin Schmitt multi-functional objects of space and light, which combine architectural requirements and communication goals with research and education. An LED display with its own pixel font extends across the lobby as an interactive information platform and technical experimental field for individual faculties. Three colossal "lampshades" float in the gallery, providing lighting and media support functions – their design is a slightly tongue-in-cheek reminder of the belief in "tradition and progress".

Project
DMC ANKARA
Gebäude
Building

Design
Tabanlioglu Architects
Melkan Gursel, Murat Tabanlioglu
Istanbul, Turkey

Client
Ortadogu Otomotiv A. S
Ankara, Turkey

Der Würfel als die perfekte Form und mehr – DMC ist ein bemerkenswertes Mediagebilde und es beherbergt die führende Mediagruppe der Türkei. Die Hauptform ist ein Würfel, der sich auf das eckige Baugrundstück bezieht. Die würfelige Form wird verzerrt und umgeordnet durch kubische Annexe und Subtraktionen, aus denen sich zusätzliches Volumen ergibt. Was die Durchsichtigkeit betrifft, ist es ein authentisches Gebäude. Die starke „In-Out-Korrelation" sorgt für eine klar definierte Darstellung, schon bevor man das Gebäude betritt. Separate Abschnitte wie die Studios bewahren die Exklusivität. Die sinnbildliche Fassade, die dem Braille-Alphabet ähnelt, betont „Kommunikation für alle".

The cube as a perfect form and more: DMC is a distinctive media figure, housing Turkey's leading media group. Main form is a cube in respect to the square site; the cube form deformed and re-structured by cubic annex and subtraction that resulted in extra volumes. A genuine building in terms of transparency; strong in-out correlation enables a well-defined description before getting in the building. Separate sections like studios preserve their exclusivity. The emblematic use of façade resembling Braille alphabet accentuates "communication is for all". The building is strongly perceived from afar and materializes as an eye-catching "sign".

Project
Fraunhofer-Jahrestagung 2008 –
Zukunft braucht Forschung
Medienband
Media strip

Design
Multitask Gesellschaft für Eventmarketing mbH
Thomas Peters, Sascha Wolf
(Beratung und Konzeption)
Frauke Harnack (Projektmanagement)
Berlin, Germany
Brandatmosphere
Medienkommunikation und Architekturdesign
Tobias Mund, Maximilian Quast
(Architektur und Design)
Sebastian Bach (Mediendesign)
Berlin, Germany

Client
Fraunhofer-Gesellschaft zur Förderung
der angewandten Forschung
München, Germany

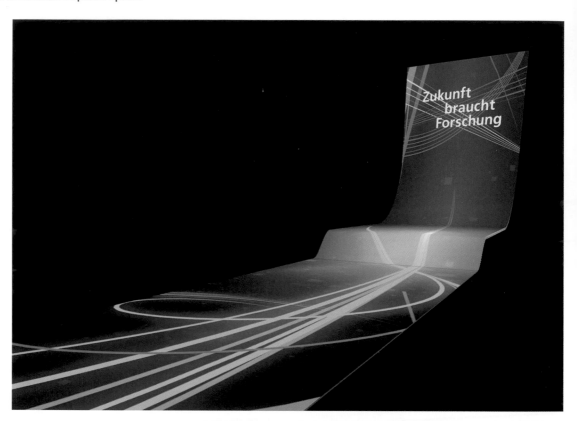

Berlin, 28.05.2008. 650 hochrangige Gäste verfolgen die Verleihung der „Joseph-von-Fraunhofer-Preise". Zentrales Element der Veranstaltung ist ein fünf Meter breites und 30 Meter langes, komplett bespielbares Medienband durch den gesamten Raum – die Fraunhofer-Zukunftsbahn. Diese nimmt im Auditorium Forschungsimpulse auf, führt diese auf der Bühne zu einer konkreten Innovation zusammen und zeigt schließlich auf einer sieben Meter hohen Rückwand die weiteren Potenziale auf. Die Preisträger selbst betreten jeweils zum Ende eines Intro-Trailers die Zukunftsbahn und nutzen diese, um das Projekt mit Hilfe von Einspielern detailliert vorzustellen.

Berlin 28 May 2008. 650 high-ranking guests attended the award ceremony for the "Joseph-von-Fraunhofer-Prize". The central element of the protocol event was a five by thirty meter projector screen surface that crossed the entire room – the Fraunhofer Runway of the Future. It collected research impulses from the auditorium, merging them into a concrete project as they crossed the stage, before finally depicting the potential of the innovation on a seven-meter tall screen. At the end of each of these trailers, the prize winners stepped onto the runway, using it as a tool to illustrate details of their specific venture by means of film-clips.

Project
Leitsystem GREY
Orientierungssystem
Signage system

Design
KW43 BRANDDESIGN
Christian Vöttiner (Creative Director)
Astrid Schröder (Art Director)
Marc Schäde (Creation)
Düsseldorf, Germany

Client
GREY Group
Düsseldorf, Germany

Thema / Aufgabenstellung:
Das Agenturnetzwerk GREY Group ist in „die Ideen-Botschaft am Platz der Ideen" gezogen. Für eine gute Orientierung auf dem neuen Gelände und in den Gebäuden soll ein umfassendes Gestaltungs- und Objektsystem erstellt werden, mit gleichsam funktionaler als auch repräsentativer Funktion.
Idee / Umsetzung:
Der Konzeptgedanke der Botschaft spiegelt sich auf dem gesamten Gelände und in allen Gebäuden wider: Die Gestaltung und Materialauswahl lehnt sich an die Optik klassischer Grenzmarkierungen an. Das Deckenleitsystem in den Gebäuden zitiert den kartografischen Stil.

Subject / Challenge:
The agency network Grey Group has moved into "the Ideas Embassy on Platz der Ideen". To help people find their way on the new premises and in its buildings, a comprehensive design and implementation for signposting, which both serve a function and is representative of the group, is to be created.
Idea / Implementation:
The underlying concept of an embassy is to be reflected throughout the premises and all its buildings The design and choice of materials thus follows the visual theme of classic border markings, supplemented by a system of ceiling signs in the buildings, which follow a cartographic style.

Project
MTZ München
Leitsystem
Signage system

Design
L2M3 Kommunikationsdesign GmbH
Frank Geiger, Sascha Lobe
Stuttgart, Germany

Client
Stadtwerke München GmbH
München, Germany

Unser Leitsystem für das MTZ verbindet mediale und grafisch-analoge Elemente zu einem Ganzen. Ausgehend von einem gedachten Mittelpunkt im Eingangsbereich ziehen sich konzentrische Kreise durch das Gebäude. Anhand einer Infowand im Foyer bekommt der Besucher einen Überblick, wo sich die gesuchte Firma befindet. Die Leuchtkuben weisen dem Besucher via Typografie-Animation den Weg zum gesuchten Gebäudeteil. Die Farben stehen für die unterschiedlichen Gebäudemodule. An den Decken in den Treppenhauskernen findet der Besucher die konzentrischen Kreise wieder. Die unterschiedliche Krümmung der Kreise definiert die Entfernung vom Mittelpunkt.

Our signage system for the MTZ combines media elements with graphical, analog elements to create a unified whole. Starting out from an assumed centre point near the entrance, concentric circles stretch out around the building. An information wall in the entrance area shows the visitor where the company he is looking for is located. Illuminated cubes point the way to the appropriate part of the building with the aid of animated typography. The colors stand for the various building modules. Visitors also find the concentric circles on the ceilings in the staircase cores. The varying curve of the circles defines the distance from the center.

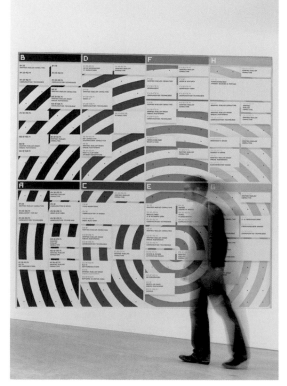

Project
smart Messe Exponate
Kommunikationsexponate
Communication exhibits

Design
spek Design
Patrick Sauter, Eberhard Kappler, Nadine Dopslaff,
Alfe Toussaint, Caterina Idler, Carola Unsöld,
Devin Teachout, Katharina Lauter, Ines Stober
Stuttgart, Germany

Client
Daimler AG, smart
Stuttgart, Germany

Am smart-Konfigurator gestaltet der Besucher sein Wunschfahrzeug mit den „RFID-Farb-Material-Würfeln" und kann sich dann seine persönliche smart-Karte ausdrucken. Das „smart-electric-drive-Exponat" kommuniziert die animierte Alltagstauglichkeit vom „electric-drive-smart". smart-Modellautos fahren simultan zu den Animationsfilmen. Mit der Schattenwand wird das zehnjährige smart-Jubiläum gefeiert. Der Besucher wird durch seinen interaktiven Schatten ein Teil der smart-Welt. Die „intelligent drive viewer" geben einen Ausblick auf die umweltfreundlichen smart-Attribute: CO_2-Champion, 3-Liter-Auto und Start-Stopp-Technik.

With the "color & trim configurator" the visitor designs his smart car by using the RFID cubes to control the screen image, before a card of the individual choice is printed. The smart electric drive city model communicates the everyday use of an electric drive car with an infotainment character. Model smart cars drive simultaneously to the animated films. The Shadow-Wall celebrates the ten year anniversary of the smart car. The shadow becomes an interactive part of the smart world. The intelligent drive viewers give an animated impression to ecological smart attributes such as: CO_2 Champion, 3 liter car and the start-stop technology.

Project
Lightscape Twin Towers
Multimedia Design

Design
SmartJoy Digital Art Ltd., Co.
Ming-tao Wang, Sheng-jer Huang, Chiu-fang Chung,
Miao-chuan Ho Hsu, Yu-ping Wang, Mei-ling Chen
Taipei, Taiwan

Client
Yuan Pu Advertising Ltd., Co.
Bank of Panhsin
Taipei, Taiwan

Die Lightscape Twin Towers sind Luxuswohnanlagen im neuen urbanen Zentrum von Taipei. Sie sind das höchste Wahrzeichen dieses neu gestalteten Stadtbereichs und werden zukünftig durch ein Skywalk-System mit ihrer Umgebung verbunden sein.
SmartJoy simuliert das Aussehen des Skywalks in einem langen Gang im Verkaufsbereich der Towers, um den Besuchern eine Vorstellung von der zukünftigen, hoch aufragenden Stadtlandschaft zu vermitteln. Interessierte können sich hier anhand eines weißen Modells inmitten des Gangs über das geplante fortschrittliche Verkehrssystem und die Wohnfunktionen sowie die Vorteile der Höhe und Lage der Anlage informieren. Auf das Modell werden per Video fließende Bilder projiziert, die den Besuchern dieser virtuellen Realität einen Einblick in die versprochene Zukunft aus einem höheren Blickwinkel ermöglichen.
Die Präsentation besteht aus drei thematischen Filmen über das Verkehrsnetz, den Lifestyle und die Szenerien der Stadt bei Tag und Nacht. Die Filme werden durch das Umdrehen von kabellosen Würfeln vor dem Modell aktiviert. Die Besucher können den gewünschten Inhalt auswählen und sich so über die zukünftige Entwicklung des Gebiets informieren und eine Vorstellung vom einzigartigen Lebens- und Wohngefühl in der Anlage bekommen.

Lightscape Twin Towers is a luxury residence architecture located in Taipeis new urban center. Its the highest landmark in this specific development area, and will connect to neighboring facilities via cityscape skybridges.
In the sale center inside the Towers, SmartJoy transformed an existing long hallway into a simulated skybridge, allowing visitors foreseeing the high rise cityscape. Furthermore, in order to illustrate the superior traffic and living environment in near future and to highlight the advantages of Towers' tallness and location, SmartJoy places a pure white cityscape model in the middle of hallway, and uses video projection to display inspiring images flowing timely and seamlessly on real model. The visitors, standing in this virtual reality, are given the access to overlook the promised future from a higher view-point.
The presentation consists of three different theme videos: traffic network, life-style and metro scenery from day to night. Each video is activated through a wireless cube in front of the model. The visitors can select desired theme by flipping cube, and proceed to visualize the future development and the wonderful residential life around the Towers.

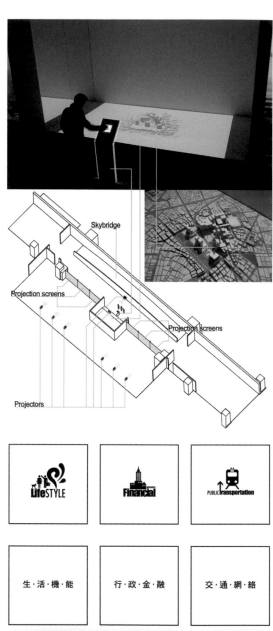

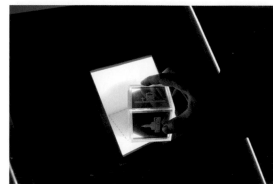

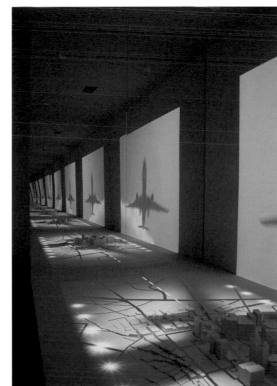

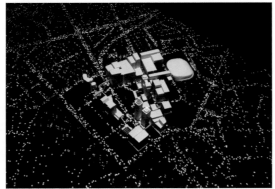

Project
Mediatektur
Mediale Fassade
Media facade

Design
ART + COM
Prof. Joachim Sauter, Dennis Paul,
Susanne Traeger, Jens-Ove Panknin,
Christine Paech, Gerd Grüneis,
Tobias Gremmler, David Siegel,
Valentin Schunack, Gert Monath
Berlin, Germany
ATELIER BRÜCKNER
Prof. Uwe R. Brückner, Eberhard Schlag,
Michel Casertano, Dominik Hegemann
Stuttgart, Germany

Client
BMW Group
München, Germany

Aufgabe in einem Museum der Mobilität war es, mit gestalterischen Mitteln eine Atmosphäre der Dynamik zu vermitteln. Die „Mediatektur", eine Symbiose aus Medien und Architektur, erweitert den Raum visuell und versetzt die ausgestellten Fahrzeugexponate in Bewegung: Zum einen durch ihre Relativbewegung zur Fassade, zum anderen durch die über die Oberflächen gleitenden Lichtreflexionen. Im reaktiven Modus reagiert die bespielte Fassade auf die Präsenz der Besucher, die so in das Geschehen im Museum einbezogen werden.

The approach was to create a dynamic environment for a museum of mobility. The "Mediatektur", a symbiosis of media and architecture, on one hand enlarges the space by extending it virtually through three-dimensional moving images. It also sets the exhibited "parked" cars into motion relative to the animated walls. In the switched reactive mode, the pattern of illumination changes according to the mere presence of visitors and thus actively involves them in the scenario.

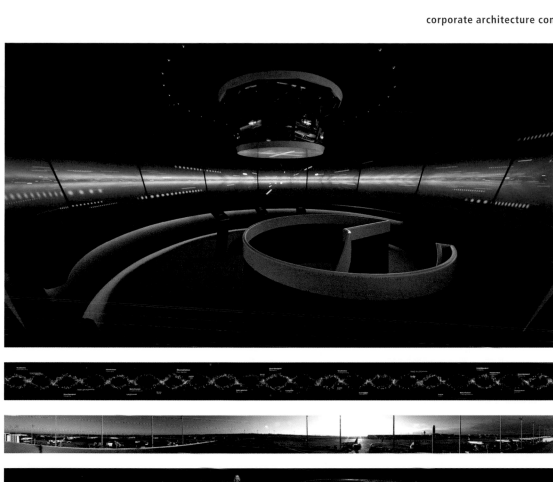

Project
Lufthansa Markenakademie Tower
360° Projektion
360° projection

Design
:: dan pearlman markenarchitektur gmbh
Steffen Armbruster, Thorsten Kadel,
Nicole Gietz-Haslinger, Patrick Bengsohn,
Gesa Gräven, Klaas Stürenburg, Sven Strassner,
Jakob Lehr, Roger Nientiet, Stefka Ammon
Berlin, Germany

Client
Deutsche Lufthansa AG
Frankfurt a. M., Germany

Lufthansa AG: mediale Rauminszenierung für die Vermittlung komplexer Konzernstrategien. Wie kann die Lufthansa AG ihre Mitarbeiter so schulen, dass sie das Unternehmen verstehen, seine Marken erleben und gegenüber Kunden stringent repräsentieren? Die Lufthansa AG beauftragte dan pearlman mit der Entwicklung einer Markenakademie, deren Kernstück die mediale Inszenierung eines Towers ist. Die didaktische Vermittlung von Kundenbedürfnissen, Marken und Strategien erfolgt in einer 360° Projektion durch audiovisuell aufbereitete Information, Interaktivität und geschulte Guides. Das beeindruckende Raumerlebnis verankert das neue Wissen nachhaltig.

Lufthansa AG: media-based spatial presentation to convey complex corporate strategy. How can Lufthansa AG train its staff to understand the company and provide an experience of the brands so that they consistently represent these brands vis-à-vis customers? Lufthansa AG commissioned dan pearlman to develop a brand academy based around the media presentation of a tower. Customer needs, brands and strategies are conveyed educationally by means of a 360° projection of audio visually prepared information with interactive elements and trained guides. This powerful 3D-experience ensures that the new material learned is acquired on a lasting basis.

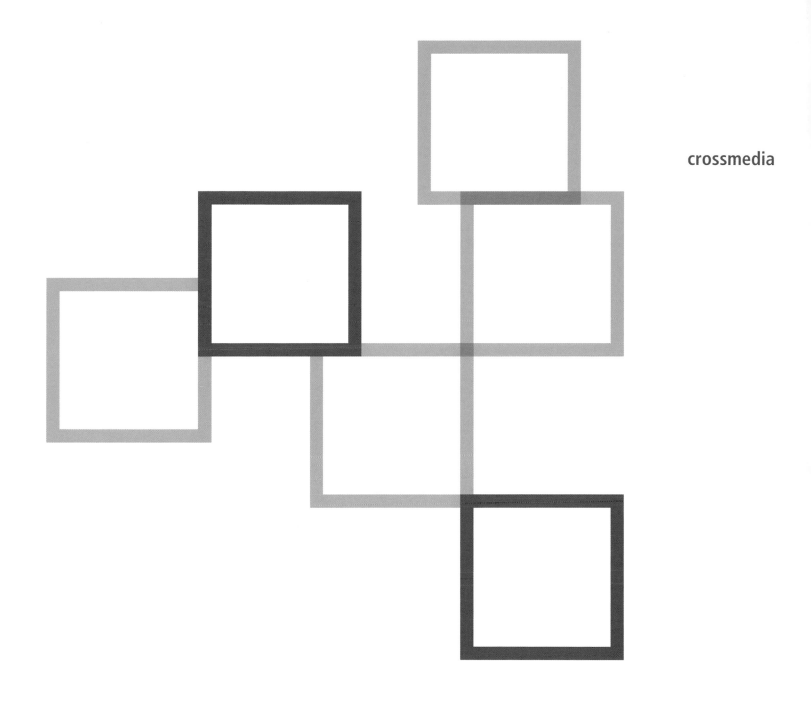

crossmedia

In Kampagnen und anderen Dienstleistungen kann schon
die kleinste Idee den Sieg bringen

Die Dienstleistungen, Kampagnen und Produkteinführungen von morgen sind ohne eine sorgfältig geplante und umgesetzte Crossmedia-Design- und Kommunikationsstrategie kaum noch vorstellbar.

Strategisch und kreativ gestaltet, optimiert die Crossmedia-Kommunikation die Schnittstelle zwischen Verbraucher, Service und Botschaft. Dies kann auf vielfältige Weise geschehen, doch das Ziel ist immer dasselbe: Service oder Produkt werden durch Kommunikationsmaßnahmen ergänzt, wodurch eine Brücke zwischen dem Bedürfnis des Verbrauchers und dem geschäftlichen Zweck entsteht.

Die Crossmedia-Kommunikation kombiniert „traditionelle" Plattformen wie Web, Print, Mobiltelefone, Media-Player, Spiele und Fernsehen und integriert zahlreiche Kommunikationskanäle, Dienste, Plattformen und sogar physischen Raum. Mehrwert entsteht, indem neue Möglichkeiten für Austausch und Interaktion geschaffen werden und der Verbraucher somit zu mehr als einem „passiven Empfänger" wird.

Die Benutzer können Informationen über ihre bevorzugte Plattform abrufen und multidimensionale Kommunikation und Service erleben – davon gehen sie heutzutage aus. Sie wollen zu jeder Zeit und über jede Plattform empfangen, sich mitteilen und am Geschehen teilnehmen können. Die nächste Benutzergeneration weist bereits jetzt schon höhere Erwartungen und neue Verhaltensmuster auf, auf die wir uns einstellen müssen.

Bei der Bewertung der Crossmedia-Kategorie kam es uns zunächst auf den Gesamteindruck an. Indem wir einen Schritt zurücktraten, konnten wir die Beiträge im Rahmen der verschiedenen Disziplinen verstehen und einschätzen. Genauso viel Beachtung haben wir jedoch auch den Details geschenkt. Selbst die kleinste Idee kann ausschlaggebend für den Erfolg einer Kampagne oder eines Dienstleistungsangebotes sein.

Even the smallest idea can be the winning factor
in a campaign or service

It's hard to imagine future services, campaigns or product launches without a carefully planned and executed crossmedia design and communication strategy.

If designed strategically and creatively, crossmedia communication optimises the intersection between the user, service and message. This can be done in numerous ways, all of which aim to supplement a service or product, thereby mediating user needs and business goals.

Crossmedia communication combines "traditional" platforms such as web, print, mobile phones, media players, games, TV. It integrates various communication channels, services, platforms and even physical space. And by creating new possibilities like sharing and interacting – allowing the user to be more than a "passive receiver" – you create added value.

Users get the chance to access information on their preferred platform and experience multi-dimensional communication or services – in fact, today they demand it. Users expect to be able to receive, share and participate at any time on any platform. And the next generation of users already has higher expectations and new behavioral patterns, which we must address.

When evaluating the crossmedia category, we took a step back. By looking at the big picture, we could grasp and appreciate the entries across the various disciplines. But we also paid attention to detail. Even the smallest idea can be the winning factor in a campaign or service.

Hans-Henrik Sørensen

Project
GENIE ESSEN | CHILLI –
Anstiftung zur Cross-Media-Cuisine
Buch/Webseite/Mobiler Dienst
Book/website/mobile service

Design
chilli mind GmbH
Oliver Gerstheimer, Hanna Faure,
Sebastian Ammermüller,
Steffen Wüst, Franz Walter
Kassel, Germany

Client
chilli mind GmbH
Kassel, Germany

64 Gestalter aus neun Ländern interpretieren 94
scharfe Genussräume. Das Design- und Erlebnis-
kochbuch ist ein kollektives Werk und adressiert Quer-
denker und Genießer, die sich gerne Geschmacks-
fragen stellen und beantworten. Die cross-mediale
Umsetzung schöpft die Vorteile der Medien Print,
Internet und Mobilfunk im Kontext des Kochens
aus: 360-Seiten-Buch; E-Book als PDF-Download
mit Weblinks; Einkaufslisten als mobiler Dienst und
weitere Multimedia-Inhalte im Internet unter www.
genie-essen.com.

64 designers from nine countries interpret 94 hot
gourmet areas. The design and adventure cookbook
is a collective work addressing lateral thinkers and
gourmets who enjoy discussing issues relating to
taste. The cross-media implementation exploits the
advantages offered by print, internet and mobile
media in the context of cooking: 360 page book;
e-book as a PDF download with web links; shopping
lists as a mobile service and additional multimedia
content available online at www.genie-essen.com.

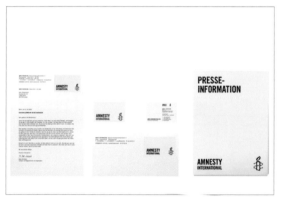

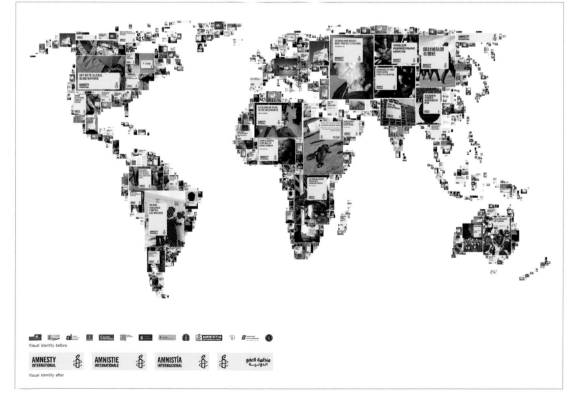

Project
Amnesty International
Corporate Design

Design
Scholz & Friends Identify
Wolf Schneider (Creative Director)
Kathrin Wetzel, Olivier Nowak,
Maria-Michaela Tonn, Vera Müller
(Art Direction)
Anna Kubitza (Beratung)
Berlin, Germany

Client
Amnesty International
Berlin, Germany

Mehr Wirkung für die Menschenrechte durch ein neues internationales Erscheinungsbild für Amnesty International: Die neue Identität ist geprägt durch ein Symbol für Unterdrückung und Hoffnung, eine Farbwelt für Aufmerksamkeit und Dringlichkeit, eine authentische und dokumentarische Bildsprache, eine Typografie für Fakten und Aktionen – für eine weltweite Wiedererkennbarkeit und einfache Anwendbarkeit. Allein im Rahmen des Einführungsprozesses für Deutschland wurden die Markenarchitektur und alle Kommunikationsmittel überarbeitet. Die mehr als 20.000 Mitglieder erhielten ein einfaches „Toolkit" mit allen Werkzeugen für die tägliche Arbeit.

More effectiveness in the battle for human rights through a new international visual profile of the world's largest human rights organization – Amnesty International: the new international visual identity is marked by a symbol of suppression and hope, a color world that draws attention and expresses urgency, an authentic and documentary-style visual language, and a typeface that is suitable for conveying facts and for campaigns – promoting global recognizability and easy applicability. During the launch process in Germany alone the brand architecture and all communication media were revised.

crossmedia

Project
KlinkenPaar I PaarKlinken
Broschüre, DVD, Website

Design
FSB-Marketing
Christian Riepe (Konzeption und Design der Bro-
schüre, DVD und Website)
Brakel, Germany
silberland medienprojekte GmbH
Christopher Langen (Film- und DVD-Produktion)
Garbsen, Germany
salient GmbH
Jörg Amthauer (Design und Realisierung der Website)
Frankfurt a. M., Germany

Client
Franz Schneider Brakel GmbH + Co KG
Brakel, Germany

Unter dem Titel „KlinkenPaar | PaarKlinken" veröf-
fentlicht FSB eine Dokumentation zu seinem gleichnamigen Design-Workshop. Thema des Workshops
mit anschließender Ausstellung und Symposium war
die Gestaltung von Klinkenpaaren, die nicht zwangs-
läufig identisch sein müssen. Während die Broschüre
auf die Entwürfe und Designer eingeht, wird im begleitenden Webauftritt die Ausstellung virtuell in
einem 3-D-Raum nachgebildet und mit Interviews
ergänzt. Die DVD rückt das Symposium in den Mittelpunkt. Es wird als vollständiger Mitschnitt bereitgestellt und kann gezielt nach Vorträgen durchsucht
werden. Eine komprimierte Dokumentation rundet
die DVD ab.

FSB is publishing an eponymous titled documenta-
tion of its "DuoHandles | HandleDuos" design work-
shop, which – together with a follow-up exhibition
and symposium – addressed the design of handle
pairs that are not of necessity identical. The brochure
covers the designs and their authors, while the at-
tendant web product recreates the exhibition in a
virtual 3D space as well as containing interviews. The
DVD focuses on the symposium. It comes unabridged
and the talks delivered can be accessed at random.
Rounding the DVD off is a condensed documentation
of the event.

Project
ACCESS ALL AREAS
Designtage Wiesbaden
Event

Design
Fuenfwerken Design AG
Wiesbaden, Germany
Die Firma GmbH
Innovative Kommunikation
Wiesbaden, Germany

Client
Landeshauptstadt Wiesbaden
Wiesbaden, Germany

Die Landeshauptstadt Wiesbaden hat mit einigen der deutschlandweit bestplatzierten Wiesbadener Kreativ-Unternehmen einen „Tag des Creative Business" ins Leben gerufen. Im Rahmen von ACCESS ALL AREAS, so der Titel der Initiative, präsentieren sich seither jeden Frühling die Wiesbadener Agenturen mit offenen Büros, Filmen, Vorträgen und anderen Aktionen in der ganzen Stadt. Für die mehrtägige Veranstaltung entwarf „Fuenfwerken Design" das Corporate Design, ein temporäres Wegeleitsystem und Mailings. Die Agentur „Die Firma" entwickelte für das Wegeleitsystem eine Online-Anwendung.

The government of the Hessian capital Wiesbaden established a "Day of Creative Business" together with some of Germany's top-ranked Wiesbaden creative companies. As part of ACCESS ALL AREAS, as the initiative was called, since then Wiesbaden's agencies have opened their offices every spring to present films, lectures and other events throughout the city. "Fuenfwerken Design" developed the corporate design, a temporary directional system and mailings. The agency "Die Firma" developed an online application for the directional system.

Project
Nokia Navigation
Navigationskampagne
Navigation campaign

Design
J. Walter Thompson
Lars Huerter (Art Director)
Jörg Bredendieck (Copywriter)
Paul Grabowski, Lopetz, Katharina Gschwendtner
(Illustrators)
Düsseldorf, Germany

Client
Nokia GmbH
Düsseldorf, Germany

Die beiden neuen Nokia Mobiltelefone können mehr, als nur ans Ziel zu führen. Lieblingsorte lassen sich markieren und mit anderen teilen. Diese Besonderheit stand im Mittelpunkt der Kampagne. Auf Plakaten, in Anzeigen und im Internet wurden 82 Millionen Menschen in ganz Deutschland aufgefordert, ihre Lieblingsorte im Internet mit anderen zu teilen. Die besten Tipps aus acht Städten wurden ausgewählt und dann als City-Light-Plakate und Anzeigen veröffentlicht, sodass die Teilnehmer die Werbung mitgestalten konnten und selbst Teil davon wurden. Spielerisch und detailgetreu luden die Plakate wie nie zuvor dazu ein, Städte zu entdecken.

The new Nokia mobile phones are not just able to navigate you where you want to go. You can also share your favorite places with others. This was the main message of the campaign. Using poster, print ads and the internet we asked 82 million people in Germany to share their favorite places via internet with others. Suggestions for eight cities were chosen and published as city light posters and print ads, so that the people actively created the advertisement. With love to detail the posters invited everybody to discover the cities like they never did before.

Project
itech
Multimedia-Kampagne
Mixed media campaign

Design
qu-int. werbeagentur
Sebastian Lange
Freiburg, Germany

Client
Hiller Objektmöbel GmbH & Co. KG
Kippenheim, Germany

itech:
Display-System für sekundenschnelle Beschriftung von Stühlen: persönliche Anrede, Platznummer etc.
Box: enthält Printfolder und USB-Stick.
Microsite: enthält Produktvorteile, 3-D-Intro, Film und Galerie.
USB-Stick: enthält itech-Microsite, Folder und Film – mit Aktualisierungsfunktion (liegt eine neue Produktinformation vor, wird sie automatisch aus dem Internet geladen und auf dem Stick installiert); lasst sich passgenau in die itech-Box einfügen; gleicht der Form des itech-Logos.
Folder: enthält Produktvorteile, technische Features etc.
Film: die Intelligenz des Systems wird durch 3-D-Animation, „Motion-Graphics" und Realbild mit musikalischer Leichtigkeit vermittelt.

itech:
Display system for caption of seats within seconds: seating number, welcoming of guests etc.
Box: contains printfolder and USB stick.
Microsite: contains key benefits, 3D intro, film and gallery.
USB stick: contains itech microsite, folder and film – equipped with an update function (if new product information is available, it is automatically loaded from the internet and installed on the stick); the stick fits accurately in the box and equates the shape of the itech logo.
Folder: contains key benefits, technical features etc.
Film: the intelligence of itech is communicated by combining 3D animation, motion graphics and shots with musical easiness.

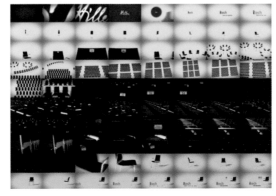

Project
Pathologie
Corporate Design

Design
identis GmbH
design-gruppe joseph pölzelbauer
Joseph Pölzelbauer (CD)
Petra Haug, Jean Mierecke, Reinhard Groh,
Janine Hauss, Bernhard Wilke
Freiburg, Germany

Client
Gemeinschaftspraxis für Pathologie
Freiburg, Germany

Design-Sprache für medizinische Leistungen: Das Corporate Design soll der Gemeinschaftspraxis für Pathologie im Markt der medizinischen Dienstleister ein unverwechselbares Gesicht geben. Dabei soll eine Wertanmutung vermittelt werden, die Seriosität mit innovativem Fortschritt sowie Gediegenheit und Verlässlichkeit mit Freundlichkeit und Offenheit verbindet. Die Basis des Corporate Designs ist eine freie, offene Farb- und Formensprache, die sich aus der physischen Realität der Gewebestrukturen herleitet. Bei aller Offenheit und Variabilität hat diese visuelle Sprache eine unverwechselbare Eigenständigkeit im Sinne eines Stils.

Visual code for medical services: the corporate design is meant to provide a unique image for the medical practice for pathology in the medical market. Beyond that it transports an impression of values. This look-and-feel connects scientific sincerity with innovative progress as well as solidity and reliability with gentleness and forthrightness. The corporate design is based on a free and open code of shapes and colors deriving from the physical reality of cell structures. Being open and variable this visual language all the same owns the distinctive originality of a coherent style.

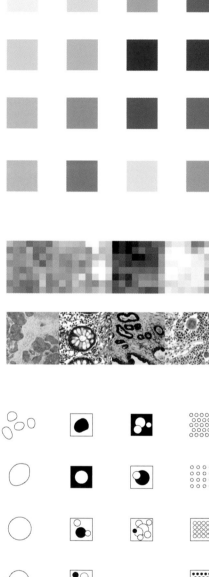

Project
Picture Press
Relaunch / Corporate Design

Design
JUNO
Wolfgang Greter, Frank Wache, Björn Lux,
Nicole Klein, Alexander Rufenach
Hamburg, Germany

Client
Picture Press / Gruner + Jahr
Bild- und Textagentur GmbH
Hamburg, Germany

JUNO erhält den Auftrag, die Bildagentur Picture Press (Gruner + Jahr) als Marke neu zu positionieren und zu inszenieren. Das Unternehmen kämpft mit Imageproblemen und sinkenden Preisen. Der neue Markenauftritt soll die Hochwertigkeit der Produkte (STERN-, GEO-Fotos etc.) unterstreichen und ein klares, positives Bild des Unternehmens erzeugen. JUNO macht Picture Press strategisch und visuell wieder zum klar erkennbaren G + J-Tochterunternehmen. Farbigkeit und ein souveräner Auftritt verdeutlichen dies. Das Logo, ein „X", soll einen Bildrahmen beziehungsweise Platzhalter für Bilder symbolisieren. Die eingeführte Corporate-Schrift für Wortmarke und Typo lässt den Markenauftritt geschlossen wirken.

JUNO is asked to relaunch the stock photo agency Picture Press (Gruner + Jahr). The company is suffering from image problems and declines in prices. A new brand identity shall emphasize the premium level of its products (STERN-, GEO-photography etc.) and a clear and positive image of the company. JUNO transforms Picture Press strategically and visually into a clearly recognizable sub company of G + J. Color and confident appearance show that unmistakably. The corporate logo, an "X", stands for frames or placeholders. The corporate typeface for the word mark and type completes the brand identity.

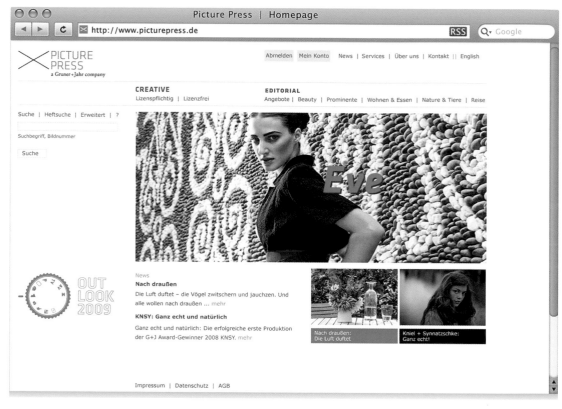

PICTUREs

PICTURE
PRESS

a Gruner + Jahr company

crossmedia

Project
Kochen ohne Grenzen
Cooking without limits

Design
artundweise GmbH
Designer der artundweise GmbH
Bremen, Germany

Client
Gräfe und Unzer Verlag GmbH
München, Germany

Unter dem Dach der Kernmarke „GU" entwickelt der „Gräfe und Unzer Verlag" gemeinsam mit der betreuenden Agentur „artundweise" mehrere Produktneuheiten in 2009, die im Rahmen einer umfassenden und cross-medialen Paid-Service-Strategie konzipiert wurden und den Markt aktiv gestalten. Zur integrierten Strategie unter dem Dachportal „www.küchengötter.de", für das sich bereits eine aktive Community gefunden hat, zählen die folgenden innovativen Produkte:
– Das Kochbuch für das iPhone und den iPod Touch
– Persönliches Kochbuch „on Demand"
– Verschiedene TV- und Video-Angebote
Ein tolles Mehrwertangebot für Menschen jeden Alters, die Spaß am Kochen haben.

Under the roof of the umbrella brand "GU" "Gräfe und Unzer", the market leader and one of the most traditional German guidebook publishers developed in cooperation with "artundweise" several new products in 2009 which were conceived in the context of an extensive and cross medial paid services strategy with the goal stimulating the market. The integrated strategy around the portal "www.küchengötter.de", which already has a huge and active community, includes the following new products:
– iPhone and iPod Touch application "Cookbook"
– Personal cookbook on demand
– Various innovative TV and video offerings
This means more fun for all of those who enjoy cooking.

WAS TRÄGT EINE FRAU, FÜR DIE EIN BISSCHEN SÜNDE DAZUGEHÖRT?

ETWAS, WAS MIT ELEGANZ BESONDERS WIRKT:

DIESEN BLICK. SIE WISSEN SCHON WELCHEN.

Project
delmod
Marken-Relaunch
Brand relaunch

Design
Skalecki Marketing & Kommunikation
Jörg Skalecki
Frankfurt a. M., Germany
ippolito fleitz group
Peter Ippolito, Gunter Fleitz, Axel Knapp,
Lisa Seidl, Johanna Rudat
Stuttgart, Germany

Client
delmod international GmbH & Co. KG
Delmenhorst, Germany

Für das Mode-Unternehmen delmod wurde ein Marken-Relaunch entwickelt, der sich von der sonst üblichen Mode-Werbung mit Mode-Foto und Logo deutlich unterscheidet. Entwickelt wurde ein Visual Device (Bügel), das zum einen in allen Medien und Maßnahmen deklinierbar ist, immer „Mode" signalisiert, aber vor allem stets eine sehr flexible inhaltliche Basis bietet: mit spannenden Elementen, die an den Bügel gehängt werden und auf die Markenausrichtung „Das trage ich. In mir." fokussieren. Für delmod wurde damit eine langfristig und breit funktionierende Basis geschaffen, wechselnde Modetrends zu zeigen, aber dennoch sofort wiedererkennbar zu sein.

A brand relaunch has been developed for the delmod fashion business that is significantly different from the usual fashion advertising with fashion photo and logo. A visual device (hanger) has been developed that is adaptable to all media and advertising measures, always signifies "fashion", but most of all always offers an extremely flexible basis for content: with exciting components that can be hung on the hanger and focus on the brand direction "That's what I bear. In me." This has created for delmod a long-term and wide-functioning basis for showing changing fashion trends, while always remaining immediately recognizable.

Project
Bella Italia Weine
Corporate Design

Design
ippolito fleitz group
Gunter Fleitz, Peter Ippolito, Axel Knapp,
Yuan Peng, Sarah Meßelken
Stuttgart, Germany

Client
Bella Italia Weine
Stuttgart, Germany

Für „Bella Italia Weine" gestalteten wir nicht nur die Räumlichkeiten, sondern auch ein neues Corporate Design. Die Raumgestaltung bildete die Basis für die grafische Welt. Großflächige Collagen, als Folienschnitte auf die Fenster aufgebracht, zitieren sizilianische Klischees und Symboliken. Diese Illustrationen finden sich sowohl in der Geschäftsausstattung als auch auf den Holzbrettchen für die Menükarte wieder. Der große gelbe Bodenkreis des Kassenbereichs wird unter anderem zur Hervorhebung besonderer Offerten in Print und Web aufgegriffen. Motive mit Aufnahmen des Fotografen Zooey Braun bilden die Basis für eine Postkarten-Edition und die Internetseite.

We have designed the restaurant interior and a new corporate design for "Bella Italia Weine". The graphic design is based on elements from the interior design. Expanses of collage, affixed to the windows with adhesive foil, cite typically Sicilian clichés and symbolism. These illustrations reappear in the business stationery and the wooden menu card. The large yellow circle on the floor of the cash register area is used to emphasize special offers in print and web. Motifs showing images from photographer Zooey Braun form the basis for an edition of postcards and the website.

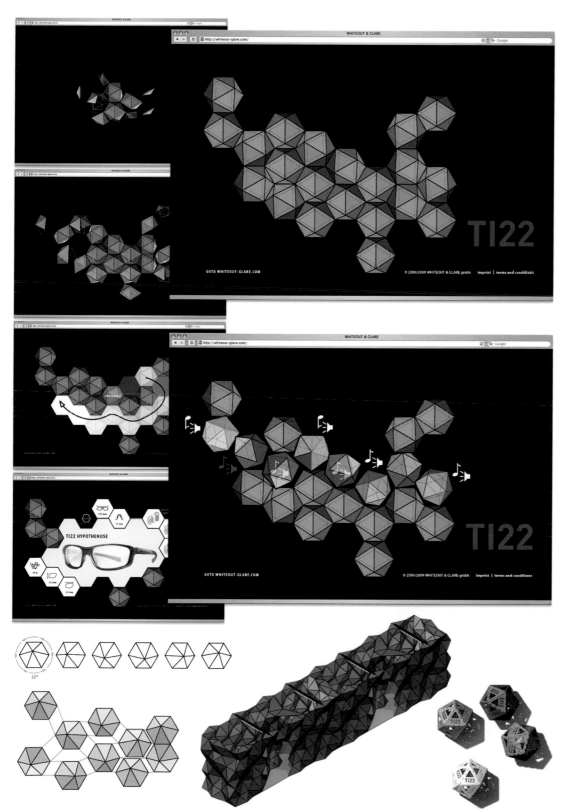

Project
TI22
Multimediale Kampagne
Mixed media campaign

Design
WHITEOUT & GLARE
Fabian Hofmann, Thomas Bischoff, Sven Kröger
Berlin, Germany

Client
WHITEOUT & GLARE
Berlin, Germany

Multimediale Kampagne für die neue Produktfamilie TI22: Das Element Titan steht im Mittelpunkt, die Ordnungszahl der Periodenliste wird zum Namensgeber. Die das Produktlogo begleitenden Medien beziehen ihre Formensprache aus der Molekularstruktur von Titan: Hexagonale Strukturen, 2-D in Printmedien sowie im Netz und 3-D im Messebau und in der Shop-Architektur verbinden alle Maßnahmen der Produktkampagne. Die Aktionen starteten im Januar 2009 und finden ihren Höhepunkt im Januar 2010 auf der „Münchner opti". Über das Jahr hinweg wird der „Look" in Farbe und Material abwechslungsreich variiert, das Motiv des Sechsecks zieht sich aber durch alle Medien.

Mixed media campaign for a new product called TI22: the periodic symbol of the element titanium inspires the name and the look is derived from the molecular structure of titanium. Hexagonal patterns, 2D in print and web and 3D in shop and booth architecture interconnect the tools of the campaign. It started in January 2009 and will come to a conclusion in January 2010 on the "opti" in Munich. During the year colors and materials will change, to keep the look fresh and inspiring, but the overall motive of the honeycomb will always interconnect the different ideas.

Project
Walter AG
Corporate Design

Design
Interbrand
Gion-Men Krügel-Hanna, Jens Grefen,
Mohamed Toutoungi (Corporate Design)
Felix Stöckle, Oliver Hopf, Jennifer Krügel-Hanna
(Consulting)
Köln, Germany

Client
Walter AG
Tübingen, Germany

Durch den Zusammenschluss der Marken Walter, Titex und Prototyp vereinen sich mehr als drei Jahrzehnte Erfahrung in der Werkzeugindustrie für Metallzerspanung zu einer starken Marke mit hoher Marktpräsenz. Es galt, eine Marken-Positionierung, eine Kommunikations-Strategie und ein Corporate Design für die neu entstandene Walter AG zu entwickeln. Die drei Firmen sollen unter der Dachmarke Walter weltweit neu positioniert werden. Während das Logo die drei Vorgängerfirmen unter einer Marke vereint, spiegeln sowohl das Layout als auch die Kommunikation die Präzision, Stärke und den innovativen Geist wider, der die Walter AG am Markt von ihren Wettbewerbern abhebt.

The merger of Walter, Titex and Prototyp united more than three decades of experience in the tool industry into a strong brand with a visible presence. The new Walter AG needed to develop a new brand position, communication strategy and corporate design. Under the umbrella brand Walter, the three companies charted a new, global position. The logo symbolizes the past of the three companies; design and communication elements illustrate the precision, strength and innovative spirit with which the new brand distinguishes itself from the competition.

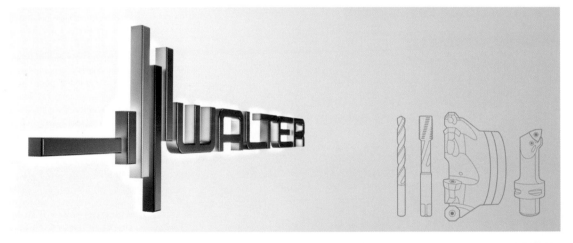

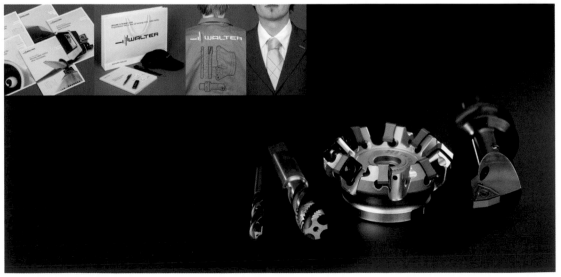

Die Substanz

USIMINAS U

Project
Usiminas
Corporate Design

Design
Interbrand Saõ Paulo
Beto Almeida, Leopold Leal,
João Marcopito, Cristiane Inoue, Jair Alves,
Rafael Cipolla (Corporate Design)
Alejandro Pinedo, Daniella Giavina-Bianchi,
Gabriela Mundim, Victoria Murat,
Laura Garcia (Consulting)
Saõ Paulo, Brazil
Interbrand Zürich
Andreas Rotzler, Iris Hänsch,
Salomon Gut (Corporate Design)
Dr. Thomas Deigendesch (Consulting)
Zürich, Switzerland

Client
Usiminas
Belo Horizonte, Brazil

Der brasilianische Minen- und Stahlkonzern Usiminas gehört zu den größten und modernsten Stahlproduzenten Südamerikas. An manchen Standorten sind bis zu 90% der Einwohner indirekt von Usiminas abhängig. Dadurch trägt das Unternehmen besondere Verantwortung. Mit dem Neuauftritt will Usiminas das Bewusstsein dafür erlebbar machen. Stahl bildet seit 4.000 Jahren das Rückgrat der kulturellen Entwicklung. Stahl ist eine zentrale Substanz unserer Gesellschaft. Usiminas ist Stahl. Usiminas ist diese Substanz. Usiminas-Stahl steckt in Gebäuden, Autos, Uhren etc. Wir alle tragen ein Stück Usiminas, ein Stück Verantwortung. Für diese Idee steht das ausgestanzte „U", das die Farben seiner Umgebung aufnimmt.

The Brazilian steel company Usiminas is one of the biggest and most modern steel producers in South America. In some areas up to 90% of the population depends on Usiminas indirectly. As a result, the company shoulders a great deal of responsibility, a point the company has chosen to address in its new brand launch. For the past 4,000 years, steel has been the backbone of cultural development. Steel is a core substance of society. Usiminas is steel. Usiminas this substance. Usiminas steel is used in buidlings, cars, watches etc. We all have a piece of Usiminas and thus carry a piece of the responsibility, an idea that Usiminas symbolizes in the movement and the changing colors of the Usiminas "U".

Project
Troika Dialog
Corporate Design

Design
Interbrand Zintzmeyer & Lux
Christoph Marti (Corporate Design)
Nicola Stanisch, Daria Gouskova (Consulting)
Moscow, Russian Federation
Interbrand
Jens-Ole Kracht, Thomas Jauss, Iris Hänsch,
Michaela Burger (Corporate Design)
Anton Isenring (Consulting)
Zürich, Switzerland

Client
Troika Dialog
Moscow, Russian Federation

„Troika Dialog" gehört zu den Gründern eines modernen Finanzmarktes in Russland zu Beginn der 90er Jahre und ist heute die führende Investment Bank des Landes. Um diese Entwicklung zu spiegeln, wurde die Marke kritisch hinterfragt. Die Leitidee des Hauses ist, dass aufstrebende Märkte „Heroes" brauchen, die Sicherheit geben und Verantwortung übernehmen. Das neue dreidimensionale Logo bewegt sich ständig – wo es möglich ist – und symbolisiert den konstanten Austausch sowie die gefundene Lösung (Dreiecke) für den Kunden – wobei drei Farben für drei Kundengruppen stehen. Die diagonale Formensprache wurde in Print, Shop-Design und Internet aufgenommen.

"Troika Dialog" has played a role in shaping Moscow's modern financial world. Since the early 1990s, it's been one of the leading investment banks in the country. To reflect on this development, the brand was scrutinized. A central idea emerged: a competitive brand in emerging markets needs "heroes", leaders who guarantee security and take responsibility. The new 3D logo is constantly moving and so symbolizes continuous information exchange. Lines representing connections among levels of interaction and processes are combined with colored triangles which signify solutions for different client groups. The bold, dynamic design is used for all corporate communications.

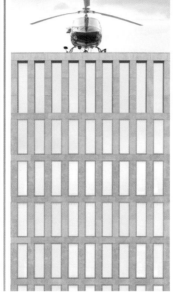

Urban Mobility

Schindler

Project
Schindler
Corporate Design

Design
Interbrand
Andreas Rotzler, Jürgen Kaske, Martina Gees,
Christoph Stalder, Janina Berger (Corporate Design)
Gernot Honsel, Anton Isenring, Dr. Ulrike Grein,
Svend Janssen (Consulting)
Zürich, Switzerland

Client
Schindler Management Ltd.
Ebikon, Switzerland

Der globale Markt für Aufzüge und Fahrtreppen ist hart umkämpft und geprägt durch technisch ähnliche Produkte. Mit einem für die Branche wegweisenden Markenauftritt wurde Schindler neu positioniert: als Dienstleister für urbane Mobilität – verlässlich, bewegend und wegweisend. Der neue Markenauftritt ist Abbild der strategischen Ausrichtung. Die Bildwelt ist ein Schlüsselelement des visuellen Auftritts: strahlend, weiß und rot. Ein Aufzug oder eine Fahrtreppe, verbunden mit einer menschlichen Handlung, stehen dabei im Fokus. Überraschende Bildausschnitte komplettieren den Gesamteindruck. Im Zusammenspiel ergibt sich eine unverwechselbare Bildsprache.

The global market for elevators and escalators is marked by a competitive struggle among producers of technically similar products. Schindler's new brand identity, recognized as a benchmark in the industry, reflects the company's business strategy with a striking collection of images. Pictures of the brand at work convey Schindler as the urban mobility provider: reliable, moving and trailblazing. Key to the brand's visual appearance is the use of bright, white and red to colorfully support pictures of elevators and escalators featuring people on the move. A surprising touch is added to each picture creating a unique message.

Project
Wataniya Airways
Corporate Design

Design
Peter Schmidt Group
Frankfurt a. M., Germany

Client
Wataniya Airways
Kuwait City, Kuwait

Die Flugzeuge der ersten kuwaitischen Point-to-Point-Airline – Wataniya Airways – mit zwei Premium-Klassen – „Premium Economy" und „First Class" – starteten im Januar 2009. Der Markenauftritt der Airline verbindet Innovation und Tradition, nationalen Stolz sowie die moderne arabische Welt. Das Herzstück der Marke ist das Logo, das mit den Elementen „Flügel", „Vogel" und „Segel" assoziiert wird. Sowohl bei den Unternehmensfarben als auch bei der Entwicklung der Typografie griff man auf Elemente aus dem arabischen und westlichen Kulturraum zurück. Wataniya Airways verspricht ihren Fluggästen ein außergewöhnliches Flugerlebnis in Bezug auf Komfort und Serviceangebot.

Wataniya Airways, which began flights in January 2009, is Kuwait's first point-to-point airline and offers a two-class premium configuration – "Premium Economy" and "First Class". The airline's premium brand identity epitomizes innovation and tradition, uniting Kuwait's proud national heritage with the modern Arab world. Its logo, the heart of the brand, creates associations to "wings", "sails", and thus "flight". The corporate colors and typography highlight elements from both Arabic and Western cultures. Wataniya Airways promises its guests an extraordinary experience of comfort and service excellence.

Project
Younicos
Corporate Design

Design
MetaDesign AG
Uli Mayer-Johanssen (Chief Design Officer)
Thomas Klein (Creative Director)
Carl-Frank Westermann
(Creative Director Sound Branding)
Berlin, Germany

Client
Younicos AG
Berlin, Germany

Younicos ist ein Zusammenschluss von SOLON Laboratories und der I-Sol Ventures GmbH mit dem Ziel Produkte mit Solarantrieb zu entwickeln und zu vertreiben. Für das neue Unternehmen standen neben der Namensfindung die Identitäts- und Markenentwicklung sowie deren Umsetzung in eine wirkungsvolle Markenwelt an. MetaDesign entwickelte gemeinsam mit ENDMARK den Namen, konzipierte den Claim „Let the fossils rest in peace." und realisierte den Markenauftritt. Corporate Design, Sound Branding, 3-D- und Interactive Branding machen Younicos multisensitiv nach innen und außen erlebbar und transportieren den selbstbewussten Auftritt einer neuen Marke.

Younicos is the result of a merger of SOLON Laboratories and I-Sol Ventures GmbH with the target of developing and marketing solar engines. The new company needed not only a name, but an identity and a brand, including implementation in an effective brand world. MetaDesign worked with ENDMARK to develop the name and the slogan "Let the fossils rest in peace." before creating the brand's look. Younicos' corporate design, brand sound, 3D and interactive branding allow the company to be experienced through several sensory channels by its employees and the public, and communicate the confident appearance of a new brand.

Project
ENTEGA
Corporate Design

Design
MetaDesign AG
Uli Mayer-Johanssen (Chief Design Officer)
Martin Steinacker (Creative Director)
Robert Schäfer, Martina Haag (Design Director)
Berlin, Germany

Client
HEAG Südhessische Energie AG (HSE)
Darmstadt, Germany

Erneuerbar und intelligent: Mit dem neuen Markenauftritt bezieht ENTEGA Stellung für zukünftige Energielösungen. Multisensuelle Kommunikations-Maßnahmen machen die Marke erlebbar und kommunizieren über eine offensive Gestaltung mit spielerischer Leichtigkeit eine eindeutige Botschaft: „ENTEGA. Energie der nächsten Generation." Eine interne Kampagne bereitete den Marken-Relaunch vor: Starterkits, Brandbooks und Schulungen verankerten die Marke im Unternehmen und machten die Mitarbeiter zu Marken-Botschaftern. Die landesweite externe Kampagne umfasst die Website, Plakate, Print- und Onlinewerbung sowie einen Radiospot.

Renewable and intelligent: with its new brand look, ENTEGA takes a stand for sustainable energy solutions. Multi-sensory communication turns the brand into an experience and conveys a clear message through an assertive design and playful light-heartedness: "ENTEGA. Energy of the next generation." An in-house campaign paved the way for the brand relaunch: starter kits, brand books and training anchored the brand inside the company and turned its employees into brand ambassadors. The Germany-wide campaign includes a website, posters, print and online advertising and a radio spot.

Project
JOB-CONFECTION.DE
Corporate Design

Design
Yellow Tree Kommunikationsdesign
Heiko Rafflenbeul, Andreas Utsch
Freudenberg, Germany

Client
Jandric M. & Jandric R. GbR
JOB-CONFECTION.DE
Siegen, Germany

JOB-CONFECTION.DE vertreibt Sicherheitsbeklei-
dung über das Internet. Als Startup-Unternehmen
ist es vor allem wichtig, im Gedächtnis haften zu
bleiben. Der kleine Budgetrahmen musste möglichst
effektiv genutzt werden, um ein starkes Branding zu
erzeugen.
Das Thema Sicherheit wird im kompletten Auftritt
durch die Farbe Pantone 804 kommuniziert. Der war-
nende Charakter dieser Farbe und die Sicherheits-
streifen in Form einer Schutzkante schreien: „ACH-
TUNG!". Wir sind uns sicher: JOB-CONFECTION.DE
hinterlässt einen bleibenden Eindruck auf der Netz-
haut.

JOB-CONFECTION.DE sells safety clothing on the
internet. As a start-up company, it is of utmost importance to make a lasting first impression. Small
budgets must be used as effectively as possible to
generate a strong brand.
The idea of safety is communicated by the consistent use of the color Pantone 804. The cautionary
character of this color and its use in the pattern of
safety stripes cries: "warning!". One thing we're sure
of: JOB-CONFECTION.DE leaves a lasting impression
on the eyes.

Project
Mohren Pfiff
Kampagne „Anpfiff zur Euro 2008"
Campaign "Starting Whistle to the Euro 2008"

Design
die3
Agentur für Werbung und Kommunikation GmbH
Mario Lorenz, Sascha Grabherr
Dornbirn, Austria

Client
Mohrenbrauerei August Huber
Dornbirn, Austria

Die Marke „Mohrenbräu" wurde in Österreich für die Fußball-Europameisterschaft genutzt und das Produkt „Mohren Pfiff" bei der Zielgruppe „16+" stärker verankert.
Die Idee lieferte das Produkt: Als Instrument eingesetzt, lassen sich mit den Pfiff-Flaschen Lieder pfeifen. Der Link zur Euro 2008 wurde mit dem Flaschenpfeifen von Fanhymnen gesetzt. Das Herz war das Web-Videoportal mit der Aufforderung, selbst zu pfeifen oder die bierig-musikalischen Werke zu bewerten.
Das Resultat: 22.465 Filmaufrufe, 700.000 zum Gewinnspiel eingesandte Kronkorken, Marktanteilzuwachs, erfolgreicher Weltrekordversuch im Flaschenpfeifen.
Die Kommunikation: Print, Hörfunk, Kino, Produkt-/POS-Ausstattung, Gewinnspiel „Kronkorken sammeln".

The "Mohrenbräu" brand was used in Austria for the European Soccer Championship 2008 and the "Mohren Pfiff" more strongly anchored in the "16+" target group.
The product supplied the idea: "Mohren Pfiff" bottles used as instruments to whistle songs. The link to the championship was established with bottle-whistling of the fans' anthem. The web video portal invited viewers to whistle themselves or to judge the beery-musical works.
The result: 22,465 film call-ups, 700,000 sent-in crown corks, market share gain and a successful world record attempt.
The Communication: print, cinema, radio, web, product-/POS materials, crown cork prize contest.

Project
Nicht jeder sieht.
Mailing, Microsite

Design
[di]Unternehmer
Marc Mundt, Jan Heinritz (Kreativgeschäftsführung)
Silke Koppai (Art Direction)
Diana Kunschke (Design)
Annette Dielentheis (Text)
Wiesbaden, Germany

Client
[di]Unternehmer
Wiesbaden, Germany

Es schien ein gewöhnlicher Brief zu sein, der da zu Weihnachten in der Post landete. Doch wer den Umschlag erwartungsfroh öffnete, stellte überrascht fest, dass es sich hier nicht um einen klassischen Weihnachtsgruß handelte. Der Text war in Brailleschrift verfasst. Nur die URL „www.nicht-jeder-sieht.com" war lesbar und schien der richtige Weg, um dem geheimen Inhalt auf die Spur zu kommen. Kurzweilig und unterhaltsam wurde auf der Microsite das Thema „Nicht jeder sieht." inszeniert. Zu erfahren war auch, dass sich [di]Unternehmer mit ihrer Arbeit für den Assistenzhunde-Verein „Vita e. V." engagierten.

It seemed to be a totally normal letter that arrived in the mail last Christmas. However, for those who opened the envelope in anticipation, came the surprising discovery that this was not just any Christmas card. The text was in Braille. Only the URL "www.nicht-jeder-sieht.com" was legible and seemed to be the only way to find out more about the letter's hidden content. The "Nicht jeder sieht." ("Not everyone sees.") theme was presented on a microsite in an entertaining and informative story. Visitors also discovered that [di]Unternehmer was supporting the guide dog organization "Vita e. V." with this year's work.

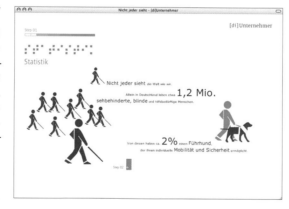

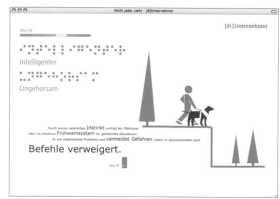

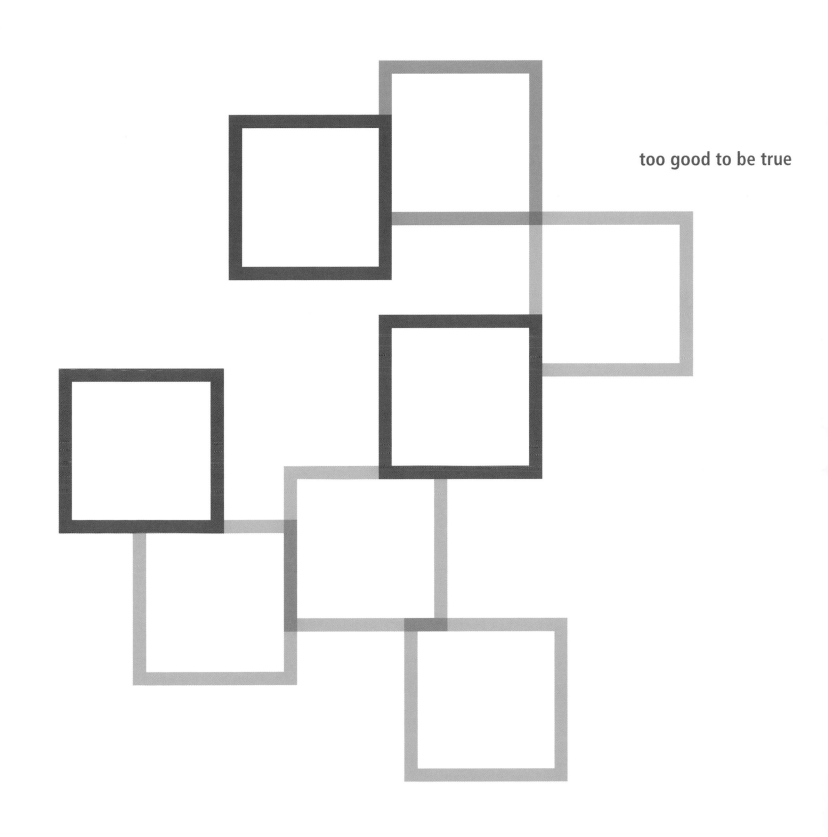

too good to be true

„Das Potenzial in dieser Rubrik liegt in der Formulierung
eines visionären Anspruchs."

Die eingereichten Arbeiten forderten mehr eigene Interpretation
und Imagination, als dass sie mit spontanem Jubel begrüßt wurden. Das Potenzial in dieser Rubrik liegt in der Formulierung eines
visionären Anspruchs, der ungestützt und offen kommuniziert
werden kann.

Der Hintergrund der eingereichten Arbeiten reichte von
Studentenprojekten bis hin zu abgelehnten Pitchbeiträgen. Unsere
Auswahl zeigt zumindest die Offenheit, nicht aber die Qualität der
Möglichkeiten in dieser noch unterschätzten Kategorie.

"The potential of this category is in the formulation
of a visionary concept."

Rather than being greeted by spontaneous cheers, the submissions
tended to require personal interpretation and imagination. The
potential of this category is in the formulation of a visionary concept which has to be communicated in an unsupported and open
manner.

The background of the submissions ranged from student
projects to rejected pitches. Our selection at least illustrates the
openness if not the quality of possibilities in this hitherto underesti-
mated category.

Arne Schultchen

Project
Leichten Herzens
Event zum Tag der Organspende
Organ donation day event

Design
D'ART DESIGN GRUPPE GMBH
Guido Mamczur, Sonja Thiemann, Myriam Tribalet
Neuss, Germany
kogag Bremshey & Domning GmbH
Michael Veidt (Konzeption)
Markus Jäger, Gunnar Oehmen (Projektleitung)
Solingen, Germany

Client
BZgA
(Bundeszentrale für gesundheitliche Aufklärung)
Köln, Germany

80 % der deutschen Bevölkerung sind laut BZgA pro Organspende eingestellt – nur 17 % besitzen einen Organspendeausweis! Es gilt, ein sensibles Thema in die Öffentlichkeit zu bringen. Mit dem Kick-Off-Event in Berlin wird Aufmerksamkeit erzeugt und das Gespräch face2face gefördert. Um den Diskurs in ganz Deutschland langfristig und regional zu sichern, tourt die Ausstellung „Leichten Herzens" quer durch Deutschland: Emotionale Aktionen und seriöse Informationen bewirken eine durchdachte Entscheidung. Ziel ist es, den Standpunkt jedes Einzelnen, ob dafür oder dagegen, mit einem ausgefüllten Organspende-ausweis zu dokumentieren.

According to the BZgA, 80 % of Germany's population endorse organ donation – only 17 % have got an organ donor card! Thus this sensitive topic must be brought to the public's attention! The kick-off-event in Berlin creates awareness and promotes the face2face dialogue. Touring through Germany, the exposition "Leichten Herzens" ensures that the discourse endures everywhere in the republic. Emotional campaigns and reliable information help to take a thought-out decision. The aim is to document everybody's opinion, be it in favour or against, in a filled-in organ donor card.

Wallpaper
The interactive driving wallpaper

EQ
The music phone
eauqlizer for classic mode

Last Carnival

Music Therapy
Recommending music to heal your emotions

'English Breakfast, Darjeeling, Ceylon
tea, Rooibos, Chamomile, Lavender'

Until The End - Norah Jones

Unlock
Unlock touch phone
interface by circling

JUN 11, Wed

Mix&Match
Recommending music by mood

'Romantic, Coffee Break, Party,
Driving, Sleep, Sports & Leisure'

Don't Know Why : Norah Jones

Project
Dancing Water
Musiktelefon-Benutzeroberfläche
Music phone graphic user interface

Design
LG Electronics, Inc.
Jae Hee Shim, Uni Young Kim, Kyung Hee Yoo,
JiHae Kim, Hyung Nam Lee, Sae Hun Jang
Seoul, South Korea

Client
LG Electronics, Inc.
Seoul, South Korea

Die größte Innovation dieser Oberfläche ist die naturgetreue Integration von Wasser in die Funktionen des Musiktelefons. Das rechtfertig den Vergleich mit echtem Wasser. Durch das visuelle und sensorische Musikerlebnis sowie die Interaktivität mit Musik wurde ein synästhetischer Musikgenuss erreicht, so dass Musik nicht nur gehört, sondern auch gefühlt und gesehen werden kann. Zudem werden durch die Verschmelzung des natürlichen Verhaltens von Wasser mit den Eingaben des Benutzers emotionale Reaktionen des Bedieners erreicht.

The most innovative part of this interface is that it merged the actual attributes of water into music phone functions so that the use of water metaphor is inevitable. And we also created a synesthetic music experience by using visual and tactile interactions along with auditory interactions of music so that users not just listen to music but also touch and see it. And in addition to this, melting in real life behaviors of water with the interactions, we tried to give emotional feedback to the interactions users make.

Project
1/2 PROJECT
Ein neues Spendensystem
A new donation system

Design
HALF PROJECT
Sungjoon Kim, Jiwon Park
Seoul, South Korea

Client
HALF PROJECT
Seoul, South Korea

Das 1/2 PROJECT ist eine gemeinnützige Kampagne mit dem Ziel, Spenden als einen Teil des täglichen Lebens zu etablieren. Spenden sollen nicht mehr als etwas Besonderes zu bestimmten Anlässen betrachtet werden, sondern als ein Teil der alltäglichen kleinen Dinge. Dies führt zu unserem Ziel, die Hürden für das Tätigen einer Spende zu reduzieren. Wenn der Kunde beispielsweise ein Getränk aus dem 1/2 PROJECT kauft – ein unbewusster und alltäglicher Kauf – gibt er die Hälfte des Kaufpreises indirekt an Bedürftige. Es entsteht ein neues Spendensystem.

1/2 PROJECT is a non-profit campaign project aimed to make donation a part of everyday life. It redefines donation from the stereotype considering it a special event, to the act of sharing the little things from our daily lives. This will lead to our objective of lowering the entry barrier to donation. As a typical example, when a customer purchases a 1/2 PROJECT beverage – something that people unconsciously pick up without hesitation – the person gives away the half to the needy who receives the monetary value of the half, creating a new donation system.

half for others, **half** for you.

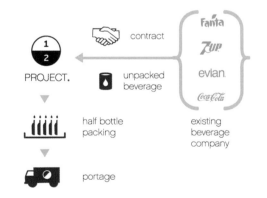

half of the selling price for **PRODUCTION**

1 2 PROJECT.

contract
unpacked beverage
half bottle packing
portage

Fanta
7up
evian
Coca-Cola

existing beverage company

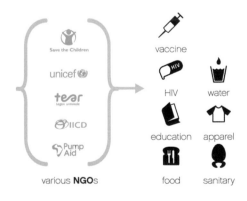

half of the selling price for **DONATION**

Save the Children
unicef
tear legær armode
IICD
Pump Aid

various **NGOs**

vaccine
HIV
water
education
apparel
food
sanitary

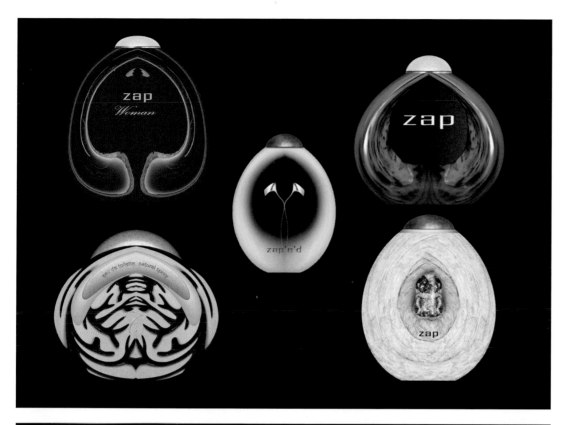

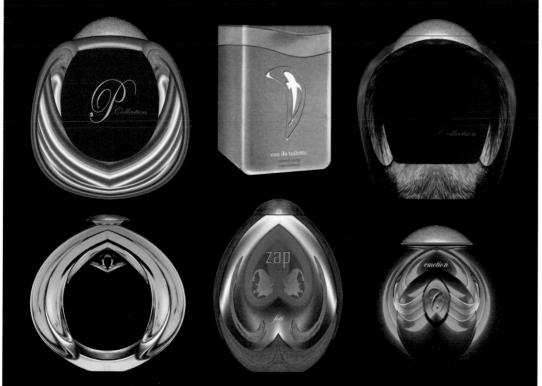

Project
ZAP Kollektion
Parfumflakons
Perfume flacons

Design
FOTI Creative Design
Patras, Greece

Client
FOTI Creative Design
Patras, Greece

Die Kollektion ZAP besteht aus neun unterschiedlichen Parfumflakons, deren Design auf einfachen Materialien basiert, die in der Natur vorkommen. Die Flakons sind durch eine Vielzahl von Themen inspiriert. Der Designprozess wurde von natürlichen Materialien beeinflusst, wie z. B. Muscheln, Kieselsteinen, Vulkangestein, Holz, Insekten, Silberblättern, Gold und Bronze. Diese Materialien finden sich in verschiedenen Gebieten Griechenlands, wie z. B. Santorin, Ionische Inseln und im Bereich des Olymps. Die Materialien wurden in einem Zeitraum von einem Jahr zusammengetragen. Sie weisen jeweils verschiedene und einmalige Merkmale auf.

ZAP collection consists of nine different perfume bottles. The design comes from a variety of different themes based upon simple materials from the natural environment. The designing process was originally influenced by images like shells, a sea stone, volcanic rocks, wood, insects, gold and silver leafs and bronze, all collected from different places around Greece, like the island of Santorini, other islands from the Ionian Sea and the Olympus Mountain. Those materials were gathered during a twelve month period. Therefore each one of them represents something different and unique.

Project
HiLight
Faltschachtel
Folding box

Design
Karl Knauer KG
Biberach/Baden, Germany

Client
Karl Knauer KG
Biberach/Baden, Germany

Durch Einsatz aktuellster Verfahrenstechnologien war es erstmals möglich, ein Leuchtdisplay umlaufend über mehrere Seiten einer Verpackung aufzubringen – und dies selbst auf gewölbten Oberflächen. Das Display erlaubt das Erzeugen mehrfarbiger Lichteffekte sowie Animationen wie Blinken oder Auf- und Abblenden. „GeHiLighted" werden können alle Teile des Verpackungsdesigns – Logos, Bilder und Texte und zwar ohne farbliche Einschränkungen. Mit der Technologie „HiLight" und ihrem hohen Aufmerksamkeitspotenzial kann eine ganz neue Dimension im Verpackungsdesign und in der Ästhetik bei der Präsentation der Marke am POS realisiert werden.

By using state-of-the-art process technology it was possible to apply an illuminated display on several sides of a package, even on arched surfaces for the first time. The display is able to show multicolor light effects and animations like flashing etc. All parts of the packaging design – logos, images and picture elements as well as words etc. – can be "hilighted" and there are no restrictions in terms of color. With the "HiLight"-technology, its brand-new aesthetics and its great impact at the POS, a new dimension in packaging design and in the presentation of brands at the POS can be realised.

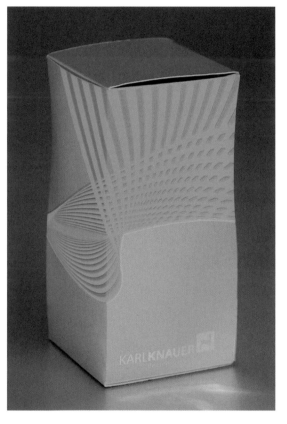
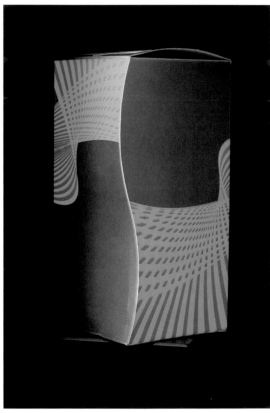

iF Industrie Forum Design e. V.
List of iF e. V. Members
Article of Association

Vorstände / Board

1. Ernst Raue, Deutsche Messe AG,
   1. Vorsitzender / Chairman iF Hannover
2. Norbert Bargmann, Messe München GmbH,
   München
3. Christoph Böninger, brains4design GmbH,
   München
4. Prof. Fritz Frenkler, f/p design GmbH,
   München
5. Ralph Wiegmann, iF Hannover,
   Geschäftsführendes Vorstandsmitglied /
   Executive Member of the Board, Hannover

Geschäftsführender Vorstand / Managing Director

Ralph Wiegmann, iF Hannover

Ehrenmitglieder / Honorary Members

1. Knut Bliesener, Hannover
2. Sepp D. Heckmann, Hannover
3. Karl-Heinz Krug, Düsseldorf
4. Prof. H. Lindinger, Hannover
5. Herbert H. Schultes, Fürstenfeldbruck

Firmenmitglieder / Corporate members

AL-KO Geräte GmbH	Ichenhauserstraße 14	89359	Kötz
Ars Nova Collection	Spenger Straße 15	49328	Melle/Bruchmühlen
Artemide GmbH	Hans-Böckler-Straße 2	58730	Fröndenberg
B/S/H Bosch und Siemens Hausgeräte GmbH	Carl-Wery-Straße 34	81793	München
BASF SE	G-KTS/EPD-H 612	67056	Ludwigshafen
BEGA Gantenbrink-Leuchten	Hennenbusch 1	58708	Menden
BEST COMPANY VIDEO GmbH	Boulevard der EU 7	30539	Hannover
BMW AG	Knorrstraße 147	80788	München
Braun GmbH	Frankfurter Straße 145	61476	Kronberg
BREE Collection GmbH & Co. KG	Gerberstraße 3	30916	Isernhagen
Carpet Concept	Bunzlauer Straße 7	33719	Bielefeld
ClassiCon GmbH	Sigmund-Riefler-Bogen 3	81829	München
Crown Gabelstapler GmbH & Co. KG	Moosacher Straße 52	80809	München
Daimler AG	Werk 059, HPC X800	71059	Sindelfingen
design report – Blue C. Verlag	Ernst-Mey-Straße 8	70771	Leinfelden-Echterdingen
designaffairs GmbH	Rosenheimer Straße 145b/EG	81671	München
Deutsche Messe AG	Messegelände	30521	Hannover
Die Neue Sammlung, Pinakothek der Moderne	Türkenstraße 15	80333	München
EnBW AG – Messen u. Events	Durlacher Allee 93	76131	Karlsruhe
EnBW AG – Marketing u. Koordination	Durlacher Allee 93	76131	Karlsruhe
Expotechnik Heinz Soschinski GmbH	Aarstraße 176	65232	Taunusstein
F. W. OVENTROP GmbH & Co. KG	Paul-Oventrop-Straße 1	59939	Olsberg
FESTO AG & Co. KG	Ruiter Straße 82	73734	Esslingen
GEZE GmbH	Reinhold-Vöster-Straße 21–29	71229	Leonberg
GHM Gesellschaft für Handwerksmessen mbH	Willy-Brandt-Allee 1	81829	München
Gira Giersiepen GmbH & Co. KG	Dahlienstraße	42477	Radevormwald

Grohe AG	Feldmühleplatz 15	40545	Düsseldorf
häfelinger + wagner design gmbh	Türkenstraße 55–57	80799	München
Hansgrohe AG	Auestraße 5–9	77761	Schiltach
HBK Braunschweig	Johannes-Selenka-Platz 1	38118	Braunschweig
Heidelberger Druckmaschinen AG	Kurfürsten-Anlage 52–60	69115	Heidelberg
HEWI Heinrich Wilke GmbH	Postfach 1260	34442	Bad Arolsen
Hiller Objektmöbel GmbH & Co. KG	Kippenheimer Straße 6	77971	Kippenheim
IBM Deutschland GmbH	Pascalstraße 100	70569	Stuttgart
iF International Forum Design GmbH	Messegelände	30521	Hannover
Interstuhl Büromöbel GmbH & Co. KG	Brühlstraße 21	72469	Meßstetten-Tieringen
Isaria Corporate Design AG	Gewerbepark Aich 7–9	85667	Oberpframmern
JAB Teppiche Heinz Anstoetz KG	Dammheider Straße 67	32052	Herford
Kermi GmbH	Pankofen-Bahnhof 1	94447	Plattling
Kochan & Partner GmbH	Hirschgartenallee 25	80639	München
Köttermann GmbH & Co. KG	Industriestraße 2–10	31311	Uetze
LOEWE OPTA GmbH	Industriestraße 11	96317	Kronach
MeisterSinger GmbH & Co. KG	Hafenweg 46	48155	Münster
Merten GmbH	Fritz-Kotz-Straße 8	51674	Wiehl
Messe München GmbH	Messegelände	81823	München
MüllerKälber GmbH	Daimlerstraße 2	71546	Aspach
Niedersächsisches Ministerium für Wirtschaft, Technologie u. Verkehr	Friedrichswall 1	30159	Hannover
Nils Holger Moormann GmbH	An der Festhalle 2	83229	Aschau
OCTANORM-Vertriebs-GmbH	Raiffeisenstraße 39	70794	Filderstadt
Panasonic Design Company	1–15 Matsuo-cho		Kadoma-city, Osaka 571-8504
Patentanwalt European Design Attorney	Flüggenstraße 13	80639	München
PH MEYER Wirtschaftsberatung GmbH & Co. KG	Mittelstraße 50	33602	Bielefeld
Philips GmbH	Lübeckertordamm 5	20099	Hamburg
Poggenpohl Möbelwerke GmbH	Poggenpohl Straße 1	32051	Herford
PRODESIGN	Turmstraße 39	89231	Neu-Ulm
RITTO GmbH	Rodenbacher Straße 15	35708	Haiger
Schendel & Pawlaczyk Messebau GmbH	Im Derdel 3	48167	Münster
SCHULTE Duschkabinenbau KG	Lockweg 81	59846	Sundern
Sedus Stoll AG	Brückenstraße 15	79761	Waldshut-Tiengen
Seibel Designpartner GmbH	Industriestraße 5	40822	Mettmann
Sennheiser electronic GmbH & Co. KG	Am Labor 1	30900	Wedemark
Siemens AG	Wittelsbacherplatz 2	80333	München
SKYLOTEC GmbH	Im Bruch 11–15	56567	Neuwied
Sony Ericsson Mobile Communications AB		SE-221 88	Lund
Steelcase Werndl AG	Georg-Aicher-Straße 7	83026	Rosenheim
Storck Bicycle GmbH	Carl-Zeiss-Straße 4	65520	Bad Camberg
TRILUX GmbH + Co. KG	Heidestraße 4	59759	Arnsberg
TROIKA domovari GmbH	Nisterfeld 11	57629	Müschenbach
Viessmann Werke GmbH Co. KG	Viessmannstraße 1	35108	Allendorf/Eder
Volkswagen AG	Brieffach 1701, Berliner Ring 2	38436	Wolfsburg

wiege Entwicklungs GmbH	Hauptstraße 81	31848	Bad Münder
Wilkhahn	Fritz Hahne Straße 8	31848	Bad Münder
WINI Büromöbel GmbH & Co. KG	Auhagenstraße 79	31863	Coppenbrügge
wodtke GmbH	Rittweg 55–57	72070	Tübingen-Hirschau
Yokogawa Electric Corporation	2-9-32 naka-cho		Mushashino-shi, Tokyo, 180-8750
Zumtobel Lighting GmbH	Schweizer Straße 30	6850	Dornbirn

Designagenturen / Design studios or Designers

Arbeitsgemeinschaft Tatorte	Moltkestraße 99a	50674	Köln
artcollin	Ickstattstraße 26/Rgb	80469	München
B:SiGN Werbeagentur GmbH	Ellernstraße 36	30175	Hannover
bgp design/Braake Grobe Partnerschaft	Lindenstraße 10	70563	Stuttgart
brains4design GmbH	Sandstraße 33	80335	München
brodbeck design	Schillerstraße 40c	80336	München
D'ART Visuelle Kommunikation GmbH	Adlerstraße 41	70199	Stuttgart
Deutscher Designer Club e.V.	Große Fischestraße 7	60311	Frankfurt am Main
Design House co., Ltd	1F., No. 2, Alley 25, Lane 118, Wusing St., Sinyi District	R.O.C.110	Taipei
design studio hartmut s. engel	Monreposstraße 7	71634	Ludwigsburg
Design Tech	Zeppelinstraße 53	72119	Ammerbuch
designfunktion GmbH	Schleißheimer Straße 141	80797	München
DRWA Das Rudel Werbeagentur	Erbprinzenstraße 11	79098	Freiburg
Eda Event Design Agentur GmbH	Gut Mönchhof, Quettinger Straße 187	51381	Leverkusen
f/p design GmbH	Mauerkicherstraße 4	81679	München
fön,design_	Schiltachstraße 40	78713	Schramberg
Fuenfwerken Design AG	Taunusstraße 52	65183	Wiesbaden
GDC-Design	Krugstraße 12	90419	Nürnberg
GUTE GESELLSCHAFT FÜR STRATEGIE, DESIGN UND KOMMUNIKATION MBH	Grafenberger Allee 126	40237	Düsseldorf
H H Schultes Design Studio	Rodelbahnstraße 1	82256	Fürstenfeldbruck
hymer idc GmbH + Co. KG	Blücherstraße 32	75177	Pforzheim
i/i/d Institut für Integriertes Design	Am Speicher XI, Abtlg.7, Boden 3	28217	Bremen
identis GmbH	Bötzinger Straße 36	79111	Freiburg
INOID DesignGroup	Reutlingerstraße 114	70597	Stuttgart
Landschaftsarchitektin BDLA DWB	Bauerstraße 19	80796	München
MEDIADESIGN HOCHSCHULE FÜR DESIGN	Berg am Laim-Straße 47	81673	München
Meisterschule für Mode	Roßmarkt 15	80331	München
.molldesign	Turmgasse 7	73525	Schwäbisch Gmünd
Network! Werbeagentur GmbH	Sandstraße 33	80335	München
Nova Design Co., Ltd.	Tower C, 8F, No. 96, Sec. 1, Xintai 5th Rd.	Xizh City	Taipei Country 221
OCO-Design O. K. Nüsse	An der Kleimannbrücke 79	48157	Münster
Olaf Hoffmann Industrial Design	Metzstraße 14b	81667	München
Philips International BV Philips Design	Building HWD, Emmasingel 24	5600 MD	Eindhoven

Pilotfish GmbH	Schleissheimer Straße 6	80333	München
Rokitta Produkt & Markenästhetik	Kölner Straße 38a	45481	Mühlheim an der Ruhr
Polvan Design Ltd.	Cemil Topuzlu cad. 79/2 Caddebostan	34170	Istanbul
PROMOTIONAL iDEAS Werbeagentur GmbH	Hessenring 76	61348	Bad Homburg
rahe+rahe design	Konsul-Smidt-Straße 8c	28217	Bremen
S + F Architektur + Design	Straße der Nationen 5, Expo-Park Ost	30539	Hannover
SAINT ELMO'S Multichannel Creativity	Kaulbachstraße 4	80539	München
SCHOLZ & VOLKMER GmbH	Schwalbacher Straße 76	65183	Wiesbaden
Strategy & Marketing Institute GmbH	Lange-Hop-Straße 19	30559	Hannover
Studio Laeis	Lindenallee 43	50968	Köln
Taipei Base Design Center	2Fl., 1. No. 49, Sec. 5, Chenggung Rd.	114	Taipei
TRICON Design AG	Bahnhofstraße 26	72138	Kirchentellinsfurt
UNIPLAN GmbH & Co. KG	Schanzenstrasse 39a/b	51063	Köln
VDID/DDV	Markgrafenstraße 15	10969	Berlin
Weinberg & Ruf	Martinsstraße 5	70794	Filderstadt

Einzelmitglieder / Individual members

Andreas Gantenhammer	Meerbuscher Straße 64–78	40670	Meerbusch
Andreas Thierry	Arthur-Kutscher-Platz 1/VII	80802	München
Bibs Hosak-Robb	Mendelssohnstraße 31	81245	München
Christoph Eschke	Admiralitätstraße 10	20459	Hamburg
Christoph Rohrer	Roecklplatz 3	80469	München
Dr. Günther Portenländer	Wolfrathshauser Strasse 77	82049	Pullach
Dr. Helga Huskamp	Schlottnauerstraße 10	81541	München
Eberhard Schlegel	Am Kapellenweg 4	88525	Dürmentingen
Gabriel Weber	Orffstraße 35	80637	München
Gerd Bulthaup	Chamissostraße 1	81925	München
Gilles Thevenot	Zieglerweg 14	76532	Baden-Baden
HD Schellnack	Mintropstrasse 61	45329	Essen
Hildegund Lichtwark	Pfarrer-Linzbach-Straße 1	52388	Nörvenich
Jens O. Brelle	Auf dem Sande 1	20457	Hamburg
Jiro Katsuta	Elsternweg 46	47804	Krefeld
Josef Hasberg	Lokenbach 8–10	51491	Overath
Michael Grüter	Hainholzstraße 17	31558	Hagenburg
Nenad Dordevic	Türkenstraße 103	80799	München
Peter Hartmann	Fasaneriestraße 10	80636	München
Prof. Gunnar Spellmeyer	c/o Fachhochschule Hannover Expo Plaza 2	30539	Hannover
Prof. Martin Topel	Fuhlrottstraße 10, Gebäude I, Ebene 16, Raum 76	42119	Wuppertal
Sebastian Le Peetz	Osterstraße 43a	30159	Hannover
Seyed Mansour Pour mohensi Shakib	No.281-Yasseman Alley-Manzariyeh-Namjo St.	41936	Rasht
Thomas Bade	Im Knick 9	31655	Stadthagen
Thomas Biswanger	Probierlweg 47	85049	Ingolstadt

Satzung des Vereins „iF – Industrie Forum Design e.V."

§ 1 Name und Sitz des Vereins
1. Der Verein trägt den Namen „iF – Industrie Forum Design e.V.".
2. iF – Industrie Forum Design ist im Vereinsregister eingetragen.
3. Der Verein hat seinen Sitz in Hannover.

§ 2 Zweck des Vereins
Der Verein verfolgt den Zweck der Förderung und Akzeptanz von Design als Teil der Wertschöpfungskette und als kulturelles Element der Gesellschaft. Die bewusste Gestaltung von Produkten und Lebensräumen für den privaten und öffentlichen Bereich sowie von benutzerfreundlichen Softwareanwendungen betrachtet der Verein als seine gesellschaftspolitische und kulturelle Aufgabe. Vereinsziele sind:
1. Die Anerkennung der Designleistung zur Erreichung von Unternehmenszielen und zur Sicherung von wirtschaftlichem Erfolg;
2. Die Organisation von Wettbewerben, Ausstellungen, Konferenzen, Vortragsveranstaltungen und weiterer Aktivitäten;
3. Die Veröffentlichung von Publikationen als Grundlage für Diskussionen;
4. Die Stärkung des Bewusstseins für Design in der Öffentlichkeit;
5. Das Angebot eines Forums zur Kommunikation auf neutraler Ebene;
Der Verein ist mit seinen Aktivitäten regional, national und international präsent.

§ 3 Geschäftsjahr
Das Geschäftsjahr ist das Kalenderjahr.

§ 4 Mitgliedschaft
1. Jede natürliche oder juristische Person kann Mitglied im iF e.V. werden. Der schriftliche Aufnahmeantrag wird von der Geschäftsführung geprüft und von ihr entschieden – in Zweifelsfällen beschließt der Vorstand mit einfacher Mehrheit über die Aufnahme des Mitglieds. Die Ablehnung der Aufnahme braucht nicht begründet zu werden.
2. Der Verein hat neben Mitgliedern auch Ehrenmitglieder. Ehrenmitglieder sind Persönlichkeiten, die sich im besonderen Maße um die Förderung und das Ansehen des „iF – Industrie Forum Design e.V." Verdienste erworben haben. Sie können durch einstimmigen Beschluss der Mitgliederversammlung zu Ehrenmitgliedern ernannt werden und haben in der Mitgliederversammlung kein Stimmrecht.
3. Die Mitgliedschaft endet durch
a) Austritt, der dem Verein gegenüber zu erklären ist. Der Austritt kann nur durch schriftliche Erklärung zum Ende eines jeden Geschäftsjahres mit dreimonatiger Frist erklärt werden,
b) Ausschluss aus dem Verein, über den der Vorstand einstimmig beschließt,
c) Tod eines Mitglieds.

§ 5 Organe
Die Organe des Vereins sind:
1. die Mitgliederversammlung
2. der Vorstand
3. die Geschäftsführung.

§ 6 Mitgliederversammlung
1. Die Mitgliederversammlung ist zuständig für:
a) Entgegennahme des Jahresberichts des Vorstandes und des Berichts der Rechnungsprüfer,
b) Wahl des Vorstands,
c) Entlastung des Vorstands und der Geschäftsführung,
d) Satzungsänderungen,
e) Auflösung des Vereins,
f) Verwendung des Vermögens bei Auflösung des Vereins,
g) die Verwendung des jährlichen Gewinnvortrages bzw. die Behandlung eines Verlustes,
h) Entscheidung über neue Aktivitäten des Vereins,
i) Festsetzung des Jahresmitgliedsbeitrages,
j) Wahl der Ehrenmitglieder.
2. Jährlich ist eine ordentliche Mitgliederversammlung durchzuführen, zu der alle Mitglieder des Vereins eingeladen werden und in der insbesondere über das abgelaufene Geschäftsjahr, über den Rechnungsabschluss und das Ergebnis der Rechnungsprüfung zu berichten ist.
3. Die Mitgliederversammlung wird vom Vorsitzenden des Vorstandes mit einer Frist von mindestens einer Woche schriftlich unter Angabe der Tagesordnung einberufen. Die Tagesordnung der Mitgliederversammlung setzt der Vorsitzende des Vorstandes oder ein anderes von ihm benanntes Vorstandsmitglied fest. Anträge einzelner Mitglieder zur Tagesordnung können nachträglich auf die Tagesordnung gesetzt werden, wenn die Mitgliederversammlung es einstimmig beschließt.
4. Außerordentliche Mitgliederversammlungen können jederzeit vom Vorsitzenden des Vorstandes einberufen werden, wenn ein wichtiger Grund vorliegt. Die Einberufung muss erfolgen, wenn dies von mindestens $\frac{1}{3}$ der Mitglieder schriftlich beantragt wird. Die Einberufungsfrist beträgt 2 Tage. In Eilfällen können die Einladungen telefonisch oder per Fax erfolgen.
5. Die Mitgliederversammlung wird von dem Vorsitzenden des Vorstandes, im Falle seiner Verhinderung durch ein von ihm bestimmtes anderes Vorstandsmitglied geleitet.
6. Die ordnungsgemäß einberufene Mitgliederversammlung ist beschlussfähig, wenn außer dem Versammlungsleiter mindestens drei weitere stimmberechtigte Mitglieder anwesend sind.

7. Jedes Mitglied hat in der Mitgliederversammlung eine Stimme. Beschlüsse der Mitgliederversammlung werden mit einfacher Mehrheit der bei der Abstimmung anwesenden stimmberechtigten Mitglieder gefaßt, soweit diese Satzung nicht etwas anderes bestimmt. Ein Beschluss über die Verwendung des Gewinnvortrages bzw. die Behandlung eines Verlustes bedarf einer Mehrheit von 80 % der bei der Abstimmung anwesenden stimmberechtigten Mitglieder. Stimmberechtigte Mitglieder können sich in der Mitgliederversammlung vertreten lassen, wobei auch die Übertragung des Stimmrechts auf den Vertreter zulässig ist. Bei Stimmengleichheit entscheidet die Stimme des Versammlungsleiters.

8. Eilbeschlüsse können im Umlaufverfahren schriftlich gefaßt werden.

9. Zu einem Beschluss über eine Änderung der Satzung ist eine Mehrheit von $^3/_4$ der Stimmen der erschienenen stimmberechtigten Mitglieder erforderlich.

10. Die gefaßten Beschlüsse werden in einem Protokoll erfasst, das vom Protokollführer und dem Leiter der Mitgliederversammlung unterschrieben werden muss. Jedem Mitglied ist eine Niederschrift des Protokolls der Mitgliederversammlung zuzustellen.

§ 7 Vorstand

1. Der Vorstand des Vereins besteht aus dem 1. Vorsitzenden sowie maximal sechs weiteren Mitgliedern. Die Vorstandsmitglieder werden von den Mitgliedern auf die Dauer von vier Jahren gewählt. Sie verbleiben bis zur Neuwahl im Amt. Die Wahlen können aus wichtigem Grund auf der Mitgliederversammlung widerrufen werden.

2. Der Verein wird gerichtlich und außergerichtlich im Rahmen des Vereinszwecks durch den 1. Vorsitzenden vertreten. Der 1. Vorsitzende ist berechtigt, für Einzelaufgaben Dritten Vollmacht zu erteilen.

3. Der Vorstand unterstützt die Geschäftsführung bei der Leitung des Vereins und beschließt über alle Vereinsangelegenheiten, soweit diese nicht der Mitgliederversammlung vorbehalten sind. Der Vorstand kann weitere zur Verwaltung des Vereins erforderlichen Personen wählen und entscheidet über sämtliche Einnahmen und Ausgaben des Vereins.

4. Über Aktivitäten besonderer Art und die Höhe der damit verbundenen Kosten beschließen nach Vorlage des Vorstandes die Mitglieder in der Mitgliederversammlung.

5. Die Mitgliederversammlung kann dem Vorstand eine Geschäftsordnung geben, nach der die Geschäfte des Vereins zu führen sind.

§ 8 Geschäftsführung

Der Vorstand bestellt eine Geschäftsführung. Diese führt die laufenden Aufgaben des Vereins nach Richtlinien des Vorstands durch. Sie ist auch zur Entscheidung über die Aufnahmeanträge der neuen Mitglieder bevollmächtigt. Die Geschäftsführung hat den Vorstand über alle Vereinsangelegenheiten von Bedeutung zu unterrichten. Sie ist an die Weisungen des Vorstandes gebunden und hat den Vorstand in allen wichtigen Angelegenheiten vorher zu konsultieren.

§ 9 Mitgliedsbeiträge

Der Jahresmitgliederbeitrag wird durch die Mitgliederversammlung bestimmt und staffelt sich zur Zeit wie folgt:

– Unternehmen: mindestens 600,– Euro
– Designer / Designbüros: mindestens 300,– Euro
– Privatpersonen: mindestens 150,– Euro.

§ 10 Revision

Mit der Rechnungsprüfung wird die Revision der Deutsche Messe AG bzw. eine Wirtschaftsprüfungsgesellschaft beauftragt. Über das Revisionsergebnis ist in der ordentlichen Mitgliederversammlung zu berichten.

§ 11 Auflösung des Vereins

1. Ein Beschluss auf Auflösung des Vereins bedarf einer Mehrheit von $^3/_4$ der stimmberechtigten Mitglieder, wobei die Mitgliederversammlung nur beschlussfähig ist, wenn mindestens $^2/_3$ der stimmberechtigten Mitglieder anwesend sind.

2. Bei Auflösung oder Aufhebung des Vereins oder bei Wegfall des jetzigen Zwecks fällt das Vermögen, soweit es die eingezahlten Kapitalanteile der Mitglieder und den gemeinen Wert der von den Mitgliedern geleisteten Sacheinlagen übersteigt, an eine Körperschaft des öffentlichen Rechts zwecks Verwendung für kulturelle oder soziale Zwecke. Beschlüsse über die künftige Verwendung des Vermögens dürfen erst nach Einwilligung des Finanzamtes ausgeführt werden.

3. Die die Auflösung beschließende Mitgliederversammlung entscheidet über die Verwendung des Vereinsvermögens mit $^3/_4$ Mehrheit.

§ 12 Überschüsse, Ausgaben, Buchführung

1. Etwaige Gewinne des Vereins dürfen nur für steuerbegünstigte Zwecke der Satzung verwendet werden. Die Mitglieder erhalten keine Gewinnanteile und in ihrer Eigenschaft als Mitglieder auch keine sonstigen Zuwendungen aus Mitteln des Vereins.

2. Es darf keine Person durch Verwaltungsaufgaben, die dem Zweck des Vereins fremd sind, mittels unverhältnismäßig hoher Vergütungen begünstigt werden.

3. Der Nachweis für die Mittelverwendung ist durch eine ordnungsgemäße Buchführung zu gewährleisten.

Hannover, 5. Juni 2008

Ernst Raue
Vorsitzender

Articles of Association of "iF – Industrie Forum Design e.V."

Article 1. Name and registered office of the Association
1. The name of the Association is "iF – Industrie Forum Design e.V.".
2. iF – Industrie Forum Design is listed in the Register of Associations (Vereinsregister).
3. The Association's registered office is in Hannover, Germany.

Article 2. Object of the Association
The object of the Association is to support and gain acceptance for design as a link in the value chain and as a cultural component of society. The Association considers the targeted design of products, public and private living spaces, and user-friendly software applications as constituting its own civic and cultural mission. The Association aims to:
1. Recognize design achievements that help companies achieve their business goals and cement their economic success
2. Organize competitions, exhibitions, conferences, lectures, and other events
3. Issue publications to serve as the basis for discussions
4. Bolster the public's awareness of design
5. Provide a forum for objective dialogue on design-related issues.
The Association's activities give it a regional, national, and international presence.

Article 3. Financial year
The financial year corresponds to the calendar year.

Article 4. Membership
1. Any natural person or legal entity may become a member of the Association. Executive Management shall examine and decide on membership applications, which are to be submitted in writing. In cases where Executive Management is unsure, the Board of Management shall decide on whether to grant membership by means of a simple majority vote. The Association is not required to justify a negative decision on membership.
2. In addition to members, the Association also consists of honorary members.
Honorary members are individuals who have been particularly meritorious in their support of "iF – Industrie Forum Design". They may be elected to honorary membership by way of a unanimous resolution passed at the General Meeting. They are not entitled to vote at the General Meeting.

3. Membership shall end
a) Through resignation, which must be declared to the Association in writing. This declaration requires a minimum of three months' advance notice before the end of the financial year, and takes effect at the end of the financial year.

b) By way of expulsion upon a unanimous resolution by the Board of Management.
c) At the time of a member's death.

Article 5. Official bodies
The Association's official bodies are:
1. The General Meeting
2. The Board of Management
3. Executive Management.

Article 6. General Meeting
1. The General Meeting is responsible for:
a) Receiving the reports of the Board of Management and the independent auditors
b) Electing the Board of Management
c) Approving the actions of the Board of Management and the Executive Management
d) Changing the Articles of Association
e) Dissolving the Association
f) Using the Association's assets in the event that it should be dissolved
g) Using the annual profits or handling of any loss
h) Setting the annual membership fee
i) Electing honorary members
2. A regular General Meeting will be held annually. All members of the Association shall be invited to attend the General Meeting. The agenda of the regular General Meeting will, in particular, include reports on the preceding financial year, on the Association's financial statements, and on the results of the auditing of accounts.
3. General Meeting shall be called in writing by the Chairperson of the Board of Management, with a minimum of one week's advance notice and with such notice containing a meeting agenda. The agenda of the General Meeting is set by the Chairperson of the Board of Management or by another member of the Board of Management appointed by the Chairperson. Topics requested by individual members may be added to the agenda if the General Meeting gives its unanimous consent.
4. The Chairperson of the Board of Management may call an extraordinary General Meeting if an important reason exists for doing so. A meeting of this kind must be called if it has been requested in writing by at least one third of all members. Two day's advance notice is required. In urgent cases, invitations may be transmitted by telephone or fax.
5. General Meetings shall be presided over by the Chairperson of the Board of Management or, in the event that he or she should be prevented from doing so, by another member of the Board of Management appointed by the Chairperson.
6. A General Meeting that has been properly called has a quorum if, in addition to the individual presiding over the Meeting, at least three other members in possession of voting rights are present.

7. Each member has one vote at the General Meeting. Unless otherwise stipulated in these Articles, resolutions of the General Meeting shall be passed by way of a simple majority of those members present and entitled to vote. Passing a resolution on the appropriation of profit carried forward or the treatment of a loss requires a majority of 80 percent among the voting members present. Members entitled to vote may appoint a proxy to attend the General Meeting in their place, including a proxy voting right. In the of a tie, the deciding vote shall be cast by the individual presiding over the Meeting.

8. Urgent resolutions may be passed by round-robin procedure.

9. Resolutions on amendments to the Articles of Association shall require a three-quarters majority vote by the attending members who are eligible to vote.

10. Approved resolutions must be recorded in writing and signed by both the individual presiding over the Meeting and the keeper of the minutes. All members shall receive a copy of the minutes of the General Meeting.

Article 7. Board of Management

1. The Association's Board of Management consists of the Chairperson and a maximum of six other members. The members of the Board of Management will be elected by the members of the Association for a term of four years. They shall remain in office until new elections take place. Elections may be revoked at General Meetings for good cause.

2. The Association will be represented in and out of court by the Chairperson of the Board of Management, who shall be permitted to delegate a power of attorney to third persons in individual cases.

3. The Board of Management shall support Executive Management in the running of the Association and shall decide on all matters concerning the Association, providing that the right to such decision-making is not reserved by the General Meeting. The Board of Management may elect other individuals required to assume administrative tasks and will decide on all of the Association's income and expenditures.

4. At the General Meeting, the members will decide on special activities and related expenditures as presented by the Board of Management.

5. The General Meeting may provide the Board of Management with rules of procedure governing the Association's operation.

Article 8. Executive Management

The Board of Management shall appoint the executive management, which will be charged with executing the ongoing tasks of the Association in accordance with the guidelines issued by the Board of Management. Executive Management is authorized to make decisions on membership applications for new members. Executive Management shall inform the Board of Management about all significant matters affecting the Association. Executive Management shall follow all instructions issued by the Board of Management und shall consult the Board of Management in advance regarding all important matters.

Article 9. Membership fees

The annual membership fee will be set at the General Meeting and is currently as follows:

– Companies:	600 Euro minimum
– Designers and design studios:	300 Euro minimum
– Individuals:	150 Euro minimum.

Article 10. Auditing

Accounting control will be assigned to Deutsche Messe AG's auditing department or to an independent auditor. The results of auditing will be reported at the regular General Meeting.

Article 11. Dissolution of the Association

1. A resolution to dissolve the Association shall require a three-fourths majority vote by the members who are entitled to vote, provided that at least two thirds of the members entitled to vote are present at the General Meeting.

2. Upon dissolution or annulment of the Association or in the event that the current object of the Association should cease to be applicable, any assets exceeding the capital shares deposited by the members and the fair market value of non-cash capital contributions made by members shall go to a public corporation that will use the assets for cultural or community welfare purposes. Resolutions on the future application of such assets may only be acted upon subsequent to consent thereto by the tax authorities.

3. The General Meeting which resolves to dissolve the Association shall pass a resolution on the application of the Association's assets by way of a three-fourths majority vote.

Article 12. Profits, expenditures, accounting

1. Any profits produced by the Association shall be used exclusively for the tax-privileged purposes of these Articles of Association. Members shall not receive shares of profit, nor shall they, in their capacity as members, receive any other forms of bestowal from Association funds.

2. No individual may be favored by receiving disproportionately high remuneration for administrative tasks not in keeping with the object of the Association.

3. Proof that the Association's funds are being used properly shall be guaranteed by way of adequate and orderly accounting procedures.

Hannover, June 5, 2008

Ernst Raue
Chairman

AXIS, das führende japanische
Designmagazin
AXIS a leading Japanese design
magazine

page, das führende design-
und publishing magazin,
page, a leading desing
and publishing magazin
Germany

w&V, Wochenmagazin für Marketing,
Werbung, Medien und E-Business
w&v, weekly magazine for marketing,
advertising,media and business
Germany

AGD
Allianz deutscher Designer
Germany

BCD
Barcelona Design Centre
Spain

BDIA
Bund Deutscher Innenarchitekten
Germany

BNO
Beroepsorganisatie Nederlandse
Ontwerpes
The Nederlands

BVDW
Bundesverband Digitaler Wirtschaft
Germany

CIDA
China Industrial Designers Association
Taiwan

ddc
Deutscher Designer Club
Germany

swiss design association

sda
swiss design association
Switzerland

Design Austria e.V.
Autria

SGD+
Swiss Graphic Designers
Switzerland

IdcN
International Design Center
NAGOYA Inc.
Japan

Taipei Design Center Düsseldorf
Germany/Taiwan

IIDA
Israel Industrial Designers Association
Israel

MFI
Hungarian Design Council
Hungary

TDC
Taiwan Design Center
Taiwan

National Institute of Design India
India

VDID

Verband Deutscher
Industrie Designer e.V.

VDID/DDV
Germany

Index

E.ON Energy Sales GmbH
Karlstraße 68
80335 München, Germany
www.eon-energy-sales.com
▲ 52

E.ON Ruhrgas AG
Huttropstraße 60
45138 Essen, Germany
www.eon-ruhrgas.com
▲ 52

E.ON Vertrieb Deutschland GmbH
Karlstraße 68
80335 München, Germany
www.eon-vertrieb.com
▲ 52

Eastern Herbal Garden Bio. Tech. Co.
No.135-3, Jhongjheng Rd., No.135-3,
Dapi Shiang
Yunlin County 631, Taiwan
Phone +886.5.5916000
Fax +886.5.5912199
▲ 328

Eberle Brand Design
Goethestraße 115
73525 Schwäbisch Gmünd, Germany
Phone +49.7171.92529.0
● 339

Eclat AG
Seestrasse 78
8703 Erlenbach/Zürich, Switzerland
Phone +41.44.91474.00
www.eclat.ch
● 269–271

EcoCraft Automotive GmbH & Co. KG
Adolf-Oesterheld-Straße 25–29
31515 Wunstorf, Germany
Phone +49.5031.97968.0
Fax +49.5031.97968.011
www.ecocraft-automotive.de
▲ 179

Eczacibaşi Yapi Gereçleri
Kanyon Ofis, Büyükdere Cad. 185
34394 Levent-Istanbul, Turkey
Phone +90.212.3717441
Fax +90.212.3747432
www.vitra.com.tr
▲ 380

Edenspiekermann
Friedrichstraße 126
10117 Berlin, Germany
Phone +49.30.212.808.14
Fax +49.30.212.808.10
www.edenspiekermann.com
● 210, 341

Edition Braus
Friedrich-Ebert-Anlage 20
69117 Heidelberg, Germany
Phone +49.6221.502966.0
▲ 305

Elastique. We design.
Moltkestraße 127
50674 Köln, Germany
Phone +49.221.35503450
Fax +49.221.35503459
www.elastique.de
● 50, 70

Elephant Seven Hamburg GmbH
Gerhofstraße 1–3
20354 Hamburg, Germany
Phone +49.40.34101266
● 114–115, 121

EONSLD.Co., Ltd
Noblesse BD. 4F. 901-10
Bangbaedong, Seochogu
Seoul, South Korea
Phone +82.2.3477.9575
Fax +82.2.3477.7917
● 408–409

Esprit Europe GmbH
Esprit-Allee
40882 Ratingen, Germany
Phone +49.2102.12345944
▲ 171

Euro RSCG Düsseldorf
Kaiserswerther Straße 135
40474 Düsseldorf, Germany
Phone +49.211.99.16.307
Fax +49.211.99.16.255
www.eurorscg.de
● 48, 146, 176, 181, 217

Euro RSCG München
Rosenheimer Straße 145 e–f
81671 München, Germany
Phone +49.89.490670
Fax +49.89.49067100
● 181, 227

Excited GmbH
Friedenstraße 10
81671 München, Germany
Phone +49.89.28806636
▲ 414

Experience Design Group
Dell Inc.
One Dell Way, PS-4
Round Rock, TX, 78664, USA
Phone + 1.512.728.1957
Fax + 1.512.728.0310
www.Dell.com
● 67

EXPOLAB GmbH
advanced communication and design
Barer Straße 44
80799 München, Germany
Phone +49.89.72989571
www.expolab.eu
● 414

F

Fabrique Communications and Design
Oude Delft 201
Delft, Netherlands
Phone +31.15.2195600
www.fabrique.nl
● 106, 208–209

Fachhochschule Augsburg
Fakultät für Gestaltung
Friedberger Straße 2
86161 Augsburg, Germany
Phone +49.821.5586.3401
▲ 190

Fachhochschule Düsseldorf
Fachbereich Design
Georg-Glock-Straße 15
40474 Düsseldorf, Germany
Phone +49.211.4351201
Fax +49.211.4351203
▲ 204

facts + fiction GmbH
Anna-Schneider-Steig 2
50678 Köln, Germany
Phone +49.221.951530.24
www.factsfiction.de
● 386

feedback media design
Hermannstraße 5
70178 Stuttgart, Germany
Phone +49.711 22070800
● 72

FEEDMEE DESIGN GmbH
Lichtstraße 43A
50825 Köln, Germany
Phone +49.221.54676.0
www, feedmee.com
● 111

Mutabor Design GmbH
Große Elbstraße 145b
22767 Hamburg, Germany
Phone +49.40.3992240
www.mutabor.de
● 249, 317, 365, 376, 389

N
namics (deutschland) GmbH
Gutleutstraße 96
60329 Frankfurt a. M., Germany
Phone +49.69.365059.228
Fax +49.69.365059.100
www.namics.com
▲ 73
● 73

NESPRESSO
Deutschland GmbH
Zollhof 8
40221 Düsseldorf, Germany
Phone +49.211.965060
Fax +49.211.96506580
www.nespresso.com
▲ 407

Nestlé Nespresso SA
1094 Paudex, Switzerland
Phone +41.21.796.96.96
www.nespresso.com
▲ 327

Netzwerk Neue Musik
Leibnizstraße 80
10625 Berlin, Germany
Phone +49.30.310180815
www.netzwerkneuemusik.de
▲ 299

Neue Digitale/Razorfish GmbH
Falkstraße 5
60487 Frankfurt a. M., Germany
Phone +49.69.70403.0
● 65, 86

Neue Digitale/Razorfish GmbH
Stralauer Allee 2
10245 Berlin, Germany
Phone +49.30.2936388.0
Fax +49.30.2936388.50
● 71

Neue Gestaltung GmbH
Gipsstraße 3
10119 Berlin, Germany
Phone +49.30.2250780
● 88

New Cat Orange
Gestaltung und Kommunikation
Hallgarter Straße 7
65197 Wiesbaden, Germany
www.new-cat-orange.de
▲ 180
● 151, 180

Nils Holger Moormann GmbH
An der Festhalle 2
83229 Aschau im Chiemgau, Germany
Phone +49.8052.90450
www.moormann.de
▲ 257

Nippon Connection e. V.
Mertonstraße 26–28
60325 Frankfurt a. M., Germany
Phone +49.69.798.22.986
▲ 150

Nirlat
hamelacha 6
42505 Natania, Israel
Phone +972.98637500
Fax +972.98637542
www.nirlat.com
▲ 323

Nokia GmbH
Balcke-Duerr-Allee 2
40882 Düsseldorf, Germany
Phone +49.210.289280
▲ 440

NOLTE&LAUTH GmbH
Breitscheidstraße 10
70174 Stuttgart, Germany
Phone +49.711.25359960
● 102–103

NOSIGNER
3-24-5-7F, Sendagi, Bunkyo
Tokyo, Japan
Phone +81 90 2935 0674
● 321

Novamondo Design
Lehrter Straße 57, Haus 4
10557 Berlin, Germany
www.novamondo.de
● 186–187, 299–300

O
Office for spatial identity. GmbH
Gasometerstrasse 9
8005 Zürich, Switzerland
Phone +41.44.27590.40
Fax +41.44.27590.49
www.ofsi.com
● 390–391

Oliver Schrott Kommunikation GmbH
An den Dominikanern 11–27
50668 Köln, Germany
Phone +49.221.3390127
▲ 70

Olympia Express SA
Piazzale Roncaà 4
6850 Mendrisio, Switzerland
Phone +41.91.646.15.55
www.olympia-express.ch
▲ 206

Omniyat Properties
P.O. Box
121926 Dubai, UAE
Phone +971.4.5115.000
www.omniyat.com
▲ 398

Open Systems AG
Räffelstrasse 29
8045 Zürich, Switzerland
▲ 238

optovision Gesellschaft für moderne
Brillenglastechnik mbH
Heinrich-Hertz-Straße 17
63225 Langen, Germany
Phone +49.6103.757.0
www.optovision.com
▲ 77

Orell Füssli Holding AG
Dietzingerstrasse 3
8036 Zürich, Switzerland
Phone +41.44.466.77.11
Fax +41.44.466.72.80
www.orellfuessli.com
▲ 271

Ortadogu Otomotiv A.S
Dumlupınar Bulvarı
No 102, Cankaya
6510 Ankara, Turkey
Phone +90.3122070000
▲ 423

Osram Opto Semiconductors
Leibnizstraße 4
93055 Regensburg, Germany
Phone +49.941.850.1601
▲ 374–375

Otto Schmid Metallbearbeitung GmbH
In den Strangwiesen 1
73529 Schwäbisch Gmünd, Germany
Phone +49.7173.6584
▲ 93

Simply outstanding.

product
design
award

communication
design
award

design
award
china

material
award

packaging
award

concept
award